William Colby

and Peter Forbath

HONORABLE MEN My Life in the CIA

SIMON AND SCHUSTER / NEW YORK

PUBLISHED BY SIMON AND SCHUSTER
A DIVISION OF GULF & WESTERN CORPORATION
SIMON & SCHUSTER BUILDING
ROCKEFELLER CENTER
1230 AVENUE OF THE AMERICAS
NEW YORK, NEW YORK 10020

PHOTO EDITOR: VINCENT VIRGA
DESIGNED BY IRVING PERKINS
MANUFACTURED IN THE UNITED STATES OF AMERICA
1   2   3   4   5   6   7   8   9   10

LIBRARY OF CONGRESS CATALOGING IN PUBLICATION DATA

COLBY, WILLIAM EGAN, DATE.
    HONORABLE MEN.

    INCLUDES INDEX.
    1. UNITED STATES. CENTRAL INTELLIGENCE AGENCY.
2. COLBY, WILLIAM EGAN, 1920–   3. INTELLIGENCE
OFFICERS—UNITED STATES—BIOGRAPHY. I. FORBATH, PETER,
JOINT AUTHOR. II. TITLE.
JK468.I6C59   327'.12'0924 [B]   78-1525

ISBN 0-671-22875-7

Contents

The End of a Career

THE plane landed at Washington's National Airport just after midnight, so it was already Sunday, November 2, 1975. I
was returning from Jacksonville, Florida, where I had gone
for a protocol meeting with visiting Egyptian President Anwar Sadat. On a trip to Cairo the previous year I had called
on him officially; now, during his visit to the United States
in line with Kissinger's policy of friendship with Egypt, I
wanted to pay my respects. But Barbara Walters had gotten
to him first and had overstayed her time, so I never did get
to see him. I was philosophical about it; plainly the Egyptian president thought it more important to get his message
out to the American people via Miss Walters's television interview than to make general conversation with me about
intelligence affairs. I couldn't quarrel with his choice.
Nevertheless, it had been a wasted afternoon and evening,
sitting in a car being unobtrusive outside his temporary residence, until the Egyptian security types and I agreed to cancel the visit. Now I was happy to be back in Washington and
was looking forward to an agreeable Sunday. My wife, Barbara, and I planned to go to Mass and then go on a picnic or
for a bike ride along the canal. But it was not to be.

The security officer with my car, waiting outside Page Air-
ways when I disembarked from the plane, handed me an
urgent message: I was to call John Marsh, Counselor to the
President, no matter how late I arrived. There was a phone

7

in the limousine, but for security's sake I went into the terminal and placed the call from a pay booth. Marsh was asleep. I apologized for waking him. No, that was all right. Could I be at the Oval Office at eight this morning? That meant a meeting with the President. Yes, of course I could. Fine, Marsh said; he'd see me then. And he hung up.

Ordinarily, on being summoned to see the President, I would ask what for, so I could bone up on whatever topic was to be the subject of discussion. But this time, I didn't. Marsh, obviously, was eager to get back to sleep and I was tired too, anxious to get home and to bed myself. And besides I could make a pretty fair guess as to what it was probably about. The previous day, Saturday, the press had broken a story revealing that the CIA had covertly been funneling aid to Kurdish rebels in Iraq. We had talked of these leaks at the usual meeting in the White House basement all that morning. So it was more than likely that the President was assembling a group of aides to discuss how leaks of sensitive material like this could be prevented. All the usual people would be there, I figured—Scowcroft; Buchen; someone from the Pentagon, possibly Schlesinger himself; Mike Duval; probably Don Rumsfeld; and Marsh and I.

But they weren't. Aside from the Secret Service on duty at the side door, the West Wing of the White House at seven forty-five that Sunday morning was deserted. The anteroom to the Oval Office was empty, until Marsh came in a couple of moments after I arrived. Apparently my guess at what this was all about was wrong. Still, I took a crack at it.

"Boy, that Kurdish story, that's some fine mess, isn't it, Jack?" I said. Marsh nodded absently. "I'd bet anything that it came from the House Committee," I went on. Marsh shrugged and looked away, clearly uninterested in pursuing the subject. I made a few more desultory remarks and then, puzzled, let it drop. We stood around in a rather awkward silence.

Promptly at eight President Ford showed up. He came from the White House residence along the enclosed porch, passed the Rose Garden and went directly into the Oval Office without seeing us. He was accompanied by two Secret Service men. After a few moments, one of them invited us in.

Ford was seated behind the huge, handsome Presidential desk, looking a bit grim and, as he was to fly to Florida to meet with Sadat later in the morning, he had a thick black briefing book on the Middle East situation in front of him. He set it aside as soon as Marsh and I walked in. I had seen the President regularly in the past year, but ours could not in any way be characterized as a personal relationship. Ford, while always cordial, dealt with me in a fairly formal manner. He did not stand up now; we didn't shake hands. I said, "Good morning, Mr. President. Jack said you wanted to see me."

"Yes," he replied, indicating that I should take a seat in the straight armchair in front of the desk. "We are going to do some reorganizing of the national-security structure."

He need not have said another word. From that sentence I realized immediately why I had been summoned: I was about to be fired as the Director of Central Intelligence.

Ford did not put it quite so bluntly. In the time-honored political tradition with sticky things of this sort, he said he wanted me to take a new job, as Ambassador to NATO. He then sketched the reorganization—which is to say, the sweeping personnel changes—he had in mind. It was what later was to be dubbed the Halloween Massacre, and it included the sacking of Jim Schlesinger as Secretary of Defense and Nelson Rockefeller's withdrawal as Ford's running mate on the 1976 GOP ticket. At the time, however, Ford didn't mention to me what was in store for Schlesinger, for the perfectly good reason that he hadn't yet mentioned it to him. But he did tell me that, under his reorganizational scheme, Henry Kissinger would give up his post as National Security Assistant to the President and move over exclusively to the State Department; that Brent Scowcroft would take over Kissinger's role as Presidential Assistant. And he told me that George Bush was coming back from

China to replace me as the new CIA chief. I said he was a good choice, and I meant it.

He then made a bit of a sales pitch for me to take the NATO post. He said that it was the job Don Rumsfeld had held before being appointed White House chief of staff. Obviously he was anxious for me to take it, if for no other reason than to have his politically explosive series of personnel changes appear to take place smoothly and uncontroversially. I would, wouldn't I?

"I would like to think about it a bit, Mr. President," I replied. "I would like to talk it over with Barbara." I was sure he would understand that, I said, as he often consulted with his wife on matters that affected them personally. But I said there and then that I had some reservations. I was concerned, for example, about the negative political impact that the naming of a former CIA Director to the NATO position could have, the political demonstrations that it could stir up in the countries of the Alliance and the disfavor with which the governments of those countries might consequently view the appointment.

Ford was quick to try to reassure me. I needn't be concerned, he said, because the appointment would be as the President's personal representative and thus didn't need the approval of the NATO countries.

"I realize that, Mr. President," I said; "nevertheless, I really need to think about it and talk to my wife about it."

"All right," Ford said. "Let us know your decision as soon as possible."

"Yes, sir, I will. I'll get in touch with Jack later in the morning," I said. He said the changes would be formally announced on Monday, and asked me to keep them to myself until then. I agreed.

There was nothing further to say. I stood up. The meeting was over. It had lasted about fifteen minutes. And in those fifteen minutes my thirty-year career as an intelligence officer had been brought abruptly to an end.

I should have been shattered, but my old discipline of thinking of the next step ahead took over. I wanted to catch Barbara, who would be leaving home in time to make a nine o'clock Mass across town. We were going to have to figure out what we should do about the NATO job offer. Marsh, at my elbow as we left the Oval Office, anxiously asked, "You are going to take it, aren't you?" revealing just how important it was that the "reorganization" go without a hitch, that all the players in it be happily in place before it was officially announced to the press. But I suspected even then that I wasn't going to oblige. (Neither was Schlesinger, I later discovered; he turned down Ford's offer to be Chairman of the Export-Import Bank on the spot, and rather angrily.)

Apart from the negative reaction that the appointment could inspire in Europe, a couple of other things bothered me. I doubted, for one, that I would be able to do anything worthwhile in the job with Kissinger as Secretary of State, with his well-known preference for conducting foreign policy personally rather than through ambassadors. And, for another, it could be a very short-term assignment, what with the President facing an uphill reelection campaign just a year away.

I didn't say any of this to Marsh just then. When he left me, I found a phone in the reception area and called Barbara. I caught her just as she was about to leave, and I asked her to skip our planned activities and wait for me as we had to discuss something important. Then, as I hurried to the basement entrance to the West Wing of the White House, I ran into Schlesinger. He was somewhat surprised. "What the devil are you doing here at this hour?" he asked. It was clear that he had no inkling as to what was afoot, but I didn't think it was my place to inform him, so I muttered that I had talked of the Kurdish exposure and hurried on my way.

By the time I got home, talked the situation over with Barbara, and called the White House, Marsh had taken off with the President for Florida to meet with Sadat. The White House operator put me through to Air Force One. "Jack, the answer is 'no,' with great respect and appreciation," I said to Marsh when I got him on the phone. "Okay," Marsh said. "I'll tell the President. I'm sorry."

That done, Barbara and I set about informing our family.

We told our children Christine and Carl, who lived at home with us. We called our grown son Jonathan and his wife, Susan, who lived in New York, and we called our other son, Paul, at Tulane University. We visited both Barbara's mother and my parents, who lived nearby. And suddenly, when I had a moment to reflect on what had happened, I realized that neither the family members nor I had been surprised. Indeed, I had been expecting this, steeling myself for it for nearly a year, the year in which the CIA had come under the most intensive public scrutiny in its history, the year in which I had spent virtually all my time facing countless Congressional investigating committee sessions, the year in which American intelligence entered a wholly new era.

That year had begun, in effect, with the publication in *The New York Times* on December 22, 1974, of a story by Seymour Hersh charging the CIA with a "massive illegal domestic intelligence operation." To some extent, of course, the ground had geen prepared for the crisis that followed. There had been Vietnam; there had been Watergate; there had been Chile. Each in its own way had raised questions that troubled the American public. Each had brought the CIA under harsh attack for one or another aspect of its operations. Each had dragged it farther out of the shadows of anonymity and secrecy, where it had preferred to function.

But the Hersh story topped them all. That *New York Times* headline—"Huge CIA Operation Reported in U.S. Against Anti-War Forces, Other Dissidents in Nixon Years"—triggered a firestorm. For in it all the dreadful fears and suspicions about the CIA, which had been building for years, suddenly crystallized. It raised the specter of a government agency running amok, becoming a Gestapo, violating the fundamental constitutional rights of the American people. It suggested a scandal equal in magnitude to the one that just recently had forced a President of the United States to resign on the verge of impeachment.

And the media seized on the CIA with an investigative intensity and preoccupation comparable only to Watergate.

Other stories, with equally sensational headlines charging equally shocking CIA activities, followed in a flood. Politicians, editorialists and ordinary citizens demanded an end to CIA's heinous practices. Devastating charges were hurled; the Agency was termed a "rogue elephant" out of control, a threat to the nation's fundamental liberties, a Frankenstein monster that had to be destroyed. Investigations were quickly underway: the regular Congressional intelligence oversight committees convened; Ford established a blue-ribbon Presidential commission, headed by Vice-President Rockefeller, to look into the particulars of the *New York Times*'s charge of alleged CIA illegal domestic spying, and the Senate and the House formed Select Committees to look into virtually everything else the CIA had ever done. The seminal year for a new and American intelligence—and my final year as an intelligence officer—had begun.

It was a grueling year. Every week I was required to spend days on Capitol Hill, facing hours of hostile questioning, struggling to keep in some sort of perspective the Agency's abuses and its accomplishments, threading the thin line between responding to the Congress's constitutional right to know and protecting legitimate intelligence secrets. I had to be alert to the prospect that whatever I said—or didn't say—could appear as a sensational headline the following day. At the same time, back at CIA headquarters in Langley, the Agency had to be kept functioning with some semblance of effectiveness in the midst of the maelstrom. I had to prevent the investigations and sensational journalism about the past from overwhelming our people and destroying their ability to do their job in the present. I had to answer younger staffers' charges that they had been lied to and misled, and senior staffers' charges that they were being sold down the river. And all had to be answered when they asked, in the wake of the latest horrendous headline, "What am I supposed to tell my children?"

Throughout this most disturbing year in my not altogether sedate career in intelligence, I now realize in retrospect, I had suspected that when the investigations had been concluded and the press and political storm had at last abated, I would almost certainly be fired. The signs were everywhere. The headlines and columns repeatedly speculated on the prospect; time and again the story went out that the White House was conducting a search for my replacement. Deep down, I admit, I hoped that it wouldn't happen. I wanted to stay on as the Agency's director; I had a number of new ideas that I wanted to apply to American intelligence. But the truth is that well before Ford actually called me in on that Sunday morning I must have known, even if I steadfastly refused to acknowledge it, that only a miracle could save me from dismissal.

Why? There were any number of reasons and all of them, to some degree, were valid. There was, for instance, the official reason—I don't question for a moment that Ford really wanted to reorganize the national security structure, at least to the extent of getting rid of Schlesinger (because his personality and his views on defense didn't sit well with the President or with Kissinger), and of dumping Rockefeller (to eliminate this red flag to the GOP's right wing), and that Ford and his advisers hoped that the political uproar over these controversial moves might be softened if they were announced in the context of a wider purge, including my own dismissal. And there was the more obvious reason that, after the damaging revelations about the CIA, it would make good political sense to name a new Agency chief to signal a turn away from the murky past toward a more promising future. For the Republicans didn't want, in the upcoming elections, to be saddled with the CIA furor.

But, however persuasive these reasons may have been, neither, in my opinion, was the main reason for my dismissal. I believe I was fired because of the way I went about dealing with the CIA's crisis. My approach, pragmatically and philosophically, was in conflict with that of the President and his principal advisers. From their point of view, I had not played the game during that turbulent year as a loyal member of the White House "team."

My strategy quite simply had been to be guided by the

Constitution, and to apply its principles. This meant that I had to cooperate with the investigations and try to educate the Congress, press, and public, as well as I could, about American intelligence, its importance, its successes and its failings. The Agency's survival, I believed, could only come from understanding, not hostility, built on knowledge, not faith. And I thought this could be done without exposing the true secrets that needed to be kept, the names of the Americans and foreigners who worked with us under cover, and the sensitive technologies that could easily be made useless if revealed to the intended targets.

In this spirit, when Hersh first called and said he had a story "bigger than My-Lai," I agreed to meet with him. And then I did not flatly deny the allegations he had dug up about improper CIA activities in the domestic field, but made an effort to put his discoveries in perspective, saying that those cases where the CIA had overstepped its legislative charter had been few and far between, had occurred years before, and had been stopped many months ago. When he nonetheless broke the story, I dictated a report for the President, detailing the entire matter without revealing names, and I added a covering note suggesting that it could be released to the press immediately, as the best way of countering Hersh's distortions and exaggerations.

Then at one of the very first Congressional sessions thereafter, when the chairman requested that my testimony—a detailed rundown of my response to Hersh's article—be released to the public, I agreed and repeated it at another committee's open session in the presence of the press and television cameras. And when the special investigating committees were formed, I telephoned the respective chairmen to say that I looked forward to a cooperative rather than an adversary relationship with them since it was in everyone's best interest, the CIA's included, that the Congress and the nation get a true understanding of the Agency's operations.

Moreover, at CIA I told my colleagues and subordinates that we could be sure the investigation would find every item of questionable behavior it sought, and that our only sensible recourse was to proffer additional evidence to try to . put those in their true (and small) proportion. And so instructions were sent to all employees to report any cases of dubious behavior in the past, so that CIA would be the one to report them, rather than have them uncovered by a triumphant investigator. Thus, when a long-forgotten vial of snake poison, and the exotic dart gun by which it was meant to be administered—which had been stored in violation of an order that such materials must be destroyed—was discovered, we reported it to the White House and then the Congressional committees; they then used it as the basis for a theatrical public hearing, but it was we who had uncovered it.

To say the very least, most of the White House staff and, for that matter, much of the intelligence community, were unenthusiastic about what I was doing. Their preferred approach, bluntly put, would have been to stonewall, to disclose as little as they could get away with, and to cry havoc to the national security about what they couldn't deny—in short, the exact opposite of mine. And I have to admit that, from the very outset, I was made aware that this was so.

Kissinger bluntly commented that he thought I should have immediately issued a flat denial of Hersh's report. My suggestion for public release of my report to the President brought only silence. Instead, the White House decided to try to contain the crisis by forming a blue-ribbon commission to investigate, although I believed that the questions would later have to be answered in public and not only behind closed doors. And soon after my first testimony before this commission, chaired by Vice-President Nelson Rockefeller, he drew me into his office in the Executive Office Building and said in his most charming manner, "Bill, do you really have to present all this material to us?" And at one of our private meetings to discuss intelligence activities, after I had become a regular performer before the Senate Select Committee, Kissinger, in a sarcastically teasing reference to my Catholicism, cracked, "Bill, you know what you do when you go up to the Hill? You go to confession." Scowcroft with his Air Force background and fierce loyalty to the Presidential command structure, didn't try to be witty about it; he flatly said I should refuse to reply to the questions the Congress was asking.

The same sort of distress over my approach existed within the intelligence community. Like administration officials, many intelligence officers argued that intelligence was strictly an Executive Branch function and must be protected from Congressional prying. Others warned that Congress could not be trusted with intelligence secrets, that release to it was the equivalent of release to the public. Jim Angleton, a onetime top CIA officer, was quoted in the press to the effect that some officials had violated their statutory obligation to protect intelligence sources and methods, and I knew he meant me. And again and again I heard the opinion whispered about that what I really was doing was dumping the crisis onto Richard Helms, my predecessor as CIA chief, in order to save my own skin.

It wasn't long before I felt very alone. Ford and his aides decided their best policy was to dissociate the White House from CIA's troubles and thus minimize their responsibility for the Agency's questionable practices in the past and bad odor in the present. I agreed with them, and thought I should take the heat, but the process added to my isolation. The wagons were drawn around—and I was left on the outside.

In the process, I too made some mistakes, such as agreeing that the Senate could release my testimony before informing the White House. The banner headlines and full text in the next day's *New York Times*, while no substantive surprise to the White House, certainly led them to reach for a tighter tactical control over my dealings with the Hill. The fact that the report essentially torpedoed the charge of a "massive illegal domestic intelligence operation," and apparently led to the denial of another Pulitzer Prize to Hersh, did not mollify the White House hard-liners. And the morning columns reporting that the White House was looking for a replacement for me made my position clear as not on its "team" and gave me warning that I would certainly go when the opportunity arose. But it also strengthened my resolve to follow what I saw as the right strategy, that of respect for the Congress's constitutional role and of fighting to show the real proportion of intelligence faults in the past against its contribution and indispensability to the nation. And some went out of their way to give a word of encouragement, as when Senator Walter Mondale drew me aside after one White House leak—or plant—and told me to stick to doing the right thing.

Despite the pressure and the end result, I do not now, nor did I then, regret what I did. I remain more convinced than ever that not only was it the right way but it was the only way.

On the tactical level, it would have been impossible to stonewall the Congress. To be sure, that wouldn't have been the case in the past. Then the traditional concept was that intelligence was the sole business of the President, a business to be conducted in total secrecy, a business, moreover, with which Congress shouldn't concern itself. One only has to recall a statement that the powerful Senator John Stennis, then Chairman of the Armed Services Committee, made as recently as 1971, to illustrate the truth of this. "Spying is spying," he said. "You have to make up your mind that you are going to have an intelligence agency and protect it as such, and shut your eyes and take what is coming." In a day when something like that could be said, obviously the President and his CIA chief could not only get away with stonewalling the Congress, they were in a sense obliged to—and could count on the leaders of Congress to support them. The Senate and House chairmen deferred to the President and were quick to shut off any Congressional attempt to pry into what they regarded as the Executive's privilege.

But by 1975 this had radically changed. Vietnam and Watergate had revealed the frightening abuses that could be—and were—committed under the cloak of the Executive's separate powers and privileges. The Congressional freshmen elected in 1974 were insistent that a new day had dawned. Congress was no longer prepared to defer to the

President. Indeed, just a few months before Hersh's article, it had forced Nixon to resign on the verge of impeachment. With its newfound muscle it wasn't about to allow itself to be defied on its investigations into the CIA. In the House, long-time CIA friend and supporter F. Edward Hebert had been unseated as chairman of the Armed Services Committee, and in the Senate the supportive chairmen and leading members who had protected intelligence in past years told me that I would have to respond to the other committees asking how intelligence had acted in areas in their jurisdiction.

Had I tried to resist Congress, we would have been inundated by a flood of subpoenas and contempt citations. The information we would have tried to withhold would have been gotten out of us anyway. Only it would have been gotten out of us in the worst possible way—dragged out, raising all sorts of suspicions about what we were trying to hide and why, and what further hideous secrets were still being covered up. The sensations, the distortions and exaggerations, the misunderstandings, the utter lack of perspective on what was revealed were only starters to what would have happened in the other event, and the damage to the Agency would have been far greater. By cooperating, by being as forthcoming as possible, we did get the chance to present the CIA's case in the most favorable light, place its few abuses in the context of its greater accomplishments, minimize the sensationalism and so protect the Agency from a slew of crippling legislation that I am convinced the Congress might have enacted in the heat of hysteria.

The best accolade for my position came from Kissinger who told me just before I left office that he had disagreed with my strategy initially but that he had come to believe that I had been right. It was a gracious thing for him to say, and he is not known to be generous with compliments.

But besides the tactical advantages, something else motivated my approach. From my early studies in Constitutional Law, I knew that Congress had the right and duty to conduct such investigations, and that they are in the best interest of our country and represent the best principles of our democracy. As a matter of conscience, I was obliged to cooperate if I were to abide by my oath to support and defend the Constitution.

I am willing to concede that I did not always believe this. I first entered the intelligence profession when all the old traditions of total intelligence secrecy held sway, and I spent the larger part of my career as an adherent of them. But during that career much happened that forced me to question and then ultimately reject them. For one thing, the intelligence profession exploded in size and in importance. In the beginning, it was a relatively minor affair, limited to clandestine operations, contributing only individual reports, involved in individual actions. Few forces required its exposure to anyone other than the President. But over the years, American intelligence burgeoned into a great academic center of scholarship and analysis, a sponsor of large-scale scientific research and technology, and a major factor in American foreign relations. It now demands the management techniques of major technical enterprises and government structures, requires mammoth financing, and must be closely coordinated with the other elements of America's foreign policy. It has quite simply outgrown the old concept of a small, secret intelligence service located at the elbow of the President and to be used by him at his discretion.

Moreover, it lost the support of the nation during those years. In the beginning, certainly during World War II and on through the Cold War of the 1950s and even into the early 1960s, a national consensus accepted the need for the CIA and, indeed, the need for the secrecy cloaking its activities in the unfriendly world around us. But, with the scandal of the Bay of Pigs, with the revelations about CIA's relations with the National Student Association, with Vietnam and Chile and Watergate, that consensus was irreparably shattered. Secrecy was perceived to cover error and wrongdoing. The once dashing James Bond image of the agent was seen as a disguise for an immoral, cynical assassin. No longer would the American public accept the statement of

Nathan Hale, one of the nation's first spies, that "every kind of service, necessary to the public good, becomes honorable by being necessary." When President Kennedy said that the triumphs of intelligence were unheralded, its failures trumpeted, he meant it in a positive sense, but the successive fanfares of failures and sensation finally deafened the public.

For these reasons I had become convinced that the CIA no longer could operate within the traditions of the past. The CIA must build, not assume, public support, and it can do this only by informing the public of the nature of its activities and accepting the public's control over them. It must convince the people that it is not some nefarious "invisible government," engaged in heinous crimes and oblivious to American democratic values, but a legitimate, controlled, and immensely valuable weapon in the arsenal of our democracy, serving to protect the nation and promote its welfare.

A public informed of the CIA's accomplishments and capabilities will support it. A public aware of its true mission and the limits of its authority will accept it. A public that understands the issues and problems involving intelligence and its role in the American government will debate and decide them. A public convinced of the CIA's value will help protect its true secrets. The only way we can have such a public is by making the CIA an integral part of our democratic process, subject to our system of checks and balances among the Executive and the Congress and the Judiciary, responsive to the Constitution and in the end controlled by the informed populace it serves.

Many good Americans in and out of the intelligence community do not agree with me. I realize that those who disagree have persuasive arguments and sincere beliefs on their side. Thus, it is the purpose of this book to show why I believe what I believe, and to do that it is best to begin at the beginning—with the origins of the CIA and Bill Colby.

CHAPTER ONE

Parachutes to the Underground

THE parachute snapped open with a reassuring jolt and the Liberator bomber *Slick Chick* from which we had just jumped at about fifteen hundred feet, veered away into the night, heading back across the Channel to England. We were on our own now, two Free Frenchmen and myself, floating down through the balmy August midnight into the heart of German-occupied France. And I suddenly realized that something was seriously wrong.

Below, I could make out the flames which the *Slick Chick*'s pilot had taken for the signal, set by the *maquis*, marking our drop zone. But it wasn't the three bonfires arranged in a triangular pattern that I had been briefed to expect. No, this was a single fire burning in a straight line. In fact, it was a train burning on a track, shot up in an air raid a couple of nights before and further sabotaged by railroad workers. We had jumped in the wrong place and were now plummeting not into a safely secluded pasture in the farm country near Joigny, but straight into an unnervingly well-built-up urban area.

I had to swing my legs out of the way to clear the tile roofs and chimney pots as I came crashing down into someone's back yard. In a burst of feathers, chickens scattered hysterically; dogs began to bark; people, startled from their sleep, flung open their shutters and excitedly asked each other about the sudden racket. My two companions, Jacques Favel and Louis Giry, having scrambled out of their parachute harnesses, joined me in the front yard of the house we had just missed.

"Where are we?" I asked Favel. A small group of French residents rapidly gathered. Favel learned from them that we had landed in the outskirts of the town of Montargis. Remembering the map of France from his school days, Favel said he thought we were twenty-five or so miles west of where we were meant to be. But what was worse, the local citizens told us, there was a German garrison just a few hundred yards up the main street.

I quickly summed up our situation as bad. We had jumped with ten supply chutes, and they had come down over a large area of the town, banging off rooftops, clanging down into the streets, hanging in telephone wires. It would take a couple of hours to round them up, and we didn't have anywhere near that amount of time. The Germans had probably heard them land, or soon would hear of the commotion, and would be looking for us in a matter of minutes. We had our side arms with us, and the codes, maps, mission instructions, and radio crystals stashed in the pockets of our jump suits. But the radio itself, the arms we had brought to distribute to friendly partisans, and the French clothing I had brought along to change into out of my U.S. Army uniform in an emergency, were in the supply cannisters scattered all around. Nevertheless, we had no choice; we had to abandon all of it and get out of there quickly, toward the east and our proper drop zone.

Our impromptu "reception committee" told us that the railroad with the burning train was a spur line from Montargis to the east, so we set off down the track. When we got into the country, we left the track, since it might be guarded, and cut off across the wooded farmlands. I don't know how far we got exactly. It must have been pretty nearly 1 A.M. when we got out of Montargis, and I don't suppose we made more than five or six miles by the time the sky began to lighten with the false dawn. We found a secluded ditch at the base of a wooded rise and hid ourselves in it. When morning came we saw that we were about a hundred yards from a road going west to Montargis.

There was no way for us to keep going during the daylight hours. The Germans had gone through every house in Montargis during the night and, with the first light, patrols moved out into the surrounding farm villages and countryside on an intensive search for us. There was nothing we could do but remain hidden in the ditch until the fall of darkness again. Once a farmer went by quite close to us, leading an oxen cart, but we didn't contact him. From time to time, we saw German trucks and armored cars moving down the road, apparently units going to Montargis to join in the manhunt. At noon we rationed out a couple of candy bars and drank water sparingly from our canteens. It was a warm summer day, the air thick with the scent of manure and wild flowers; bees and flies buzzed around us drowsily and one by one we would doze off for a few moments, each with his own private thoughts.

Jacques Favel, lieutenant in the Free French forces, brilliant cardplayer and irresistible lady's man, code name Galway. Louis Giry, sergeant in the Free French forces, tough, simple workman from Nancy, and excellent radio technician and operator, code name Piastre. And me. I was twenty-four at the time, a major in the U.S. Army Parachute Field Artillery and my code name was Berkshire. We three formed Jedburgh Team Bruce, one of some ninety such three-man multinational teams (others included Britons, Belgians and Dutchmen) that had been parachuted behind German lines in the first days and weeks following the Normandy D-Day invasion with the object of organizing an uprising of French resistance groups so as to wreak the maximum havoc in the German rear and undermine German defense against the advancing Allied armies. Team Bruce's mission was to contact *réseau* Jean-Marie, a *maquis* network operating in the Department of Yonne in central France, arrange for weapons and supplies to be parachuted to it, and coordinate its activities with that of Patton's Third Army, blowing bridges, ambushing patrols, attacking depots, sabotaging communications, blocking roads and rail lines, in a ceaseless series of hit-and-run harassing raids.

It was a dangerous mission. Just a few weeks before, the German High Command had broadcast this warning: "Whoever on French territory outside the zone of legal combat is captured and identified as having participated in sabotage, terrorism, or revolt is and remains a bandit or franctireur and shall consequently be shot, whatever his nationality or uniform." And they weren't kidding. The leader of one of the first Jedburgh teams to drop into Brittany, Major John Bonsal, had been stopped at a German checkpoint, identified, and executed on the spot.

Under the circumstances, and not surprisingly, I couldn't help asking myself during that long, hot summer day, hiding in a ditch while German soldiers scoured the countryside looking for me, just how in the world I had gotten into this. It was a question I have often asked myself, in comparably sticky situations, in the thirty-odd years since, because that Jedburgh mission was what started me on the path that, with just one brief interlude, I was to follow for the rest of my life. For the Jedburghs were an operation of the Office of Strategic Services, and the Office of Strategic Services, the first comprehensive intelligence organization in America's history, was the precursor of the Central Intelligence Agency. My experience as a Jedburgh made me a natural recruit for the CIA's world of espionage, sabotage, covert operations, and intelligence. But what got me to become a Jedburgh in the first place?

Probably my being an Army brat of a somewhat unorthodox sort had a lot to do with it. My father, Elbridge Colby, became an Army lieutenant shortly after I was born on January 4, 1920, in St. Paul, Minnesota, returning to the Army after World War I service. But he was not at all your typical spit-and-polish career officer. He had, in fact, set out in life to be exactly the opposite—a writer, a teacher of English literature, an independent thinker. As a young man at col-

lege he had converted to Roman Catholicism out of intellectual conviction and to the distaste of his New England family, had won a Master's degree and Phi Beta Kappa key from
Columbia and had taught at Columbia and the University of
Minnesota before the outbreak of World War I. His interest
in that conflagration was not unlike so many other young
writers of that generation, and like them he went to what is
now Yugoslavia in 1915 on a war relief expedition deliver-
ing food. With America's entry into the war, he joined up
and was commissioned, but was frustrated to be sent to Panama to guard the Canal instead of to France to fight in the
trenches. He took with him from Minnesota to the faroff
tropics his wartime bride, Margaret Mary Egan, a lovely
Irish Catholic girl from St. Paul, whom he had met at the
University of Minnesota.

But there was something else about my father. He came
from a family that had fought hard to stay respectable despite poverty—his own father, a junior chemistry teacher at
Columbia, had died when he was a boy and my father had
watched his mother scrimp and scrape to educate his two
sisters and him, and this had made him extremely conscious
of economic security. When the war ended, he returned to
teaching at Minnesota, but he became anxious about his
ability, as a struggling writer and underpaid teacher, to support his family of my mother and myself. And so, partly for
the financial security it offered, he returned to the Army for
his career (he retired in 1948 as a full colonel, to establish
and head a department of journalism at George Washington
University).

But he never stopped being that writer, teacher, independent thinker. He regularly produced books on military history, served as press officer and editor of post journals, and
wrote editorials for Army weeklies and articles for a prominent Catholic journal. The Army valued his qualities
enough to send him back to Columbia to get his Ph.D. But it
also had reason to rue them. In 1925, while my father was at
Fort Benning, Georgia, a black soldier from the Fort (this, of
course, was in the days when the Army was strictly segre-

gated) went to nearby Americus. It seems that while walking down the main street he refused to step off the sidewalk to let a white man pass. The white man pulled a gun and shot the black soldier dead, and then was acquitted of the crime by an all-white jury. My father was outraged and thought that soldiers should stand together against such a crime against any one of them. As "publicity officer" for the garrison, he wrote an incensed article about the incident for the extremely liberal *Nation* magazine. A furor broke out. The black press came to my father's defense, praising him for his sense of justice and decency. But the Georgia press and Congressmen, predictably, attacked him viciously. The Army reacted by assigning him to the 24th Infantry Regiment, an all-black outfit, and though he was later reassigned to a Northern post, the incident haunted his career for years.

My mother's contribution was no less significant. To her strong Irish Catholicism, she added stories about the Irish Democratic Party politics which her father participated in in Minnesota, and of his days as a post trader in the Dakota Indian territories as a young man. Her discipline and devotion rubbed off on me.

So, this combination of contradictory forces shaped my character in my earliest boyhood. On the one hand, I was fascinated by the military life all around me, with its pomp and pageantry, weaponry and *machismo*, its discipline and patriotism, its grand and heroic deeds. At the same time, I was profoundly influenced by my father's unorthodoxy, his outspoken independence, his respect for good scholarship in English and history, his interest in a wider world than the narrow life of an Army camp.

There were also other forces at work on me during those youthful years. There was, for example, all the traveling we did. In my first sixteen years, my father was posted back and forth across the world and all over the country, from the Panama Canal Zone to Tientsin, China, from Minnesota to Georgia to Vermont. And surely one of the effects of this was to develop in me a curiosity about the world and its peoples and an eagerness always to be off to new places and to experience different things. But it also had the concomitant effect of making me feel an outsider everywhere, with roots really nowhere. The longest period of settled life that I experienced in my youth was the three years I spent at high school in Burlington, Vermont, where my father had been assigned as an ROTC instructor at the University. And even there I have the clear memory of being the new boy in town, and a Catholic in Protestant Establishment circles. It was a feeling I brought with me when I was admitted to Princeton in 1936.

There had been a vague understanding that I might follow my father into the military, as many of my fellow "Army brats" did. But, because of my constant shifting from one school to another as a result of my father's repostings, I graduated from high school at sixteen, a year too young to apply to West Point. Then the next year when I did apply, after a year at Princeton, I was rejected by the Academy because of my nearsightedness. I was delighted, for that one year at Princeton had disabused me of the idea of a military career.

It was not that at college I had found a place in which I at last belonged. In those days, Princeton was a very social and socially conscious place, still dominated by the snobbish F. Scott Fitzgerald tradition. And I was still very much the middle-class type, the son of an Army officer from a public school, who, to help with his tuition, had to wait on tables in the college dining halls, tutor in some of the courses I did well in, and serve as altar boy in the Catholic chapel. I wasn't invited to join one of the more fashionable eating clubs. And since I wasn't much of an athlete either—at five feet, eight inches, one hundred and thirty pounds, and wearing eyeglasses—I wasn't taken up in the social whirl. No, I remained still pretty much the outsider, content to go my own way quietly, with a few friends, involved in a few extracurricular activities, but a leader in none. Only in ROTC did I achieve any real prominence, as a cadet captain.

What excited me about Princeton was the intellectual stimulation and challenge of my studies—sharing a campus with Albert Einstein, participating in seminars held by Edward S. Corwin and Alpheus T. Mason on constitutional law and political theory. And now that other influence in my background surged to the forefront—my father's love of books and ideas, his and my mother's liberal principles and concern about the world. A course in anthropology turned me on in my freshman year. I took courses in the new School of Public and International Affairs, doing independent study and research on such problems as black education, the Cuban sugar trade, and civil liberties in Jersey City under Boss Hague.

This was the time of Franklin Roosevelt's New Deal, a time of liberal idealism and political innovation domestically. These were also the years of the growing threat of fascism in Europe, the Austrian *Anschluss*, the rape of Czechoslovakia, the flawed Popular Front in France, the Spanish Civil War—a time of rising debate between American isolationists and interventionists. I was a liberal, an antifascist, an interventionist, and I wanted to get involved in everything in that eager, urgent way only a young college student can.

In the summer after my junior year (1939) I decided to spend my vacation in France as much to have an adventure and learn the language as to get a chance to find out what was happening in Europe politically. My father arranged for me to live with a French family in the Loire Valley. It was a magnificent summer. I spent much of my time happily bicycling around the beautiful château country, visiting lovely little farm villages, learning to drink wine in the small cafés, developing a deep affection for the French people. And it was also an incredible summer because while I was there World War II broke out. I made my way across the Channel to England and returned to New York aboard an armed British ship, dodging German submarines in the North Atlantic. My intellectual antifascism had acquired a very personal dimension.

As the subject for my senior thesis, I chose French policy toward the Spanish Civil War as a vehicle for examining the question of why the democracies were so weak in the face of the rise of fascism. It came down hard on the side of the

Republic and condemned the democracies for failing to support the Republic against Franco, their fear of war paralyzing them into watching Hitler and Mussolini carry the day. This, however, did not put me on the side of the Communists, who also supported the Republic. I was perfectly convinced—which of course many supporters of the Republican cause were not—that it was possible to be antifascist without becoming pro-Communist. Indeed, if anything, I was as anti-Communist as I was antifascist, and for the same reason—a conviction that freedom is a transcendent value. In part, I am willing to concede, my Catholicism may well have kept me from the emotional antifascism that pushed many of my time into the ranks of the Communists. But I had also read Lenin; and the Hitler-Stalin pact made it clear that Communism represented the same cynical totalitarian threat to liberal democracy as did fascism. It was just that, at the moment, fascism was the more immediate danger.

France fell the year I was graduated from Princeton, and I was convinced, and indeed hoped, that America would soon enter the war against Hitler. I might have joined the Army right then had not one of those curious influences from my background held me back. Despite my ROTC graduation, I could not be commissioned as an officer until my twenty-first birthday in January 1941. That peculiar class consciousness bred into an Army officer's son made me rather wait for that date than go into the less consequential duties of an enlisted man.

I had by this time chosen to be a labor lawyer as the most practical way of getting into the excitement of New Deal politics, and Columbia Law School had accepted me for the class starting in the autumn of 1940. I decided to spend the summer until then in Washington (where my father had been transferred) examining the political scene at close hand. I got a job at a gas station and quickly made contact with the local Oil Workers' Union. Gas station attendants weren't unionized, and I enthusiastically joined in the effort to organize them in the best tradition of New Deal liberalism.

Then it was off to law school for a year, during which the

most memorable event was my meeting (on a blind date arranged by a mutual friend) a Barnard junior by the name of Barbara Heinzen. We saw each other during that year, although both of us had other interests as well. I suppose I knew that she was the girl I would marry. But I also knew that I intended to join the Army when I was twenty-one, so the subject was never broached. We had splendid times together, racing around New York, dancing, partying, endlessly arguing politics with our friends. A memorable event was a Communist demonstration in which mock coffins were carried around the campus in protest against Roosevelt's policies of aid to Britain. (This was during the Nazi-Soviet "friendship" period, dramatizing Communist cynicism in its reversal of its earlier antifascism.) Then, at the end of the school year, I applied for active service. And in August 1941 I reported for duty.

As an ROTC second lieutenant, I was sent to a replacement training center at Fort Bragg, North Carolina. While I was there the Japanese attacked Pearl Harbor, and Hitler foolishly (but, to me, happily) declared war on the United States. I was then assigned to Fort Sill, Oklahoma, for field-artillery training. Apparently I did well at it—in fact, too well for my taste, for instead of being assigned to a combat unit going off to war, I was selected to be an instructor at the Field Artillery Officer Candidate School. After six months in that job, I was afraid that the war would be over before I got a chance to fight—a repetition of my father's frustration in Panama during World War I. But an Army notice appeared on the bulletin board one day, calling for volunteers for a new type of military training—parachuting—and saying that applications could not be blocked by commanders trying to keep their personnel. Instantly I volunteered. I realized that my weak eyes, which had kept me out of West Point, might keep me out of the paratroops, so when the time came for the physical examination, I arranged to undress near the eye chart and memorized the 20/40 line. When I stumbled on reading it backwards with my left eye, and couldn't see the 20/50 line at all, a wise doctor asked if I really wanted to be a paratrooper, and waved me on with the comment that he thought my sight was good enough so that I could see the ground.

I was sent to parachute school at Fort Benning in the fall of 1942 but, because I broke my ankle on my second jump, it wasn't until March 1943 that I was assigned as a staff officer in a combat outfit of the parachute field artillery. But this was still not to be my vehicle for fighting fascists. Just before the unit was to be shipped out with the 82nd Airborne, the battalion's commanding officer, a reserve lieutenant colonel, was relieved of the command, apparently for lack of the *gung-ho* dynamism expected of paratroop commanders in those days, and the colonel who replaced him brought in his own personal staff. I was suddenly out of a job and back again in the officers' replacement pool at Camp McCall, watching enviously as the units prepared to go off to war. And then along came the man from OSS.

The Office of Strategic Services had been in existence at this time for less than two years. Previous to that, hard as it is to imagine for a great power, America had no intelligence service at all. While America had, of course, used spies in wartime since the days of Nathan Hale, it had always gotten out of the intelligence business during peacetime. During the 1920s, after World War I, for example, then Secretary of State Stimson had closed a code-breaking unit in his department with the righteous comment that "Gentlemen do not read each other's mail." After that, whatever intelligence the United States government obtained came in a haphazard way from a scattering of uncoordinated, understaffed and inadequate sources such as diplomats in American embassies abroad, military and naval attachés, a dedicated group of military-communications intelligence specialists, and the gleanings of foreign press and radio broadcasts. By 1941, however, as war neared, Franklin Roosevelt saw the need for intelligence and did something about it. He created the Office of the Coordinator of Information, and chose the prominent and well-connected attorney William J. Donovan to head it.

The choice was both inevitable and brilliant. Wild Bill Donovan, though then already fifty-seven, was a vigorous, brilliant, adventurous man with just the right combination of romanticism, sophistication and intellectual keenness to be perfect for the job. He had been commander of New York's fabled Fighting 69th in World War I, winning the Congressional Medal of Honor for valor in the field, had founded one of Wall Street's most successful law firms, had traveled widely in Europe, and had in fact already undertaken intelligence missions for F.D.R., having made fact-finding visits to England and the Mediterranean in 1940 to assess the military and political situations there. He campaigned for a new intelligence service to comb through the mass of disorganized intelligence information and summarize its meaning, and to perform the political task of meeting the new fifth column tactics that the enemy had developed. Once given the mandate to produce a real intelligence effort, there was no stopping him. He set about building a central agency that not only would coordinate and analyze intelligence coming in from existing sources, but also would put its own agents into the field to conduct a broad range of espionage, counterespionage, sabotage, paramilitary and propaganda activities.

A year after Donovan's appointment (and six months after Pearl Harbor), the Office of Coordinator of Information formally became the Office of Strategic Services, which reported to the Joint Chiefs of Staff, and was well on its way to recruiting some 12,000 of that generation's most extraordinary men and women to participate in the war's most spectacular adventures. By the time I joined up, OSS had run operations in North Africa to prepare the way for the Allied invasion there, had agents working in Spain and Portugal to keep those countries neutral, had spies in Berlin stealing the secrets of the German High Command, had guerrilla teams working with the partisans in the Balkans, had clandestine radios broadcasting from Sicily and Italy, and now, with preparations shaping up for Operation Overlord, the Normandy invasion, was beginning to put together the Jedburgh teams.

At the time, however, I knew none of this; in fact I had never even heard of the OSS. And the OSS recruiter did very little to enlighten me. All he said, in effect, was that he was looking for qualified parachute officers, especially those with some proficiency in French and other foreign languages, willing to volunteer for a highly hazardous mission. Practically every man in the replacement pool that day stepped forward.

I have often felt that the true act of heroism occurs when a person volunteers for a dangerous mission in the first place. Later on, when the mission itself is underway, all sorts of irresistible factors come into play that require a man to behave bravely, independently of his will, very often without a second thought—peer pressure, instinct for survival, or solidarity with comrades in dangerous circumstances. But in the tranquillity of an office, before any of these factors begin to have any force, a man does measure his courage and decide whether he is willing to risk his life, and why. In my case, the urgent desire to escape the replacement depot was in part produced by my antifascism. It was fortified by the need not to be left out of the action, indeed to be in the forefront of the fighting, that almost every young man felt at that time. And then too, all those other influences of my youth came into play: an inclination to unorthodoxy in military service, an interest in the political aspects of war, a habit of going my own way and seeking my own band of kindred souls where money or social status, or the prep school you went to, didn't matter; where only your spirit, what you were made of, and what you could do mattered. And the Jedburghs were certainly that sort of band.

Of the hundred-or-so parachute officers who volunteered for the mission, only some fifty survived the initial screening process. Those who did survive were a mixed, spectacular, and exuberant lot. There were Stewart Alsop, who went to fame as a writer; Lucien Conein, who later sat with the generals who overthrew Diem in Saigon; Douglas Bazata, a red-haired soldier of fortune, who called all colonels "Sugar"; Phil Chadbourne, who became Consul General in Marseilles, and in later life, public-relations agent for Prin-

cess Grace of Monaco; Hod Fuller, who had sailed around
the world in a small boat, fought in the French army until
the fall of France, and then with the First Marine Division
on Guadalcanal; Bernard Knox, a Cambridge classicist, who
had fought in Spain; René Dussaq, before the war an Argen-
tine stunt man in Hollywood. I have to say that in this colorful company I was regarded as a quiet one.

Just before Christmas 1943 we sailed for Britain aboard
the *Queen Elizabeth*. By this time we realized that our mission would involve parachuting behind enemy lines in
France, but little else. We debarked in Glasgow and were
taken to a British commando training center in western Scotland. Within two weeks we were on the move again and
settled in a magnificent country estate in the south of England near Peterborough called Milton Hall. And it was
here that we truly turned into Jedburghs and discovered at
last what we were expected to do.

At this stage in the war, America had little experience in
guerrilla operations, so our training at Milton Hall was conducted mostly by British commandos and intelligence personnel, organized in a "Special Operations Executive" directed, in Churchill's words, to "set Europe ablaze." From
them we learned all the dark arts—the secrets of silent killing, demolition, operation of clandestine radios, infiltration
and exfiltration, judo, cryptography, and how to live on the
run, use forged papers, dress, eat and otherwise behave like
Frenchmen. Night after night we ran mock exercises in the
surrounding countryside; day after day the patient British
women radio operators tried to get our Morse code speeds
above twelve words per minute; and several times a week
we attended lectures on the workings of the French *maquis*
networks or on the tactics the Germans used to combat
them—talks given by agents and commandos who had been
behind the lines and had come back alive. On one occasion
we were given a talk by a British spy who had been captured by the Gestapo: in typical British low key he described his capture and escape, casually glossing over his
torture and success in withholding his secrets from the Ger-

mans. It made for riveting, hair-raising variations on the traditional academic lectures we recalled from far-off college
days.

But despite this sort of thing, morale was incredibly high.
By now, along with the fifty of us, there were some two
hundred and fifty at Milton Hall—English, French, Belgian,
and Dutch officers and enlisted men, as well as some fifty
American enlisted radio operators—from which the multinational teams would be assembled. None of us dwelt on the
dangers of what we were preparing to do. The usual young
man's conceit that he is invulnerable and immortal
enveloped us all. Everything was dealt with as a joke; in a
sense we were far too much caught up in the adventure that
we were undertaking to be afraid. We had weekend passes
to London, where we could pose as heroes and chase girls.
There were endless poker games and interminable discussions of the fine points of explosives and weapons. On one
trip to London I took time off to visit Foyle's great book-
store, where I bought a copy of T. E. Lawrence's *Seven Pil-
lars of Wisdom*, which I read voraciously for its account of
how an outsider operates within the political framework of a
foreign people. I suppose I fantasized myself as becoming,
if not exactly a Lawrence of Arabia, then at least as Colby of
a French Department, but it was the closest thing I could
find for training in the political aspects of our mission.

By June we had gone through our training scores of times,
and it had long since become second nature; it was clear
that we were now just marking time, just being kept busy
until the operation was activated. Supreme Headquarters
(SHAEF) was concerned to use the Jedburghs at precisely
the right moment. It didn't want us to go in and spark the
French uprising so early that the Germans could put it down
before it would do any good. And it didn't want us to go in
so late that the uprising would be of no help to the advancing Allied invasion. So we continued our training, honing
ourselves to the sharpest edge humanly possible, and began
forming our three-man teams.

This was done by a system of engagement, marriage and,

occasionally, divorce. The commanding officer at Milton Hall had decided that for an operation like this the men themselves should choose the partners they felt they could best work with under the harrowing conditions ahead. The only criterion was that, beside the radio operator, who could be of any nationality, each team had to include one British or American officer, and one French or Belgian or Dutch officer. Throughout the previous weeks all the Jedburghs had been mixed together in all training exercises, but there was a natural enough tendency for each of the nationalities to stick pretty much to themselves socially. As a consequence, Jacques Favel (his real name was Camille Lelong, but all Frenchmen used pseudonyms to protect their families under German occupation) was the only one of the French Jedburghs I knew really well. The reason for this was that he had gone to high school in Louisiana, where his father had owned a cotton plantation, and he enjoyed socializing with the American Jeds.

He and I got along particularly well. He was lively and outgoing, a dazzler with the English girls, an extremely deadly poker player, tough, quick with a native intelligence and an ability to handle himself in tight places. He had gone to Algeria after the fall of France and joined the Free French forces after the Allied invasion of North Africa. We quickly agreed to an engagement (a trial period to see how we liked working with each other), then decided on marriage (formalized by the command officially posting our names as a team) and were assigned Louis Giry (whose true name was Roger Villebois) to join us as the radio operator for Team Bruce. To show the informality of the operation, Lieutenant Favel was named team leader and Major Colby his deputy.

In the second week of August we finally were tapped to go. Ten Jedburgh teams had jumped into Brittany on D-Day and in subsequent weeks some twenty more had followed. On August 12, after the St. Lô breakout of Patton's Third Army, we were summoned to London. In a nondescript row house, a British officer told us we would be dropped to a *maquis* network led by Henri Frager, who was known as

Jean-Marie, in the Department of Yonne, southeast of Paris. "Go in, make contact, report the situation, and build up the resistance strength," we were told. We didn't need more precise instructions; we knew the basic drill from our training, and the mission of attacking Germans to turn them away from the Allied invasion was obvious. We were to take off at dusk from the air base at Tempsford. But the weather closed in, and the next day there was a sudden change of plan. We were told that word had come that Henri Frager had been arrested by the Gestapo. No one had any good information on how it happened. Later we heard that he had been picked up by a street patrol, quickly identified, and sent off to Buchenwald (where he was subsequently executed). We were briefed to meet and work with his deputy, Roger Bardet, who had taken charge of the network. We accepted the new order as simply as the first, as though our announced hostess had taken sick and was replaced by a cousin. The friendly British girl escort officer took us to Tempsford to check our equipment, and at dusk we climbed into the Slick Chick.

And so now, with dark fallen once again, we climbed out of the ditch in which we had been hiding and continued on our way to find Roger Bardet. A summer thunderstorm sprang up; the fields turned into a muddy morass, and the night became so unfathomably dark that the three of us fastened ourselves to each other with our pistol lanyards so as not to become separated and lost. Slogging and stumbling along a compass course in this awkward fashion, staying clear of farmhouses where dogs would bark at us, we made pretty poor headway. I realized that it would take us forever proceeding like this; we had to get help.

Then, toward 2 A.M., we suddenly heard muffled voices a short distance off in the darkness. A lightning flash revealed a lone farmhouse. It was far too late an hour for ordinary farmers still to be awake. We decided to chance it. With Giry and me covering him with our pistols, Favel knocked on the door. The voices within stopped abruptly. Then, after a moment: *"Qui est là?"* Favel replied, *"Un français."* A few moments more of silence. Then the door opened. Favel went in. Giry and I waited tensely. Then Favel opened the door and said, "It's all right. Come on in."

As luck would have it, we had stumbled on a *maquis* radio post, manned by an agent who had been parachuted in from England just eight days before. He sent a signal to London, reporting Team Bruce's position and disposition. We spent the following day hidden in the house and the next morning were driven in a beat-up, charcoal-burning Citroen the fifteen remaining miles to our proper drop zone, where we went to the "safe house" emergency contact point. There we arranged to be passed on through the Jean-Marie network to Sommecaise, a small farm village twenty miles to the east, where Roger Bardet had set up his "headquarters."

We met in Sommecaise's sole café. Bardet was seated at a table in the corner, a bottle of red wine and a plate of food in front of him, while armed resistance fighters lounged about eyeing us as we came in. Bardet stood up and we shook hands.

"Where have you been?" he asked. "We've been waiting three days. We had the signal fires ready but no plane came."

We explained about our misplaced jump and close call in Montargis. Bardet nodded, had extra chairs pulled over to the table, invited us to sit down, then snapped orders to the others to have food brought to us.

"We're here to help you fight the Germans," I said, and pulled out my map and spread it on the table. "Where are they? How many are there? Where are your men? How many do you have? What about the other networks in the region? Who are their chiefs? These are the things we need to know so we can bring in more arms, coordinate our actions with the invading Allied armies, and hurt the enemy as much as we can."

I smoothed out the map, located our position on it, and expected Bardet to begin eagerly filling me in. But there was only silence. I looked up. Bardet was staring at me with small, black, beady eyes.

I cannot pretend that I was suspicious of Bardet then or, for that matter, at any time during our association. And when he was arrested after the liberation for being an agent of the Germans, the traitor who had sold out Henri Frager, and was convicted of treason and sentenced to death, I was as surprised as everyone else in the network. But there was something about him right there at the very start that didn't feel right. He had the look of a minor civil servant, a petty functionary, going through the motions instead of leading, wearing puttees and a beret, though he was anything but energetic, let alone daring, in his role of resistance leader. He never initiated the actions, but found reasons to oppose or delay those that others did, and forever pleaded ignorance about information we needed to know. I had the feeling that the intense and dedicated men under him gave his "leadership" lip service out of respect for Frager's memory, but were in fact autonomous.

In retrospect, of course, considering that he had been a German agent, one can understand his passivity. That he didn't turn us in to the Gestapo is also understandable: he realized by this time that he was on the wrong side of the war. With Patton's tanks now blasting across France, he was trying to disengage from the Germans and come over to the victors without attracting too much attention to himself from either. Only Nicole, the pretty English girl who had parachuted in April to serve Jean-Marie as a courier, had doubts about him. Of mixed British-French parentage, she had been recruited for the job when a British officer overheard her perfect French in a restaurant in London, and, after receiving one training jump from a balloon, she had come to the Yonne to help Frager run his network. Surrounded and barely escaping from a German roundup once, she had ever since harbored a suspicion that Roger Bardet's absence from that night's rendezvous was not entirely coincidental, and after our arrival she looked to us for orders to run messages through the German patrols to other *maquis* groups, always carrying a submachine gun hidden in her car.

But we were stuck with Bardet for the first few days be-

cause, having lost our radio in the drop, we needed the use
of his. I wasted little time contacting other *maquis* networks in the region and hunting out other more effective
resistance leaders with whom to coordinate our operation. I
found an over-all chief in the person of Colonel Chevrier
(his real name was Adrien Sadoul), a sixty-year-old former
French Army reserve officer and lawyer from Metz, with an
imperious manner, who proclaimed himself appointed by
de Gaulle's headquarters as the *maquis* chief for the entire
Department of Yonne. In actual fact, and certainly compared
with Bardet, who had some five hundred armed men in his
network, Chevrier commanded very little, perhaps a score of
personal associates. But what he did command, in a way
Bardet never could, was respect. He was flamboyant, charis-
matic, constantly on the move, in touch with all the other
resistance chiefs in the Department who themselves commanded some two thousand or more fighters. He was a potent political force, a spellbinding orator in tune with the
emotional times, a man I certainly could work with. We
soon shifted Team Bruce's activities to him and only once
had to intervene diplomatically to suggest that he rule as
"chairman" of a departmental committee of resistance leaders rather than as "commander" of such locally raised and
proud groups.

The first thing we had to do was get weapons and ammunition parachuted to the various networks. With Chevrier
we picked the most likely drop zones, secluded fields and
pastures in the outlying country. Each was given a code
name—Binnette, Pelle, Engrais, Rateau—a signal letter and
these with the map coordinates locating the field were ra-
dioed to London. Each code name corresponded to a prearranged code phrase, some nonsense statement like, for example, "Le Vieux Monsieur de Gaie Sentiment," or "Le Vin
Est Rouge." What we then had to do was listen to the "*Messages personnels*" that followed Beethoven's Fifth Symphony theme on the nightly news that the BBC broadcast to
France. And when, in the course of that, we heard one of
our nonsense phrases, we knew that a drop was scheduled

that night for the field to which the phrase corresponded. So we'd go out to that field about midnight, listen for a plane, light the signal fires, flash the arranged identifying letter, and then duck to avoid the arms-filled containers crashing down in the dark. I have never heard Beethoven's Fifth Symphony theme since without thinking of those messages.

In the first two weeks behind the lines we arranged for at least a dozen such drops, bringing in several thousand rifles and carbines, mortars and bazookas and machine guns. And with those arms, the numbers of resistance fighters in the region was doubled, then tripled, as farmers and farm maids flocked to the *maquis* now that the war at last was going against the Germans. The uprising was underway. *Maquis* units ambushed patrols, attacked convoys, blew up supply depots. At one point a German plane was forced to make a landing in a field because it had run out of fuel, and I joined the *maquis*'s attack on it, shooting it up thoroughly, but learning the lesson that guerrillas should not make frontal attacks. The harassment of our hit-and-run actions was continual, forcing the Germans to divert their attention from their main tasks of defending against Patton's advancing Third Army and withdrawing their forces from southwestern France. One day, near Montargis, past the outposts manned by Lieutenant Colonel Creighton Abrams' tanks, we visited Patton's headquarters to relay intelligence on the state of the German forces and the movement of their troops. Since Patton was moving with such phenomenal speed north of the Yonne, he was leaving his right flank wide open to German counterattack, so we took the job of helping protect that flank by establishing posts and occupying towns along it, blowing up bridges on the Loire, and doubling our harassing raids on German units in that area.

It was an explosive, exciting time and, though it didn't seem so then, remarkably brief. By the second week of September, the liberation of Yonne was complete. The *maquis* units took over the towns of the Department, wine, champagne and oratory flowed like water in celebration of the liberation. Team Bruce went on to Paris (with a slight detour to pick up an old girl friend of Favel's) for a grand gathering of the surviving Jedburghs, including a great meeting with Bob Anstett, a fellow Columbia law student, whose Jedburgh mission "liberated" Vichy Premier Pierre Laval's black Cadillac, which he turned over to me as he climbed on a plane to England.

For Favel and Giry, who rejoined the French Army, the war in Europe was over. (Favel served as a liaison officer with the Americans and after the war, following in his father's footsteps, went back to Louisiana to run a cotton plantation, and there he lives today. Giry, unluckier, was sent to Indochina, where he was killed in 1945.) But the war wasn't over yet for me. I was slated to command yet another OSS mission behind enemy lines.

I returned to London wondering what new mission I might draw. A plan to drop into Alsace was abandoned when the Germans withdrew across the Rhine, and my one year of college German was not enough for me to be considered for a mission into the hostile Reich. Then Gerry Miller, our London Jedburgh chief, called me in and said they needed a major who could take command of OSS's Norwegian Special Operations (NORSO) Group. This was a group of a hundred or so Norwegian-Americans who had been used in France and were now destined for a drop into northern Norway, to sabotage the Northland Railway over which the Germans were moving 150,000 troops toward the final battle of Germany after having been pushed out of Finland. I quickly accepted, as it seemed an interesting and important mission, and better than the long delay and confusion that a move to the Far Eastern theater might involve.

"By the way," Miller said to me, "do you ski?" We both belatedly realized that the Norwegian mountains were deep in winter snow, but I assured him that my days as one of the first members of the Burlington High School ski club in Vermont had taught me how to climb the then chairliftless Green Mountains, and to maneuver safely, if not swiftly, back down.

My first command was a bit dubious about this non-Norwegian who arrived to lead them. They were at the time living in a pleasant country house north of London, resting and refitting after their operation in France, where they had been led by the colorful Colonel Serge Obolensky, who had learned his military lore in the St. Petersburg Imperial Guards and had met Donovan in New York society circles. Now a Fort Benning graduate, I, arrived to put them through miles of double-time jogging, begin the preparations for the drop into Norway, and select the few who would be taken on the long flight over the North Sea. I quickly moved them to the Scottish Highlands, where they could toughen up with long treks in the mountains and refresh their ability to shoot and ski. The area had the benefit also of being fifty miles north of the nearest American military police post and among sympathetic Scots who could understand the effect of their national drink on soldiers let out only on Saturday night. We even survived a field exercise when, living off the land, we shot and roasted one of the royal deer from the preserve around Balmoral Castle, the King's highland retreat.

Night drops into enemy country can take place only during a favorable "moon period," when the darkness is lightened so that rivers and lakes can be seen for navigation. We were ready to go in January, but bad weather dominated that month's moon period. In the February period, we dispatched an advance party of my second in command, Captain Tom Sather; our best radio operator, Borge Langeland; Arne "Tank" Listeid; and "Hans Hoel" (in truth Herbert Helgesen), a Norwegian liaison officer with the resistance, who had been smuggled back from the area through Sweden to go with us. But the long flight was turned back by the weather and reached base only after jettisoning all equipment. By the next moon period, we had changed our target and drop zone when the Norwegian exile newspaper in London reported that the Germans had strengthened the defenses of exactly the target area we planned to hit—the press had revealed the first of many intelligence leaks I would have to contend with in my career.

Finally, on March 24, Gerry Miller came out to the Harrington air base to bid me goodbye as our eight black Liberators revved up for the flight to the snow-white Norwegian coast and the drop zone on frozen Lake Jaevsjo in the wooded mountains north of Trondheim. Operation "Rype" (Norwegian for *"ptarmigan,"* which is white in winter, brown in summer, like our parkas) was at last underway.

The immense distance to the target zone was one of the main difficulties of the mission. Only four of the eight planes dropped anywhere near the target; one dropped fifty miles into neutral Sweden, and three were forced to return to England. I was in one of the successful four planes and landed easily on the frozen lake. It was midnight. I saw a bonfire built on a bed of logs, burning through the ground mist. I walked toward it. A tall figure was waiting. I took my pistol in hand, just in case. The prearranged password was, "Is the fishing good in this lake?" I said that in my rudimentary Norwegian. The proper response was, "Yes, particularly in the winter." But the fellow looked at me rather quizzically and said, "To tell you the truth, it's no good at all." I suppose I was meant to shoot him for giving the wrong answer, but my instinct was to look for a real explanation, such as his not knowing the password. So I went with him to meet the others who had jumped with me, and Helgesen vouched for his old friends.

We spent Palm Sunday collecting our supplies and the chutes scattered over the lake, hoping the Germans would not send a spotter plane to see what the midnight air activity had been all about. We established a camp in the woods with our parachutes for tents, so that we would not be seen by Easter skiers. Our local Norwegian reception committee, six resistance team members, a reindeer herder and guide, and an isolated farmer, told us the Germans were in the Snaasa Valley, twenty miles west. Our strength was only sixteen of the thirty-six who had left Scotland, not enough to blow the Grana Bridge as we had planned. The three planes that had returned to England would try again, and I decided to await them before moving out on the operation.

So each night we tuned in on BBC's personal messages, this time in Norwegian, to learn if they were coming. After two trials, with bad weather aborting the drops each time at the last moment, the moon period ran out and London told us to go ahead with what we had. Headquarters at the same time informed us that they had canceled all further air operations to us; two aircraft had crashed, and that convinced them that the mission was just too long a distance.

So we set out on our first sabotage mission. With six of the Norwegian resistance fighters, we took off on a hundred-mile, six-day cross-country ski trek—each man carrying a fifty-pound pack and taking turns pulling the small toboggans carrying sixty pounds of explosives. It was a brutal journey, often through blinding blizzards in zero temperatures and involving the climbing of ice-covered, boulder-strewn mountains and the crossing of lakes and streams. One of my concerns was that one of the men might break a leg, leaving me an impossible task of evacuating him through the mountains and facing the problem of where to find medical care for him. So I told them all to sit down on their skis if they went out of control, and I guaranteed them against shame by assuring them that I would be the first to do so at the head of the column. It was a slower way to proceed, but it worked—not even a sprain.

At last we reached the Northland Railway. I took two men and went down to look at our target, the Grana Bridge. The defenses were substantial, and the German force was too large for our small band. So I left my two men to reconnoiter further and skied over the mountain emptiness alone to rejoin the main group. I picked a smaller bridge off the map and railway chart; it was at Tangen. We arrived about dawn, set our charges and waited for a possible train, in hopes of repeating the sabotage operation that our Norwegian colleagues had pulled off nearby some months before. There a German troop train had run straight into the stream at Jorstad, some hours after the bridge had been blown. But I posted lookouts with walkie-talkies to ensure that we didn't blow the bridge in front of a train full of Norwegian civilians. Finally, the wait becoming too long, we blew the bridge and left our small American-flag shoulder patches to show who had done it and, hopefully, protect the local population from German reprisal. This time the trek was serious; we knew the Germans were after us, and our escape depended on moving east before their truck-borne patrols could cut us off. I named one long, steep climb Benzedrine Hill, in honor of the stimulant that got me up it. But we made it ahead of the patrols, thanks also to the indefatigable trail breaking of Hans Leirmo, our elderly timber guide whose legs were made of spring steel, and Herbert Helgesen, who showed the cross-country stamina that he later applied as chairman of the Norwegian Olympic cross-country skiing team.

We turned north along the Swedish border, and I left the main group and went ahead with Langeland and Helgesen to the Jaevsjo base to report to London by radio, after a week of silence. On the lake before our farm hideout, Leif Oistad, the leader of the five who had been dropped in Sweden, embraced me in welcome; they had, with a conspiratorial wink from the Swedish intelligence authorities, been spirited up from an internment camp in Sweden to join us.

A few days' rest in mid-April, and off we went to the railroad again, this time to take out, by small charges, as many rails as we could. In the dark of the moon we split into teams, silently crept to the line, placed our charges, and at midnight sharp the first went off. My team hadn't quite finished, but we quickly did so when a German flare went off fifty yards from us. A bullet kicked a pebble against my forehead, but I told Sivert Windh not to fire his Browning automatic rifle; I didn't want the Germans to know that a regular unit with automatic weapons was near them. We jumped the fence, retrieved our skis, and made fast tracks on the hard snow crust up the trail back into the mountains. Applying the lesson of my drop in France, I made the group keep going all the way back to base, taking a roundabout route to point the German patrols in the wrong direction until a friendly snowstorm covered our tracks.

Day and night our radio brought news of the progress of the final battles in Germany, but our concerns were more immediate. Our food had run out, despite an occasional reindeer. Friendly Norwegians had come to join us (and had to be fed), and the Germans were still seeking us. One five-man patrol found us, but they were shot down after its chief shot one of our Norwegians. But if the war had lasted, the follow-up patrols would surely have caught us.

Meanwhile, I argued with my operations chief in the London headquarters. During my Jedburgh days and after, I had visited our headquarters a few times; but I had never learned the intricate procedures of a multinational command. I urged a political gesture: let's seize the mountain redoubt of Lierne and declare it the first step of Norway's liberation, with the NORSO Group and the friendly Norwegians who would flock to us, replaying France's liberation. Headquarters replied that the idea was not feasible at the time. My repeated arguments were automatically distributed in multiple copies to allied British and Norwegian officers, instead of going as personal arguments to my chief. The argument ended when I received a message that said sharply that my orders were to stay in hiding and that "any unauthorized contact by you with enemy will subject you to immediate disciplinary action." Headquarters was right— the delicate political procedure of securing the surrender of the remaining Germans in Norway was not to be upset by a flamboyant action in Lierne. I also learned that complex headquarters operate through joint knowledge and coordination, not by "personal messages" from subordinate unit commanders to individual staff officers.

One mission completed during this period was an unhappy one. A Lapp reindeer herder told us that he had found a crashed plane on the top of the tree-bare Plukkutjonnfjellet. We went to it and there found and buried our four team members and the air crew, who had hit the hilltop trying too hard to drop to us.

On May 11, four days after V-E day, we were ordered by London to move down to the Snaasa Valley. With two six-foot sergeants as escort—and the rest of our unit covering, against the possibility that the German troops, defying their leaders' surrender, might take over our entire group—I approached the German garrison's gate. The German commander was more nervous than I, and he quickly assured me that all German units would remain in their camps in perfect discipline. The highway to Trondheim then became an excited parade through each small community as the normally stolid Norwegians cheered the Allied victory and the end of the German occupation. The NORSO Group was a prominent element in the National Day parade before Crown Prince Olaf in Trondheim.

But its duties in Norway were not over. The town of Namsos sixty miles up the coast had been destroyed in 1940 by German bombers and still had some ten thousand German troops in it. The population asked for some visible reassurance that the war indeed was over. The NORSO Group was chosen for the job, about thirty strong. We rode the same railroad we had blown up, somewhat chastened at the short time in which it had been repaired by Russian POW's. I billeted the men in friendly homes in the town and hoped that a combination of American confidence and German discipline would do the job. I soon realized that a problem was developing as our men reported shoulder brushes on narrow sidewalks with proud German soldiers, but one evening the problem was made clear as the crew of five German naval craft circled the harbor chanting *"Sieg Heil!"* My orders, wisely, were that we should show ourselves in Namsos, inspect at will, but under no circumstances give a German an order or attempt to arrest or disarm him. This was an order easy to follow, as I had not the slightest idea of what I could do if a German refused to obey me. But I could and did have a responsibility to demonstrate that the war was over, so I phoned the German commander to announce that at 9 A.M. the next day I would visit the naval ships "to inspect them." Taking three NORSO members, all former Norwegian merchant mariners, I climbed aboard each ship, despite the sullen looks of the crewmen. And that put an end to all demonstrations; the message was clear to all that the war indeed was over. Inspection made the point to German as well as Norwegian.

I spent a few days in Oslo, took a sunny daytime flight back to London, contrasting with our midnight flight to German-occupied Norway, and made a kindly arranged duty visit to OSS headquarters in Paris, where just by coincidence my father was also then stationed at SHAEF. I made one proposal for a new assignment in Europe before departing for China, asking OSS chief Russell Forgan if I could be put to work on anything OSS might be planning to complete the liberation of Europe from fascism by operations against Franco's rule in Spain. He quickly said no, and I learned that America's mission in Europe was not purely ideological. A slow ship back to the "Welcome Home—Well Done" sign in New York harbor followed in short order.

The first thing I did when I landed in New York was look up Barbara Heinzen. She had graduated from Barnard and was working for Abraham and Strauss in Brooklyn as a copy-writer. I wasted no time, and we were engaged within two weeks. I was assigned to the Pacific Theater, due to be shipped either to China (because of my boyhood sojourn there) or to Indochina (because I could speak French). Most of the Jedburghs, after their operations in France, had been sent into action behind Japanese lines in China, Vietnam, and Thailand, while I was on the Norwegian operation.

Among the groups that the OSS supported to fight the Japanese was a small faction of Vietnamese Communists led by an intense and dedicated Ho Chi Minh. Several of the photos of the time incongruously show Ho, Vo Nguyen Giap, Pham Van Dong, and others in friendly solidarity with their American-uniformed OSS-team colleagues. And there my OSS counterparts, looking to the ideology of the war for freedom, also urged support for Ho and his movement against French attempts to reimpose its old colonial rule as the Japanese moved out. In this they had the sympathy of Franklin Roosevelt, who had vigorously said, "France has had the country—thirty million inhabitants—for nearly a hundred years, and the people are worse off than they were in the beginning." He looked to a trusteeship leading to independence. But Roosevelt died, and Truman was preoccupied by the problems of Europe in which a reborn France and the British grand alliance were important factors. So the OSS link with Vietnamese Communism was broken off, and America supported the revival of French and British colonialism and only later sought non-Communist nationalists to slow the momentum that Ho had first developed with OSS. This deference to the demands of statecraft over the ideology of freedom would have enormous consequences with which I would have to deal twenty years later. But I was far from this issue then.

While I was in New York on leave, the atomic bombs were dropped, and the war in the Pacific came to an end. That ended my self-discipline not to marry during the war and risk leaving a widow, and Barbara and I were married on September 15 at St. Patrick's in New York. I stopped in advance at a quiet Catholic church to confess the lively bachelor life I had lived as a paratrooper for three years and resolved again to follow the Catholic discipline I had strayed from during the war—because I knew that Barbara was firm in her faith, for which my Irish mother thanked all the saints. She came with me down to Washington, and we looked into our future.

I was to be transferred to a military unit and assigned to Fort Leavenworth to attend the Command and General Staff School in preparation for a regular military career. Since I would be starting as a major at twenty-five, the prospect seemed promising. But in truth, I had no intention of doing that; I was eager to get out of the Army and resume my studies at Columbia Law School. In those turbulent weeks after V-J Day, I had no idea how long it would take to get my discharge; so, figuring that it would be a more fruitful way to spend my last months in the Army than any other, I agreed to enroll at the Staff School. But then a point system was introduced as the scheme by which it would be determined who got out of the Army first. I had won the Bronze Star and the Croix de Guerre for the Jedburgh operation in France, and the Silver Star and St. Olaf's Medal for the Norwegian operation. Those, combined with my length of service, dating from before Pearl Harbor, gave me enough points to be eligible for discharge immediately. I checked with Columbia. They said they would enroll me for the fall semester if I could make the classes on the next Monday. Sure I could make it.

But we had one final task to perform for OSS, to provide the backdrop for OSS's last assembly. It occurred in the skating rink next to the brewery behind the Washington headquarters of OSS on the Potomac River. The Commander of OSS, Wild Bill Donovan, wanted to dramatize the work of his OSS brainchild by showing what great things the men and women of his command had done to meet the wartime challenges. It was the first time that I had met this legendary figure. When he pinned the Silver Star on me, he stopped for a moment to comment that he had always wanted that decoration himself. I replied, somewhat embarrassedly, that it would indeed have complemented the Medal of Honor, Distinguished Service Cross, and Distinguished Service Medal already on his chest. He smiled, then moved on down the line to decorate the mild-looking man standing beside me for his service in Bangkok under Japanese occupation as the link to a "Free Thai" leader.

As he passed down to others, the thought struck me how lucky I was to be alive. If the landing in France had been a few hundred yards to the north into the German garrison, if we hadn't walked far enough that night, if Roger Bardet had turned me in, if I had been in one of the planes that crashed in Norway, if we hadn't outrun the Nazi ski patrols, if . . . if . . . if the war had not ended when it did and I had been sent to China, my luck might not have held on a third try at operating behind enemy lines. But it had, and I was still alive and married to a wonderful girl and ready to turn to the serious business of getting a law degree and getting on with life. Intelligence was over. The ceremony meant that America had discarded it for the better days of peace, as it had always done at the end of a war. In two years I'd be a lawyer, eager to get into the liberal causes of the period ahead after the defeat of fascist totalitarianism and aggression.

But OSS was more than an episode or an adventure. It had a major impact on me personally of course, transforming the young and somewhat shy student I was before into a man with confidence, knowing that I could face risk and danger and hold my own in a company of free spirits exulting in their bravery. I had seen at first hand the political commitment to freedom of my French and Norwegian colleagues translated into courageous actions against a brutal Nazi occupation. A girl in Norway, who told me she had not attended a movie in the five years of German occupation and censorship, gave me an idea of the power of political commitment even in those unable to play more active roles.

But I learned that bravery and commitment are not enough alone. If they are not accompanied by wisdom, they can lead to futile, and fatal, wastage. The heroism of the French resistance had to be scheduled carefully or it led to such disasters as at the Vercors Plateau, where a premature uprising was crushed mercilessly by the Germans. Furthermore, it would have been of little avail to France without the massive military power of the Allies landed at Normandy, and its real value lay in its contribution to their move across France. My own mission's greatest worth probably was in lifting one worry from General Patton, whose single-minded drive across France could proceed in confidence that his flank was secure, or that he would know in good time if it was not.

I couldn't help but wonder whether the pinpricks of the small bridge and half-mile of rails we had destroyed in Norway, fixed in short order by the prisoners and slave laborers of the Germans, were really worth the lives of our comrades and the plane crews who had crashed with them. The political fact that Americans had fought and died in Norway dramatized the new alliance between America and this fatherland of so many of our citizens, but I wondered how much our costly mission really contributed to such a major political relationship. In this field, however, the actions of a few could produce potent political results, independent of their physical contribution. Thus, the final worth even of the bravery of our men lay in the political dimension.

But had we been wiser, sooner, in this case in identifying and meeting Hitler's threats politically before he was so powerful that he could be met only militarily, we might have produced the same results for the cause of freedom without all the death and destruction that procrastination required in the end. Although my own OSS role was in the guerrilla field, the secret techniques of intelligence surrounded me, and drummed into me the lesson that knowledge is vital to action, and that it can forestall the need for frantic heroism. Dropping into France or Norway was premised on the fact that even mistakes were not fatal among a populace friendly to our cause. Dropping into Germany was a different question; there a united and disciplined populace would have turned me in.

As I stood at the ceremony in my uniform, I realized that the OSS experience had been valuable in other ways. Rather than being lost in the rigidities of the great military machinery, I had been remarkably free of its procedures and had been individually responsible for my job. I had associated with free and brave Americans and allies, and drew from them and the crises we faced the psychic rewards from meeting great challenges. The experience convinced me of the importance of freedom, personal as well as political, and my survival had given me hope that similar efforts to further it in the future could be successful.

During the final ceremony, Donovan referred first to his scholars and research experts in describing the OSS "team" and only secondly mentioned the "active units in operations and intelligence who engaged the enemy in direct encounter." In this he reflected his unique contribution to American intelligence, that scholarship was its primary discipline, that the acquisition of information was to serve it, and that its paramilitary adventures were an adjunct to its authority and expertise in secret machinery. If anyone other than

Donovan had started American intelligence, these three elements might not have been combined in it. But he did, and they reappeared in later uneasy alliance in this new discipline for America.

The surge of "now it can be told" stories about the OSS, which flowed into the mass media after the war, concentrated on its adventurous aspects almost exclusively, however. These glamorous aspects of the OSS resistance and guerrilla experience thus came to dominate its public image, submerging the analytical contribution and the more refined clandestine discipline of secret intelligence. To be sure, the research analysts were mentioned in the official and semiofficial accounts of the OSS experience, but the great innovation they brought to the intelligence profession in those years was not given the public prominence it deserved.

This was to have long-term effects. For one thing, in the intelligence profession a split developed between the scholars and analysts on the one side and the paramilitary and covert operatives on the other. For another, the rash of publicity of the OSS's glamorous adventures confirmed the spy-fiction stereotype of intelligence and developed an appetite for such stories of intrigue and sensation in the American public. The consequence of both would have a powerful effect on the practice of intelligence in the decades ahead.

CHAPTER TWO

Intelligence or the Law

Peace. In the autumn of 1945 the nation heaved a collective sigh of relief and satisfaction at the successful end of the years of combat and destruction, its unity and effort fully justified by the shocking revelations of Hitler's death camps. It sadly but proudly buried its dead, including my closest Burlington High School friend, Jim Cooke, outside Manila; my parachute artillery companion from Texas, Carrol Willis, in Italy; my Norwegian-American comrades in England. In the space of a few months, the greatest naval, air and army force ever assembled to fight two wars simultaneously melted away through demobilization, and the nation looked ahead to a world free of the menace of Fascist aggression.

But one wise man was concerned. For months Bill Donovan had argued vigorously that the United States would need a centralized intelligence service in the years ahead as much as it did during the war. In November 1944 he wrote to his Columbia Law School classmate President Roosevelt exactly what should be done:

> Once our enemies are defeated, the demand will be equally pressing for information that will aid us in solving the problems of peace. This will require two things: 1. That intelligence control be returned to the supervision of the President. [During the war, the OSS had been under the direction of the Joint Chiefs of Staff.] 2. The establishment of a central authority reporting directly to you, with responsibility to frame intelligence objec-

tives and to collect and coordinate the intelligence material required by the Executive Branch in planning and carrying out
national policy and strategy.

More specifically, Donovan proposed that this central authority should coordinate the functions of all government intelligence agencies (e.g., Army G-2, the Office of Naval Intelligence, State Department); collect intelligence through
its own network of spies and counterspies which it would
recruit, train and run itself; evaluate, synthesize and dissem-
inate all the intelligence needed by the government to determine policies "with respect to national planning and security in peace and war, and the advancement of broad
national policy"; conduct "subversive operations abroad";
have its own independent budget; and exercise "such other
functions and duties relating to intelligence as the President
from time to time may direct." What the authority, however,
would not have—and Donovan made quite a point of excluding it—was any police or law-enforcement function,
either at home or abroad. In effect, what he outlined in this
memo was the Central Intelligence Agency.

But Donovan and the OSS had made powerful enemies
and jealous rivals with their free-wheeling, flamboyant style.
The military repeatedly resisted an independent intelligence service during the war. (MacArthur, for example,
banned the OSS entirely from his Pacific Theater of operations, and the OSS was formed only after Donovan consented that it report to the Joint Chiefs of Staff.) The military
certainly would not be subservient to him and his organization in the intelligence field in peacetime. Nor was the State
Department about to surrender its primacy in the processing
and analysis of information in the field of foreign affairs.
But Donovan's most adamant and potent foe was J. Edgar
Hoover.

Before Roosevelt established the OSS, he had given the
FBI the job not only of protecting the nation against sabo-
teurs and spies at home but also of running espionage and
counterespionage operations in Latin America, and it had
continued these operations after the OSS was formed, and to

the exclusion of the OSS, throughout the war. Now with war's end, Hoover was eager to expand this mandate. Donovan's scheme directly threatened his ambitions and, with the enthusiastic support of G-2, ONI and the State Department, Hoover set about sabotaging it.

On February 9, 1945, under the byline of a certain Walter Trohan, the *Washington Times-Herald* and its sister newspaper, the *Chicago Tribune,* carried a startling story.

> Creation of an all-powerful intelligence service to spy on the postwar world and pry into the lives of citizens at home is under consideration by the New Deal. . . . The *Washington Times-Herald* and the *Chicago Tribune* yesterday secured exclusively a copy of a highly confidential and secret memorandum from General Donovan to President Roosevelt . . . setting up the general intelligence service, which would supersede all existing Federal police and intelligence units, including Army G-2, Navy ONI, the Federal Bureau of Investigation, the Internal Revenue Agency . . .

The article then went on to imply that the proposed intelligence service would have secret funds for spy work "along the lines of bribery and luxury living described in the novels of E. Phillips Oppenheim." It was an inspired hatchet job, obviously meant to raise fear in the public mind that what Donovan was intent on forming was some sort of Gestapo. And how had Trohan got hold of Donovan's memo to Roosevelt in the first place? Hoover had given it to him.

There is every reason to believe that Roosevelt favored Donovan's idea of converting the OSS into a peacetime central intelligence agency. But, because of the flap caused by Trohan's article, he decided to postpone taking any action on it for a few weeks, until the furor calmed down. But by the time it did, it was too late. Roosevelt was dead and Truman had stepped into the Presidency. Donovan made one last try to save the OSS. Calling on such talented writers as Stewart Alsop, Tom Braden and John Shaheen within the OSS's ranks, he launched a propaganda campaign from which came a flood of glamorous adventure stories of the OSS's wartime exploits. But it didn't do any good. In fact, if anything, it probably did harm. Truman was annoyed, interpreting the campaign as just so much self-aggrandizement on Donovan's part, designed to launch the colorful hero of two wars—and a Republican—into national politics.

And, besides, the new and inexperienced President had other, far more urgent matters pressing on him. In his first months of office, he had to deal with the surrender of Nazi Germany, the decision to drop the atomic bomb, the capitulation of Japan, the meeting with Stalin and Churchill at Potsdam, and all the problems of organizing the peace in the postwar world. In this perspective, the future of the OSS seemed minor indeed, a niggling irritant, and the best way of dealing with it was simply by getting rid of it. On September 20, 1945, he did just that, disbanding it.

Under his Executive Order terminating the OSS, Truman hit upon a rather Solomonic solution as to how to dispose of the organization's functions and personnel: he ordered that the baby be cut in half. The researchers and analysts, men like William Langer, Sherman Kent and Ray Cline, who had toiled quietly during the war in Washington, evaluating and synthesizing intelligence from all sources, and who were to go on and make distinguished careers as intelligence officers in later years, were assigned to the State Department. There, under Presidential order, they were meant to "take the lead in organizing peacetime intelligence." But State wasn't in the least pleased to have these outsiders thrust upon it, and rather than have them function as a single expert unit, it scattered them haphazardly throughout the Department where their value was diluted and eventually wasted.

As for the OSS's clandestine operatives, the spymasters and counterspies like Richard Helms, James Angleton, Harry Rositzke, Tom Karamessines, John Bross and Lyman Kirkpatrick, who too were to become major figures in the American intelligence community in the years to come, they were transferred to the War Department. There they fared a bit better than their colleagues at State. They were at least kept together by a proper Army officer, William Quinn, who knew their value from firsthand exposure in southern France. His Strategic Services Unit at the War Department pushed and supported them to keep their old OSS spy networks in Eastern Europe, the Balkans and China and to begin developing confidential liaison with friendly foreign intelligence services.

Despite their relative impotence, these two groups must be credited with keeping the flame of intelligence burning in America during the first postwar year. At State, the group of historians, political scientists and other scholars dedicated to transforming raw information into "intelligence" to alert the President to the realities and complexities of the postwar world, held fast to the ideal of independent and objective analysis. They fought hard against being integrated into the regular diplomatic service. And the SSU group at the War Department dedicated itself to demonstrating the need for professional secret espionage and counterespionage operations even in peacetime, especially in those countries where the Communists were in power or threatening to become so. The dedication of both groups unquestionably had a long-term, positive influence on the practice of intelligence gathering in the subsequent decades.

But there was another long-term effect—and this quite a negative one—as a result of the split of OSS functions and personnel between the State and War Departments. The separation of the research and analysis scholars from the clandestine operatives encouraged and exacerbated the growth of two "cultures" within the intelligence profession, cultures severely compartmented from each other and often hostile to or contemptuous of each other—a condition that has plagued and complicated intelligence work to this day.

There was, of course, yet a third group of OSS personnel that had to be disposed of at war's end: the paramilitary types, the parachutists and guerrilla fighters and covert propagandists like Michael Burke, Tom Braden, Stewart Alsop, John Shaheen and me. As there seemed at that time to be absolutely no use for us or our special skills in peacetime intelligence work, we were given the choice of making our careers in regular military service or going home. Some, such as Jedburghs Aaron Bank, Jack Singlaub and Bill Pietsch, chose the military and went on to play important roles there in developing and refining the techniques of ir- regular guerrilla warfare that would one day lead to the for- mation of the U.S. Army Special Forces—the Green Berets. But most chose to go home and look ahead to the challenges of civilian life. Walter Mansfield returned to the law; Stew- art Alsop joined his brother Joe in writing a political news- paper column; and I returned to school to prepare for a ca- reer as a liberal-leaning labor lawyer.

Barbara found and fixed up a dark and rather dingy apart- ment on Manhattan's upper west side so that we could be near Columbia. To supplement the $80-a-month GI Bill (which just paid our rent), she supported us editing a house organ for the New York State Department of Labor until the first of our children came along. During this period I disap- peared all day and night into the library and law-review of- fices, and had no connection with the cloak-and-dagger world of intelligence. To be sure, from time to time, the Jed- burghs would get together in a rather haphazard sort of alumni evening on the town and light-hearted nostalgia about the good old days of derring-do. And from time to time we would see Donovan. As irrepressibly romantic as ever, he liked to stay in touch with his "boys," especially those who had participated in the more spectacular adven- tures, and he occasionally invited Barbara and me to join him in the seats allotted him as a trustee of Columbia for a football game, or for a dinner at his Sutton Place apartment. And out of this contact came an offer of a job. When I gradu- ated from Columbia Law School in February 1947, Donovan invited me to join his firm of Donovan, Leisure, Newton, Lumbard and Irvine.

The firm occupied three floors at 2 Wall Street and exuded the successful air of brilliant legal minds working on the great corporate problems of the day—antitrust counsel and defense, company mergers and stock issues and the tax con- sequences of trust arrangements. But there was something more. Walter Mansfield, Otto Doering, Dick Heppner and others had returned to the firm from service with Donovan in OSS, and they supported him still in his continuing campaign to convince the nation to establish a permanent professional intelligence service, and worked also on the legal problems of Donovan's international contacts.

As the most junior associate, I wrote drafts of legal briefs, reviewed minutes of trade-association clients to ensure that they did not transgress the Sherman Act, and took notes as the partners met with the clients to outline their cases. And at times there was the chance to deal with one or another of Donovan's OSS subordinates who had a new problem— helping with a book, straightening out a claim for disability, or just drafting encouraging letters. When Donovan was retained to determine the facts behind the murder of newsman George Polk in Greece in 1948, Barbara and I received his lovely young Greek widow, Rhea, and eased her arrival in America. And, in another case, I learned that the strict letter of the law does not always govern, when my careful legal pleadings were brushed aside by one exile Rumanian financier, who abruptly settled his intense dispute with another exile Rumanian financier on realizing that neither was apt to obtain access to some timberland now under Communist control in Rumania. (I noted that the opposing counsel was Frank Wisner, three floors above in 2 Wall Street, who had also been in OSS and had left in disgust at the low level to which the intelligence service had sunk in 1946.)

In the best Wall Street tradition, the individual lawyer's politics were his own affair. Most of the partners were Republicans, like Donovan, but my own Democratic leanings were respected, and my initial activities in that direction even encouraged. After all, a Wall Street institution must look with realism on the shifts in political direction in the United States, and it could only help to have friends and associates in both camps. So I went beyond the ritual membership in the downtown New York Young Democratic Club of lawyers and investment counselors to join my local Robert B. Blaikie Regular Democratic Association of the 7th Assembly District. In that outpost of Tammany Hall I rang doorbells to urge the voters to support Harry Truman for President in 1948, and helped as a watcher at the polls on the night of his victory. And with a kindred band of Democratic liberals such as Joe and Vince Broderick, I joined a rump group of "Fair Deal Democrats" in that traditional endeavor to purify Tammany from within that is a cyclical feature of New York's Byzantine politics, and to support the campaign of Franklin D. Roosevelt, Jr., for election to Congress. Another extracurricular activity was being an Army Reserve officer with fellow Wall Streeter and later Undersecretary of State and Ambassador to France, John Irwin, where we planned guerrilla exercises on maps of the West Point area and I took two weeks duty with the 82nd Airborne on a winter maneuver in the snow.

But peace was proving to be fragile. Stalin presented a new threat to the world, and Donovan had added a warning of danger to his appeals for a proper intelligence service. Gradually the political issues I dealt with included more international matters, and not merely the need for equal rights for blacks and unionization of labor. Soviet Communism had revealed itself as a new totalitarian threat to democratic people everywhere. Stalin had plainly reneged on the Yalta Agreements and was aggressively pushing his ambitions in much the way Hitler had done a decade before. Virtually every day one read in the newspapers of yet another Soviet move; the Communist coup in Czechoslovakia and Masaryk's shocking "suicide"; Communist insurrection in Greece; the Red Army's refusal to withdraw from Iran; Communist-inspired strikes and subversion in Italy and France—not to mention the unnerving examples of Soviet espionage in the United States and Britain as revealed in the trials of the Rosenbergs, Klaus Fuchs, Alger Hiss and Judith Coplon.

My dislike of Soviet Communism dated back to my college days, to my studies of the Spanish Civil War, to my reading of Lenin, to my awareness of the Stalinist purge trials, to my disgust with the Hitler-Stalin Pact. During the war I had heard from fellow Jedburghs of the ruthless Communist attempt to seize power in southern France. And I was shocked to learn of the Red Army's delay outside Warsaw to permit the Nazis to massacre the non-Communist Polish partisans so as to clear the way for a takeover by Polish Communists. The increasingly brazen events of the early Cold War years and the flood of books like *Darkness at Noon* and *Homage to Catalonia* brought Communist cynicism into clear focus. But, in fact, it took a personal experience in New York to show that the Communist threat was close to home.

I got a call one day in late 1946 from Mickey Boerner of the American Veterans Committee. The AVC had been formed to provide an alternative veterans' organization for former servicemen and servicewomen too liberal to join the conservative American Legion. In the early postwar period, the Communists were determined to play a role among veterans, but their efforts to penetrate and dominate the American Legion had, not surprisingly, failed. And so, just around this time, they had turned their attention to the fledgling, liberal AVC, and the struggle was in full bloom in Manhattan Chapter No. 1. In order to stave off a takeover by several Communist rank-and-file members, Mickey was trying to recruit additional liberal non-Communist veterans, and a law-school friend had suggested my name. I quickly agreed to come to the next meeting. It was an enlightening if disturbing experience.

About thirty members showed up, and after I joined and paid my dues I listened to the program. At issue was a Communist proposal that the Chapter adopt a resolution, to be submitted to the national convention, that called for support of the continued revolt by the "democratic forces" of Greece against the "Fascist-dominated" government there. An angry debate raged. On one side were those who recognized that the Communists had played a major role in the resistance against German occupation, but who did not want to see a repetition of the Communist takeover of Poland. On the other were the Communists, who argued that the real objective of the resistance sacrifices should be to sweep away the old regime entirely and replace it with a new society led by those hardened in the battle. The discipline and stamina of the Communists provided a classic example of the organizational techniques outlined by Lenin. And as the hour grew later and the wrangling continued, it was clear that only Mickey's band of special recruits would stay long enough to prevent the Communist victory on the resolution while the ordinary members left in disgust or because of the call of home and family. The Communist resolution did not pass, but neither was the AVC able to do or say anything constructive, and the dream of an organization of liberal veterans became a casualty of the new cold war.

This sort of struggle, of course, wasn't limited to the AVC. In the tradition of the Popular Front movements of the thirties and forties, Communist efforts at penetrating, subverting, and taking over liberal organizations (such as Henry Wallace's Progressive Party, where in great part they succeeded, and Walter Reuther's United Auto Workers, where they failed) were going on all over the world during this period. And this raised a crucial challenge and dilemma for liberals like myself: how could we resist real Communist aggression, which threatened to destroy our liberties, without falling into that hysterical, demagogic anti-Communism, which would soon go by the name of McCarthyism and clearly represented just as much a threat. It was a challenge, no matter how difficult, liberals had to meet; a dilemma, no matter how tricky, they had to solve. For in my view, what was happening in the late forties was a dangerous replay of what had happened in the late thirties. I was convinced that the Communists were as ruthlessly intent on expanding their totalitarian power and taking over the world as the Nazis had been a decade before. And I was just as eager now as I had been then that the United States and the other democracies collectively counter and contain this expansion before it grew to military conflict.

I was, of course, hardly alone in this view. Whereas for some liberals the desire to avoid the excesses of anti-

Communism or out of a confused nostalgia over Communism's erstwhile antifascism resulted in a kind of political paralysis and intellectual blindness, many leading Americans were clear about the danger. Harry Truman, George Marshall, Henry Stimson, Averell Harriman, and Bill Donovan called for a positive stand against the new totalitarian menace, a move to a new United Europe, economic recovery, support to Greece and Turkey, and a North Atlantic Alliance. As one step in this direction, James V. Forrestal called for the modernization of America's defense establishment to apply the lessons learned in World War II.

Just a few months after disbanding the OSS, Truman had come full circle to call for a central intelligence organization. As he later told Merle Miller and was quoted in the latter's oral biography, *Plain Speaking*, "The President needed at that time a central organization that would bring all the various intelligence reports we were getting in those days, and there must have been a dozen of them, maybe more, bring them all into one organization so that the President would get *one* report on what was going on in various parts of the world." Even before he dissolved the OSS, Truman had said to his naval aide, Clark Clifford, that, "If we had had some central repository for information, and somebody to look at it and fit all the pieces together, there never would have been a Pearl Harbor." * His view was reinforced by the recommendations of the Congressional Joint Committee on the Pearl Harbor Attack, which found the fragmentation of such American intelligence as existed in 1941 responsible in good measure for our lack of preparedness and called for a unified intelligence service.

But the problem of forming such a unified service was just as difficult then as it always had been. The Army, Navy, State Department and FBI, jealous of their own prerogatives in the intelligence field, opposed the creation of a strong central agency that would take precedence over them, whether led by Donovan or led by anyone else. Under the

* Tom Braden in *American Heritage*, February 1977.

circumstances, the best that Truman could arrange was a weak compromise. On January 22, 1946, only four months after OSS had been disbanded, by Presidential directive, he set up the National Intelligence Authority comprised of the Secretaries of State, War and Navy, as well as the President's personal representative (Admiral William D. Leahy). The NIA was charged with planning, developing and coordinating all "Federal foreign intelligence activities," and its operating arm was to be an organization called the Central Intelligence Group, whose personnel would come from the intelligence services of each of the overseeing departments. Its director, appointed by the President, was instructed to "accomplish the correlation and evaluation of intelligence" by making full use of "the staff and facilities of the intelligence agencies of (the) departments."

While the CIG was clearly the first step toward a CIA, it was nowhere near the independent, central authority that Donovan had visualized. In the first place, and crucially, it did not have its own budget. What funding it got, as well as its personnel, came from the departments and at their pleasure. And by this—as well as their overseer role on the NIA—the departments assured their autonomy and preeminence in the intelligence field. Moreover, the CIG, whose total staff at the outset numbered only eighty, was meant to concentrate on research and analysis. It was not to have an intelligence-gathering capability of its own, but would gather its facts from the State Department's overseas embassies and depend on the Army and Navy for military information. And to reassure the military that the CIG would respect the secrets to which it was given access, the NIA and the director were directed to be "responsible for fully protecting intelligence sources and methods." Nor, moreover, was the CIG meant to engage in any clandestine political or paramilitary operations of the sort that had made the OSS's reputation. To be sure, Truman's directive did say the CIG would "perform such other functions and duties related to intelligence affecting the national security as the President and the National Intelligence Authority may from time to time direct." But this was regarded as a catch-all phrase, borrowed from Donovan's memorandum to F.D.R. two years before and added to give flexibility for unforeseen contingencies in the future. And finally, to reassure the FBI and overcome any fears of an American Gestapo, Truman made a point of stressing that the CIG would deal only with foreign intelligence. It was to have "no police, law-enforcement or internal-security functions" (a paraphrase of another Donovan point) and was not authorized to conduct "investigations inside the . . . United States."

But as the Cold War intensified in the year following the CIG's formation, its inadequacy became increasingly apparent, and attempts were made to strengthen it for the job it had to do in an increasingly threatening world. The Strategic Services Unit at the War Department, with its old OSS spies and counterspies, was transferred (under the new designation of Office of Special Operations—OSO) to CIG. With that the Group got a small but highly professional independent clandestine collection capability with men like Richard Helms and Harry Rositzke operating in Germany, James Angleton in Italy, Alfred Ulmer in Austria. Moreover, it took over the FBI's intelligence-gathering function in Latin America. And the research-and-analysis staff was beefed up; an Office of Reports and Estimates was created to produce daily intelligence summaries and conduct economic and scientific research. And the Foreign Broadcast Information Service was brought over from the State Department to provide an overt collection capability on foreign affairs. By 1947 the CIG's staff had mushroomed to nearly two thousand (of which about one third were overseas). Even so, the general consensus of professional intelligence people was that the CIG was a disorganized assembly of parts, not a working machine, bigger but not much better than before. What was worse, it even failed to perform the specific function for which it was created. Separate intelligence reports from G-2, ONI, the State Department and a host of other agencies still flooded the President's desk. The

CIG merely added one more, albeit an interesting one, to the unstanchable stream.

This situation wasn't corrected until Forrestal's campaign to modernize the national-security structure finally succeeded. World War II had taught the wisdom of a single line of military command covering land, sea and air forces. The *ad hoc* and informal arrangements by which the nation had conducted that war had to be put on a formal and permanent basis if it were to pursue the Cold War effectively, and be ready for a hot one. How this should be done was debated all through 1946 and well into 1947. There were those who believed that the Army and Navy should be merged, with a single Department of National Defense, one chief of staff and one unified general staff. There were those who argued that the services be kept separate (the Air Force becoming independent) with a Joint Chiefs of Staff organization and a civilian Secretary of Defense coordinating them. So, when the Congress finally passed the National Security Act and the President signed it on September 15, 1947, the focus of attention was on the provisions coming from this debate: the creation of the National Security Council, establishment of an independent Air Force, and formation of the Department of Defense under which the separate Departments of Army, Navy and Air Force were unified. Little attention was paid to another provision in the Act. With virtually no discussion or debate, the Act also created a Central Intelligence Agency, giving the United States the first peacetime, coordinated and comprehensive intelligence service in its history.

The statutory charter establishing the CIA repeated much of the wording of Truman's Presidential directive, which had created the CIG eighteen months before. For example, the new agency was assigned the tasks of advising the National Security Council on matters related to national security, of making recommendations to the NSC on the coordination of the intelligence activities of all departments, of correlating and evaluating intelligence and providing for its appropriate dissemination, carrying out "services of common concern" (which was understood to be a euphemism for espionage and clandestine counterintelligence) and performing "such other functions and duties related to intelligence affecting the national security as the NSC may from time to time direct." Thus, in effect, the CIG was expected to carry on without major change under the new Agency name, collecting intelligence, both overtly and covertly, doing research and analysis and producing intelligence summaries and estimates.

But there were some crucial differences between CIG and CIA. Under the Act, the CIA was an independent department of the Executive Branch of government created by Congressional legislation. It was responsible directly to the NSC. Since the President presided over the NSC, and since the Cabinet members of the NSC had only advisory powers, this meant that the Agency had a direct channel to, and was under the control of, the President. The various competing intelligence services of the departments no longer could control the Agency's activities. And the CIA was given its own budget—a secret one at that—and was authorized to hire and train its own personnel.

There was one thing, however, the new agency did not get at this time. In his original memorandum on the subject to F.D.R. in 1944, Donovan had proposed that a central intelligence organization be authorized to conduct "subversive operations abroad." Truman had not taken up this suggestion in setting up the CIG, nor was it now included in the CIA's charter. American intelligence was launched instead toward a quiet future.

But with the rising intensity of the Cold War and the clear use by the Communist world of infiltration, subversion and guerrilla techniques—in Greece, in Western Europe, and in the Philippines—an increasing number of voices argued that the United States had to have not only the intelligence-collecting and -analysis capability to report on the Cold War, but also the political and paramilitary capability with which to fight it. In December 1947 a small step was made when President Truman gave CIA a charter to conduct small-scale covert psychological and propaganda operations. But others

called for broader political and even paramilitary action, re-
calling the wartime success of OSS support to people resisting Nazi totalitarianism. The issue was soon raised whether
and how America could provide large-scale covert assistance
to people who were struggling against Communist subversion and expansion in a Cold War, so that a hot war would
never be needed to free them.

Of especial concern at that moment—and a dramatic example of a situation where the need to meet Communist
subversion was particularly acute—was the 1948 election in
Italy. There the Soviet Union, employing a host of subversive techniques, was providing massive political support to
the Italian Communist Party in its campaign to overcome
the Italian Christian Democrats and the other center democratic parties. The fear was great that Italy could go the way
of Czechoslovakia, and by the same means, and if it did, as
George Kennan wrote at the time, "our whole position in
the Mediterranean, and possibly in western Europe as well,
would probably be undermined."

What was to be done? Private Italian-American groups organized letterwriting campaigns to urge friends and family
in Italy to reject the Communists. Economic and military aid
under the Marshall Plan was shipped to Italy to shore up
Gasperi's government. But clearly something more was
needed, something more than diplomacy and governmental
assistance, if Communist ambitions in Italy were to be frustrated. The democratic political parties and private groups
had to be helped, as the Soviets were helping the Communist ones. The something more needed was covert political
and propaganda support and operations of the kind with
which the OSS had helped the resistance grow in World
War II.

CIA's legislative charter did not contain Donovan's charge
to conduct "subversive operations abroad." But the need
was there, and, with a sudden stroke of ingenuity, the CIA
fixed on that catch-all phrase that had first appeared in Donovan's memo to F.D.R. and had been carried over to the
CIG and then to the CIA: "perform such other functions and

duties related to intelligence affecting the national security as the National Security Council may from time to time direct." Although CIA's general counsel first demurred, the feeling was that this wording could be construed to authorize the clandestine subversive operations needed now. The matter was put to Truman. He agreed. And in June 1948 the National Security Council issued Directive No. 10/2 authorizing the CIA to undertake secret political and paramilitary operations. A special unit, euphemistically entitled the Office of Policy Coordination (OPC), was set up to carry them out, under the direction of the Secretaries of State and Defense with the Director of CIA. And Frank Wisner, the intense New York lawyer who had seen Soviet tactics at first hand for the OSS in Rumania, was named to head it. Wisner landed like a dynamo, read all the intelligence and set out to form a clandestine force worldwide. By hard work and brilliance, and by reaching widely for similarly activist OSS alumni, he started it operating in the atmosphere of an order of Knights Templars, to save Western freedom from Communist darkness—and from war.

The creation of the OPC completed the formation of the CIA. There were the analysts evaluating information from all sources and drawing their conclusions. There were the spymasters and counterspies, recruiting and exploiting agents and working with foreign intelligence services. And now there were the covert political and paramilitary activists, reveling in risk, commitment and secret influence. Together these three "cultures," severely compartmented from one another, which were to dominate the intelligence community for the next two decades, formed an agency almost precisely like the one Donovan had proposed that his OSS become.

But as all this swirled at the high level, I remained deep in the law. Responsive to my long interest, the Donovan firm assigned me some labor-law work and sent me to the Legal Aid Society at Manhattan's Criminal Courts to learn something of courtroom procedure by giving poor defendants arrested in New York for misdemeanors a basic defense. And most of the defendants were indeed poor, as well as minorities, dramatically demonstrating the correlation between economic misery and crime. I continued my outside political activities and joined the American Civil Liberties Union to help write briefs in civil-liberties cases. But I became restless, despite the intellectual stimulation of daily contests with the fine minds drawn from throughout the nation to Wall Street.

I could see pretty clearly what the future held: promotion from associate to partner, more responsibility writing briefs, counseling clients, and arguing corporate, antitrust, or labor-law cases, an always rising income and, as Barbara and I by now had two children, Jonathan and Catherine, and had every intention of having more, whom we didn't want to raise on the streets of New York, the inevitable move along with all the successful young families of our time out to some proper suburb like Scarsdale or Greenwich.

Now this future might, from time to time, be enlivened by some government or political work such as my help to Donovan on the Polk case or the trip we took together in 1949 to attend the unveiling of a monument to the dead of the Rype operation on that lonely hill of Plukkutjonnfjellet in northern Norway (a trip, incidentally, during which I overheard a tantalizing conversation between a Norwegian and an American intelligence officer at an Oslo reception about their efforts to run down a mysterious supply of uranium that had been offered for sale). But such glimpses of the world outside New York only made my predictable Wall Street future that much more unappealing, and I could confidently predict the decline of my political idealism in exact step with the rise in my status and responsibilities.

So I began casting around for a break in the pattern. My interest in politics was as keen as ever, my concern with such liberal issues as labor relations and unionization as sincere as ever, and so I hit upon the idea of applying for an attorney's job at the National Labor Relations Board, rationalizing the drop in salary as only a sabbatical to get the kind of litigation training available in government but only rarely experienced on Wall Street. So in the autumn of 1949 we moved to Washington, where I embarked on a career as a government lawyer, preparing and arguing briefs, mainly on appeals brought by employers against NLRB decisions. It was an extremely short career; it lasted barely a year.

For Frank Wisner's new Office of Policy Coordination had moved into high gear and was engaged in a major recruiting campaign for personnel. Naturally enough it turned to the reservoir of old OSS types with experience in its kinds of covert operations. Indeed, the OPC's early leadership was studded with the names of those who had played prominent roles in OSS during World War II, men like Franklin Lindsay, Kermit Roosevelt, Tom Braden—men who were anxious to return to the forefront of the struggle against the new totalitarian threat. And it recruited new men like Cord Meyer, whose liberal activism had taken him high in the World Federalists and the American Veterans Committee. Among them was Gerald Miller, the OSS civilian who had been my commander in Western Europe and who had come to the airport to bid farewell to me and my Norwegian-American ski troops when we departed for our mission to Norway.

Shortly after we arrived in Washington and I had dived into my NLRB work, I got a call from Gerry. He said he had heard that I was in town, and suggested that we lunch to refresh our acquaintance. When we got together, we spent only a few moments on the old days and then turned to the problems of the world of today. He said that he had become so concerned at the direction events had taken that he had decided to drop the idea of going back to the Michigan banking business and had returned to the "old firm" with its new name of CIA. He was vague enough, following the rules of secrecy, which limited what he could say to an outsider like me, but between the lines I could tell that he was talking essentially of a peacetime continuation of our earlier work together. And after a while he came out flatly and said he would like me to join up again with him.

The offer was certainly tempting, evoking the challenge of great international events and struggles on behalf of the same freedom we had defended against Hitler. But it just wasn't possible. I had only been with the NLRB a few weeks, and to pick up and leave would neither be fair to my new bosses there nor good for whatever career record I was building. At the same time I couldn't quite let the opportunity pass entirely. So I told Gerry that I would like to offer my services as a part-time consultant if that were possible. "Go ahead and run the clearance check on me," I said. "Then let's see if there's anything you'd want me to do from time to time." He agreed, and I filled out the long forms, giving all my former addresses, the eleven schools I had attended, and the twenty-four associations I had joined, from the Association of Catholic Trade Unionists to the Museum of Modern Art.

So I continued the NLRB work, arguing my first case in Philadelphia for hosiery workers trying to organize, and writing a brief against agribusiness efforts to block strike activity by grape pickers in California. As extracurricular work outside the quiet bureaucracy, I helped write an American Civil Liberties Union brief in a Supreme Court case involving the harassment of a left-wing California group protesting the Marshall Plan.

But then, in June 1950, the Korean War broke out. Suddenly the entire situation was changed. The Cold War had turned hot; Communist aggression had revealed itself brazenly as a dire and immediate danger. Once again the United States was caught up in a new mobilization, as it met the first Communist assault squarely rather than appease, as we had done in the 1930s. As an Army Reserve officer with the rank of major, I had no doubt that I would soon be called back into active service. My work at the NLRB was clearly of secondary importance against this new threat to world peace and freedom. All I had to decide was whether, in the fight against Communist totalitarianism, I could be of more use on regular military duty or in the ranks of the CIA's paramilitary service. Barbara and I talked about it, and her strong sense of propriety and loyalty reinforced my own belief that my duty lay in only one direction. Given my OSS experience, given my special political interests, given my taste for adventure, the CIA was the answer. Shortly after the North Korean attack across the 32nd parallel, I called Gerry Miller to offer my services. And a few months later, I embarked on a CIA career, as CIA ballooned in strength to fight the Cold War.

Hard as it may be to imagine nowadays, considering the attacks on the Agency in recent years, joining the CIA back in 1950 was a highly esteemed, indeed a rather glamorous and fashionable and certainly a most patriotic thing to do. In those days the Agency was considered the vanguard of the fight for democracy and it attracted what nowadays we would call the best and the brightest, the politically liberal young men and women from the finest Ivy League campuses and with the most impeccable social and establishment backgrounds, young people with "vigor" and adventuresome spirits who believed fervently that the Communist threat had to be met aggressively, innovatively and courageously. These activists (in the best sense of that word), for all their anti-Communism, equally rejected the right-wing hysterical demagogy of the likes of Joseph McCarthy. In fact, it can quite accurately be said that the CIA at that time was perceived as the high-quality, liberal vehicle in the fight against both Communism and McCarthyism.

CHAPTER THREE

A Scandinavian Spy

Every weekday morning, for over a year, I had ridden to work at the National Labor Relations Board with a car pool of fellow civil-servant neighbors from the housing development in Washington's Southeast District, where Barbara and I and our children, Jonathan and Catherine, lived. And it was just the same in early November 1950—except that then, after I was dropped off at Fourth and Independence and after the pool car had driven well away, instead of going into the NLRB building, I caught a bus that dropped me off down the Mall near the Reflecting Pool, where the ramshackle barracks of the Central Intelligence Agency were. I had entered the double life of the cloak-and-dagger world; I was trying to maintain a "cover."

As far as anyone was supposed to know, I had quit the NLRB to take, at the same GS-12 civil-service rating (the CIA was forbidden to raid other government agencies by offering higher pay), some not too clearly specified job having to do with foreign policy and defense. For a few months, I had no formal cover. The administrative burden of providing such for every new member of the burgeoning CIA was just too much, so we were told to take refuge in vagueness, saying only that we worked for the "U.S. Government," so as not to establish a public CIA tie. But in the one-industry town of Washington, where government is the name of the game, this vagueness quickly was recognized as meaning you worked for the CIA. The atmosphere of the times, however, assured that the vagueness also closed off conversation as to what exactly the job might be, and friends and strangers alike rallied to protect even this thin layer of "cover."

My new secret job was different from the old OSS one in this respect. Then I had lived and worked almost exclusively with a band of brothers who shared their secrets, and I had had little contact with outsiders. But now I was married and had to live in two worlds, one of secret activity and one of co-op nursery schools, vacation-home communities, and good friends in other professions. Barbara bore the heaviest burden of this dual life, knowing that I was engaged in some mysterious work but not knowing precisely what it was, or how dangerous it might be. But her own discipline and dedication took over. She accepted that intelligence work had secrets, and that these had to be kept, even from her, as she did not "need to know" them, in the jargon of the trade. We talked over any major decisions, overseas tours and the like that affected our lives, but she adapted to my not discussing my work and adjusted to her exclusion from a husband's usual office gossip that could be explained to her only by describing entire operations. Her own warm outgoing personality carried her through quiet dinners with foreigners whose names were slurred, secluded picnics with Americans we never saw elsewhere, and large official receptions where she had no idea what my real relations were with the other guests.

And our friends were also supportive in this. I am sure that most of them eventually figured out where I worked. But they never were impolite enough to put me on the spot and try to get me to confirm their conjectures. In fact, it seems to me, they rather enjoyed the idea that I had a secret and often went out of their way to help me protect it, diverting the conversation when an occasional antagonist at a party would start giving me a hard time, wanting to have me say more specifically what exactly it was that I did for a living. Their protective attitude was not surprising, though. One has only to remember that this was during the height of the Korean War, when a very real sense of danger to the nation's security was once again abroad in the land and when the CIA was widely perceived—and applauded—as an elite, rather glamorous vanguard force created to defend that security.

And that sense of elitism and glamour reverberated nowhere more excitingly than in the ramshackle halls of the CIA buildings that first day I reported for duty.

The atmosphere there was once again that of wartime and the urgency of mobilization. The halls were full of earnest and worried men and women, rushing to meetings, conferring on the run, issuing crisp instructions to assistants trying to keep up with them. New people, full of enthusiasm, mingled with OSS veterans, Jedburgh colleagues with the elite of the postwar era, fresh from the Ivy League campuses in their tweed jackets, smoking pipes, and full of daring, innovative ideas, who had flocked to the Agency as the most effective place for a non-Communist liberal to do battle against the Communist menace. It would, of course, be misleading to suggest that only liberals joined the CIA. Certainly plenty of conservative anti-Communists came into the Agency in those days. But over all, the liberal coloration was so strong, especially among the analysts and in the Office of Policy Coordination, that Joe McCarthy a couple of years later, having decimated the State Department, turned his hysterical attacks against the CIA. But that only served to enhance the Agency's sense of elitism, of its specialness, of its standing in the forefront of the struggle for freedom. I was glad to be back within this dedicated and stimulating band, and I was filled with the spirit of impending adventure as I made my way down the chaotic hallways and through the maze of makeshift cubicles to Gerry Miller's office.

General Walter Bedell Smith, Eisenhower's former Chief of Staff and Truman's former Ambassador to Moscow, had just become Director of Central Intelligence. He had chosen Allen W. Dulles, the OSS's superlative spymaster, who had run an extraordinary espionage network from his headquarters in Switzerland into Hitler's Germany during World War II, as his Deputy Director. Under them, the CIA constituted a loose confederation of three compartmented and competing "cultures." The scholars and academicians collated, evaluated, synthesized and disseminated intelligence from both covert and overt sources. The Office of Special Operations ran espionage and counterespionage networks abroad for the clandestine collection of intelligence. And there was the Office of Policy Coordination, the Agency's paramilitary, propaganda and political-action arm, which I had just joined. Under Frank Wisner, the OPC was in turn divided into functional staffs—dealing with political, psychological, and economic warfare, and with paramilitary operations— and into geographical divisions covering the world. Gerry Miller, my old OSS boss during the Norway mission, was deputy chief of the Western Europe Division.

When I reported to his office that morning, he had with him Lou Scherer, a former Army officer, who was head of the Western Europe Division's Scandinavian Branch. But before we got together there was a formality that had to be attended to. My security clearance had come through rapidly enough because of my OSS background (and I did not even have to take the polygraph test most new people went through). But I could not be accepted as an intelligence officer until I signed the secrecy agreement (which binds me still) that stated I would not reveal, without the CIA's authority, any secrets I would learn while working for the Agency. I had no compunction; it was the sort of thing any employer dealing in valuable and competitive materials would require, and I signed. And then we got down to business.

Somewhat to my disappointment—I had been expecting to get involved in the Korean War—Miller informed me that he was assigning me to Scherer's Scandinavian Branch. The reason was obvious—he wanted to make use of the experience I had gained operating behind enemy lines in that part of the world on the OSS NORSO mission. For, as it turned out, one of the main fields of the OPC's work then was planning for the not unlikely possibility of a Soviet invasion of Western Europe. And, in the event the Russians succeeded in taking over any or all of the countries of the Continent, Miller explained, the OPC wanted to be in a position to activate well-armed and well-organized partisan uprisings against the occupiers. But this time, unlike the Jedburgh and similar OSS paramilitary teams that went in to help the French *maquis* and other resistance movements during World War II, the OPC didn't want to have to arm and organize those partisans after the occupation, using such dangerous and fallible operations as night flights, supply drops, and parachute infiltrations behind enemy lines. No, this time Miller said, we intended to have that resistance capability in place before the occupation, indeed even before an invasion; we were determined to organize and supply it now, while we still had the time in which to do it right and at the minimum of risk. Thus, the OPC had undertaken a major program of building, throughout those Western European countries that seemed likely targets for Soviet attack, what in the parlance of the intelligence trade were known as "stay-behind nets," clandestine infrastructures of leaders and equipment trained and ready to be called into action as sabotage and espionage forces when the time came. And the job Miller was assigning to me was to plan and build such stay-behind nets in Scandinavia.

The situation in each Scandinavian country was different. Norway and Denmark were NATO allies, Sweden held to the neutrality that had taken her through two world wars, and Finland was required to defer in its foreign policy to the Soviet power directly on its borders. Thus, in one set of these countries the governments themselves would build their own stay-behind nets, counting on activating them from exile to carry on the struggle. These nets had to be coordinated with NATO's plans, their radios had to be hooked to a future exile location, and the specialized equipment had to be secured from CIA and secretly cached in snowy hideouts for later use. In the other set of countries, CIA would have to do the job alone or with, at best, "unoffi-

cial" local help, since the politics of those governments
barred them from collaborating with NATO, and any exposure would arouse immediate protest from the local Communist press, Soviet diplomats and loyal Scandinavians who
hoped that neutrality or nonalignment would allow them to
slip through a World War III unharmed.

But in both cases, whether CIA worked with or without
local cooperation, we would have to operate with the utmost
secrecy. Obviously, if the preparations ever leaked to the
Russians, they would be in the position to destroy the nets
directly after they occupied the country and so the whole
point of the work would be lost. But there was another,
more subtle reason for the need for secrecy, which Miller
was at pains to impress upon me. In all the countries, despite their greatly different political relations with the
United States and the USSR, public knowledge that the CIA
was building stay-behind nets there in anticipation of a Soviet occupation would oblige the governments to put an end
to the project forthwith. For whether it would merely violate
the government's official policy or suggest that its defense
against a Soviet invasion had been discounted as hopeless
in advance, the result would be a disaster not only to CIA's
plans but to NATO's hopes to deter an attack. Therefore I
was instructed to limit access to information about what I
was doing to the smallest possible coterie of the most reliable people, in Washington, in NATO, and in Scandinavia.
Did I understand that? Miller pressed. Yes, I did.

"All right, Bill, get on with it, then," Miller said. "What
we want is a good solid intelligence and resistance network
that we can count on if the Russkis ever take over those
countries. We have some initial planning, but it needs to be
filled out and implemented. You will work for Lou Scherer
until we see what more needs to be done."

I was assigned a broken-down desk in a particularly rattle-
trap area in one of the corridors, smack in the middle of all
the hectic activity, and Scherer cheerfully dumped on it all
the materials that had so far been assembled for the operation: old OSS operations reports, country and geographic

studies, NATO thinking, espionage stuff from the OSO boys, and transcripts of tentative discussions with Scandinavian officials. I pinned a map of Scandinavia on the wall behind my desk and got to work. However far-fetched the plan might seem, it just might forestall a repetition of the kind of air-supply problem that had been fatal to some of my NORSO friends in 1945. So it was worth a try.

It was clear that at some stage of the game I would have to go to Scandinavia to help implement the operation. But for the moment, and indeed for the next few months, my job was to work up a rough outline of proposed infrastructures for the stay-behind nets, determine what their missions ought to be, what kinds of supplies and how many people they would need and in what sorts of units they should be organized. I had to locate the key bridges, rail lines, river crossings, straits, and other vulnerable sabotage and geo-graphical choke points, pick the most likely places for sup-ply caches, guerrilla redoubts and secret radio transmitters, set up training programs for resistance leaders, develop scenarios for a variety of guerrilla actions and figure out how long it would take to put the nets into operation and how much the whole thing would cost, so the amounts could be budgeted.

I turned to my colleagues in OSO for help in finding good potential resistance leaders and to pass my messages to the Scandinavian intelligence officials with whom I began to talk about the stay-behind nets. The OSO was also in the stay-behind business, but on a far smaller scale, putting only a few spies and counterspies and their communications in place, rather than the weaponry, explosives, food, clothing and shelter that were required for the OPC's guerrilla forces. And the plans for these, as plans tend to be, were grandiose and overoptimistic, and I made enormous de-mands on CIA's logistics and procurement offices during those months. And I also learned my first lessons about deal-ing with allies. For example, my first dispatch to an OPC field representative, instructing him to make a personal in-spection of an installation reported to us by Scandinavian officials, brought the response that the local government did not want him to be seen in contact with the people or places being prepared for the resistance effort. He ascribed that attitude not only to concern over security by the Scandinavians but also to an anxiety on their part that the sovereignty of the local authorities could be diminished by direct dealings between members of the nets and Americans. Another aspect of my work at this time was a trip to Europe to confer with our allies in the venture, to settle the details of our collaboration, arrange the secrecy rules, the logistics requirements, and the training to be given Scandinavian trainers (who in turn would train the guerrillas so they would not know of the American participation). That trip brought my first try at operating under cover internationally. I used my old private passport, which indicated that I was an attorney, and I said that I was on legal business whenever I went through immigration at the various foreign airports.

During this period I also undertook secret-agent training. Although in those days all new intelligence officers were required to go through parachute school (so they wouldn't feel like lesser daredevils among all the tall-talking OSS veterans) and learn judo, weaponry, demolition methods, the techniques of silent killing, and all the rest of the smash-and-bang stuff, I was excused from that part of it because of my wartime training and service. But I still had a lot to learn if I hoped to function effectively as a secret agent. Clearly the kind of work I'd be expected to do in the future, living under cover and engaged in clandestine activities in a peacetime situation, would require far different skills from those needed by a guerrilla fighter behind enemy lines during a war.

High on the list of these skills was what we called trade-craft. I attended classes on how to pass messages via letter drops and cut-out agents, how to set up rendezvous, plant bugs, approach safe houses, and shake tails, how to process the chemicals used in invisible writing and raise the information contained in microdots, how to work miniature cameras and other sophisticated spy equipment. Then, too, I was trained in that special branch of psychology and human relations that teaches how to spot and recruit foreigners to serve as agents and then how to be sympathetic but in control, building on their personal problems or political doubts about their loyalty to their own country. I was impressed by the subtleties and ingenuities in the training, but was equally distressed by the emphasis on the mechanics of contact instead of developing simple relationships of trust and friendship, which I felt were the keys to successful secret collaboration. We also were given an introduction to Communist theory and practice, designed to teach the agent the methods of his enemy, how he works, what can be expected of him and the best ways of countering him.

Although I thought the material used in these courses considerably inferior to what I had been exposed to at Princeton, the training was valuable on how to fight the Communist apparatus through the recruitment of good local leaders, on the importance of the circulation of ideas, coming apparently from local rather than American sources ("covert psychological warfare"), on the role of organizations (local offices, activists, training, etc.) in building a mass political base and the ways these could be assisted and even stimulated secretly by American intelligence officers behind the scenes. But here I had less to learn, since my own experiences as a Jedburgh and in New York's political maze had given me firsthand exposure to this sort of thing.

But perhaps the most complex lesson I had to learn—and one that really could not be taught in training or anywhere else—was how to live the double life. And I have to say that there was an enormous temptation to not even try. Considering the importance and all-consuming nature of the work I was doing at the Agency; considering the missionary zeal, sense of elitism and marvelous camaraderie among my colleagues there; considering above all that I was strictly forbidden to talk about what I was doing with anyone outside the Agency and thus couldn't share my concerns or just sit around shooting the breeze in shop talk with anyone in the outside world—considering all of this, one can see how easy it would have been for me to drop out of that world and immerse myself exclusively in the cloak-and-dagger life. And some of my colleagues at the Agency did just that. Socially as well as professionally they cliqued together, forming a sealed fraternity. They ate together at their own special favorite restaurants; they partied almost only among themselves; their families drifted to each other, so their defenses did not always have to be up. In this way they increasingly separated themselves from the ordinary world and developed a rather skewed view of that world. Their own dedicated double life became the proper norm, and they looked down on the life of the rest of the citizenry. And out of this grew what was later named—and condemned—as the "cult" of intelligence, an inbred, distorted, elitist view of intelligence that held it to be above the normal processes of society, with its own rationale and justification, beyond the restraints of the Constitution, which applied to everything and everyone else. As I saw this develop, I remembered a talk I had had with Donovan several years before. I had asked him how you get young paratroopers to behave like choir boys on Saturday night after spending six days learning to be aggressive, devious and heroic. He answered that he didn't know, but nevertheless it just had to be done. It would be many years before I would have to develop a better answer than Donovan's.

That I didn't fall into this "cultist" attitude—at least not to the degree I might have—I have to attribute solely to Barbara. She was resolutely determined to maintain a normal life for us and the children, no matter how peculiar my profession might be. She retained close contact with our friends from my NLRB days; she cultivated new ones from among our neighbors in the Southeast District housing development, most of them young junior civil servants like ourselves, and arranged joint parties and picnics with them; and despite the fact that she was pregnant with our third child, Carl, she remained vigorously active organizing a commmunity play school. Indeed, we associated infrequently with CIA people outside the office, so that my off hours were filled with normal affairs having nothing to do with secret operations, which helped me to keep my CIA work in perspective, a perspective that served me in good stead a quarter of a century later.

Early in 1951, Gerry Miller called me in to say he wanted me to open an OPC representation in Stockholm, with a continuing connection to other parts of Scandinavia until representatives could be assigned there too. An OSO "station" was already established in Stockholm and I would be loosely attached to it, but I would still report directly to OPC Washington. I was again surprised; I had expected to be posted to Norway to follow up on my wartime mission there, but I accepted after Barbara and I talked it over, agreeing that this was an opportunity to get to know yet another part of the world, and one even closer than Norway to the main action of the Soviet Union. We planned to leave shortly after our third child was born.

But I needed a real cover for this assignment. Those squadrons of civilian employees of the military, under which CIA covered its people in such centers as Germany and the Far East, did not exist in Sweden and our stay-behind preparations in Scandinavia might be exposed if I was too readily identified as a CIA employee there. So it was decided that I would ostensibly join the Foreign Service and serve as a junior political attaché in our Stockholm Embassy with only a few key Scandinavian and NATO intelligence services knowing of my CIA mission.

The matter of cover has always been most difficult for American intelligence. The intelligence services of other countries, and certainly of the totalitarian ones, have always been able to provide their agents with the deepest and most protective of covers. Because they can dictate to all the other agencies of their governments and, for that matter, to the society at large, they are able to plant their agents credibly wherever they choose, fabricating for them solid false identities as foreign-service or military officers, newspaper reporters, ministry officials, or staff members of international organizations. This is also true in most democratic countries, where long tradition had made intelligence activities, and their necessity for good cover, fully accepted and normal.

But various legal restrictions, plus the exceptionally open character of United States society, do not permit the CIA to do anything comparable. Arranging for an American intelligence officer as a diplomat entails a number of bureaucratic hurdles. In addition, the Foreign Service is a close fraternity, whose members bristle at the intrusion of outsiders into its ranks at any level other than the bottom. Much the same problem arises with any attempt to place a CIA officer into a large American corporate enterprise, for despite the patriotism of the management, which may be thoroughly agreeable to the deception, the employees are bound to be dubious of the intruder and will quickly notice that he is not spending full time on his work nor producing business results that might justify his tenure. Moreover, as a result of the often nefarious view of intelligence in America, constraints have progressively been established against the use of a number of other obvious possible covers, such as the Peace Corps, the Fulbright program and even, in recent years, the Agency for International Development.

The solution in 1951 was to make me a Foreign Service *Reserve* Officer, a category that had been developed for members of other government departments such as Treasury or Agriculture, temporarily assigned to embassies abroad. But their designation was not as *political* officers. Mine was, and this title, plus the Reserve status, would soon have fellow diplomats and unfriendly foreign intelligence services guessing that its owner probably belonged to CIA. But for lack of any better cover, I went through the procedures and filled out all the forms necessary to obtain that appointment and early in April Barbara and I, with our three children, flew to Stockholm.

But my cover proved to have an extra dimension that I hadn't counted on—Barbara. She jumped into the job of the junior diplomat's wife with her typical enthusiasm and charm, and soon had leading roles in the local American women's association and the American community play, established a wide circle of Swedish friends at all levels of Swedish society from the Court on down, and was involved in studies of women's and consumers' affairs in Sweden with Esther Peterson, later President Carter's Consumer Affairs Adviser. In the meantime, I sought out interesting political figures in Swedish life, such as the Secretary General of the Social Democratic Party and the leading advocate of the right of Swedes to declare themselves out of the established church and therefore no longer have to pay the taxes that supported it. Together in this way we did much to shore up my weak cover and convince most people that I was in fact what I said I was—a diplomat—since these activities were strictly along diplomatic lines and had no CIA connotations.

One area in which I acted out my role as a junior diplomat, however, did have some intelligence value. In Stockholm at the time was a large colony of refugees and exiles from Communist Europe, mainly from the Baltic states, Poland, Hungary, Rumania and the Ukraine. Under Swedish law, enacted to protect Sweden's strict neutrality, asylum had been granted them with the understanding that they would not engage in political activity. Still, it was within appropriate diplomatic limits for me to meet with these people; and as an impressionable young man I found it an exhilarating experience to develop friendships with exiled East European cabinet ministers, dissident intellectuals and would-be political leaders. I spent hours discussing with them the situations in their homelands and their hopes and dreams of freedom from Soviet rule, and whether this could come about without war. Their links to home were then still fresh enough—and were from time to time renewed by the arrival of new exiles—so I gleaned an occasional tidbit out of these innocent conversations about what was going on behind the Iron Curtain to pass back to the CIA in Washington. But chiefly, I felt that I was fulfilling a CIA function by encouraging these people to maintain their morale and their links to dissident movements in Eastern Europe. And though I myself could not provide any direct assistance, I was able to steer some of them to the correct channels in Europe through which they could get support for anti-Communist activities such as the publication of their news-letters and the maintenance of their exile organizations.

Perhaps the greatest value of these contacts, though, was in what I learned from these people about the nature of Communist rule, especially of the difference between it and the Nazi rule, since they had experienced both. An Estonian woman journalist drew the comparison in this way. The Nazis, she said, demanded two things of the people they ruled: that they not oppose the authorities and that they do the jobs assigned to them to contribute to the economy. But the Communists added a third demand: that the occupied peoples actively support the new regime by participating in indoctrination sessions and attending public rallies. The awful thing about this, she said, was not so much the time it wasted and the bother it caused, but the danger that it would ultimately work. Hammered at long enough and persistently enough, she feared, even such intellectuals as herself among the occupied peoples of Eastern Europe would eventually be brainwashed and trapped in the ideology of their occupiers. And so, when the second Soviet occupation of her country loomed, she sought refuge in exile.

To me, trying to set up resistance networks in anticipation of just such an occupation, the message was chilling. I had to wonder if, no matter how well prepared the physical aspects of a resistance movement were, it could survive the ideological and political pressures, or whether we had to think in new and revolutionary terms. The model we were using of the European resistance against the Nazis might not be adequate in the face of a totalitarian threat that sought to enlist and not merely subjugate the peoples it overran.

The CIA operation in the Embassy, as at all its stations abroad in those days, was divided into two components. There was the OSO "side" engaged in the clandestine collection of intelligence through so-called "unilateral" United States nets to Eastern Europe, exchanging information with friendly intelligence services and dealing at arm's length with services bound by their national policies to stay clear of involvement with the United States. And there was the OPC contingent that I established. On the basis of length of residence and precedence, the OSO man in Stockholm was my senior and the principal CIA representative. In theory, I was independent of his command, since OPC was a separate entity in Washington set up to implement propaganda, political and paramilitary projects, taking as its starting point the information that OSO might collect but going on to influence the outcome of the conflict with the Soviets rather than merely report on it. But even then, the theory didn't make sense. To the foreigners I dealt with, America was one country, and they were not particularly interested in the fine points of its bureaucratic divisions. To Ambassador W. Walton Butterworth, hidden in Sweden from the wrath of the China Lobby, CIA was one agency, engaged in secret activities, and he was properly impatient of any attempt to draw subtle distinctions between OSO and OPC responsibilities. So I made a point of making sure that my OSO colleague knew all of what I was doing, often consulting with him to make sure that we did not cross lines in our foreign contacts and always playing as a member of the CIA and embassy teams rather than as a solo performer.

It was just as well that I did, as Director Walter Bedell Smith was moving in the same direction in Washington. He insisted that if he was to be responsible for OPC's support and maintenance then he must have full authority over it. After getting that authority he then demanded that the two secret operational cultures end their splendid bureaucratic independence from each other and be merged into one operation. A measure of the power of bureaucratic institutions in Washington and of the cultural chasm within intelligence was that it took him two full years to merge even these fledgling OSO and OPC entities, at first by appointing a "senior representative" over the OSO and the OPC erstwhile independent chiefs at the overseas stations. In Stockholm, it would have been absurd to send an additional officer for that job, so the OSO man was named chief. But the seriousness with which the decision was viewed in headquarters is shown by the fact that Louis Scherer made a special trip to Stockholm to tell me about it to assuage any wounded feelings I might have had. In fact, I had none; bureaucratic wiring diagrams are not my passion in life, and the OSO chief was a close personal friend, so I was convinced that anything useful I wanted to do I could do and that if he would have an objection it would be a real one for valid reasons. In Washington, the merger was accomplished by making Frank Wisner of OPC the CIA's "Deputy Director for Plans" and Richard Helms of OSO his second in command, thus combining flamboyance and professionalism at the top; it would, however, take years to bring about their full integration at the working level.

My job of developing stay-behind nets in Scandinavia differed markedly from country to country. In one country, which must remain nameless, I could work freely and frankly with the local intelligence authorities in the selection in each region of good potential leaders who were to be sent abroad for training in guerrilla, sabotage and psychological operations at schools run by CIA or our NATO allies. In another, equally nameless, the local intelligence authorities, with their government's approval, designated one representative to work with me on the development of the guerrilla net and one on a political and psychological warfare net. In another, again nameless, I found, with the help of the local OSO representative, reliable resident Americans whom I could approach and from whom I could get assistance in the recruitment of local nationals willing to join such a network directly, without their government knowing anything about it. I cannot specify which nation is which, as it would violate not only my secrecy agreement with CIA but the understanding upon which our cooperation took place then, and on which any future cooperation must rest. And thus in the following description of my work, I will merge the separate operations into one story, so that amateur (and some professional) cryptologists will not be able to identify the specifics of the activity.

One of the rules of relations between intelligence services, and even more with agents, is that offices are off limits, since they are too easily observed. So as soon as I had completed the embassy paperwork I left it to make contact with the first of my "stay-behind" contacts in a mutually convenient apartment, parking my car a few streets away and walking aimlessly around a couple of blocks to make sure I wasn't being followed. We were introduced by the local OSO chief and spent some time getting acquainted. He obviously had been told about me and my Norwegian operation during the war. For my part, I knew that he was a regular army officer and that he also had fought in the snow during World War II. He proved to be a friendly, outgoing fellow, proud of his family, and full of amusing stories of his rides with the cavalry of the Hungarian Army before the war—and of the "girls of Budapest" he had met in the process. We talked of the need to prepare against the eventuality of a Soviet occupation, which we devoutly hoped would not occur, and of the need to keep the whole matter totally secret. And while we did not try to get down to precise details, it became clear what our relationship would be. He was very much in charge of the operation, and would be letting me know only as much of it as I would "need to know" to arrange the exile base connections, the logistics stocks, and to furnish the special equipment, such as radios, which could not be obtained locally. He would go through the CIA training himself and then decide whether he would send others.

We both understood that I would not learn the names of the members of the net, since I did not need to know them, and we did not want to risk their exposure through some leak, Soviet penetration, or misuse at some future time. (In a similar relationship elsewhere, I later heard that we had insisted on the names and had been given false ones, which we had no way of checking, so my lack of interest was correct.) But I did make it clear that I would have to know enough to be sure that something was really happening, that the nets we said we were building, supplying and relying on really existed. This made sense to him, and we agreed to work out ways to do this without showing my participation.

My second contact was quite a different type. A modest and successful businessman, he had been selected, I guessed, to develop the psychological warfare nets because of his ability as an organizer. He was totally loyal to his country, but he gave no hint of whether he voted with the conservative parties or the Socialists so prominent in all Scandinavian countries. He was much interested in learning the mysteries of our clandestine tradecraft, and we discussed in great detail the comparative merits of different small printing presses, the need for an exile editorial staff to man overseas radios and how to transmit to the network editorial direction and material that it could pass by word of mouth or in clandestine publications under Soviet occupation. My relationship with him was the same as with the guerrilla net officer in terms of what I would know about his operations. He was quickly convinced of the need to develop an exile library of national reference material, photographs, and recordings of national music for use when and if the country was occupied by Russian soldiers, and to arrange to deposit these with CIA. And as confidence grew, he and the guerrilla chief both agreed to turn over heavily sealed lists of the members of their nets for safekeeping in the event they were forced to destroy their own copies to keep them from the Russians. I made it clear to Washington that these must be kept away from our "flaps and seals" experts, who claimed that they could open and reseal such material without ever showing a trace, since we could not risk any violation of the confidence we had built, despite the hard-nosed professional doctrine that all is fair, or at least done, in intelligence work.

A third contact was the chief of the intelligence service of his country, whom I met together with my OSO colleague in that country. A quiet, intellectual, self-effacing gentleman of the old school (and the "school" in his country stretched back a century or more), he was the prototype of the silent spymaster, his head full of exotic secret adventures, while he maintained the image of a nondescript and not particularly exceptional middle-grade civil servant. With splendid tact he played the game of pretending that he recognized the separate and independent nature of our OPC and OSO missions and dealt scrupulously and separately with each of us, until with a well-concealed sigh of relief he received the news that our headquarters had merged us into one unit and that my OSO colleague was the single point with which he had to maintain contact. We remained friends, but he certainly appreciated CIA's decision that we were one service, rather than a vague coalition of independent baronies.

My periodic meetings with these gentlemen, the reports they generated for headquarters, the map studies and planning they involved as we worked out our ideas of where nets should be established and how they should be supported hardly amounted to a high-pressure task, even with the related "cover" work I did as an eager young diplomat. The remaining time I put in on CIA's so-called "unilateral" work—done without the knowledge of the governments of the area. Some of this involved building the same sort of stay-behind network in those countries in which the local government would not, or felt it could not, collaborate even secretly with the American CIA. And some of it involved the building of independent "assets" within those countries in which the governments built the nets jointly with us, as back-up capabilities in case the original operations were exposed and eliminated just when they were needed, or the governments in power at the time of the invasion decided that collaboration was the better part of valor, accepted the occupation, and betrayed the net.

A further "unilateral" action involved building the basic elements of a clandestine structure to be used for whatever purpose the United States and the CIA might need them for in the future. In a country where information is open, where the government's policy is friendly to the United States, or where it clearly is the best possible one in the circumstances it faces, and where our intelligence exchange with the local services provides more valuable information than could be gathered secretly, there is no need for CIA to engage in clandestine intelligence or political operations aimed at the local nation. Several in Scandinavia fitted this description perfectly. But even in such countries, some secret activity is often required—for example, to make contact with nationals from other countries visiting there and free of the strict surveillance of their home countries and so able to meet with American intelligence officers to pass on information or to receive help for their work to take back to their homes.

For such purposes, a clandestine apparatus is necessary, and it was my chore to build it in some of the Scandinavian countries. Headquarters supported the effort by sending over American agents to reside in Scandinavia under private cover, which is to say as ordinary businessmen or persons of some other nonofficial status. In the theory of the time, the American government, through its President or its Ambassador, would then be able to issue a "plausible denial" of its involvement in the activities of these nonofficial Americans, so long as no link could be shown to exist between these nonofficial agents and the official officer, such as myself, in the Embassy. That meant that my contacts with these agents had to be in the same clandestine manner as with a full-fledged foreign spy.

For this purpose, I applied the tradecraft lessons I had learned, contacting them only from odd pay phones, identifying myself with aliases, making dates in codes and by passwords, meeting them in safe-house apartments, and arranging those meetings so that we arrived and departed at least ten minutes apart and thus were never seen together. With some of these agents, with whom a casual acquaintance could be credibly claimed—both of us might be members of the same local American club for example—a drive through the city in a car would be a satisfactory way of meeting and talking in an inconspicuous fashion, since few people really look at two men riding in a car, although they will immediately notice them parked. But this meant that the car had to be inconspicuous, and that the pickups had to be made right on time and in natural locations so that local citizens wouldn't take note of a figure waiting on an isolated and strange corner to be picked up by a car that was obviously out of place in the neighborhood. The perfect operator in such operations is the traditional gray man, so inconspicuous that he can never catch the waiter's eye in a restaurant, and I believe my deliberate cultivation of this quality produced habits and attitudes that hung with me even under the television cameras in later years.

I had to do more than just run these "outside" officers who were sent from headquarters, however. I had to cultivate some locally, too. I did this by following the rigid procedure of "spotting" those local Americans who appeared to have the qualities and patriotism necessary to engage in intelligence operations. Then some specifics of the prospect's biography had to be extracted from the local records of the American community and the consulate without drawing attention to my curiosity. And this material had to be sent to headquarters for a check against its security files and possibly for a field check of the prospect's prior jobs and residences to ensure that he was indeed reliable enough to be entrusted with secret operational information. Once "clearance" was received, I would then gingerly sound him out on the prospect of giving me some help on a few simple tasks that I could not do myself, and test him with some operation that could be bungled without causing much trouble. This accomplished, and he by then fully aware that he was engaged in secret intelligence activities, I could move along to the next step: giving him the tradecraft training that he would need. And I would also now impose a tighter discipline on our relationship, usually cooling off any open connections we might have established until then and replacing them with clandestine contacts, or in some cases moving him entirely to the control of another outside officer so that no contacts would remain between him and the embassy. With this done, he could now be used operationally, for example, to pass funds to a visiting foreigner he would be instructed to meet at an outlying streetcar stop, identifying him by a description and the rolled-up magazine the foreigner carried in his left hand, plus an exchange of passwords in the local language, with me watching the whole exchange from a neighboring apartment prepared to jump in and repair anything that went really wrong.

Gradually my "stable" of such outside officers grew. The cover of one was that of a journalist on the staff of a technical publication whose management was patriotic enough to allow the use of their name by CIA. Their international interests were sufficient to explain the assignment of a correspondent to Scandinavia. In dealing with him, I made clear that his work for the journal was his alone, and that I would have no voice in what he submitted to it, as CIA's mission was abroad, not in influencing what appeared in the American press. But as an inquiring reporter, he could go into circles and ask questions that would certainly not be appropriate for an embassy officer such as myself to do, and in the process he could "spot" likely candidates to help CIA's operations: travelers behind the Iron Curtain, experts in the "middle way" political techniques so needed in underdeveloped nations, distinguished cultural leaders to participate in free international organizations challenging Communist fronts—all of these could help in CIA's cold-war strategy without in any way transgressing their own country's laws or interests, and those that agreed to do so acted out of conviction, not CIA bribes.

Another of my agents, recruited locally, was an American graduate student combining his studies with various odd jobs in Scandinavia, including acting as an occasional stringer or free lance for American media. Again, I had nothing to say about his work for these employers, who judged his performance strictly on his merits and knew nothing of his CIA connections. But in the process he could be alert for information or contacts that might be valuable to CIA. Another agent was an American who had returned to the land of his forefathers, where he ran a modest business and operated a farm he had inherited. He arranged to cache a well-preserved radio in an obscure spot at the farm so that it would be there for whatever "unilateral" use CIA might want to make of it during a Russian occupation. In another country, a similar American resident helped locate several local citizens who agreed to serve as the nucleus of a resistance organization in the event of war, and we sent a trainer from the United States, ostensibly just on a pleasant summer tour, to teach them the techniques of clandestine radio communications. Then I took Barbara and our oldest son, Jonathan, on an auto tour of that country as well, ostensibly to visit its lovely historic castles. But the trunk of the car was heavily laden with carefully packed radios and in a remote forest I passed them to my friend for distribution to the people he had recruited. My only real problem on the trip was seeing the rear of the car sag alarmingly under the weight of the radios as we boarded a ferry, but my diplomatic passport got it through the customs inspectors.

I have always wondered whether the stay-behind nets we built would have worked under Soviet rule. We know that last-minute efforts to organize such nets failed in places like China in 1950 and North Vietnam in 1954. We know that efforts to organize them from outside were penetrated and subverted by the secret police in Poland and Albania in the 1950s. So it is possible that my nets might also have been lost in a real Russian invasion of Scandinavia. But I believed then and still believe that at least some of the caches we laid down, and carefully recorded in CIA's files, would have survived and been of immense value to some heroic souls who would have risen to keep the flame of freedom burning.

While my assignment remained on the "action" rather than the "intelligence" side, the shotgun marriage of OSO and OPC by Walter Bedell Smith opened my eyes to the world of espionage. I saw the value of exchanging information secretly with Scandinavian intelligence services who could not admit publicly that they were helping the United States during the Cold War. And on a duty visit to the CIA station in Germany I got a sense of the great effort being made to develop agent sources behind the Iron Curtain, to give us some idea of what the Soviets and the Eastern coun-

tries were planning, and even to tell us of what weapons
they had, where their forces were located and what areas
might be fruitful targets for our forces if war broke out. This
showed, too, the importance of recent defectors and exiles,
who could be debriefed to provide direct accounts of new
trends and developments, but who had to be handled carefully to note the stage at which their memory began to be
supplemented by their imagination and their strong political
views. And I also learned of the frustrations and weaknesses
in such activities, as when a Polish exile, who had arranged
to have a friend in Poland mail to one of our cover addresses
in Scandinavia reports in secret writing about naval forces in
Gdynia, finally confessed that he prepared the secret writing
reports in his own home and out of his own imagination,
then mailed them to his friend in Gdynia who reposted
them from there to our cover address.

Another experience gave me a still greater insight into the
nature of intelligence and the bureaucratic problems that
can affect it. The political section of one of our embassies
had hired a refugee to read the local Communist press, to
see what he might learn from it of the role of the Communist
Party in the country. This conscientious student not only
collected all the publications issued by the party and its
fronts, he meticulously carded every reference to individuals and to organizational units. Within six months he produced studies and diagrams of the complete Communist
Party and front structure, identified its leaders, membership
and supporters, its principal strategies and issues, and its
relationships with many non-Communist political, syndical,
and cultural groups. Using secret sources, the local CIA files
had nothing nearly as comprehensive as this. But at this
point the embassy political section suffered a budget cut
and decided to terminate this study, since coverage of the
Communist movement was considered a CIA function. But
the CIA station could not take over the conscientious employee to continue his work, because his was merely an
"overt" operation and thus did not fit into the clandestine
mission of CIA abroad. So this valuable program was

stopped, a tribute to the impact of bureaucracy on intelligence—of the art form over the art. Whether that degree of knowledge of the local Communist Party was really essential can be argued, but not the artificial way in which the decision to terminate was made.

I made one other foray into the "intelligence" field. Allen Dulles paid Scandinavia a visit shortly after he succeeded Smith in 1953 as the new Director, making calls on his counterparts there, and entertaining all concerned with his rich collection of stories and his Santa-like "Ho, ho, ho" laugh. Before going out one evening, he luxuriated for a few moments in his tub at a Stockholm hotel while he carried on his conversation with me discreetly behind the door. In the course of it I asked if he had given any thought to the idea of producing CIA's reports and assessments in Washington in a newspaper format, instead of on the typewritten letter-size pages traditionally used. I said I thought it would make it easier for the reader to use a form familiar to him, allowing him to choose how deeply he wanted to go into any one subject rather than having to proceed *seriatim* through the successive pages, and would give more flexibility for the use of maps and graphs to clarify the matter being reported. He listened, but closed the subject with the comment that the news format would dilute the impact of "intelligence."

I enjoyed the work in Scandinavia. It certainly provided a measure of excitement and a sense of accomplishment far greater than what I would have had if I had been really just a regular political officer. I had the feeling that I was doing something valuable, was actually engaged in the battle against the Communist threat rather than merely reporting on events or attempting to influence them by the representation of policies formulated in Washington, which is, after all, the lot of the diplomat. Most of all, I could enter, albeit indirectly, into the life and political struggles of these countries, instead of observing them from the detached platform of the American Embassy. And the foreigners, with whom I shared the excitement of a secret relationship and the commitment to freedom for their homelands and mine, became close friends despite the vast differences in our backgrounds. The fraternity of freedom enveloped us both and gave us satisfactions beyond mere jobs.

For all of this, though, I was perfectly aware that I was operating on the periphery of the main game. Despite its reputation from spy novels, Stockholm was not a major intelligence center in the early 1950s. The neutrality of Sweden had to be respected, which meant limiting our activities to those that would not embarrass the Swedish government. Moreover, Stockholm geographically and politically did not provide particularly good access to what were then the CIA's high-priority targets in Europe, the Communist countries. The great challenges to secret intelligence gathering were elsewhere, in Berlin, Vienna and Hong Kong, and the need for covert political or paramilitary action hardly existed in Scandinavia. The dominant Social Democrats excluded the Communists from all but a tiny percentage of the political spectrum through good and socially advanced government, leaving the Communists with few issues other than Scandinavia's links, overt or secret, with the West, and the call for support of a Soviet-sponsored "peace" movement. Since many in Scandinavia had experienced Nazi "peace" and saw the similarities in Soviet Eastern Europe, this had little appeal. Thus, my work was less in the present than in building and training a CIA covert-operations framework for use in the future in the event that the current situation in Scandinavia was radically altered. Not surprisingly, after a couple of years of this, the novelty of the assignment began to wear off and I became increasingly restless for more action.

And action there was aplenty in those days. For those were the years of the most explosive growth for the CIA and most especially for its paramilitary and political-action mission. Despite the merger of the OPC and the OSO, the paramilitary and political-action "culture" had unquestionably become the dominant one in the CIA, much to the chagrin of its bureaucratic bedfellows. The research-and-analysis scholars may have sympathized with the liberal thrust of much of the effort. But they grumbled over being held at arm's length from knowledge of what in many countries was a major political force at work, the CIA station. And the spymasters and counterspies feared that the high-risk, flamboyant operations of the "cowboys" jeopardized the security and cover of their carefully constructed clandestine networks. But there was little that either could do about it. Under the impetus of the Korean War, in a time of fierce anti-Communist and anti-Soviet sentiment and rhetoric, covert paramilitary and political action was the name of the intelligence game.

One main arena of action, of course, was Korea and there, in emulation of OSS derring-do, paramilitary teams were dropped behind North Korean and Chinese lines to organize resistance and sabotage in the enemy rear (during which John Downey and Richard Fecteau were shot down and began twenty years of incarceration in Chinese jails). The CIA was also active in other parts of Asia. For example, in an effort to pick up the pieces after mainland China's fall to Mao, CIA was hard at work supporting Chiang Kai-shek's Taiwan government and sending guerrillas to the mainland, as well as trying to develop a "third force" alternative to both Chiang and Mao. In the Philippines, where the Communist Hukbalahap movement was threatening that country, the CIA's almost legendary Ed Lansdale identified Magsaysay as a decent and honest alternative to Communists on the left and corrupt quislings on the right and provided him imaginative political counsel and other forms of Agency help, to see him elected president. And in Indochina, the CIA ran two stations, one working with the French in their war against the Viet Minh and the other helping a little-known nationalist politician by the name of Ngo Dinh Diem to become president of a fragmented but nationalist South Vietnam.

The activity in Europe was just as vigorous at the time. For example, the CIA clandestinely supported the development of an anti-Communist resistance movement in the Ukraine and occasionally by parachute or PT boat delivered agents to the Baltic countries. A major effort to break Albania out of the curtain by stirring up a revolt against the Communist regime there was underway. The intensity of that effort was in no way diminished by the fact, as we later learned, that Kim Philby, the British double agent, sold out the partisans to his Soviet masters. The CIA also helped build an ingenious tunnel under Berlin to tap into the telephone communications in the Soviet sector and supported a variety of intelligence organizations from Gehlen's in West Germany to exile Russian organizations with real but weak links to their homeland. And CIA became the vehicle by which the United States supplemented its "official" Voice of America, with the ostensibly privately funded and operated Radio Free Europe and Radio Liberty to carry honest news behind the Iron Curtain.

Probably the CIA's greatest impact during this period was in the field of international front organizations. The Soviets had spawned dozens of international political fronts to influence and control labor, student, women's, journalists', cultural, lawyers' and veterans' groups throughout the world. To counter this effort CIA called back from OSS days or recruited new liberal activists like Tom Braden, Cord Meyer, and a host of others, and put them to work organizing rival front groups. To operate in the international field these men needed Americans fully qualified to speak for the various constituencies. In labor there was no question; the AFL-CIO was, if anything, ahead of the government in identifying the danger posed by the Soviet threat to free labor and in building an international movement of free labor unionists in opposition to the government- and party-controlled officers of the Communist countries. Over the years CIA never provided financial help to the AFL-CIO; the shoe was on the other foot as the movement did indeed watch carefully what was happening with foreign labor movements, and had plenty of access to the White House if something displeased them.

But in the other fields, the Americans were disorganized or did not have the resources and capability for conducting a worldwide contest with the Soviet front groups. Thus, CIA found American leaders who could organize such movements, wanted to contest the false Soviet-founded fronts claiming the field, and saw no problem in receiving assistance for that work from a variety of anonymous donors and foundations serving as covers for the CIA. Gloria Steinem has been wrongly accused of being a CIA tool in her work with movements of this type. As she has replied, the CIA only helped her and others go to foreign political conferences, where she presented the kind of independent, spontaneous position and image that is truly representative of America's freedom. This kind of support constituted CIA's "operation" in a number of fields, from the National Student Association to the Congress of Cultural Freedom, and it met and defeated the Communists with their own organizational tactics, different only in that ours espoused and incorporated freedom as its key. In particular, it knocked down the Communist attempt to monopolize the cause of "peace" by giving voice and strength to those who denounced the hypocrisy of Communist pretensions to "peace" after Czechoslovakia, East Berlin, and especially Hungary. Never again would the Soviet Union be able to pretend that it is the home of the "peace-loving" working class, as it did in the 1930s, when it achieved the leadership of the "anti-fascist" cause despite the Stalin purges, the slave camps, and the totalitarian press of the Soviet brand of fascism.

And these CIA activities received the wholehearted support of any American who became aware of them. Prestigious establishment leaders were glad to serve on the boards of CIA-owned corporations and foundations. Business managers and publishers agreed on the spot to provide "jobs" for CIA officers in their subsidiaries abroad. Labor chiefs, leaders of cooperatives, and prominent American figures from every profession and art joined in the important task of extending their influence to foreign countries to contest the threat the Communists posed there.

The Agency thus enjoyed almost unqualified backing from the American people and government. As a tool of the Executive Branch, the CIA needed to get approval for its projects only from the President. Ideas dreamed up in the field, at lower levels in CIA in Washington, or pressed upon CIA by eager outsiders, were carried up to the Director, who then presented them to a special committee of the National Security Council, consisting of the deputy secretaries of Defense and State, the National Security Adviser to the President, the chairman of the Joint Chiefs of Staff, and the Director himself, who reviewed them for the President. If he said go, they went; and in those days he rarely said otherwise. The Congress' part was limited to the appropriations process. At that time the concept of Congressional oversight, the idea that Congressmen should know of and scrutinize CIA projects simply did not exist. Rather a selected group of senior members from the Congressional Armed Services and Appropriations Committees met *ad hoc* to review the CIA's over-all budget and virtually automatically voted the funds requested. They knew few of the details of what the funds were used for—and wanted to know less. The need for clandestine covert action to fight the Cold War was accepted as an article of faith. They equally accepted the need for secrecy to protect those activities, so Congress abstained from questioning too deeply about the details of what was really going on. The CIA under the President essentially had a free hand to engage in the widest range of activities and to undertake the most daring and controversial projects.

At my station in Stockholm, it is true, I was only vaguely aware of the range of CIA's activities or the details of the many projects. But the gossip that I picked up from the cable traffic and from other intelligence officers who passed through from time to time was enough to confirm in me the feeling that a lot of exciting things were going on that I was being left out of in the Scandinavian backwater and to increase in me my restlessness for action. Then, in the summer of 1953, when I had been in Stockholm just two years, Gerry Miller invited me to meet him in Rome and there offered to transfer me to the CIA's Italian operation. I accepted with an almost shameless enthusiasm—because, if there was one place just then that was in the heart of the action, it most certainly was Italy.

CHAPTER FOUR

Covert Politics in Italy

Our move to Rome, in the autumn of 1953, marked the start of a great experience both for the family personally and for me professionally.

Indeed, Barbara to this day remembers our five years' residence in the Italian capital as among the most fascinating and enjoyable times of our lives (and still keeps up her Italian-language studies in nostalgic anticipation of a day when we can go there again). And no wonder. In the eyes of a young American couple, Rome was never more breathtaking than it was in the middle 1950s. There was, of course, the sheer beauty of the place and the overwhelming power of the Eternal City's history and antiquity, where the ruins of the Roman Forum stood a stone's throw from its modern replica in the monument to Victor Emmanuel II, where the Mamertine Prison, which once confined Saint Peter, contrasted with the great basilica honoring his name, where at every corner you were overcome by yet another lovely fountain or architectural jewel. And beyond physical beauty, there was the impact of being at the center of world Catholicism, with the rich ritual of the Vatican and the earnest seminarians of every race and nation showing the depth of our religion over the centuries and its breadth over the continents. And apart from all that, one has to remember that the 1950s were the glittering years of Rome's fabled *dolce vita*, when the Via Veneto overflowed with bizarre and colorful modern characters, when fabulous parties brightened the nights and glamorous stars of Italy's resurgent movie industry brightened the parties.

We hardly could have asked for anything more. And yet, to make the experience well-nigh perfect, I did get something more: one of the most exciting challenges the Agency had to offer, running what was by far the CIA's largest covert political-action program undertaken until then or, indeed, since—an unparalleled opportunity to demonstrate that secret aid could help our friends and frustrate our foes without the use of force or violence.

That dazzling, accomplished precursor of women's liberation, Clare Boothe Luce, had just arrived in Rome as American ambassador. Gerry Miller had come out from the Agency's Western Europe division to serve as CIA chief of station under her, and I had been named to head up the political-operations side of the station under him, coequal with the head of the regular intelligence-collection operations. My job, simply put, was to prevent Italy from being taken over by the Communists in the next—1958—elections and thus prevent the NATO military defenses from being circumvented politically by a subversive fifth column, the Partito Communista Italiano (or PCI).

The possibility of a Communist takeover of Italy through a victory at the polls had worried Washington policymakers before the 1948 Italian elections. Indeed, it was primarily this fear that had led to the formation of the Office of Policy Coordination, which gave the CIA the capability to undertake covert political, propaganda, and paramilitary operations in the first place. And the last-minute, frantic assistance that the CIA had provided in Italy at that time had had a positive effect. The Vatican-backed Christian Democratic Party, under Alcide de Gasperi's leadership, had polled almost half the electorate and had obtained an absolute majority in the Chamber of Deputies. This had been followed by Gasperi's wise move of insisting that the Christian Democrats govern in coalition with smaller, anticlerical center democratic parties—the Liberals, the Social Democrats and the Republicans—rather than rely only on the Catholic Church and polarize Italy along clerical-versus-secular lines, which would have given the Communists the chance to pose as the champions of modern social freedom.

But the compromises necessary to hold these different parties together, and for that matter the separate Christian Democratic factions, prevented them from moving ahead with the dynamic social program needed in the increasingly secularized postwar Italian society. And thus the June 1953 national elections saw a substantial setback for all the center parties, arousing Washington's and Western Europe's concern about the future of Italy. In that election, the Christian Democrats actually lost over two million votes from their 1948 totals, dropping to just 40 percent of the total cast. Their Liberal, Social-Democratic and Republican allies also slipped badly, so that together the four parties collected only 49 percent of the votes and a razor-thin majority in the Chamber of Deputies. The lost votes went partly to the Right, the reviving ex-Fascist MSI and the old-line Monarchists of the South, and partly to the Left, the allied Communists and Socialists, who together polled about 35 percent of the electorate, gaining some 1,400,000 votes over 1948.

Thus, by the time of my arrival in Rome, there was good reason to fear that, if the voting trend between 1948 and 1953 were allowed to continue, the governing center democratic coalition would become weaker and increasingly unstable, while the combined Communist and Socialist vote would grow to become the largest political force in Italy and take it down the same popular-front path that had preceded the Communist seizure of power in Czechoslovakia and other Eastern European countries.

CIA had not been idle during these years of deterioration. But plainly something more was needed than the sporadic election-year support it had given to the center democratic parties and to the Social Democrats and Christian Democrats when they split from Socialist and Communist political and syndical groups. And this especially since Moscow was covertly pouring in massive support to the Italian Communist Party—according to our estimates at the time, to the tune of over fifty million dollars a year. Because of the intimate relationship between party and government in the Soviet Union and in the East European countries, and because of the old Communist International's tradition of mutual support among parties, the Russians had a variety of mechanisms by which to do this with relative ease. Among the most effective was the host of party-controlled export-import firms that had been set up in Italy to engage in trade with Soviet-bloc countries and from whose profits funds could be siphoned to finance Communist organizational, political and propaganda activities in Italy. For example, one such company enjoyed a virtual monopoly on the Sicilian citrus trade with the Soviet Union; others similarly dominated the Italian traffic in Hungarian meat products and Polish coal. Just as often, though, the money was "black-bagged," which is to say that direct cash subsidies to Italian Communist officials and party organizations from the Soviet Party treasury were funneled in through the diplomatic channels of the Russian and East European embassies in Rome and distributed covertly by their agents in nontraceable United States dollar bills. In a country where most businesses kept at least two sets of books, the Italian Communists had no difficulty in concealing the sources of this extra cash, while fiercely boasting of the voluntary contributions their elected officials made to the Party from their government salaries.

And the funds were well used. A massive network of Communist organizations covered Italy both horizontally and vertically. In every region of the country there was not only a Party office with its paid organizers and activists, but for every segment of the population there was an appropriate front organization. Women, youth, labor, artists, farmers, veterans—each had an organization that loudly asserted its support of the particular interest it represented. And each was richly supplied with national and local journals, training schools and neighborhood offices, paid staff, subsidized congresses, posters, leaflets, and research, with a lavishness that completely outclassed that of the democratic parties, when they existed at all. This massive Communist organizational apparatus was matched in Italy only by the Church and its parish and lay organizations, but their clerical character reduced their appeal among the voters whom the Communists hoped to attract. Communist power of this scope, through the Party and its many fronts, facing a fragile democratic governing coalition doomed to immobility and internecine partisan squabbles, presented the clear threat of increased Communist strength in the elections ahead, and the loss of the first nation in the world to Communism by subversion rather than by the force of a Red Army.

This was a prospect that Washington could not—and would not—abide. The Cold War times simply wouldn't allow it. To be sure, by this time the Korean War was drawing to a close, but this did little to diminish the fear of Communist aggression. By now the Indochina conflict, with the Communists scoring startling successes against the French, was heating up to take its place. And while Joseph Stalin had just recently died, the succession struggle then going on in the Kremlin boded the ascendancy of an equally dangerous Soviet chieftain; after all, Beria seemed to be a major contender. Moreover, China and Russia were still wedded in what seemed an unshakable alliance, and the neutralism of newly independent former colonies like India seemed aimed more at reducing the power and influence of the free world than merely avoiding involvement in great-power rivalry. Communism was on the offensive in many areas, from Malaya and the Philippines to the so-called "peace" campaign in Europe against NATO and the Marshall Plan. Indeed, if anything, the Cold War seemed to be gaining in intensity and spreading in dimension, and in the United States the hysterical anti-Communism of Senator Joseph McCarthy was reaching a fever pitch.

In such an atmosphere, it was obviously unthinkable that Washington could allow Italy to be lost to Communism, and Clare Luce had all the personal strength needed to see that it would not happen. The only question was how it was to be saved, not whether, and it soon was clear that the CIA would have to play a key role. The Marshall Plan had revived Italy's economy, NATO protected it against Soviet military attack, but only CIA could furnish the tools to meet the Communist political campaign at the organizational level, where the threat was greatest.

CIA's Italian political operations, and several similar ones that were patterned after it in subsequent years, notably Chile, have come under scorching criticism, especially recently. The charge has been leveled that the United States and, most certainly, the CIA have no business "interfering" in the domestic political affairs of another sovereign nation, that their assistance to one side or another in an election there is not only illegal but immoral. Now, there can be no denying that "interference" of this sort is illegal. Under most countries' laws, as under American law, a foreign government is strictly prohibited from involving itself in that nation's internal political processes. But its illegality in this respect does not settle the matter. Espionage also is illegal under the laws of most countries, and yet most countries consider themselves justified by the inherent right of sovereign self-defense to engage in espionage in order to learn of possible secret threats to their safety. Moreover, "interference" through direct political and paramilitary aid via secret channels has been a characteristic of interstate relations for centuries. Indeed, such aid helped obtain the independence of the United States. Benjamin Franklin, one of our first representatives in France, used there a small "private" company which provided arms and funds to the American colonists struggling against King George III, but kept secret from the British that the French government was their source. That such "interference" took place to our benefit does not, of course, make it right, but it does require of us careful consideration before we throw the first stone of reproach.

Now, whether such illegal action also is immoral raises another question. The sovereign-state system of the modern world has long given to each state the moral right to use

force in its own self-defense in such degree as may be necessary for that purpose. If such *military* "interference" is
accepted, then surely lesser forms of interference can be justified under the same conditions. The test involves both
ends and means. The end sought must be in defense of the
security of the state acting, not for aggression or aggrandize-
ment, and the means used must be only those needed to
accomplish that end, not excessive ones. In this moral and
philosophical framework, assistance to democratic groups in
Italy to enable them to meet the Soviet-supported subversive campaign there can certainly be accepted as a moral
act. It was clearly for the defense of the United States and
its NATO allies against the danger of Soviet expansion, and
the financial and political support given was plainly a low-
key and nonviolent means of acting for that end. This framework cannot justify every act of political interference by CIA
since 1947, but it certainly does in the case of Italy in the
1950s.

But if the United States was justified in undertaking the
operation, it has been legitimately asked, why then did it
have to be the CIA that handled it? The short answer is that
the United States had no other mechanism then—nor, for
that matter, does it today—for doing the job effectively.

Before the creation of the OPC as the CIA's covert-action
arm, Washington did in fact try to support Italy's center
democratic forces by other means—through the Marshall
Plan, for example. But we discovered that our government
aid must go to or through the receiving government, and
that the receiving government's legislature must know how
the funds were disbursed. This made it impossible to funnel
the funds only to democratic forces, for, obviously, the Communist deputies in the Chamber would block it or demand a
share. If we tried to pass such government aid directly to
our friends in the open, the Italian government itself, no
matter with how much sympathy it might view what we
were doing, would have to stop it, because it was illegal.
And, finally, the recipients of such open aid would be accused by the Communists of being in the pay and control of

Washington. Thus it became quickly apparent that for an operation of this sort to succeed, the fact that the American government was the source had to remain a secret. Unlike the Russians, who have the Party apparatus, which they "plausibly deny" is an arm of their state, the only way for the United States to do it was by turning it over to the clandestine operators of the CIA either to pass the funds in secret directly or to create the ostensibly private sources behind which our government's hand could be concealed. And in a major operation such as in Italy, the amounts involved required the first method, as they were beyond any believable private funding.

To be sure, the political-action operation wasn't the only CIA activity in Italy at the time. My counterpart in the OSO area was engaged in an array of espionage and counterespionage activities, including liaison work with Italy's intelligence services. But the political-action program that I headed was the CIA's major assignment in that country, and certainly the several millions of dollars involved constituted the largest sum of money the Agency ever pumped into a single political-action operation.

The operation's primary purpose and effect was to provide support to the center democratic political parties. As obvious as this may seem, it is a point worth underscoring, because of so many misconceptions about it. The underlying philosophy of the CIA was to be *for* a democratic Italy, not just *against* a Communist one. The program in Italy gave aid to the democratic forces to obtain *their* goals. It did not "bribe" them to follow American direction, nor did it merely engage in "dirty tricks" in order to undermine the Communists. What's more—and this too deserves emphasis in light of latter-day misrepresentations—the very deliberate and conscious policy was made both in Washington and in Rome that no help of any kind go to the Neo-Fascists or Monarchists. The unanimous view was that, with the right kinds and amounts of assistance, the center parties could be strengthened sufficiently to form and maintain a stable, viable, and truly democratic governing majority, and thus the

United States did not need to back right-wing groups in its campaign to stop the rise of the Communists. To a large degree the reason was ideological; after all, what we wanted was democracy in Italy, so we could not very well support antidemocratic groups, whether on the Left or on the Right. But there was also a pragmatic reason; any strengthening of the Neo-Fascists and Monarchists, we recognized, would inevitably weaken the Liberals and Christian Democrats, for that was the only place from which added strength could come to them, not from the Communists.

The CIA's support to the center forces was provided mainly in the form of direct payments, money to help them finance the usual variety of political activities: publication of newsletters, leaflets, posters, and other propaganda materials, staging congresses and public rallies, conducting membership drives and voter-registration campaigns and the like. In addition, though, perhaps because of my earlier experience in the New York Democratic Party movement and my studies of the Communist "organizational weapon," I was particularly concerned with the fundamentals of party organization and operation, and so I insisted that not only funds but also advice be given for training programs, research and study groups, local party offices and activities, and so on. In particular I worked to establish firm long-term budgets, so that the groups supported could maintain a regular schedule of activities and services to their voters, rather than only frenetic electoral campaigns and promises. I felt that smaller expenditures each year for these purposes would be more effective than a single large crash funding for an election campaign.

But it was also clear that to confine our efforts strictly to the purely political arena would be to keep the operation entirely too narrow, especially in light of the way Moscow was functioning. Past masters in the art of wielding the organizational weapon, the Russians poured their aid not only into the Italian Communist Party itself but also to the host of Party-controlled or Party-front organizations that the Communists had set up throughout the Italian social and economic structure: the huge and highly effective Communist trade union, for example, consumer and farmer cooperatives, cultural societies, youth and student groups, veterans organizations, and local committees of all kinds. This kind of support had to be vigorously matched, and therefore much of the CIA effort also went to strengthening the free trade-union movement, building competitive democratic cooperatives and supporting a variety of cultural, civic and political groups. A strategy had to be developed into which the individual groups to be supported could fit.

In Italy, it was clear that the Church still was an important force, and its lay activities, from the associations of Christian workers to parish-based discussion groups, still could pull voters to the democratic center. At the same time, though, it was clear that the Church's political influence was waning, that a program based on it alone would be destined to failure; and in any event that these groups drew on the Church's own financial sources, so CIA aid was less needed. But other, secular groups, whose interests led them to support center democratic government, did need help in their competition with Communist organizations in the same sector. Thus, fishermen, farmers, resistance veterans and other groups had to be identified and a decision made whether and how they could use CIA assistance effectively to increase their appeal and to provide a broader base for a center democratic government.

Our task was much more difficult than that faced by the Communists, whose support of such groups was designed single-mindedly to aid the Party to extend its influence into sectors where the purely political organizations could not penetrate. As our strategy was based on center democracy, we had to deal with a number of parties and groups quite fiercely insistent on their independence and with interests sometimes quite opposed to one another. Thus we had to accept the fact that on occasion a group being supported by the CIA might be in tactical opposition to the very government and parties supported by the CIA. Any attempt to dictate the tactics of such a group would conflict with the basis of our relationship, that we were assisting it to flourish as an element in a pluralistic, democratic Italy, and would risk discrediting our own strategy as well as the appeal the group offered to its followers. But this explanation was frequently a difficult one to get across through cables to Washington or even sometimes to the senior members of the embassy reviewing our progress.

Propaganda was a particular arena of contest in Italy. The Communists and their front groups were amply supplied with journals and leaflets of all descriptions, and the wall poster was a firmly established vehicle for pressing the party line not only on the faithful but also on the independent passer-by, in every village and city in Italy. These had to be answered, not only by the democratic parties themselves, but also by the organizations facing the front groups. I viewed posters with some distaste, as they were expensive, their effect was rarely more than fleeting, and they had a terribly intoxicating effect on American officials, who continually urged that a poster be put out with whatever pet idea they had at the moment. I believed that our funds were much better spent on local offices and activists, training schools and similar organizational work, even including organization journals to ensure that the cadre and membership were well armed with arguments they needed to contest their Communist associates orally. But I also accepted the need for a presence on the walls, and often approved the necessary large funds for posters.

A feature of life in Italy was the periodic rumor that a general-circulation magazine or newspaper was in the process of being acquired by some well-funded people who planned to make it anti-American in character, promote a neutralist line, or otherwise pose a threat to United States interests. The suggestion would then be made that this problem could be obviated either by arranging to purchase the controlling interest ourselves through intermediaries or by starting up a competing journal. The sums involved were invariably large, the pit into which the first installment would be placed was clearly bottomless, the problems of controlling the editorial content on a daily basis to the satisfaction of covert would-be publishers in Rome and Washington were insuperable, and I could confidently predict that the feared anti-Americanism would appear in other journals even if we blocked it in this one. By a combination of these arguments and some traditional bureaucratic foot-dragging, I managed to divert most of these proposals into more productive channels for our support.

But Washington expected action in the press field. It was acutely conscious of the fashion in which the worldwide Communist propaganda apparatus functioned, placing a story in some obscure journal in Bombay and then picking up and replaying the article throughout the world, at which point even the non-Communist wire services and journals began to treat it as a real story. To match this, Washington wanted the ability similarly to place stories in non-American media around the world and then cause its other "outlets" to pick up and publicize it; the apparatus was irreverently dubbed the "Mighty Wurlitzer." And in Italy it was arranged in a way that reflected some of the CIA culture, and later produced problems of its own. We turned to the OSO "side" of the station and its friends in the Italian security field. With their help, we located an editor interested in publicizing little-noticed facts about life in the Communist countries (the bulk of Washington's interest) and some other occasional tidbits of international politics, with particular attention to highlighting material about Communist worldwide activities.

The material we supplied this editor was fundamentally true, to maintain the news agency's credibility, and the local press began to use it regularly. Washington was happy with the clippings we sent in, I was happy that the affair required minimum investment in time or money, and the station was happy at this evidence that the OSO and OPC cultures had merged to conduct this operation. None of us noted the danger of thus encouraging some of the Italian security leadership to believe that CIA might be sympathetic to their playing an active political role in Italy. And while CIA in 1954 had nothing to do with the political activities that later caused the head of the Italian intelligence service to be indicted (although ultimately cleared in 1971), even the small earlier activity might have been used by opponents to place the entire blame for his actions on CIA.

For all these activities the essential ingredient was secrecy; there simply couldn't be any evidence that the support was coming from the United States government. Therefore that support, whether money, materials or simply advice, was passed to the recipients via intermediaries who ostensibly had no connection whatsoever with the CIA, or for that matter even with the United States embassy. These intermediaries, of course, were so-called CIA "outside officers," agents living under private cover in Rome and elsewhere throughout Italy. It is true that in two of our larger operations, because of their importance in the country's over-all political spectrum, I or one of my "inside officers" maintained direct contact with the Italian recipients of our aid, meeting in carefully selected and well hidden safe houses, after the traditional circuitous approach, although even in these cases the funds would actually be passed by an outsider, so that no funds were handed over by an acknowledged United States official. In every other case, the contacts went through an outside agent, using a good cover reason why the two would be together. Indeed, this sort of thing was so effective that often the Italian recipients of our aid themselves were not certain where the aid was coming from. Some believed that they were in contact with private American groups who had taken an interest in their cause. And those who had an inkling that they were in touch with the United States government in some way, though not knowing exactly in which way, were discreet enough not to ask.

Compared with Scandinavia, planting and running outside agents in Italy was a virtual piece of cake. In the *dolce vita* atmosphere of the time, Americans of every shape, form and description had flocked to Rome and other major Italian cities and were constantly roaming all over the Italian landscape. Thus, the half-dozen-or-so outside officers I ran, most of them sent over by the Agency from Washington headquarters and each assigned to a different political group, attracted no more attention than the tens of thousands of other Americans on the scene then. And what's more, there was very little problem establishing credible covers for them. Americans could present the flimsiest reasons for being in Italy at that time without raising a single incredulous eyebrow. They could be businessmen, free-lance journalists, students, artists, aspiring film actors, or just well-heeled drifters who had come to partake of the sweet life.

Which is not to say that that sweet-life atmosphere didn't present some problems. On one occasion one of my outside contacts, in the best *dolce vita* spirit, got into a fight with his wife's lover and wound up in the local jail, thereby creating some fairly anxious moments for me about what he would reveal concerning his real work during his trial. On another occasion, we discovered that one of our officers was requiring the recipient of CIA funds to receipt for a larger sum than he actually received, and was pocketing the difference. When he was confronted, he ran, and a wild chase ensued, with the officer getting as far as Mexico before he was finally induced to surrender and repay the stolen funds. But CIA and the Justice Department concluded that he could not be prosecuted without exposing his entire operation and the Italian recipients, and destroying them among their associates.

This incident, I must quickly add, was by no means usual. In fact, corruption of this sort was really quite rare in the CIA, despite the obvious opportunities for it that covert operations afforded. Extremely strict internal procedures had been designed by the Agency to prevent, or at least severely limit, such abuse. Funds were handled by a separate finance office with its own channels of reporting; signed vouchers and receipts were required, even using aliases where necessary, to conceal secret recipients, or an officer's certificate on those occasions where a receipt could not be obtained; and detailed accountings and audits made every officer aware that precise control of funds was vitally important to the Agency. Allen Dulles had warned that the CIA's power to dispense secret funds would undoubtedly be cut off if the Congress ever suspected that the power was being abused. This is not to say that some chiefs of station did not use funds to entertain quite lavishly, nor that some of the "operational expenses" involved in an officer's cultivation of potential agents did not include providing that officer with some of the better brands of alcohol in the Embassy commissary. But in such incidents CIA's activities did not differ substantially from those of the military and foreign services during those years, nor indeed from the accepted mores of the corporate-expense-account world.

But most of the problems presented by the indirect way of operating were simple ones: being certain that the agents were properly briefed and that they were saying only what was approved United States policy. Isolated as they were from the official American community, in frequent and sympathetic contact with only one of the facets of the intricate Italian political scene, they quite naturally tended to take on the views of their contacts. Thus, on a daily basis I would wander out of the Embassy, drive across town and pick up one of them at a street corner for a discussion, sometimes merely driving aimlessly through beautiful Rome, sometimes stopping at a discreet safe apartment, sometimes taking a chance, on a sparkling spring day, to have a quiet lunch at a remote country restaurant. We would discuss the political scene and the latest government crisis in fine detail, he would explain how his contacts could not possibly do anything other than what they were doing without losing all their political appeal, and I would tell him he had to urge them to change their position slightly, so that the government could survive and I could answer the furious cables I was receiving as to how headquarters could possibly continue giving any further aid to such a recalcitrant group. We would then separate, and each would try to present the other's arguments to an unsympathetic reception, yet obtain enough movement on each side to keep the project alive.

Despite the tension, it was stimulating and enjoyable work for one who liked politics and the fine Roman atmosphere.

Clare Boothe Luce took an intimate interest—and hand—in the CIA operations run out of her embassy. When I first arrived in Rome, she was heavily involved in what was to become her most brilliant diplomatic accomplishment: negotiating a peaceful settlement of the dispute over Trieste between Italy and Yugoslavia. But she soon turned her attention and keen intelligence to my political action program. She set up a regular Tuesday afternoon skull session in her beautifully gilded office in the Embassy—the former residence of Queen Mother Marguerite—which wonderfully and somewhat theatrically set off her blond hair, the pastel colors she favored in her clothing and her regal bearing. And, later when she became ill and temporarily bedridden, rather than cancel the session, she would hold court in her bedroom. And either there, clustered about the foot of her bed, or seated in her spacious office, those senior officers of the embassy who were entitled to know of CIA's activities— her deputy chief of mission Elbridge Durbrow, one of the Foreign Service's original Soviet experts; Francis Williamson, the head of the political section; and Tom Lane, the labor attaché, who had come to Italy in 1943 and had the confidence of both American and Italian labor leaders— would question Gerry and me for the details of our activity and the reactions of our contacts.

Extremely attractive, intelligent and knowledgeable, full of confidence and poise, quick and decisive, leaving no one in doubt about who was in charge, Mrs. Luce still stands high on my list of strong and effective ambassadors, taking command of her mission as the President's representative, willing to take sensible risks and not succumbing to a nervous concern with minutiae. My great regard for her, however, did not mean we always agreed. In fact we had some substantial disagreements.

Our disagreements were not over our basic policy. Mrs. Luce made no secret of her conservative leanings, but she fully supported the center democratic parties as the best answer to the Communists in Italy, and never suggested any kind of turn to the Right. But she never really accepted my strategic approach of building the democratic organizations on a long-term basis, aimed not only at the next election contest but the next one after that. She approached the relationship in a much more tactical vein, and saw little merit in providing support to groups who were acting against a particular American interest at any one time. Thus at our Tuesday sessions we would frequently argue over whether the regular installment of aid to some small party, for example, should be held up and the word passed that there was deep concern that the recipient was not acting as we would have wished and that we thus had doubts about the utility of continuing our support. This policy was not limited to the CIA program, however. Perhaps its most public expression was when Mrs. Luce stated that no "off-shore" Defense Department procurement contracts should be awarded to firms whose employees had voted to be represented by the Communist labor union. Applied to Fiat, this worked, and the Communist union's vote promptly fell from 60 percent to 38 percent. But the lesson was also learned by management, which two years later engineered a split in the free union and replaced it with a company union, which hardly strengthened the cause of center democracy in the area.

A larger issue arose over the constitutional status the Communist Party and its front organizations enjoyed in Italy. Prime Minister Mario Scelba, who as Minister of the Interior had met the full blast of the Communists' violent reaction to a madman's attempted assassination of their chief, Palmiro Togliatti, in 1948, spoke of the desirability of placing legal restraints on the Communists as disloyal to the Constitution. To American policy circles, this seemed both logical and an effective way to hold down this threatening force. But Scelba was able to do little about the matter, because his minor-party partners saw the answer to Communism more in social and economic policies, and the Christian Democrats were divided among themselves between those who agreed with Scelba, those (the dominant factions) who agreed with the minor parties, and those who thought it impossible to take such actions against one out of five Italians, and the best-organized ones at that, without stirring riots and revolution.

As the Americans debated this issue, the Italian parliament in 1955 elected Giovanni Gronchi, considered a Leftist among the Christian Democrats, as the new President of the Republic, and the party clearly set out on the road of social and economic reform as its appeal for the support of the populace in the next elections. But the Americans held to the need for anti-Communist measures. And my long-term program of aid to build center democracy was once again suspended—until nationwide local elections neared and the need for that aid became critical, whereupon I was authorized to fill the back seat of my Fiat with millions of lire and pass them on through my outside agent, an ostensible student, in one rather tense evening's work.

But 1955 opened a new issue, around which an intense American debate would swirl for many years. The Socialist Party, under Pietro Nenni, began a long, slow process of separation from the Communists. The center parties' social programs, the Socialists' junior-partner status with the Communists, the prospect of being in opposition forever and the change in the European atmosphere from Stalin's menace to the Marshall Plan's hopes, all contributed to Nenni's move. But he took no dramatic nor even clear steps such as the Social Democrats had done when they broke off from the Communists and their Socialist allies in 1948. Whether from a natural supercaution, a tactical design to extract the greatest possible number of concessions from the Christian Democrats, a sincere fear of dividing the Left for the benefit of the Right, or because the web of his supporting organizations in labor, cooperatives, and elsewhere were under Communist control and would be used against an independent Socialist Party, the moves he made were so ambiguous and imperceptible that they raised the immediate question whether they were in good faith or merely a stratagem through which the Communists could enter the center political arena by proxy.

This ambiguity produced the debate over whether the

center, and especially the Christian Democrats, should con-
template an "opening to the Left"—that is, an arrangement
for collaboration with the Socialists separated from the Communists. The proponents of this, of which I was one,
pointed to the fact that some 15 percent of the combined
Left vote was Socialist, and that if this (or even a major part
of it) could be separated from the Communists, they would
be reduced at one blow to a mere 20 percent of the Italian
electorate, and a very minor threat to the Western alliance.
The opponents, including Mrs. Luce, pointed to the ambiguity of the statements and steps of the Socialists, and insisted that they make a clear break with their erstwhile allies before they could be received as respectable members
of Western democracy. And in the background, the problem
of Christian Democratic unity loomed. A clear turn to the
Left and an alliance with the Socialists might lead, in many
opinions, to a split of the right wing of the Christian Democrats into a separate party hoping to add enough rightist
strength from the Monarchists and the ex-Fascists to govern.
The prediction was that they would fail, but the result
would be to weaken the Christian Democrats in the face of
the Communists, spell the end to center government, and
lead to the type of coalition instability endemic to France.
As usual in important political questions, good arguments
could be offered in support of both sides.

There was an operational dimension to the debate. The
Socialists for years had relied entirely upon the Communists
for their network of supporting organizations and, some said,
for their basic financial livelihood as well. Whether or not
the latter was true, it was apparent that one of the inhibitions to a clean break by the Socialists from the Communists
was where their future financial and political support would
come from. But if this could be assured by a combination of
an outgoing attitude among the center democratic forces recognizing the return of a prodigal to the tenets of Western
democracy *and* an assurance of a continuing source of financial support from unspecified and understanding "friends"
in America, then the inhibitions might be eliminated and

the Socialists might take the step that would end American concern over the slim majority that stood for Western democracy in Italy. Some of my outside officers had little trouble striking up acquaintances with Socialist leaders, and in their discussions with them of the objectives and plight of the Socialists, they were close to offering to survey friendly and understanding sources "in America" to see whether some assistance might be found to help the Socialists through their dilemma.

But it was not to be, as American policy remained solidly against the opening, even after Mrs. Luce departed in November 1956 after the bizarre but very real experience of suffering from arsenic droppings from the paint in her residence at the Villa Taverna. Under her successor, James David Zellerbach, the Embassy and Washington remained insistent that the Socialists prove their conversion by separating themselves not only at the party level but from all the supporting organizations they shared with the Communists. I was never authorized to permit my outside officers to open a conversation with Socialists about the possibility of locating friendly American sources to assist the Socialist Party gradually to wean itself from the massive support it had received from the Communists.

Paradoxically, my operations also had to contend with Americans of exactly the opposite political persuasion from Mrs. Luce. At this time the CIA's International Organizations Division, headed by Tom Braden and his deputy, Cord Meyer, had a firmly liberal coloration and viewed the principal struggle with the Communists internationally as one over the loyalties of voters attracted to social and political change and even Socialism—whether they would be lured by the false promise of the Communists or could be brought to support the democratic socialism of the West. This division's primary work was in helping to organize and support internationally such groups as free labor federations, free student societies, the Congress of Cultural Freedom, and a series of other free associations from jurists to lawyers to veterans, to counter the similar "front" organizations the

Communists ran in the international field. But these international organizations were based on national ones, like the American National Student Association, and they needed to demonstrate their strength and reality at home before they could speak effectively in the international arena. Thus, from Braden's division came suggestions that Italian Social Democrats and independent cultural groups be especially helped, and that the opening to the Left could be a major tactical victory in the East-West struggle.

This thesis, however valid on the international plane, had two complications in Italy. Most of the individuals and groups Braden suggested for assistance were outspoken in their criticism and opposition to the Christian Democrats, and even of the necessary compromises that permitted a coalition center government in Italy. Since this was the linchpin of American policy, it made no sense to us to support those who opposed it, even for whatever unmeasurable help that might give to our international programs. The coalition was too fragile to permit much internal conflict, and we had enough as it was. Secondly, these activities raised a problem over lines of authority and responsibility. Ambassador Luce was charged with the management of our Italian relations, and she was highly competent to do so, whether I agreed with her every decision or not. But independent CIA-supported activities from other areas could have a major impact there, and I believed it important that she have a major voice in determining what they might be—under Washington's over-all control, of course. So my own liberal sympathies and understanding of these proposals took second place to the pragmatics of Italy's politics, and the structure of the American government—I had to agree that we not turn from the Christian Democrat bird in the hand to the Socialist birds in the bush, at least not until they were fully grown and we could better see their plumage.

Considering the amounts of money we were spending—at least relative to the CIA budget—it is not surprising that there was an almost constant demand by Washington for accountings on what we were accomplishing. Impatient staff reviews repeatedly complained of the size of the subsidies disbursed in Italy (although they were but a small fraction of the economic and military aid flowing in simultaneously); there were many at headquarters who were suspicious that all we were doing was handing out our money in a free-wheeling happy-go-lucky way; and time and again I was visited by senior Washington officials for detailed briefings.

One such visitor was Joseph P. Kennedy (father of the future President), a member of the President's Foreign Intelligence Advisory Board (PFIAB), who was particularly inquisitive about the program. Headquarters informed me of his coming, told me to brief him fully, but said not to tell him the names of our agents and outside officers. But the desk officer in Washington who gave these instructions obviously didn't know Joe Kennedy, a man who hadn't amassed his fortune and imparted to his sons the wit and drive to reach the top by accepting anodyne descriptions of the activities of bureaucrats. While I briefed him in Gerry's office, he suddenly and gruffly demanded to know the name of the outside officer handling the labor program that I was describing. Following my instructions, I described the officer's qualifications but did not name him. But Kennedy bore in; clearly, he was out to prove that he was entitled to know all and every secret. And, after some further fencing on my part, he sharply said that either he would be given the name of the outside officer or he would return to Washington and resign from the PFIAB. At this point, Gerry Miller intervened and solved the impasse by giving Kennedy the name he wanted, and Mrs. Luce saved my hide by vouching for me to Kennedy. I had learned my first lesson about outside supervision of the CIA: that while such supervision must have limits if it is both to work and to keep secrets, the Agency itself cannot set those limits.

It was admittedly difficult to show "hard returns" for the money we were spending. We could—and did—monitor the work being done by the parties and groups we were supporting, checking on the functioning of their local organizations, attending their meetings, rallies and congresses, reading their papers and propaganda materials, auditing their books, seeing whether their posters appeared in the villages or just the major cities. We also kept a close watch on the local, municipal or regional elections to get readings on how our friends were doing. But it was clear to me that our accomplishments could not be measured in short-term ways. As I argued repeatedly, we had to realize that we were in this for the long haul, that our objective had to be the continued vitality of the center democratic forces and that it would not be until the 1958 elections that we could have even a benchmark of whether we had succeeded in halting the trend toward waning Christian Democratic strength and rising Communist strength.

Despite all this political work, I was still in the world of intelligence. Our outside officers, by virtue of their relations with leaders of the political parties and other organizations at the center of Italy's political life plus a wide variety of other politically involved Italians, had access to the most intimate aspects of Italy's political life. This was "intelligence" in the sense of information and judgments necessary to the Embassy and to Washington as they made American policy vis-à-vis Italy. It was supplemental to the product of our "intelligence" spies and counterspies on the OSO "side" of the station, who concentrated on Soviet and other Communist actions with respect to Italy, and who worked with their Italian counterparts. But our approaches differed—theirs the secret techniques of intelligence professionals, mine the tactics of the cloakrooms and political dealings familiar from ward politics to state legislatures. And sometimes the techniques clashed.

One day Gerry Miller called me into his office. He said he wanted me to meet a very secret American contact whom I should handle for him in the future. We went out to a small bar where no one would notice us and shared a *cappuccino*. I learned that my new friend (and he is still my friend) had come to Italy with the OSS and had gotten to know a number of young political leaders when they were trying to establish their new political system. A liberal Catholic by background, and fluent in Italian, he had befriended a number of them and had helped them to formulate their ideas on how Italy should develop. He had returned to the United States after the war, but had kept his friendships not only with the Italians but with some of the OSS veterans who also had operated in Italy during the war and later had helped to form CIA, in particular James Angleton. They had asked him to return to Italy from time to time to keep in touch with his old friends and report to Washington on their views and hopes. He had done so regularly, but it was clear that the struggle in Italy was moving into high gear, and Washington had sent him to Rome to live, so that his information could be continuous. Gerry had tried to meet with him and keep him compartmented from the rest of the station, and from my political operations, but had come to the conclusion that it could not be done. The problems of briefing and debriefing him, ensuring that he both understood and thus followed the ambassador's policies, yet operated without apparent connection with the embassy were too demanding in time and too difficult to conceal for one in Gerry's prominent position as one of Mrs. Luce's principal advisers as well as in official liaison with the Italian security services. So Gerry obtained Washington's approval to bring me in on the secret of his friend's activities and authorized me to help in handling him thenceforth.

"Charlie," as we referred to him when necessary, was a fascinating individual. Totally devoted to Western freedom and the United States, he had a circle of Italian friends that made me green with envy, as they covered a number of political currents. Well-educated and widely read, he could discourse with ease on medieval philosophy and the Pope's social encyclicals. But his very closeness to his Italian friends had an impact on his judgments about them. He looked as much at their personal attributes as at their political roles, and he formed strong opinions about whether their personal standards were of the high quality needed, inevitably measured by his own, which were high indeed. As raw information feeding into an over-all assessment of Italian affairs, his contribution was of great value.

But I learned that it was more than this, and in my view

dangerous; I heard that the secrecy of his operation as a classic "singleton," an individual agent operating alone rather than as a member of a net or through a chain of intermediaries, produced the impression in Washington that it reflected the direct truth about events and personalities in Italy. And the professional intelligence operators who managed him, to ensure that this direct truth reached policy levels, had arranged that his reports be forwarded in their raw form in sealed envelopes to Washington and laid on the desk of senior policy-level officials as the real story direct from the source. No Washington official could resist reading or being impressed by his lively, informal and personal accounts of his meetings with senior Italians, and on one occasion I learned that he had even been picked up on a Washington street corner by a black limousine so that he could orally brief the Secretary of State, John Foster Dulles, as they drove through the city.

Obviously such a meeting and the dramatics of clandestinity that surrounded it enhanced the impact of Charlie's views, vastly beyond the effect of the judgments of the many other reports, also from direct conversations with Italian leaders, but passed through the careful screening and collation process of the corps of experts on Italian political affairs not only in the editing staffs of our station, but in the analytical components of the embassy, the State Department and the CIA.

Gradually, I set about changing the situation. I adhered to Washington's strictures that his identity be kept totally hidden, but I began to insist that his product (but, of course, not his identity) be circulated to those who needed to know the results of his unique access in Italy. This began with the Ambassador and the political officers of the embassy, and then spread naturally to the other CIA officers in the station, the operational desk at home, and finally the analytical staffs of CIA's Directorate of Intelligence and the other intelligence "customers" in Washington. Charlie's material then reached all its proper readers, but arrived without a special aura of mystery, and was put in proper proportion in the

jigsaw-puzzle collection of information needed to understand the variegated Italian political scene. I could not be
accused of suppressing it, but only of ensuring that all
points of view were reported. To the extent that Washington
or the embassy adopted his views and his recommendations
for policy, even over my arguments to the contrary (and they
were many as the opening to the Left loomed), I at least
knew that the policies he espoused had official approval.
Moreover, Italians were not subject to confusion at hearing
one policy from the embassy and its unofficial spokesmen
and another from a mysterious representative of some un-
stated authority in Washington, perhaps the CIA.

The contrasting political and "professional" approaches to
intelligence had other encounters. At the Twentieth Congress of the Communist Party of the Soviet Union, Khrushchev made his famous speech denouncing Stalin. CIA obtained a copy through its excellent professional operators,
despite Khrushchev's intention that it remain a Communist
family secret. The question then arose as to what was to be
done with this obviously valuable weapon in the struggle
between Stalin's successors and the free societies of the
West. The more conspiratorial elements of CIA, led by the
counterintelligence experts, saw it as the basis for an operation to spread confusion and deception among the Communists of the world. As one move in this program they turned
to the Italian station and its press outlets to plant a copy of it
sourced in Italy, with subtle variations in the original text to
increase suspicions and backbiting among Communists. But
before it was published, more politic heads prevailed
(among them Ray Cline, as an analyst looking at the over-all
impact it could have on world political trends), and Allen
Dulles delivered the true text to the State Department to
release officially to *The New York Times*. It is clear that the
political approach was right, and that the speech marked a
watershed in the appeal of the Soviets to other peoples
throughout the world, unblemished by doubts as to how an
obscure Italian publication might have obtained such a document, or as to the accuracy of its text.

Perhaps the most dramatic, if not indeed most important, effect of the worldwide distribution of the Khrushchev speech was, of course, its contribution to the Hungarian uprising of 1956, and its brutal suppression by Russian tanks. From the point of view of the Rome station, without minimizing the great admiration and sense of deep tragedy we felt for the Hungarian freedom fighters, that event provided a wonderful propaganda opportunity. All the hypocrisy of the Communist claim to be building workers' paradises and all the brutality of the Soviet method of maintaining those "paradises" were incontrovertibly revealed. The CIA and its allies did everything they could to reinforce the impact in Italy. Thousands of posters were plastered in every city, leaflets were distributed everywhere, meetings organized, memorials to the fallen Hungarian heroes arranged, and a nationwide program to receive and resettle the wave of refugees who escaped, including one who married the fine nursemaid of our Rome-born son, Paul. Although the British-French attack on Suez diluted the effect of Hungary in much of the world, in Italy the lesson was driven home.

The Hungarian Revolution had an additional significance for the CIA. Ever since the creation of the OPC under Frank Wisner's direction, the Agency had had—or at least believed that it had—a mission to assist militarily, in the OSS tradition, resistance groups—call them freedom fighters in the Hungarian case—seeking to overthrow Communist totalitarian regimes. And certainly it had tried to do so in Albania, Korea and China. Although I was in no way personally involved in headquarters planning at the time, I do know that the CIA did not provoke the Hungarian revolt, as Communists have variously charged, by its then front operation Radio Free Europe. But once the uprising was underway, there can be no doubt that Wisner and other top officials of his Directorate of Plans, especially those on the covert action side, were fully prepared with arms, communications stocks and air resupply, to come to the aid of the freedom fighters. This was exactly the end for which the Agency's paramilitary capability was designed. And a case can be made that they could have done so without involving the United States in a world war with the Soviet Union.

But President Eisenhower overruled them. Whatever doubts may have existed in the Agency about Washington's policy in matters like this vanished. It was established, once and for all, that the United States, while firmly committed to the containment of the Soviets within their existing sphere of influence, was not going to attempt to liberate any of the areas within that sphere, even if the provocation was as dramatic as that in the Hungarian situation. And, in fact, no CIA aid was sent into Hungary to support the freedom fighters. Starkly, we demonstrated that "liberation" was not our policy when the chips were down in Eastern Europe, and the price might have been World War III.

Wisner went to Vienna at the end of the uprising and traveled to the Hungarian border to watch, at least symbolically, the fleeing Hungarians cut down by Russian guns as he and America stood helplessly aside. He came to Rome from there to make a routine visit to the station and it was clear that he was near a nervous breakdown. Shortly after, he resigned from the Agency for health reasons, and Richard Bissell succeeded him as Deputy Director for Plans. Wisner never fully recovered, and his eventual suicide was as much a casualty of the realities of the Cold War as was that of Secretary of Defense James Forrestal.

The main test of our Italian political program finally came in the national elections of 1958, and, in the best Italian political tradition, the results were arguable. The facts were that the Christian Democrats gained a bit more than two percentage points of the electorate over their setback in 1953, the Communists were held to the same 22 percent that they had achieved then, the three minor center parties came out about the same, the Right lost substantially and the Socialists gained. One school stressed the strength shown by the Christian Democrats as the result of their organizational effort, managed since 1954 by Amintore Fanfani, and pointed to the rise in Socialist votes as an indication of the potential of a Socialist party separated from the Communists in an alliance with the Christian Democrats, an argument for the opening to the Left. The other school pointed out that the Communist organizational machine, unrestricted by the anti-Communist laws that they contended should have been passed, had held its voters almost intact despite the negative political impact of the Khrushchev speech and the Hungarian revolt, that the Christian Democrats' gain had come principally from the losses by the Right, and saw the Socialists as only a stalking horse to keep enticing the Italian electorate leftward to weaken the center and resume the new alliance with the Communists in a stronger position.

Washington auditors of the funds I had used saw no clear-cut result in the statistics of the elections, were uncomfortable with the differing interpretations they heard, and found insufficient precision in the argument that the results might well have been substantially different if no aid had been given, either in the form of a larger swing to the Left or a polarization of voters into a Right and a Left at the expense of democracy in the center. Again the real value of the project could be understood only in the light of a long-term strategy: gradually to strengthen center democracy, stop the move of voters toward the Communists, and split the Socialists from their unity of action with the Communists. From this viewpoint the program did succeed, and the few millions expended on such direct political action compared favorably with the many more millions spent on economic and military aid. The defeat of the Right meant that Communism's threat would be met through democratic politics, not a reversion to Fascism. The strength of the Socialists, even without aid from outside, meant that left-wing sentiment looked toward a democratic form of socialism. The stabilizing of the Communists, despite their lavish electoral campaign and the real social problems of Italy, meant that there was no inevitability in their electoral trends and that they would have to change their allegiance from Soviet Communism if they were to contest the kind of social program the Christian Democrats and Socialists could mount together. Even the Communist success in holding their previous level showed what a similar long-term organizational effort on the democratic side could produce in terms of a well-served and loyal mass base. Thus, the way was open for dramatic steps to consolidate democracy in Italy and move against the social and economic inequities that encouraged authoritarianism of both Right and Left.

It did not happen that way, of course. Fanfani's leftward-leaning postelection government ran into a series of sabotage actions from the right wing of the Christian Democratic Party. He was soon replaced as Prime Minister by Antonio Segni, with whose government the Monarchists and ex-Fascists were so happy that they voted for it, although they did not participate in its majority. Fanfani was removed as Secretary General of the party, and replaced by Aldo Moro, who altered Fanfani's drive to create a disciplined party machinery to a relaxed view of the many currents in the party, compromising in order to placate all of them. The opening to the Left stalled, as the Vatican threw the weight of the Church against it, and in 1960 Ferdinando Tambroni brought Italy nearer to Right-Left polarization than it had been since 1948. With his government actually resting on ex-Fascists in his majority, he authorized them to hold a party congress in the strong resistance center of Genoa, sparking riots and violence in a series of Italian cities. He met this by a program of police surveillance of the Communists through wiretaps, surveys of their mail, and even troops in the streets.

The situation became so dangerous that Tambroni was finally forced to resign, and the process of the opening to the Left could again proceed, albeit at the slow pace dictated by the difficulties within the Christian Democrats and by the Socialists' continued sharing of organizations with the Communists. The "opening" was not actually consummated until Pietro Nenni finally became Deputy Prime Minister in December 1963. But the move was not accompanied by any dynamic social or political program, as the divisions within the Christian Democrats continued to limit that party's moves in that direction, despite Pope John XXIII's new spirit in the Church (which in Italy meant a reduction of its role in Italian political affairs, rather than a new direction of it) and John Kennedy's support for the opening to the Left, which he managed to press onto a reluctant State Department only after a series of internal struggles. The Johnson years were obviously preoccupied with Vietnam, and the political niceties of Italy were only a secondary matter, so the lack of forward progress continued to characterize the government, and the Socialists eventually were discredited by their coalition with the Christian Democrats. The Communists, under a new and clever leader, Enrico Berlinguer, absorbed the fundamental lesson of the times and themselves talked about an "historic compromise" between themselves and the Christian Democrats as the two major Italian political forces, squeezing out the Socialists and asserting their independence of Soviet control in a new Eurocommunism. And today the same debate over their *bona fides* and the effect of carrying out that historic compromise rages as it had earlier raged over the "opening to the Left" for the Socialists.

But I was long gone from Italy when all these events transpired. After the 1958 elections, I had been there five years—long enough to have become knowledgeable about the country, but not long enough to have become more oriented to it than to United States interests—and I had asked for a transfer. Whether I could have made a difference is doubtful, but my departure reduced by one those arguing for the opening to the Left within the embassy policy group, and the early sixties saw the reduction and phasing out of our support to any of the Italian democratic forces, on the premise that they had been helped during the fifties and should have become self-sustaining by now. The Rome station turned to professional intelligence work against the Communist foreign missions and similar espionage and counterintelligence targets, and the CIA budget for Italy dropped. But the nagging thought remains in my mind that, if we had fully supported the opening to the Left and provided the assistance it needed to contest the continuing rich resources of the Communist Party, we might have helped it gain the momentum that President Kennedy hoped for it. We might also thus have freed the Christian Democrats from the pressures of finding their support in government corruption and freed the Socialists from their unhappy dependence on the Christian Democrats for political cooperation and on the Communists for their supporting organizations.

But despite this outcome, I believe that the five years between the elections of 1953 and 1958 showed that the long-term strategy of covert political help to democratic forces can work and can frustrate the hopes of authoritarians to capture democratic voters for a nondemocratic cause. It cannot be used to justify every CIA intervention abroad, but it does demonstrate the utility, and even the morality, of such secret assistance to foreign friends faced with a subversive challenge. It showed that the United States can conduct such a struggle on a political level rather than wait until it must be confronted on a military one. It also demonstrated that such programs can be conducted in full compliance with the policy of the President and his ambassador, even though I had a few differences with the latter as to what the policy should have been.

Both the successes of the program and its limitations show the value of a long-term policy and program of support *for* our friends, in contrast to more conspiratorial activities *against* our adversaries through deception or propaganda attacks. The real weaknesses of the program were perhaps ones of omission rather than of commission—its failure to seek out good young leadership cadre and to help them directly to grow in expertise and political prominence, so that they could take the leadership of the center forces from those who controlled them until the 1970s; its failure to take a stronger position with respect to forward-looking policies of social change and anticorruption and perhaps even a deeper involvement in longer-term political policies for an economically changing Italy (thanks in good part to the Marshall Plan) such as dismemberment of the vestiges of Mussolini's corporate state, which combines the inefficiencies of socialism and the corruption of uncontrolled corporate management. But this sort of influence could not be exerted just because we thought so and were supporting the effort. It would have to depend on a close and cooperative working relationship with the Italians actually engaged in the fray. And this would be difficult without constant, obvious contact between Americans and key leaders in a sophisticated and somewhat suspicious country like Italy. But CIA could and did maintain such relations, while keeping secret the specifics of the aid and advice, in many less-developed nations, and I looked forward to participating in those programs.

CHAPTER FIVE

Strategic Hamlets
in Vietnam

In 1956, while still in Italy, I received a cable from CIA headquarters in Washington proposing that I transfer from the Rome station to South Asia, where, operating under private cover, I would act as the CIA's adviser to a very prominent political leader. In deference to Agency discipline, I replied that of course I would go if headquarters insisted, but that I thought it made little sense to pull me out of Rome before the 1958 Italian elections, the outcome of which was the main reason I had come there in the first place. Gerry Miller forcefully seconded my view; headquarters thought it over and concurred, leaving me in place to finish my five-year tour.

After the elections, however, I reactivated the idea and applied for a transfer to the Far East. I didn't have any place in particular in mind. My boyhood sojourn in China, when my father had been stationed in Tientsin, had produced a vague yearning to return some day to that part of the world. I was prepared to go virtually anywhere in Asia if the Agency had an appropriate opening for me. And where they had that appropriate opening—as deputy chief of station— was in Saigon. And so it was, in this rather desultory, coincidental, virtually unthinking fashion, that I began more than a decade and a half of intense involvement in what was to be one of the most traumatic and tragic experiences in modern American history, the Vietnam War.

When I arrived in Saigon with the family on Tet of 1959, after a few months of reading on the Vietnam situation in Washington, the war had not yet begun, and the scene before us on the short drive from Tan Son Nhut airport was remarkably peaceful and calm. Saigon was a gracious colonial city with tree-lined boulevards, bustling marketplaces, pedicabs racing to and fro, and wonderfully pretty women gracefully gliding by in their beautiful *ao dais*. But it was a deceptive peace and calm, a peace and calm between storms.

Less than five years had passed since the fall of Dienbienphu. The Geneva Agreement of July 1954, formalizing the French defeat in Indochina, had divided the country between the rival governments of Ho Chi Minh in North Vietnam and Ngo Dinh Diem in the south, had arranged for an exchange of populations—about 90,000 southern Communists went north and some 900,000 northerners, largely but not exclusively Catholics, went south—and had set 1956 as the date for elections for the reunification of the country.

To be sure, at that time, both sides had made arrangements for a resumption of war. The Communists had left a stay-behind net in the south, consisting of perhaps 5,000 to 10,000 cadre and guerrillas, and had put into training as future guerrilla leaders the southerners who had gone north. And the CIA's Ed Lansdale, coming fresh from helping Magsaysay of the Philippines put down the Communist Hukbalahap insurrection there, and Lucien Conein, my old Jedburgh buddy, who had served out the rest of World War II with the OSS in Indochina, had tried to set up a similar anti-Ho underground network in the north. But neither amounted to very much. Lansdale and Conein's effort involved a few sabotage strikes just before the Geneva Accords were signed, but the net they left behind faded away or was destroyed by Hanoi's forces during the next few months. As for the Communist underground in the south, which was in time to be known as the Viet Cong, it remained essentially quiescent. Ho and his colleagues at the time were far too preoccupied with consolidating power and applying Communist ideology to the economic, social and political structure of North Vietnam to start up the war in the south again. Besides, and more to the point, Ho didn't think he had to. He believed that he was going to be able to take over South Vietnam by peaceful means—through the internal collapse of the Saigon government and the reunification elections scheduled for 1956.

That, in 1954, was a view that was widely shared. Indisputably, the Saigon government was extremely weak and precarious. Diem's power and authority in those days didn't extend much farther than the gates of the Presidential Palace. Beyond, he was challenged on every side by a host of dissident and powerful factions, quite apart from the Communists. The armed religious sects—the Cao Dai and Hoa Hao—were in a virtual constant state of revolt, and the Binh Xuyen, best described as a gang of bandits, controlled the Saigon police and freely defied Diem. In addition, the army and the civil-service bureaucracy, which had been established and trained by the French colonialists, were still very much under French influence—and no two groups disliked each other much more than Diem and the French. Finally, Diem had no mass popular constituency; his Mandarin Catholic background gave him no base among the Buddhist peasant population. His only appeal lay in his nationalism, which had led him to exile rather than accept French colonial rule, and the fact that his non-Communist nationalism seemed a more hopeful prospect than Ho's Communist version.

Not surprisingly, with so much going against him, hardly anyone gave him much chance of surviving, and virtually no one (including himself) gave him any chance at all of winning the reunification elections against the Communists in 1956. And this included the Americans. A national intelligence estimate, dated August 1954 (and quoted in the Pentagon Papers), stated: "Although it is possible that the French and Vietnamese, even with firm support from the

U.S. and other powers, may be able to establish a strong regime in South Vietnam, we believe the chances for this development are poor and moreover, that the situation is more likely to continue to deteriorate progressively over the next year."

And yet, Diem pulled it off, by taking on his enemies one by one. He first asserted his authority over the army. He purged its pro-French chief of staff and put his own man in, ended the assistance it received from the French, and welcomed an American Military Assistance Advisory Group (MAAG), some 350 strong, to take over its training and supply. Then, during 1955, he successively took control of the Saigon police from the bandit Binh Xuyen, fended off, split, and ultimately defeated the Cao Dai and Hoa Hao private armies. Next he organized a referendum to depose the Emperor Bao Dai, and establish a Vietnamese republic with himself as President. And finally he arranged elections for a South Vietnamese National Assembly and formally rejected the 1956 elections for the unification of the country, because they obviously would be won by the more populated Communist-controlled north.

Through all of this, Diem unquestionably benefited from American aid, both economic and military, as well as from the political support of President Eisenhower, who saw in him a firm line of resistance to the spread of Communism in Asia. Moreover, the dramatic exodus of Catholic refugees from North Vietnam during this period, demonstrating in this way their preference for a society in which their religion could flourish, also added to his support in the United States, especially from Cardinal Spellman. And then, too, there was CIA's backing: Ed Lansdale proffered political advice (for which he was pilloried by Graham Greene in *The Quiet American*) and the Saigon station helped to train Diem's bodyguards and provided him with a direct channel to the Dulles brothers, John Foster at State and Allen at the Agency, in Washington. But for all of this the main accomplishment was truly Diem's, the result of his toughness in crisis times, his firm use of authority amid anarchy, his monastic devotion to his mission of non-Communist nationalism and even his prickly refusal to accept counsels of caution and compromise when the situation appeared bleak. By 1958 not only had he put down his opponents, he was well launched on an extensive development program for South Vietnam. Roads were reopened, schools proliferated in the countryside, a five-year DDT-spraying campaign was started to eliminate malaria, rice production began to climb, and light industry grew in the Saigon suburbs.

But despite this success, there were in Diem's approach flaws that would prove critical in time. The fact of American aid, for example, cast a shadow over Diem's nationalism and allowed the Communists to claim to be the only true nationalists, the ones who had ousted the French and the ones who still sought to free the country's soil of all outsiders. Paradoxically, this was a chief reason behind many of the difficulties that Americans had in dealing with Diem and others of his government; on occasion they resisted the Americans merely to demonstrate their independence, to themselves if to none other. Moreover, during the days of anarchy, Diem discovered the value of keeping a firm grip on all the levers of power, and he developed the view that it would be dangerous to release even small bits of it, especially to opposition groups who appeared to him at least irresponsible if not actually disloyal to the fragile new state and its leaders in the face of the mortal threat from the north.

Thus, Diem functioned as a Mandarin administrator, a benevolent dictator, forcing his people into development for their own good, whatever they thought of it, authoritarian and undemocratic, using but complaining about the French-trained bureaucracy he employed to do so, believing that it could gradually be reformed and replaced by the graduates of American public-administration training programs. The vacuum that this produced in Saigon's political life was partially filled by noisy Saigon opposition groups and by mass rallies organized regularly by government officials to impress the Palace. But to a far greater degree it was filled among the elite by groups loyal to the suppressed sects and to regional chieftains, and by rumor and conspiracy theories about the real course of events behind the Palace's façade, especially the machinations attributed to Diem's brother, Ngo Dinh Nhu, Nhu's wife, and the secret services serving them.

In the countryside, more worrisomely, the vacuum was filled by the Communist stay-behind networks. Since the Diem regime had not collapsed as expected, and the 1956 reunification elections had not taken place, the nets were put to work, and during 1957 and 1958 there was a gradual rise in their activity—agitprop teams lectured hamlet residents in the evening, guerrilla squads attacked villages and executed isolated government officials, and recruiters took young men into the forests for political and guerrilla training. Their political campaign stressed the continuation of the struggle for Vietnam's independence, now against the "American Diemists" instead of the French, whom they had defeated. But this activity was still at a low level. It certainly was not yet a war and had not stalled the government's development drives nor yet affected the life of the cities.

This, then, was the situation when we arrived in Saigon in February 1959, a situation so quiet and uneventful that I could bring my family with me without worry about their safety. We moved into a lovely former colonial villa, located on a handsome tree-lined boulevard near the Presidential Palace, with spacious rooms, high ceilings from which graceful fans whirred, a well-manicured garden, and the appropriate number of charming Vietnamese servants to look after our needs. The children—there were now four; Paul had been born in Rome, and soon there would be a fifth, Christine, born in Saigon in 1960—were enrolled in the local French and American schools. We joined the Cercle Sportif, and the family would gather there weekly for lunch at poolside. Barbara plunged into a host of church and community activities with diplomatic and Vietnamese women's groups. There were dinners in Cholon, Saigon's Chinese quarter, for some of the best Chinese food in Asia (or anywhere else, for that matter), weekend picnics in the outlying rubber plantations, and outings to the beautiful beaches of the coast—a measure of the sense of security we had, not only in Saigon itself but also in the countryside. Only the old grilles outside one or two restaurants reminded one of the days of confusion and danger so few years before. Indeed, it had all the makings of a pleasant and comfortable life, more exotic than Rome but every bit as delightful.

My job promised to be just as challenging and interesting, and no more dangerous or dramatic. In transferring to the CIA's Far East Division I had moved into a new atmosphere and tradition in the Agency. Desmond FitzGerald had just become chief of the division, and his spirit permeated it. From an impeccable New York establishment background, he had gone to China during World War II and served as adviser and liaison officer with Chinese troops, although not with OSS. He came to CIA when OPC was formed and served in Japan and the Philippines, working on China operations. With a lovely Gerogetown house and a country residence in Virginia, he was well connected throughout Washington, where his romantic activism produced great dinner talk. In the Far East Division and at its stations in Asia, he had a rich stable of immensely colorful characters from "ugly Americans" like Lansdale, swashbucklers accustomed to danger, to quiet students steeped in the culture of the Orient. Some were old China hands, raised there in missionary or commercial families, who had taken part in the struggle between Mao's revolution and Chiang Kai-shek's regime, and more recently in the Taiwan Straits crisis. Some had helped win the fight against the Hukbalahaps in the Philippines, some had shared in the failure of the revolt against Sukarno in Indonesia and some had worked with the British in the long struggle, just then drawing to a successful close, against the Communists in Malaya. Almost all had been affected by the Korean War, and many had been through the political coups and countercoups of Thailand, Laos and Burma. They were a brilliant corps of officers, unparalleled in their ability to operate in the special Asian environment, accustomed to the unrelenting presence of open and secret violence and conspiracy there, schooled profoundly in the politics of underdeveloped and authoritarian societies and understanding the need to work as often through military as civilian channels in that part of the world.

Ebullient Elbridge Durbrow, an old friend from Rome—he had been Clare Boothe Luce's Deputy Chief of Mission—was United States Ambassador in Saigon at the time with Joseph Mendenhall as his political counselor and Arthur Gardiner the head of the AID mission. And although Durbrow was nominally in command of the over-all United States effort in South Vietnam, there can be no question of the importance of the military mission even then. Growing out of the Army and Navy's long, distinguished and pervasive influence in the Asian theater, from the Pacific war in the 1940s through the Japanese occupation and the Korean War, the 350-man MAAG in the country, commanded by Lieutenant General Samuel ("Hanging Sam") Williams, enjoyed considerable, indeed disproportionate, clout not only within the United States official community in Saigon but also in Washington. By comparison, the CIA mission in those days was relegated to a relatively minor role.

The chief of station was a dynamic Greek-American who had served with the OSS in Italy during World War II and then with the CIA in Greece during the Communist civil war there. He was a strong-minded leader and an excellent manager of people, evoking fierce loyalty from them, and running an operation of about forty people when I got there to be his deputy. Unlike the CIA breakdown in Europe, the station wasn't split into the two cultures of foreign intelligence (FI, formerly OSO) and covert action (CA, formerly OPC). In effect, despite the Far East Division's derring-do tradition in paramilitary and political-action operations, we were somewhat paradoxically all FI here. The division of the station organizationally was between "liaison" and so-called "unilateral" operations.

The "liaison" officers, as the name implies, were engaged

in the work of maintaining liaison with the local authorities, especially SEPES, the South Vietnamese intelligence service. Their jobs involved primarily the exchange, coordination and analysis of information about the Communist apparatus and its activities both in the north and in the south, the interrogation of refugees from the north and of Viet Cong cadre captured in the south, and the development of better techniques for the collection of intelligence on the Communists, including the possibility of infiltrating agents into North Vietnam. To do this job, these officers didn't need deep cover; they operated fairly openly, with only a pretense at cover.

As for the unilateral officers, their job was to establish and maintain connections with the whole array of political factions working openly or subversively in South Vietnam, from the fanatic religious sects and bandit gangs on the extreme right to the liberal groups on the left who opposed Diem for his authoritarianism and antidemocratic ways. These officers, obviously, required better cover for their work than their liaison-section colleagues, and most of them were scattered throughout the American community, ostensibly as officials, and even one or two private businessmen. They recruited and ran Vietnamese agents in the various groups they were assigned to keep tabs on. But in whichever section, liaison or unilateral, the object of the CIA officers was the collection of intelligence in the strictest professional sense of the word. None was involved in covert action, political, paramilitary, propaganda or otherwise, at the time, except to the extent that training South Vietnamese intelligence personnel in CIA's techniques strengthened them to face their Communist (and sometimes non-Communist) adversaries.

The first problem I had to deal with hit me on my first day in Saigon, in fact on the drive into town from the airport. The wife of the officer who met us flagged us down on the street to tell him that a message had just come in that he had to handle immediately. A "flap"—the CIA word for crisis—was ahead in Cambodia. Neutralist Prince Sihanouk, who had recognized China only a few months before, was thought by the Thai and South Vietnamese to be an advance agent, or at least a supply channel, for the spread of Communism to their borders. And they had found a sympathetic Cambodian general who thought the same way and whom they were assisting in his preparations for a coup against the Prince. CIA was well aware of these machinations through its "unilateral" sources in both those countries and, in response to the White House and State's policy, was doing its best to dissuade the Thai and Vietnamese from this venture, which we felt was unlikely to succeed and would only exacerbate the problems of dealing with Sihanouk. But to be certain that we would know what was happening among the coup-makers, CIA had recruited an agent on the Cambodian general's staff, and had given him a radio with which to keep us informed. And we were indeed informed.

But our efforts to dissuade our allies did not work, and they went ahead with the coup. And it came out as we expected, a failure. Unfortunately, in putting down the coup, Sihanouk had captured our agent and his radio. And, not unnaturally, he drew the conclusion that CIA was one of the participants, and that the gold and arms furnished from Bangkok and Saigon to be used against him were only part of the over-all plot of which the radio was a key element. In his mind, his "War with the CIA," as he titled his book, had begun, and the Agency was taught a vital lesson—that our operations would be judged as much for what they seemed to be as for what they really were. It was a lesson many of us had trouble learning, and it would plague us in later years as well.

After this flap, the situation cooled down enough so that I could devote my first few months in the Saigon station to familiarizing myself not only with the general situation in Vietnam but also with the finer points of the FI culture and doctrine. My chief, who had come up in that culture in the Agency, was a firm believer in the importance of recruited and "controlled" agents in the best professional sense, and he made a particular ceremony of congratulating officers who successfully brought a prospect to sign on the CIA's dotted line. So I decided to try my hand at it. One of my Vietnamese contacts was an aspiring and rising politician, who fitted somewhere in the spectrum between the sycophant supporters of Diem and those who were downright unhappy with him. As an agent, he could give us direct insights into the attitudes and activities of a potentially significant sector of Vietnamese political opinion. So, in a series of quiet talks with him I gradually built up a case for the importance of the United States being accurately informed of events in Vietnam, in view of its influence there, and our need for help from good Vietnamese like himself concerned about their country and America's relations with it. I stressed that such a connection needed to be secret, so that he would be protected against adverse criticism or other retaliation for maintaining it, and I assured him that we would indeed protect the secrecy of our relationship. He signed the rather innocuous paragraph I drew up summarizing what I said, and he became one of the station's agents. The chief of station was pleased, and I was happy that I had shown that I could accomplish a real FI task.

It wasn't until much later that I realized that getting an agent's signature on paper didn't make any real difference, that the test of his loyalty and value was instead in the accuracy and importance of his information and how it fitted into the picture we were building up from all our contacts, including those of other American agencies and, of course, the press. Moreover, while I believed that my friend would not report my proposal to the Vietnamese government, I realized that I could be wrong, and if he did, it might adversely affect my relations with the Vietnamese officials with whom I dealt. And that would make the undertaking ridiculous. For surely, far more important to my assignment than signing up agents was to develop friendly, persuasive and helpful relations with Vietnamese officials so as to be able to convince them to follow American policy rather than to engage in such counterproductive actions as the attempted coup in Cambodia. Such recruiting, then, really was a job for our unilateral officers, who, if exposed, could be disowned as not part of the station's work. So, as a result, I didn't especially pursue this sort of activity and instead concentrated on the other aspects of my job.

For example, I was anxious to learn as much as I could about the real situation in Vietnam; so I traveled about the country as much as possible. I accompanied a Vietnamese legislative delegation to the new areas in the highlands that were being opened for settlement by refugees from the north. I drove to the southernmost province and in a muddy delta village watched the inauguration of a school that had been reestablished there after having been abandoned for four years because of the war, which had dominated the area before 1954. I took the family for a happy Sunday picnic to the Cao Dai sect's holy city, driving past the unused small forts on the road, which had been the scene of some of Graham Greene's *Quiet American* episodes. And our son Jonathan and I rode the train from Saigon north to Hue and from there drove to the Lao border over Route 9 and then to the DMZ to see the North Vietnamese flag flying on the other side of the bridge. The only dangers we encountered on these excursions came not from hostile forces but from things like a train jumping its track, which forced us to spend one night in the jungle of Central Vietnam, where the children swore they heard tigers, or from the huge shark that our son Carl saw circling the small fishing boat we once hired for a ride in the harbor of the southern island of Phu Quoc. Aside from the pleasure of seeing the magnificent scenery of the country, these trips taught me something of the life of its people, and gave me a chance to try out some of the rudimentary Vietnamese, which my language teacher, who came to my house regularly, so laboriously drilled into me.

But, because of my long-term interest and experience in politics and political action, I devoted most of my time to deepening my knowledge of and cultivating my contacts with the Saigon government and especially the triumvirate that dominated it: Diem himself, his brother and *éminence*

grise, Ngo Dinh Nhu, and his wife, the controversial dragon
lady, Madame Nhu. According to protocol, Ambassador Durbrow was the one who maintained the ongoing, personal relationship with Diem, while the CIA station chief was the
principal American contact with Nhu. And so my initial contacts with them were only on ceremonial occasions, plus the
time when my chief introduced me to Nhu so that I could
brief him in the event of the chief's absence. But a quirk of
luck brought me into close touch with his wife under more
private circumstances almost right away.

Madame Nhu had, just a few months before my arrival,
forced through the legislature a new "Family Code." Press
coverage of it had left the impression that its main purpose
was to introduce into Vietnamese law the Catholic proscrip-
tion against divorce, and Saigon rumor had it that Madame
Nhu's main motive was to prevent the divorce of her sister
by a wronged husband. In order to set the record straight,
she wanted to have the law translated into English and circulated among international women's organizations to show
that there was a great deal more to it than that. After I had
met Nhu, and she learned that I was a lawyer, she asked me
to help her with this task.

So, on a series of afternoons I went to the Nhus' wing of
the Palace to sit with her and work through the code, seeking the right legal language, in English and French, to accurately express the thrust of the Vietnamese text. In the process, she and I discussed the traditional social structure of
Vietnam which her new Family Code was designed to
change, and she made clear her revulsion over such old established practices as the right of a husband to control his
wife's property after marriage and to legitimatize a child
born of an extramarital affair despite the protests of the wife.
Intelligent, sharp both in mind and manner, and brilliantly
groomed from lacquered hair to bejeweled fingers, she ex-
hibited the imperious manner of the empress that she in fact
was in the Vietnamese power structure at the time. But in
these sessions as well as on other occasions when our families later met, she also showed a very real human side—her

pride in her four children and her hope for the betterment of the lot of the women of Vietnam. She was a complex and impressive character. But she had a fatal flaw, a complete lack of tact, and this led her to make the combative and outrageous statements that were to help bring down her husband, his brother and her in later years.

My first private encounter with Nhu himself occurred not long after I finished working with his wife and proved every bit as fascinating. My chief took a well-deserved home leave the summer after I arrived, and while he was away I sat in for him at his regular weekly meetings with Nhu. They were quite a ritual. I turned up before the appointed hour at the rear gate of the Presidential Palace, in deference to intelligence anonymity and the precedence given to President Diem's visitors, and was escorted to the West Wing, where the Nhus lived and he had his office, cluttered with books and dossiers of all descriptions. After a short wait, Nhu came in, thinner than his brother, delicately handsome, informally clad in a white sport shirt, and very soft-spoken, giving the impression of being extremely shy. He lighted a cigarette, the first of a continuous chain, and what ensued was a rambling and revealing four-hour discussion in French, touching on virtually everything from his first contacts with CIA during pre-Dienbienphu days, to his belief in the need for an ideological base for all politics, with stops along the way to make biting and, unfortunately, accurate cracks about various members of the Saigon government and opposition.

I usually brought with me a short checklist of matters that I wanted to raise at these meetings, primarily about what the CIA was doing with various Vietnamese officials of the security and intelligence services, in order to be sure that Nhu was aware of and approved them, in part to keep his confidence and in part to be able to impress those officials that our work was truly important, since it had Nhu's imprimatur. I also would have a number of developments on which I wanted his comments, since his views would be an important indicator of likely government reaction and action in the future and thus constituted "intelligence" that our embassy and CIA's analysts should have. And on some occasions I carried a message as to the American attitude on some matter that the Ambassador wanted me to get directly to Nhu, either to reinforce his (the Ambassador's) telling President Diem the same thing, or as a means of saying something that could not be said on the formal diplomatic level. Thus I would try—usually futilely—to dissuade him from badly concealed efforts to unseat Cambodian Prince Sihanouk or to allow the political opposition in Vietnam some better possibilities of expression.

But no matter how much such business I brought with me, I always let Nhu take the lead in our conversations, counting on a few Socratic questions from time to time to make my points or on the probability that in his rambling he would raise a subject closely enough related to what I needed to talk about that I could gently nudge him around to it. The process certainly added to the length of our meetings, and the numbers of cups of tea we consumed, but I learned a lot about Nhu and his thinking and my points could be made in a way that I thought put them across much more effectively.

Nhu then actually held no official post in the Saigon government, and his only title was that of counselor to his brother. But he was unquestionably the second-most-powerful person in the regime, the closest to Diem and the greatest influence on him. Yet he was utterly unlike Diem both in his ideas and his methods. Nhu was the intellectual, interested in theoretical concepts and political forces. He tended to be overly fascinated with intrigue, seeing plots and conspiracies at work all around, especially by the French, and thinking in these terms as well. He was also rather something of a mystic, developing abstract and abstruse philosophies and seeking to infuse a kind of spiritualism into everything. But for all of that, he was a man who thought in political terms. And, unlike his brother, he recognized that the political survival and stability of his brother's government and the future of a viable non-Communist Vietnam depended on building a political base for it. Nhu had adapted the obscure French Christian philosophy of "personalism," which stressed the human person rather than the state, but which also held that the person is fulfilled through participation in his family and community. This philosophy was intended to serve as the regime's ideology, and a center had been established in the Delta for the indoctrination of ambitious civil servants. For the practical side of politics, he had turned to Marxist-Leninist concepts that he had learned during his days in the trade-union movement, and he organized a core elite party, the Can Lao, in which membership was supposed to be secret, to provide guidance and leadership to mass front organizations and even the government. His opposition to Communism was deep-seated, sharpened by the assassination of the oldest Ngo brother by Communists in 1945 and his own experiences struggling simultaneously against them and the French in North Vietnam.

Three other brothers completed the family. Can resided in the ancestral home in Hue with their mother, whence he served as the hidden overlord of Central Vietnam. Thuc, the senior Vietnamese Catholic Bishop in tenure, was Archbishop of Hue. And lastly there was Luyen, playing the least role in his post as ambassador to London. Together, the family was truly an imperial one, anachronistically operating as a feudal monarchy amid the trappings of a constitutional republic.

But Washington, and CIA headquarters, were committed to their success against their rival Ho Chi Minh's Communism. The Cold War made the struggle between these adversaries more than a local one; it was just one more element in the larger effort that we were making to contain the spread of Communism worldwide. Diem's "miracle" of survival in the dark years of 1954 and 1955 gave hope that we would succeed here, and the pace of economic and social development under his regime in South Vietnam seemed to promise a better future for its citizens than the Communist rule in North Vietnam. I saw my job as one of understanding the country and its political forces and helping them fend off the threat from the north while influencing its leadership to follow American policy whenever we differed. I did not then see the dimensions to which this job would grow, but I soon realized that it would be a far more complex assignment than Italy.

And the complexities began in short order. On July 8, less than six months after my arrival, a small MAAG billet was attacked outside Bien Hoa, about twenty miles north of Saigon, and two Americans were killed. My chief, in Washington on home leave, cabled to ask whether any of our sources had warned us in advance of the attack. I had to reply that they had not. Now the low level of violence, which we had been reporting from the countryside, suddenly took on a more personal American aspect. And we had to wonder whether the Communists had decided on a change of tactics from their rather patient waiting for the South to collapse. During 1958, Diem had rejected the last proposal from the north to arrange steps toward reunification of the country, and had clearly set out to establish a permanent and independent South Vietnam, and his economic and political progress since then suggested that he might be successful in doing so. The attacks in the countryside, and now this direct one against Americans, seemed to indicate that the Communists had decided to move the contest from the political to the paramilitary level.

But they had one last political opportunity. On August 30, 1959, elections were scheduled for the National Assembly, the first since the Constituent Assembly elections of March 9, 1956, in which 3 of the 123 seats went to parties opposing Diem and 19 to independents. The Communists were not allowed to run in these new elections, but our CIA sources reported that they had instructed their followers to vote for the more leftist of the candidates presented, as a step toward influencing the political life in Saigon, at least indirectly. In its reading of these reports the government saw a danger of Communist infiltration through such candidates. And so the apparatus of the Saigon bureaucracy went all out to produce the maximum favorable vote for Diem, and elected 121 of the 123 seats from among his supporters. It then indicted and convicted the two successful opposition candidates of electoral fraud and refused to seat them, even though one of them, Harvard-educated Dr. Pham Quang Dan, had gained the largest plurality of any candidate.

The lesson to the Communists was clear: they would not be allowed to work their way into the political life of South Vietnam through elections, in their own name or through intermediaries. The Diem government was dedicated to eradicating their influence, and it launched both military and political campaigns to do so. The social and economic improvements then coming to the countryside also supported the cause. In particular, Diem's pet project of 1959, the "agroville," got off to what seemed a promising start. Agricultural "cities" were established on land taken from large landowners under a land-reform program and divided into population centers and rice fields. The land was to be purchased on long-term contracts by the farmers, but they were assisted in setting up their homes and the garden plots around them in a community center sufficiently large to support a market, a school, a medical center, and the like. But the project proved to have an Achilles heel: the garden plots around the houses widely separated them from each other, and the resulting size of the whole community made it impossible to defend against infiltrators. The rise in Communist violence simultaneously with the inauguration of the program doomed it to failure.

On January 27, 1960, the Communists attacked an army regimental headquarters near the Cambodian border. What later came to be known as the Ho Chi Minh trail was opened, and the some 90,000 southern Communists who had gone north in 1954 began reinfiltrating into South Vietnam—along with arms and supplies and some North Vietnamese as well. The stay-behind net was activated. The numbers and effectiveness of the guerrilla raids, assassinations, terrorist strikes and kidnappings escalated. In the final four months of 1959, for example, 119 assassinations of local government leaders were reported, as compared to 193 in all of 1958. In May 1960, Hanoi's Central Committee formally decided that "the time has come to struggle heroically and perseveringly to smash" Diem's government, and its supporters in South Vietnam began to drive the government presence from the rural areas, attacking teams spreading antimalaria chemicals, village authorities, and the rudimentary local defense forces of barefoot soldiers manning mud forts.

Another of Diem's troubles emerged at just about the same time. A group of leading civilian political figures formed a "Committee for Progress and Liberty" and on April 30 met in Saigon's Caravelle Hotel to issue a petition that charged that Diem's regime was copying Communist dictatorial methods and was filled with nepotism and corruption. He was urged to liberalize the regime and grant fundamental civil rights in order that the struggle against the Communists might be more effectively waged. Diem and Nhu contemptuously rejected the petition, remarking on the plush surroundings of the Caravelle Hotel in which this group of Saigon politicians had gathered, and on their lack of contact with the rural areas where the real battle against both the Communists and underdevelopment were underway. The effect of this petition was to start a political war within Saigon to go along with and complicate the guerrilla war in the countryside.

The immediate consequence of both these wars, especially from the CIA's point of view, was twofold. First, as the Viet Cong insurgency gained momentum, the Diem government came under increasingly severe strain and pressure, both from within and without, to counter that insurgency. And second, the official United States community, both in Washington and in Saigon, fell to quarreling bitterly about what to do to meet the challenge, starting the long, bloody and tragic debate over the American role in the Vietnam war.

The United States military took a predictable stand. It viewed the escalation of the Viet Cong insurgency as the outbreak of a war, with General "Hanging Sam" Williams arguing for measures to shore up South Vietnam's ability to defend, in effect, against an invasion from the North. To this end, MAAG stepped up its efforts to re-form the South Vietnam Army in line with the American model and in 1959 secured the reorganization of the Vietnamese Army into seven divisions under three corps headquarters and a general headquarters, so that coordination with an American force would be facilitated if the war escalated to a real invasion. The military also urged the increase of size of the Vietnamese Army from 150,000 to 170,000 men, with the enthusiastic support of Diem, and secured Washington's approval for an increase in the American MAAG from 327 to 685 in strength.

But the embassy objected. The State Department officers in Saigon looked at the problem as one of building political confidence in the Diem regime among the Vietnamese people, and they believed that this could be done only by forcing Diem to make his government less authoritarian and more democratic and so enlist popular support for the fight against the Communists. Thus, the increase in the Army was held up in hope of pressuring Diem to undertake the reforms the embassy thought needed, which included exiling Nhu as an ambassador far from Saigon, disbanding his Can Lao party, appointing one or two ministers to the cabinet from among the political opposition, and stimulating the National Assembly to conduct legislative investigations of the government. The contradiction between these ideas and the reality of the Diem regime did not discourage the Foreign Service officers. They even went so far as to recommend that the United States might have to consider alternatives to Diem and Nhu in order to achieve our objectives, that we not "sink or swim with Ngo Dinh Diem," in the phrase of the time. Thus, the "country team" meetings at the embassy became barely civil, as "Hanging Sam" vented his fury at AID's Gardiner and State's Mendenhall for presuming to interfere in such military matters as determining the proper force levels with which to defend the country, while Gardiner and Mendenhall argued for reforms, especially the removal of Nhu.

The CIA station pretty much stayed out of these disputes, taking the traditional position that intelligence does not participate in the determination of policy, but only contributes information and assessments to the policymakers. In its own field, the station began to develop ways to improve the intelligence operations of the Vietnamese, including convincing the Saigon government to set up its own central intelligence organization to bridge the gaps between its military and other intelligence services, and to begin training and preparing for operations into North Vietnam as a means of improving our intelligence coverage of the source of the problem. But listening to the heated arguments at the country-team meetings I could not help but begin to formulate my own ideas of how the insurgency should be met and countered. And, influenced by the growing discussion in those days of doctrines of counterinsurgency, coming from the post-mortems on the French failures in Vietnam and Algeria and the British success in Malaya, I soon found that I didn't agree with either the military or the diplomats.

In the first place, it seemed obvious to me that the Communist strategy was anything but a traditional war. Vo Nguyen Giap, Hanoi's military genius, had written of how he had fought the "people's war" in North Vietnam and, although its culmination was in the set-piece battle of Dienbienphu, it had begun just as it was beginning now in South Vietnam in 1960. Clearly, this was the first stage of the "people's war," the mobilization and organization of the forces with which to fight. And clearly at this point the challenge was a political and subversive one, and not something for divisions and corps headquarters to contend with. On the other hand, though, the political challenge was not one that could be met by a well-meaning, intellectual elite with no political base issuing manifestoes from the Caravelle Hotel, calling for an "honest and just government," "a valiant army animated by a single spirit," and an economy which will "flourish" provided that the government changes its ways. And thus, in my view, the embassy prescriptions of appointing oppositionists to the government and advocating American-style Congressional investigations seemed largely irrelevant.

The real contest, it seemed to me, was in the villages,

where the issues were more fundamental. Did association with the Saigon government offer a better future, both economic and political, for the villager? Or did the national and revolutionary appeal of the Communist organizer, reinforced by the authority of guerrilla squads, convince the villager or leave him no alternative but to join the revolt? My travels in the countryside had shown how wide was the gap between the French-influenced urban class and the traditional Vietnamese villager. But it had also shown the latter's enthusiastic acceptance of economic and social development and his willingness to work hard toward it. In the long term, villagers would certainly insist on more of a voice in their national affairs, even along the lines advocated by the oppositionists in Saigon, but in the near term they were far more interested in the practical improvements that could be made in their lives and in the life-and-death issue of protection from the armed bands circulating in their regions. Thus, the real way to contest the Communists, it seemed to me, would be to mobilize, organize and involve the villagers in the economic and social improvements that the government was providing and to strengthen them so that they could help defend themselves against Communist pressures. The question was which side they would join, and whether they would be free to join the government's if they wanted to. The answer, I was convinced, would be found only in the villages, not in political circles in Saigon or in General Staff Headquarters.

In June 1960 I got a chance to try to implement some of my ideas on this score. For my chief was transferred to a new assignment and I was named to succeed him as CIA chief of station. It occurred at a moment when we were still furiously debating which of the many recommended policies the United States ought to pursue in Vietnam, and while each agency was still pretty much allowed to try its own thing. MAAG was energetically training and supplying the South Vietnam Army to engage in large-scale maneuvers so that it would be well prepared to fight a Korean-type war. The State Department officers in the embassy were busily engaged with the convoluted political disputes in Saigon. AID was immersed in its elaborate programs for administrative, economic and social reforms. And none of it was working to set the Communists back. Day by day the situation continued to deteriorate.

The Viet Cong were making gains everywhere, establishing their authority in more and more of the countryside and denying it to the government and its programs. And all our intelligence reports revealed that their forces were growing—both through increased infiltration from the North and the recruitment of villagers in the South.

To make matters worse, a coup attempt was launched against Diem, led by a disaffected parachute colonel, who believed that Diem wasn't fighting the Communists aggressively enough. A number of the anti-Diem opposition politicians in Saigon joined him to provide a political element, and for a day and a half Diem was besieged in his Palace while the rebel paratroopers surrounded it. Because of the proximity of our residence, the Colby family got their baptism of fire on that occasion. Bullets whined through our windows, and I barricaded Barbara and the children in a hall on the top floor. Some hours later, the situation had quieted and I could get down to the embassy, where the Ambassador needed all hands and heads. By midafternoon we alerted Barbara that it would be a good idea to take advantage of the lull and leave the premises while it was still daylight, in case there might be another fight that night. She gathered the children, collected a small assortment of hand baggage and proceeded to the nearest American neighbors in a direction away from the Palace.

For several hours, nearly a full day really, it wasn't clear which way the coup would go, whether or not Diem could survive it, and the United States embassy took a hands-off stance. CIA officers, however, were in touch with all the factions involved, from the Palace to the military coup leader, to the political committee led by Diem's opponent, Pham Quang Dan, and our radio net kept us up on every minute's move. At one point Nhu sent me a message, asking that I attend a conference between the contestants at the Palace gate to warrant the safety of both sides. But by the time it took place Diem had rallied troops from outside Saigon, including the 7th Division under Nguyen Van Thieu, and the parachutist colonel fled to Cambodia in a plane he obtained from Air Force Transport Commander Nguyen Cao Ky. Dr. Dan and most of the politicians were arrested, but one showed up a day later on the doorstep of the CIA officer who had been with him during the coup, pleading for help to avoid Diem's retribution, which he feared would be harsh. CIA's loyalty to its sources was at stake, so I had him hidden for several days in a house temporarily empty as a result of some CIA personnel transfers, and later arranged a courier flight abroad onto which he was loaded in a mail sack, to be passed through CIA's covert channels for resettlement in Europe.

Nhu became aware of CIA's contacts with the coupmakers and was greatly annoyed. He particularly focused on one of my unilateral officers who, following the Ambassador's and my instructions, had been in continuous contact with the civilian politicians with the coup leadership. Nhu said that his actions had been unacceptable and that he would have to go. "All nations conduct espionage," he said, "and this is not a matter to get upset about. But what no nation can accept, and our government no less, is interference with its political authority and processes." I stuck to the cover story that my officer was not a CIA man, that he had merely been reporting what he knew and not encouraging the coup group, and we were at a stalemate. But Nhu resolved it: he arranged for a letter to be dropped in my officer's mailbox, allegedly from the participants in the coup, which threatened him and his family with retribution for the way his assurances of help had vanished when the coup was over, leaving them exposed to the government's reprisal. I saw through the stratagem and took advantage of it to report the letter to Nhu with my conclusion that the safety of the officer and his family made it necessary that he leave. He and his family were given a police escort to the plane in order to "protect" them, and everyone's face was saved.

The coup attempt, despite its quick defeat, had real effects. The embassy's neutrality, while the outcome was still in doubt, showed Diem and Nhu that they could not absolutely rely on the full support of the Americans. They realized that they would have to deal with us as yet another outside force affecting the situation, with a potential for help but also for opposition. Nevertheless, they believed that CIA and I were sympathetic to their position and represented a channel outside the hostile embassy straight to Washington. Moreover, the key role played by the Vietnamese Army in putting down the coup highlighted its importance as a political factor in Vietnam, both to Diem and to others. And, finally, the coup's rationale of calling for a more effective fight against rising Communist strength in the countryside, intensified the debate among the various American factions as to how that was to be accomplished. The Communists added to the pressure; in December they established the National Liberation Front as the political framework for their fight against South Vietnam's government, in effect a clear declaration of revolution if not war. It was in this atmosphere, then, that I decided to experiment with an idea we in CIA had about how that revolution should be combated.

The idea had grown up among several of us. There was Gilbert Layton, a gruff, straightforward paramilitary specialist who had arrived in Vietnam in an Army colonel's uniform to manage our program helping the Vietnamese Special Forces develop operations against the North. He had run across a young man I will call Ben (because he is presently with the CIA), who at that time, however, was a member of the International Voluntary Service, a precursor of the Peace Corps, which, I must emphasize, had absolutely no connection with CIA. Ben was working with the Rhade tribe of Montagnards in the region around Ban Me Thuot in the Highland Plateau, had learned its language and culture, and was concerned by the growing Communist guerrilla strength in the area. Layton and he came up with a scheme by which the Rhade villages could defend themselves against the Communists. They asked if CIA could get the villagers weapons so that they would not have to depend on the Vietnamese Army units in the area, which were never there when needed and whose idea of how to defend them was to conduct great "sweeps" through the region before which the Communist forces simply vanished. CIA certainly could help; in fact it was the only American agency with the flexibility that could respond to such a local request directly and did not have to set up a complex program through Vietnamese government channels, which might or might not pass the material to the place it was needed.

But there were some problems. The Vietnamese government was worried about the Montagnards. In 1958 there had been a movement among them advocating their autonomy, rather than their assimilation, as sought by the Vietnamese, and the Communists were actively promising them that sort of tribal autonomy. So I believed it essential that CIA's help be put in a political framework. Layton and I came up with the idea of combining the self-defense concept with economic and social improvement for the villages that joined the program, and furthermore recommended that the Vietnamese Special Forces be in charge of the effort, with Americans in a supporting role only. In order that CIA not be thought to be developing its own private army, we turned to the U.S. Army Special Forces to provide the tactical training needed. And we called on the regular medical, educational, and other developmental agencies of the Vietnamese government, supported by AID (with some direct CIA supplies to break through bottlenecks), for the economic- and social-improvement part. With this joint approach we had no problem securing approval from the American Country Team, nor from Desmond FitzGerald at CIA headquarters at home, who understood immediately the importance of combining security, economic and social features into one program. But the real question was whether the government would permit it, and the answer to that lay with Nhu and Diem.

My weekly sessions with Nhu by now had covered the entire history of his and Diem's rise to power, and we had moved on to discuss matters that clearly revealed the differences between Diem's essentially administrative and military approach and Nhu's own belief in the need for a political answer to the Communist challenge. I made no secret of my sympathy with his views, and as a result he and his subordinates were convinced that my only objective was to help strengthen them against the Communists and that I was willing to respect their authority and leadership in the effort, whether they accepted my ideas totally or not. So when I outlined my plan for an experiment in the small Montagnard community of Buon Enao outside Ban Me Thuot, to be undertaken in collaboration with the Vietnamese Special Forces and in coordination with the local authorities, Nhu quickly agreed. He understood the essentially political aim of a project to get villagers to participate in their own self-defense and social and economic improvement, and saw it as a means of building a new political base for the Vietnamese Government.

Once Nhu approved, and assured me that he would obtain Diem's approval as well, Ben (who left the IVS and was put on our payroll) sat down and talked with the village elders at Buon Enao about enlisting the village in an effort to improve both its security and its welfare, and doing it for themselves with some help from the Vietnamese and Americans rather than depending on the administrative and military authorities in Ban Me Thuot. They cautiously agreed, and Ben and a small group of Vietnamese and American Special Forces personnel moved to the village and began to train the local young men and women in a program of defense and development. Trenches were dug in which the families could hide during an attack; a basic sanitation survey was conducted to separate the water supply from sewage; the log houses were dusted with DDT; a small stock of carbines was delivered, and the young men were trained to use them on patrol and in defense positions; some of the girls were taught simple first aid; and an emergency radio contact was set up with a nearby military center to pass the word if an attack occurred. While a Vietnamese flag was run up over the village, the political message of the program was deliberately downplayed; the interests of the village itself and not the Saigon regime was the main theme.

It worked. The villagers enthusiastically joined in the various activities, and a sense of confidence grew. We had deliberately chosen a village in a comparatively safe area, to permit it to build some strength before coming under pressure. But neighboring villages quickly heard of the activities in the best word-of-mouth tradition and sent their leaders to inquire how they could join the program. Thus the strategic principle developed by Marshal Lyautey in Morocco almost a century before was applied, and the "ink spot" grew. As more and more villages were included, it became clear that something more was needed than individual centers protecting themselves. So, from among the young men trained in the different villages, groups were chosen to serve as "strike forces," patrolling the empty territory between population centers and reinforcing any community that came under attack. But the principle was one of defense; the strategy was to gradually expand the area and people defended, to exclude the Communist organizers and guerrillas from both. The approach was the opposite of the traditional military. There was no stress on attacking the enemy; indeed, the ideal was for him quietly to fade away in the face of this program, or even to abandon the Communists and join the newly self-sufficient and confident communities participating in it.

Nhu was impressed. On one of the first trips he had ever made to the countryside (other than those to the hill palace at Dalat), he came to Buon Enao to see for himself and, as a result, approved the expansion of the program not only in the Highland area, but to a number of other villages along the coast and in the Delta as well. The initial villages in those areas were generally Catholic, to reassure Diem that we would not be arming Communists, and the priest-leader of one told me of discussion at an annual diocesan retreat in

which the priests talked about the comparative effectiveness
of the American carbine versus the Russian AK-47.

CIA's experiment spread with such rapidity that I decided
to give it a name, Citizens' Irregular Defense Groups, to
clarify to the U.S. Special Forces units that implemented it,
under CIA's over-all control, that it was a citizens' and not a
military operation, that its objective was defense rather than
offense, and that it should be kept irregular to meet the different needs of the different communities in which it was
being carried out. But as it expanded—30,000 weapons were
eventually distributed—it raised qualms in military circles
about its lack of coordination with the regular military forces
and their operations, and the familiar cry for a single chain
of command (military, of course) began to be heard. Meanwhile, in our weekly conversations, Nhu became more and
more enthusiastic over the political revolution he could see
as the result of the program, starting at the local community
level, building upward and gradually replacing the French-
trained bureaucracy and urban elite with a new, uniquely
Vietnamese society and leadership. It was, he said, what Ho
had accomplished with his Vietnamese brand of Communism but what Diem had not with his non-Communist nationalism. The seed of his "Strategic Hamlet" campaign had
been planted.

The CIA station was not wedded to this one approach. Its
curiosity to find ways to contribute at the local level to the
real contest with the Viet Cong led it to other programs too.
Working with the Vietnamese Army commander of the Second Corps, for example, we supported his idea of recruiting,
training and running "mountain scouts" of Highlanders to
patrol deep into the unpopulated areas along the Cambodian and Lao borders to bring back intelligence of Communist infiltration there. And under Diem's brother Can in
Central Vietnam, we assisted a so-called "Peoples Force" of
politically trained teams in their program of moving into rural communities to live with, work with, and help the peasants in their community efforts. These teams were armed,
but only in order to defend themselves if necessary. Their

real work was to establish a sense of identity with their fellow peasants. Because of Can's insistence that only peasants be recruited for the program, it worked well and was later approved by Diem for expansion to a national level, where it merged with an early experiment in civilian "civic action teams," and CIA's support grew there too.

There was another aspect to CIA's work as the paramilitary problem grew: action against North Vietnam itself. With our experience in Korea and against China, CIA was the natural agency to which the job of penetrating North Vietnam should be assigned. The Vietnamese Army had established a Special Forces unit to develop the capability for such operations, but little had been done with it beyond basic training and selection of volunteers. But as the pressures from North Vietnam grew in South Vietnam, both Saigon and Washington pressed for actions that would "do to the North what it was doing to the South." So CIA undertook to help to build up South Vietnam's ability to conduct such "covert" operations, particularly the air, sea and communications support they would need. The station was augmented by air officers skilled in contour flying at night over hostile areas during the "moon period," frogmen to teach how to infiltrate beaches clandestinely, and U.S. Army Special Forces to teach how to live off the land in enemy territory. We turned to the Vietnamese Air Force Transport Squadron, commanded by then Colonel Nguyen Cao Ky, for the flying operations, and he convinced me of his skill as a pilot and his steady nerves by taking me on a flight over the ocean at wave-top height to elude radars; I told him I'd bring my fishing pole the next time.

In order to provide a "plausible denial" that the Vietnamese or the American government was involved in these operations, I set up an alleged Vietnamese private air-transport corporation—VIAT—and arranged that it contract with some experienced pilots from the Agency's old friends on Taiwan (despite the bitter complaints of CIA's own "proprietary" there—Air America—which I thought too exposed to provide an effective cover story). But Ky insisted that if he was the air commander he must fly the first mission over the North. It was a violation of doctrine, but I understood exactly how he felt, and agreed—and was relieved when he returned safely and told me of having seen the lights of Hanoi off his wing tip.

As press and Washington attention to Vietnam grew, a steady stream of visitors from the United States came to inspect our efforts. And in January 1961 a special one arrived, to whom I paid particular attention.

John F. Kennedy had, of course, just been elected President and was developing policies he would use to "pay any price, bear any burden, meet any hardship, support any friend, oppose any foe to assure the survival and success of liberty," as he was to pledge in his Inaugural Address. And the visitor he sent out to Vietnam to help him in this was the "Ugly American," Ed Lansdale, who had returned to the Pentagon after his service in CIA. I understood that his fertile imagination and his deep knowledge of Southeast Asia had been enlisted by the new administration to help it determine what it should do in Vietnam. I had never met him. But I knew from the lore of the Far East Division of his brilliant work with Magsaysay in the Philippines and in Vietnam during the anarchy of 1954, and I was determined that he understand the essentially political nature of the operations I was carrying out in the countryside and the importance of not diverging into a purely military or urban political approach. CIA headquarters was suspicious that his assignment represented a Pentagon move to assume authority over the Agency's activities in Vietnam, and some in the Pentagon feared that he was about to be named as Kennedy's ambassador to Vietnam, with an inevitable conflict with the regular military ranks of MAAG. But I welcomed the chance to make my case about the real nature of the war at a level where it might have some effect, and I knew that Lansdale was enough of a political thinker to appreciate it.

Lansdale didn't know me, either, and our first session together, at which I gathered the senior officers of the station to discuss the situation and explain our programs to him, was a shambles. He obviously thought he was being subjected to some form of shell game and said hardly a word during the whole evening. But he did go out into the countryside to take a look at what we were doing, and he did talk to Vietnamese. And so he did learn that the station's activities were both welcome and effective and came away with the conclusion that I hoped he would: that the conflict was essentially a guerrilla war and that the military approach was not the answer.

Lansdale's message did get through to the new administration, even if he was torpedoed as ambassador. In April I was called to Washington to participate in an interdepartmental "task force" drawing up a "program of action for Vietnam" for the new President. And a number of my ideas were included in it: the need to provide MAAG support and advice to the territorial forces as well as the Army, to press the economic-development program in the countryside, to expand intelligence operations in both South and North Vietnam, to carry forward CIA's program of village defense and to support the growth of "independent or quasi-independent organizations of political, syndical or professional character" (a reference to my Rome experience to be gradually applied in Vietnam). In the process I also met our new ambassador, Frederick Nolting, and had a chance to put some of my ideas to him as well. The President approved the program, which mercifully had almost none of the State Department's favorite rhetoric about "reforms."

Something else was going on in Washington during my visit. Just a few days before, the CIA-organized invasion of the Bay of Pigs had ended in total disaster, and the President and the Agency were reeling from the shock of it. Now, while I was certainly sorry that the Agency had been involved in such a fiasco, I must admit that I didn't give it much thought. It was, at the time, just too far away and remote from my immediate concerns; it seemed to have very little relevance to Vietnam. I was dead wrong. For, in fact, the Agency's failure at the Bay of Pigs was to have a profound and sweeping effect not only on the CIA generally but also on its role in Vietnam specifically. But it would take me a few months to discover that.

Meanwhile, back in Vietnam my requests for increased people for the station were met, and we pressed ahead with our operations throughout the country and with our operations against the North. Flights left Danang in the dusk headed north with Vietnamese trained and equipped to land in isolated areas, make cautious contact with their former home villages and begin building networks there. Boats went up the coast to land others on the beaches, and we started leaflet drops and radio programs designed to raise questions in North Vietnamese homes about their sons being sent to South Vietnam to fight and about the vices of Communist rule. We lost one plane, which did not give the crack radio signal that it had passed the coastal checkpoint, and a few weeks later Hanoi issued a press release containing confessions by the crew and team that they had been trained by Americans and sent by South Vietnam. No plausible denial there.

But Washington was undeterred. Quite the contrary; we began to talk about how the effort could be stepped up to a higher intensity with the help of more U.S. Army Special Forces assigned to and supported by CIA's flexible logistics and financial system. And meanwhile, the debate began as to whether United States forces should be deployed to Vietnam to train and to support the Vietnamese with aircraft, helicopters, communications and similar modern equipment reflecting the American preoccupation with technology and gadgets. As the level of this debate grew, the CIA's gradual expansion of its activities was regarded as moving too slowly, however correctly, and Washington began looking for ways to accelerate the process to reverse the rising curve of Communist activity. At the same time, in my long, rambling discussions with Nhu, he began talking about how our experiments in the countryside could be turned into a major weapon for the war and for the political regeneration of Vietnam.

Two other visitors from Washington arrived in Saigon in October 1961. They came to assess for President Kennedy the situation on the ground and help him choose among the conflicting views he was hearing, each urging some different tactic in Vietnam, from the Joint Chiefs' recommendation to send American troops and Diem's request for a formal defense treaty, to CIA's national intelligence estimate that the real problem was still very much a guerrilla one and that the arrival of American troops would give the Communists a psychological advantage and probably stimulate them to increase rather than diminish their efforts. The senior of these visitors was Maxwell D. Taylor, the courageous commander of the 101st Airborne during the Normandy invasion, who had retired as Army Chief of Staff in protest against the Eisenhower administration's reliance on nuclear deterrence at the expense of regular combat forces, and whom Kennedy had named as his chief military adviser. The second was Walt Rostow, the brilliant and forceful economist on Kennedy's National Security Council staff. And they brought with them a radically new view about the CIA.

Taylor had conducted the official post-mortem on the Bay of Pigs for Kennedy, and one of his most important conclusions about that fiasco was that the CIA was not staffed nor did it have the necessary logistics backup to carry out large and difficult paramilitary operations, such as that landing on a hostile Cuban beachhead, and that, therefore, whenever a paramilitary operation grew to such a scale it should be transferred from CIA to the Department of Defense for its management, with the CIA assuming only a supporting role. And Vietnam obviously presented just such a large-scale operation; it was, in Taylor's analysis, beyond CIA's capabilities and thus ought to be given over to the Pentagon.

I never got a chance to talk to Taylor about our activities, nor to show him on the ground how they worked. Unfortunately, before he arrived, I had to attend a gathering of the area's station chiefs at Baguio, in the Philippines; there we briefed the new CIA Director, John McCone, who had replaced Allen Dulles in the post-Bay of Pigs reshuffle (which also saw cool, professional Richard Helms replace brilliant, intense Richard Bissell as Deputy Director for Plans). Although I cut my visit in Baguio short, by the time I got back to Saigon, Taylor and Rostow were just about ready to depart for the United States, and I had only a few harassed minutes with them to discuss what CIA was doing and what our experience showed about the kind of strategy we needed. Thus, the thrust of their report and the intense discussions it generated in Washington emphasized conventional military action and made little of the CIA's activities. And soon thereafter the first American helicopter units arrived to provide "combat support," and a series of other steps were taken to increase the military side of the effort, including the upgrading of the U.S. Military Assistance and Advisory *Group* (MAAG) to the U.S. Military Assistance *Command* Vietnam (MACV) under four-star General Paul Harkins. Moreover, the Taylor-Rostow mission revived the State-Department–stimulated debate over Diem's political and administrative weaknesses and the failure of his authoritarian government to rally popular support.

But all decisions were not Washington's to make. In September, Diem welcomed a British Advisory Mission, headed by Sir Robert Thompson, who had been Secretary of Defense of the Federation of Malaya when the insurgency there was finally put down. He brought with him an experienced police officer, Desmond Palmer, and an accomplished colonial administrator, Dennis Duncanson, who together constituted perhaps the highest ratio of talent to numbers seen in Vietnam previously or since. Some Americans resented their presence, but I welcomed them. I had studied enough of the Malayan Emergency to have gained great respect for the priority the British had given there to the local-level struggle, in which they used only 80,000 troops and 60,000 police but some 400,000 home guard. The British team concentrated their advice on the need for an over-all strategic counterinsurgency plan, the importance of improving the intelligence on the enemy through careful penetrations as well as methodical interrogations, and on the augmentation and improvement of the police as a means for bringing the rule of law to the countryside.

On these I agreed fully. Not so the American military; they were restive about the Britishers' assertion of a role with respect to a strategic plan and about their thoughts with respect to the police. In this latter, they stepped into an almost impossible American and Vietnamese web of controversy and competition. AID had for many years worked with the Vietnamese police, but had been hampered by the Vietnamese military's suspicion of such a separate armed force and of the American approach to the problem as analogous to that of a state police in the United States instead of a constabulary on the European model. Relations between the American military and the AID police advisers were anything but cooperative, with the Vietnamese police the sufferers.

We in CIA, and I in particular, had really only one point of difference with Thompson and his team. The British experience in Malaya had led them to conclude that the most important feature of rural village operations was a good, fair but firm central administration through which discipline could be imposed on local communities, cutting them off from contacts with the insurgents and thus starving the latter of recruits and even of supplies if possible. My own conviction was that the guiding principle must be political. We had to enlist the active participation of the community in a program to improve its security and welfare on the local level, building cohesion from the bottom up rather than imposing it from the top down. Thus, in specific terms, we disagreed on the question of arming local communities. I advocated it and was, of course, heavily involved in doing so. Thompson believed that a more measured approach was required through a well-coordinated over-all plan, involving the effective integration of the police and territorial and military forces with the government's social and economic services to produce the result of security and welfare *for* the people.

But, these differences aside, the Saigon government was willing to move in the general direction that Thompson recommended and I was supporting. With Diem's approval, Nhu began to develop his plan for a nationwide campaign of "strategic hamlets," as his political answer to the Communists, the activation of the smallest local community unit to take part in its own defense and development. He held a series of seminars to explain the concept to the military and civilian officials of the government, leaving many of them thoroughly mystified over his convoluted theories about Vietnam's necessary rise from colonialism, underdevelopment, and dependence on outside aid to self-sufficiency. Most of them simply seized on the physical features of the program he described, such as the need for a defense work around each hamlet to fend off hostile outsiders (a significant difference from the Malayan barbed-wire enclosures that were meant to keep the villagers in). And while they expressed concern over his stress on the need to build a new leadership class, they responded to the Palace's directions by complying at least with these physical aspects of the program and submitted roseate reports of their success.

After a momentary shock over this unilateral Vietnamese initiative, the American official community fell in behind the program, thanks especially to the good sense of Ambassador Nolting, who saw it as what was really wanted: a Vietnamese effort aimed at the Communist threat in the rural communities. With his support, and as a result of Washington's interest in counterinsurgency, all the American agencies joined the effort. AID established an Office of Rural Affairs under a former member of Lansdale's 1954 CIA team, Rufus Phillips, to furnish barbed wire, bring its national development programs to bear in the local areas and to report through its regional and provincial representatives what was needed. In particular, AID made an effort to articulate to its own officers the political and social objectives of the program, as nearly as they could ascertain them from Nhu's explanations. MACV set up a special office to support the program and tried to reassert its primacy as advisers to the

Vietnamese by pressing onto its counterparts its concept of the program. And CIA began to fit its own rural projects into the over-all strategic-hamlet program in coordination with AID's office, and to discuss how its by now large-scale paramilitary operations might be integrated with MACV in accordance with Taylor's Bay of Pigs conclusions. The program as a whole began to gather momentum and reports came in of Communist concern that it was succeeding in blocking their access to rural communities from which they had hoped to recruit guerrillas for the fight against Diem.

By early 1962, the prospects for a favorable outcome looked so promising that when Desmond FitzGerald requested that I return to Washington to become his deputy in the Far East Division, I asked that he leave me in Vietnam for one more year so I could see the situation well along toward success. But he insisted. He had appointed John Richardson as my successor, and as I knew that John thought about insurgency strategy in much the same political terms that I did, I agreed to come home that summer, fairly well satisfied with what I had accomplished in my three and a half years in Vietnam. For one thing, I could feel that CIA had played a key role in helping to find a proper strategy by which to fight the war. Moreover, the station had contacts and influence throughout Vietnam, from the front and rear doors of the Palace, to the rural communities, among the civilian opponents of the regime and the commanders of all the key military units. Even when, on February 27, two maverick Vietnamese pilots bombed the Palace and blasted out all our windows (by which time Barbara and the children and servants were, thankfully, safely under the stairwell), I did not change my optimistic assessment. They had the same complaint as the paratroop colonel had in November 1960—that is, that the war was not going well enough. But I was convinced that the strategy the CIA had pushed forward would soon prove them wrong.

I made a series of farewell visits to the good Vietnamese friends I had made, flying up to the A Shau Valley above Hue with General Staff Chief Nguyen Khanh and Corps

Commander General Tran Van Don, receiving a tiger skin from Highland Corps Commander General Ton That Din, visiting Father Hoa in his well-armed redoubt almost at the southern tip of Vietnam in Ca Mau, letting Barbara and Catherine drive over the Hai Van pass between Hue and Danang with one of the officers leading our northern operations, and taking the family (without our baby Christine, who was born in Vietnam, and Jonathan, who was at school in the United States) for a final call on President Diem, where they watched and listened while he explained his satisfaction with how things were going.

Before I left I wrote a report for Washington on who might take over if Diem, like Magsaysay, were killed. I discounted Nhu, because of the hostility he and his wife evoked, the civilian politicians because they had no political base, the titular senior Army General Duong Van (Big) Minh because of his lack of political force and strength of personality, and Nguyen Cao Ky because he was an airman. I chose instead General Nguyen Khanh, finding him bright, aggressive, and with a political sense. (I had not yet met Nguyen Van Thieu.) And then, in the early summer we packed up the family, leaving Vietnam and heartened by the situation later described by that prominent Australian Communist journalist and apologist for North Korea and North Vietnam, Wilfred G. Burchett, that "1962 must be largely credited to Saigon."

CHAPTER SIX

Washington Assignment— and a Secret War

AFTER a delightful halfway-round-the-world holiday with the family (the Taj Mahal, Jerusalem, the Greek Islands, Rome—where I found my friends still arguing about the opening to the Left—Lourdes, and the bull rings of Spain), I returned to Washington from Vietnam in the summer of 1962, to discover a radically changed atmosphere both within and without the CIA. The Bay of Pigs fiasco, which I had thought of only as it affected our programs in Vietnam, had turned out to have had a far more profound impact on the Agency than I had realized. For it had triggered a wave of public and political criticism of a sort that the Agency had never been subjected to before. And it had led to internal changes that were to have a major effect on the Agency's techniques and programs.

Until the Bay of Pigs—indeed, ever since the glory days of the OSS in World War II—the Agency had enjoyed a reputation with the public at large not a whit less than golden. After all, we were the derring-do boys who parachuted behind enemy lines, the cream of the academic and social aristocracy, devoted to the nation's service, the point men and women in the fight against totalitarian aggression, matching fire with fire in an endless round of thrilling adventures like those of the scenarios in James Bond films.

Now, to be sure, during that period, the public's understanding of what the CIA really was and did was, to say the least, very vague. It would be a fair guess that a majority of the general public wasn't even aware of the existence of the Central Intelligence Agency—as distinct from a hazy realization that the United States probably had spies just like every other country. But this worked, if anything, to enhance its favorable image. The total secrecy surrounding the CIA added the appropriate touch of mystery to its romantic reputation and, what's more, it was perceived as an altogether necessary condition of its dangerous occupation. From the public's point of view, it was more than sufficient to know in a general way that the CIA's spies and counterspies were out there somewhere slinking through the dark alleyways of the Cold War outwitting the Russians and stealing their secrets, that its covert operatives from time to time were engaged in such cunning coups as ousting the pro-Communist Arbenz government in Guatemala or restoring the Shah to the Peacock Throne in Iran. But as to exactly how they did these things or, for that matter, what they might be planning to do next, well, the less said about that the better—at the risk of blowing their cover, endangering their lives and hampering the vital work they performed in the interest of "national security." If intelligence was an exception to normal constitutional procedures, then so be it; the public was willing to accept that it was essential to the protection of our society in a dangerous world, and those who did this work were to be admired and not interfered with.

To a remarkable degree, this essentially naive and uninformed popular view of the CIA had been shared by the press and the Congress. The press, by and large, willingly accorded the CIA a privileged position among government agencies and refrained from inquiring into and reporting on its activities as a self-imposed act of patriotism. There is perhaps no better illustration of this than in the case of the Bay of Pigs itself. *The New York Times* actually had come upon information about the CIA's preparations for the Cuban invasion before the event. But President Kennedy persuaded the editors that running the story would jeopardize the national security, and they suppressed it. A number of news organizations during those years saw no inconsistency in hiring CIA officers as ostensible correspondents so that they could have the benefits of journalist cover overseas.

Nor was the Congress any more inquisitive or investigative about CIA's activities, nor any less in the thrall of the Agency's mystique. It shared the universal belief that intelligence was "different," that it had to operate by special rules. And under the powerful seniority system in the Congress, CIA affairs were handled only in the utmost secrecy and only by selected senior committee members whose integrity, concern for the nation's safety, and long service allowed them to protect the Agency from outside interference. The National Security Act of 1947 and the CIA Act of 1949 had provided broad enough authorization for the CIA to go about its work in its special and secret ways, requiring only that there be discreet contact between the Director and the carefully chosen members of the Congressional committees that had jurisdiction over it—Armed Services and Appropriations—to provide assurance that the Agency was hard at work in the delicate and dangerous field of intelligence collection and the related activities of political and paramilitary operations performed in the nation's interest. As for the recurring need to obtain appropriations for these activities, the CIA budget annually was submitted to carefully selected leaders of the Congressional Appropriations Committees, which permitted them to warrant to their colleagues that they had reviewed the sums requested and approved them, while burying the specific CIA activities in the over-all budget so that these could not be ascertained by an enemy. And the judgment of these highly respected Congressmen was never challenged. Occasional attempts to establish new committees to supervise CIA or to expand the membership of the existing ones were regularly voted down. The prevailing opinion of the times was put by Senator Richard Russell when he remarked that, while he could obtain information as to intelligence sources and methods of the CIA, "I want to be very frank . . . I do not want the information except in the very rarest of cases . . ." And when Senator Leverett Saltonstall expressed his "reluctance, if you will, to seek information and knowledge on subjects which I personally, as a Member of Congress and as a citizen, would rather not have, unless I believed it to be my responsibility to have it because it might involve the lives of American citizens," Senator Mike Mansfield replied that, "The Senator is to be commended." In short, the Congress was satisfied to consider the CIA the particular preserve of the Executive Branch, a tool for the President alone to use as he saw fit in the interest of the nation's security, and it voted the Agency its funds with little or no discussion about the kinds of operations for which those funds were used.

Even the occasional exposure of CIA failures did not substantially change this general picture. Charges of CIA responsibility for espionage and sabotage operations against China, Albania and Eastern Europe were passed off as the natural rhetoric of the Cold War. And even that most clamorous event, Gary Powers' crash of a U-2 spy plane in the Soviet Union was not blamed on the CIA after President Eisenhower announced that he had authorized the flight. Eisenhower's remark that intelligence is "divorced from the regular visible agencies of government . . . a distasteful but vital necessity" asserted the common understanding at the time, and Khrushchev himself pointed out in his memoirs that Eisenhower's acceptance of responsibility for the intrusion, not the flight itself, had been the consideration that led him to cancel the Paris Summit Meeting. In fact, the incident probably evoked more admiration than blame for CIA, admiration for its development of the U-2, in Kelly Johnson's secret Lockheed "skunkworks," which flew so many successful missions over the Soviet Union and brought back so many valuable photographs and launched a whole new era of secret intelligence operations from the sky.

But all that changed—or, more accurately, began to

change—with the failure of the Bay of Pigs invasion. In the first place, the Agency's long-standing, widespread, and immensely comfortable anonymity was shattered. From that time forward, one would have had to be deaf, dumb and blind not to be aware of the Agency's existence. Indeed, it is not too much to say that, more than any other single event, it was the abortive Cuban invasion, with all the attendant *brouhaha* in the United Nations and elsewhere, that imprinted the initials CIA onto the general public's consciousness. And, what's more, it imprinted them in the most negative way possible, at a moment of such shock and outrage that President Kennedy himself said that, in his anger, he was tempted to "scatter CIA to the winds."

Suddenly the Agency appeared to be, not an elite corps of slick, daring James Bond operatives, but rather a collection of bunglers, launching harebrained escapades and leading men uselessly to their death. And suddenly, too, its vaunted secrecy seemed easily penetrable by its opponents, effective really only to hide its failures and misdeeds from official and public view and to trick such a reputable figure as Adlai Stevenson into the humiliating situation of lying to the United Nations about the operation in order to cover up the Agency's debacle. And suddenly also the public abroad acquired a perfect scapegoat; from now on, when anything went wrong, it could be conveniently blamed on the CIA.

As the Agency's public reputation declined, the press, perhaps not coincidentally, moved into the attack, becoming critical and investigative in a way it had not dared in the previous decade. The letters CIA now virtually guaranteed a banner headline, even on the obituary page when a clerical employee died in an auto accident. The Bay of Pigs fiasco was dredged up and reported in countless articles and postmortems. Other CIA failures—the capture of CIA agents John Downey and Richard Fecteau in China, for example, the discovery that KGB agent Heinz Felfe had been at the center of the West German *Bundes Nachrichten Dienst* (intelligence service), the aborted coup against Sukarno in Indonesia—were gone over in exquisite detail. And questions

were raised about its fundamental procedures: Was its secrecy really necessary, or a vehicle to bar outside criticism?
Did its administrative and logistics flexibility hide waste
and inefficiency? Did its personnel outnumber and subordinate the normal foreign service overseas? Were its programs
self-originated, self-controlled, and unknown to the policymakers who were publicly responsible for foreign policy?
In short, was it a second and "invisible government," as
one book termed it, incompatible with our Constitutional
system?

Under the drumbeat of this sort of critical reporting, the
Congress became uneasy about its responsibilities vis-à-vis
the CIA. The senior Congressmen most immediately involved with the Agency, who were by and large conservative in their outlook, remained adamant that the existing
Congress-CIA relationship was correct and satisfactory. But
nevertheless some of the Congressmen outside that inner
circle, such as Eugene McCarthy, Mike Mansfield, Hubert
Humphrey and Wayne Morse, began to press for an expansion of the circle to include the Foreign Relations Committee and even to establish a formal intelligence or national-
security committee to replace the selected Armed Services
and Appropriations Committee members who held the monopoly of CIA oversight. But the jurisdictional and seniority
arrangements of the Congress held firm, and the system remained unchanged.

None of this—the public's disenchantment, the press's
criticism, the Congress's uneasiness—reached the fever
pitch that it would in the middle 1970s. But it did mark the
start of the CIA's slide from being one of the most prestigious and admired agencies of government toward one of its
most denounced and condemned. And this despite the fact
that even at the time every effort was made to arrest the
slide by undertaking the first serious overhaul of the Agency
since its founding.

In the first instance, two days after the Bay of Pigs, President Kennedy turned to his brother Robert, the Attorney
General, and to General Maxwell Taylor, his personal mili-

tary assistant, to make an official post-mortem of the Bay of Pigs disaster, which, as we have seen, came to the conclusion that the CIA was unsuited, both in staff and logistics strength, to carry out an extensive paramilitary operation such as the Cuban invasion, and that any such activities in the future should be transferred from the Agency to the Defense Department—a doctrine that was to have a major impact on the CIA's role in Vietnam. At the same time, Kennedy reestablished the President's Foreign Intelligence Advisory Board, with James Killian as its chairman, and gave it a broad mandate to examine the whole range of activities of the entire intelligence community. And then, after a discreet interval to spare personal feelings, he purged the CIA's top leadership, replacing Allen Dulles with John McCone as Director, and Richard Bissell with Richard Helms as Deputy Director for Plans, appointments that were to have major effects on the Agency and its style of operations in the future.

McCone was a Republican and, in part, Kennedy chose him in order to remove the furor over the CIA from the arena of partisan politics (after first offering the post to Taylor, who turned it down because he thought it inappropriate for a military man). But more to the point, McCone, a millionaire wartime shipbuilder and engineer who had served as an Air Force Undersecretary and as Atomic Energy Commission Chairman, was a brilliant manager and hard-driving executive who could shape up the Agency's sprawling bureaucracy and establish firm lines of responsibility. Unlike Dulles, the legendary spymaster, McCone was more interested in the research and analysis side of the business and in advancing the technology of intelligence gathering. Under his leadership, a separate Directorate for Science and Technology was created to increase emphasis on space and other technological aspects of intelligence and he moved to bring the estimators and analysts into direct contact with the policy questions being wrestled with in the White House. In this he was helped by Kennedy's style of open committee discussion of the issues before him, and by his own unerring instinct for pushing himself into the Oval Office to assert his position. He was, I have long felt, the best director the CIA ever had.

But the more immediate and direct effect on me of these changes came from Dick Helms's appointment to head the Directorate of Plans. Unlike his predecessors, Frank Wisner and Dick Bissell, who leaned to the covert political and paramilitary action culture, Helms came from the Foreign Intelligence side of the DDP house. And predictably, both because of his own background and because of the reaction to the derring-do attitude that had been responsible for the Bay of Pigs debacle, he set about stressing the need to develop more professional espionage and counterespionage operations, and to tighten the discipline in the covert-action arena. It wasn't an overnight job. After all, the covert-action culture had grown by leaps and bounds during the preceding ten years and, by the time of the Bay of Pigs, about half the total CIA budget was being spent on political, propaganda and paramilitary operations. But by the time I returned to Washington, just about a year after the Bay of Pigs, it was clear that the FI culture was in the ascendancy and CA no longer had the glamorous advantage it once had. Indeed, the corridor gossip among my colleagues was that large-scale covert-action operations were now things of the past. The Italian program that I had run, for example, was being phased down, assistance to the international front organizations of students, lawyers and cultural groups was being gradually cut, and our paramilitary efforts from Taiwan were stopping.

But once I had a chance to familiarize myself with the Washington scene after more than a decade abroad, I found a peculiar contradiction in this picture. And the contradiction arose from a fundamental feature of the Kennedy administration—its vigorous commitment to advance the cause of freedom in the world. It was plain to Kennedy and his circle that the Agency had a particular capability to contribute to this program, especially in its skills in covert political and paramilitary work, which put it in the lead in the growing field of counterinsurgency, and through its well-developed techniques of secrecy by which its actions could be veiled from diplomatic and political complications. And there was one particular area where the Kennedy brothers turned especially to CIA to use these skills and techniques: to carry out an intense program against the Castro regime that had humiliated the United States in the Bay of Pigs.

Within a few days of the failure of the Bay of Pigs invasion, President Kennedy flew to Miami to meet with the remnants of the invasion brigade and pledged to them that he would, in a free Havana, return the flag they presented to him then. Soon after, Bissell was being "chewed out in the Cabinet Room by both the President and the Attorney General" for not doing enough against Cuba. And in November 1961 Kennedy authorized Operation Mongoose, "to help Cuba overthrow the Communist regime," bringing in that veteran covert-action hand, Ed Lansdale, as its chief of operations and assigning Robert Kennedy and Maxwell Taylor to oversee it personally. While Lansdale's wildly imaginative initial 30-odd tasks—ranging from simple intelligence and propaganda operations to sabotage of Cuban factories and rail lines, to spreading nonlethal chemicals in sugar fields to sicken cane cutters—which he set for Mongoose were cut back to intelligence operations alone, a year later authorization for sabotage was given to a new special CIA Cuban Task Force. And pressure for operations of this sort was intensified by the Cuban Missile Crisis in October 1962, and the Kennedy reaction to that near-successful effort to put the United States under direct nuclear threat.

The missile crisis is a much-told tale, documented in great and dramatic detail by many of the participants, and since I played no part in it, the only points about it that I want to make here are those that affected the profession of intelligence.

For some months before the missile crisis, I was aware, the Agency had been getting reports, from various exile groups and through journalistic pronouncements, that the Soviet Union was making preparations to place offensive nuclear missiles in Cuba. The Agency's analysts, by and large, tended to discount these reports as exaggerations or figments of overheated imaginations. A particular point of confusion was the difference between defensive and offensive missiles, with the intelligence estimators certain that Khrushchev would not be so reckless as to place the latter for the very first time outside the borders of the Soviet Union. But the definitive intelligence finally came from the U-2 and its photographs, which on October 15 showed offensive missiles in the process of erection. With this "hard," indisputable intelligence in hand, Kennedy in the next few desperately intense days was able to rally national and international support, confront the Russians eyeball-to-eyeball and force them to withdraw.

One of the most important consequences of the missile crisis was on the morale of the Agency: it soared. The CIA had done just the sort of thing it was supposed to do in the defense of the nation, and done it well. And that splendid performance did much to repair the damage done to its reputation by the Bay of Pigs debacle. Beyond that, the photographs and the like demonstrated the value to intelligence of the most sophisticated advances in science and technology, and they spurred McCone to push for new work in this area, including spy-in-the-sky satellites and ultrasophisticated electronic equipment. Increasingly, as a result, the customers of intelligence began demanding "hard" evidence of this sort on all information and in just such indisputable technical and measurable forms, instead of generalized academic conclusions, and Kennedy's pleasure at seeing the raw photographs themselves produced an appetite for the same sort of raw reports, direct from the source, in field reporting as well.

But from my own point of view, the most significant consequence of the Cuban Missile Crisis was that it exacerbated the Kennedys' fury over Castro and intensified their determination to use the CIA and its covert-action capability "to get rid of him," with all the ambiguity the phrase includes. For this purpose, that ace clandestine operator Desmond FitzGerald was transferred to head the special Cuban Task Force, and I succeeded him as Far East chief. While Operation Mongoose under Lansdale's "outside" direction was soon disbanded, FitzGerald under Robert Kennedy's close scrutiny launched a series of operations involving economic warfare, sabotage and infiltration against Cuba. And this campaign included renewed attempts to assassinate Fidel Castro, which had started in 1960 and were sporadically prosecuted from 1961 to 1963, and which, although I had nothing to do with them at the time and indeed didn't even know about them, I would find myself trying to explain to the press, the public and Congress fifteen years later.

The Castro problem and the threat he appeared to present to the United States were not so easily resolved, however. Indeed, Kennedy's assurances that the United States would not invade Cuba gave Castro a sense of stability, and he continued to posture as the David who had succeeded against the American Goliath, trumpeting the success of his revolution and asserting its inevitable spread through Latin America. His envoy in this cause, Che Guevara, traveled through the underground nets of the continent encouraging others to emulate the Cuban revolution, and his romantic image as the insurgent guerrilla began appearing on posters throughout the world. Thus, FitzGerald was appointed to head CIA's entire Latin American Division to press the Agency's part in the anti-Castro program, which included State's diplomatic efforts to ostracize Castro through the Organization of American States, AID's Alianza para el Progreso for economic development, the military's training and equipment of counterinsurgency forces, and CIA's intelligence and political and paramilitary support throughout *all* of South America.

Inevitably Kennedy's activism and his use of the CIA in this regard then spread from there to much of the rest of the world. While in Europe the political division between East and West had stabilized (in the East by the Berlin Wall and the firm internal hold established by Communist governments, and in the West by the obvious success of the Marshall Plan and NATO, and Kennedy's firm *"Ich bin ein Berliner"* pledge), the contest intensified in the Third World. Khrushchev's pledge to support "national wars of liberation," Castro's external ambitions and the rise of Mao's theory of rural Communism, all drew especial attention to this area of challenge. In Chile a CIA covert political program, modeled on the Italian one that I had run, was launched to strengthen the center democratic forces—parties, cooperatives, women's groups, etc.—against the leftist challenge of Salvador Allende and his advocacy of alliance with Castro's revolutionary drive. In the Congo, the chaos that followed the Belgian withdrawal evoked CIA and diplomatic action to find a stabilizing compromise middle solution between colonial puppets and Communist-supported extremists. And in the Far East, which FitzGerald had left to me, I faced plenty of situations calling for CIA's covert-action talents and energy. In Vietnam, the Agency's station was fully engaged in carrying out the programs I had started; in Thailand similar moves against insurgency in the northeast were underway; and Malaysia faced the danger of a new Communist subversive attack from Sukarno's Indonesia. But the contest that called the most on my efforts in my new post was in Laos.

Just when I had returned to Washington, the Geneva Agreements on Laos (July 1962) were signed. After years of bloodshed and byzantine political turmoil in that tiny Southeast Asian country, Kennedy had obtained Khrushchev's agreement that neither wanted a confrontation there. And through the skill and hard work of Averell Harriman, then Assistant Secretary of State for Far Eastern Affairs, an agreement had been struck at Geneva recognizing the neutrality and independence of the little war-torn nation. Under the accord, fifteen nations agreed to withdraw all their military forces, cease their paramilitary assistance to the three contending factions in Laos, and recognize neutralist Souvanna Phouma as the leader of a three-part coalition government. The "count-out" began. The Soviet planes, which had been dropping supplies to Communist Pathet Lao and North Vietnamese troops, stopped their missions and went home. The Agency's Air America planes, which had been dropping weapons and supplies to tribal armies in the mountains of the north, ceased their flights. The White Star training teams of the U.S. Army's Special Forces withdrew. All the nations followed the agreed script, except one: North Vietnam. According to CIA's intelligence reports, there had been some 7,000 North Vietnamese troops in Laos at the time of the Accord. But during the so-called count-out, only 40 went through the formalities of leaving the country. Since they had never been acknowledged as being there, they could hardly in theory be officially counted out, but our intelligence showed that they were there nonetheless.

Now Harriman had made it forcefully clear to the CIA as well as the military that he (and the President) insisted on full compliance with America's commitment to abstain from providing any further assistance, military or paramilitary, in Laos. He was playing a larger game than Laos—if we and the Soviets could successfully draw back from confrontation there, we might be able to apply the same technique elsewhere, and indeed reach the world of "coexistence" that Khrushchev was talking about. So when I brought him the first intelligence reports revealing that North Vietnamese troops were still in the country, he insisted that we hold to our position of not sending paramilitary help, despite the pleas of the Lao tribal leaders that we help them drive the North Vietnamese out if they were not going to leave in accordance with the agreements. Each week, I would go down to Harriman's office in the State Department to brief him on what CIA was doing throughout the Far East, and gradually our sessions spent more and more time on Laos. He insisted on knowing in detail of our activities there, and of approving or disapproving every step we took so as not to permit any differences to arise between CIA's policies and his. I agreed wholeheartedly—America had to speak according to one script, not in different ways through its overt and covert outlets.

But gradually our weekly intelligence reports became

more ominous. The North Vietnamese troops were not only still there, they were moving out to expand the area they and their Pathet Lao puppets controlled, pushing the tribal Meo away from their settlements, or absorbing those who did not flee, as well as attacking the neutralist forces. Meo resistance was weak, as the stocks of munitions they still held from the period before the Geneva Agreements diminished. My arguments became more forceful, reflecting the intense cables I was receiving from the two CIA officers who were still up in the hills observing and reporting on what was happening. It was plain to them that the North Vietnamese were out to crush the Meo by military force and that the truce the Meo had accepted at our urging was collapsing, with the Meo unable to defend themselves for want of resupplies of ammunition.

However hard Harriman wanted the coalition to work and for Laos to be neutralized, he had had enough dealings with Communists to know that they did not respect weakness. So he at last approved the secret dispatch of a minimum quantity of ammunition, with strict instructions that our officers make clear that it was only to be used for defensive fighting, and that they make sure that the Meo were not initiating actions against the North Vietnamese or the Pathet Lao. That proved easy, since the fighting was taking place then only in areas that had not until then been occupied by the Communists and the stream of refugees from there attested dramatically to who was putting the pressure on whom. Harriman insisted that he specifically approve each and every clandestine supply flight, and its cargo, that lifted off from a friendly Thai air base with a load of weapons and ammunition, and crossed the border to dodge among the jungle-covered mountains of Northern Laos to find the secret drop zones our officers had chosen.

Harriman was not nicknamed "The Crocodile" for nothing. During some of our weekly sessions he would ostentatiously turn off his hearing aid in the middle of my arguments, or bait me mercilessly until we were engaged in a shouting match, to test how firmly I believed in the proposals I was advancing. But it was plain that he had the President's full confidence with respect to Laos, and convincing him that he was indeed in charge of our operations was the best thing I could do for our friends in the mountains, and for CIA itself. He had the strength to do what was really needed, he had the good sense to put what CIA could do into its proper place in American policy, and he knew that CIA offered a unique capability to do what needed to be done quickly, effectively, and under discipline, without the bureaucratic and institutional problems other agencies, military and civilian, presented.

While it became clear that the Soviet Union had indeed accepted the idea of removing Laos from the American-Russian contest, it also became clear that the North Vietnamese were not part of the bargain. Although the Russians never said so, it was obvious that they had little influence over the North Vietnamese, who insisted on making their own decision, which was to continue to expand their control in Laos, both in the area nearest to Hanoi's Red River Delta heartland and on the Ho Chi Minh Trail to the Communist forces in South Vietnam. And so Harriman was increasingly understanding of the need of CIA's tribal forces to fight, and to fight in the way they fought best: as guerrillas behind the North Vietnamese lines. It was obvious that the lowland-bound Royal Lao Army, despite American military aid, was not going to go outside the narrow limits of the Mekong plain to engage the Communists. And the American military, which at that stage saw South Vietnam as the real theater of contest with North Vietnam, had no desire to set up the long logistics lines a regular American military force would require in Laos.

Thus the task of meeting Hanoi's pressure in the area would have to be undertaken by CIA's tribal friends, if at all—and the Kennedys had no doubt that it had to be undertaken. Another feature made the use of CIA even more attractive: the letter of the Geneva Accords could ostensibly be kept, the Soviet Union could turn a blind eye to the "covert" support CIA would supply. Thus the issue of Laos did not have to be brought back to the main negotiating table between Moscow and Washington, and the original deal to set it aside could be respected. The distinction Khrushchev had made in the U-2 incident between what Moscow knew and what Washington officially admitted was applied to this field, and the USSR even kept its embassy in Vientiane as the "secret war" escalated.

And escalate it did. The North Vietnamese forces gradually grew to the 70,000 we would count in 1972, and CIA was authorized to revive, supply, and increase the tribal units it had started to build before the Geneva Accords. Moreover, it was authorized to send its harassing parties deep into areas "controlled" by the North Vietnamese to locate its depots, ambush its trucks, mine its roads and mortar its outposts. The tribal patrols, who knew the country and were fighting against its invader, were airlifted to battle in Air America's helicopters and put down in isolated clearings or villages, reported the exact enemy dispositions through the radio nets set up and supplied by CIA and were supplied (and their families supported) through CIA channels that bypassed corrupt Vientiane middlemen to bring funds and weapons direct to them in the mountains.

CIA was not alone in the work; AID jumped in to help with magnificent men like "Pop" Buell, a retired Indiana farmer with a burning desire to help his fellow man, who worked with superhuman effort to bring food and shelter to bedraggled refugees fleeing from North Vietnamese "sweeps" through their villages, and signaling Air America planes exactly where to airdrop rice sacks to villages cut off from outside help. AID's medical program was equally effective, establishing field aid stations and rude hospitals where treatment could be given to wounded tribal fighters, captured enemy soldiers, and bewildered families alike.

In North Laos, a mirror image of Vietnam thus appeared. The North Vietnamese and the Pathet Lao conventional military forces clung precariously to the road network and contended with assaults and ambushes from evanescent guerrillas; indeed, CIA's tribal forces roamed freely over the mountain terrain to take such a toll on enemy logistics and rear areas that the latter's occasional frontal assaults often ran out of steam. The conflict seesawed back and forth, but the war stayed far from the river valley where most Lao lived. In South Laos, however, where there was almost no local population in the mountain areas near Vietnam, the Ho Chi Minh Trail gradually expanded with only little harassment from the teams which CIA sent from the Mekong area into that unfamiliar territory. And CIA's attempt to turn those teams into spotters of Hanoi's convoys for United States Air Force attack bombers proved of only minor value. The Air Force developed its own technical sensors to report the targets electronically, and became impatient with the bombing restrictions imposed in order to protect the teams CIA sent in.

Throughout this "secret war," I insisted on the importance of the political element. American policy was clearly one of support to the Royal Lao government and its neutralist Prime Minister Souvanna Phouma. CIA had no interest, and Harriman would have vigorously vetoed any that it might have developed, in supporting the right-wing leaders we had helped in the pre-Geneva period. But CIA's direct lines of communications and supplies to the tribal areas could create a problem: belief by the tribal Meo in their autonomy from corrupt and faraway Vientiane. After all, they were carrying the brunt of the fight and got little or no help from the lowland Lao Army. But such sentiment compromised the authority of Souvanna Phouma and could have caused a formal rupture of the Geneva Accords, bringing down the carefully erected structure of American policy in Laos and complicating the whole picture in Southeast Asia. Thus CIA's officers in Laos were instructed to use their political as well as their paramilitary skills to ensure that the forces we were supporting understood clearly that they were being helped as a part of Laos, and that Souvanna Phouma's approval of CIA's support was as necessary as Harriman's. The CIA-supported forces were in theory integrated as units of the Lao Army, and the officers given regular ranks, although direct CIA financial, logistical and advisory links remained. A radio station was set up with CIA help, and transistors were distributed throughout the mountains to broadcast the appeal of the "Union of the Lao Races," to unify the different tribal elements and the lowland Lao. And the king was induced to pay a ceremonial visit to the tribal force headquarters to show the symbolic unity of his kingdom.

There was another political aspect. The traditional leadership of the tribal areas was no less corrupt and weak than that in Vientiane. But guerrilla fighting required better men. CIA had identified an officer of the Lao Army, originally trained by the French, who had not only the courage but also the political acumen necessary for leadership in such a conflict. He represented a new approach, sharing the dangers of the front instead of sending orders from the rear, he was a native of the area and the tribe instead of a diluted, weak cosmopolitan hybrid of French and Lao, and he was fiercely dedicated to the defense of his people and their homeland. His name was Vang Pao, and he had the enthusiastic admiration of the CIA officers, who knew him well from their time together in the mountains, as a man who would have been leader of the struggle whether or not he received CIA aid and advice; he knew how to say no as well as yes to Americans. And under his over-all command (confirmed when the king made him a general), the process of selection and training of a new breed of tribal leadership could go on, men chosen for courage in the field and sympathy for the refugee villagers, rather than because of their aristocratic inheritance.

But the process also required the subtle expression of external deference to the old leaders, so that they would not be stimulated to react against this clear threat to their positions and privileges. In the same way, CIA also moved against such old corrupt practices as the opium trade, which had been an economic mainstay of the Lao mountains for generations. Bringing in new crops and cattle, teaching better nutrition and sanitation, and resolutely refusing to permit Air America aircraft to carry drugs, CIA kept free of contact with the trade (as a Congressional inquiry in later years confirmed), although it certainly continued to exist in Laos and especially among some of the lowland leadership, where it became an issue when it began to have an impact on our troops in Vietnam.

Despite the scope of this CIA effort, numbering some 36,000 armed forces throughout Laos, involved in everything, from village defense to teams infiltrating far behind enemy lines to specialists collecting intelligence on South China, the CIA station conducting it never rose above two or three hundred in strength. They were supported, of course, by Air America, which served the entire American establishment in the area and by the close integration of AID and other American programs under Ambassadors William Sullivan, and McMurtrie Godley. Moreover, the CIA officers were under strict instructions not to engage in combat, which they did not, despite their unhappiness at not being able to share dangers with their Lao and tribal friends whom they had trained and worked with; the policy worked to limit CIA casualties during this long war to only about five killed. What's more, the CIA's budget for the operation measured in the tens of millions instead of billions of dollars, and was less than the military aid that went to the valley-bound Royal Lao Army.

And the result: the battle lines at the end of ten years of fighting, against an enemy whose strength increased from 7,000 to 70,000 in that time, were approximately where they were at the outset, and the Communists were forced to accept a second agreement to recognize a neutral and independent Laos and the coalition government that America had pledged to support in 1962. To be sure, the end was not victory, but neither was it the defeat that the Communists had sought. (But when the Communist forces resumed military and subversive pressure *after* the 1973 agreement, CIA was *not* directed to respond, and Laos is under Communist rule today, with CIA's tribal friends in exile, dead, or living under oppression.)

To accomplish even this much was not without its difficulties, of course. Flying hop, skip and jump through the karst mountains during tropical rainstorms, skittering along the Mekong at a ten-foot altitude under a twenty-foot ceiling, searching for an airfield on a flat stretch of the river's bank, and carrier-type landings in a swirl of dust on mountaintop airstrips called for a certain equanimity of spirit from the CIA officers who did them every day rather than on the semiannual visits I made. Flying in such conditions required care as well as daring from the magnificent Air America pilots and the installation of a complex of navigational and meteorological aids to supplement its swashbuckling image. Also, CIA's doctrines of clandestinity had to be stretched a good way to cover the "secret city" of 20,000 that grew up of the families of the tribal forces grouped around its headquarters. Moreover, appropriate uniforms had to be devised for the Thai officers and men who arrived to help with communications and training, since they could not officially be Thai and they certainly were not Lao. And a fine line had to be drawn between helping the tribal groups in their struggle and avoiding participation in some of the more primitive practices of those mountain peoples so far from civilization, including politely tasting but not ingesting the locally fermented rice "wine," keeping clear of the ritual bull-baiting that preceded feasts and tactfully turning down the maiden offered by the local chief to ease the strain of a mountain village visit.

One problem was fundamental to guerrilla war, only partly brought about by the actions of the other side. Some immutable principle provides that a barefoot guerrilla force must inevitably grow to become a conventional army. Tito's struggle against the Germans, Mao's against Chiang, and our Minutemen's against the British, all exemplify this. And it occurred in Laos as well. The successful teams in North Laos against the North Vietnamese requested heavier weapons first to improve their effectiveness and then to defend against North Vietnamese attacks on their villages instead of fleeing before them and harassing them from the rear. A few captured artillery pieces turned against the enemy from the magnificent mountain ring around the Plain of Jars generated the demand for more, and successful forays by squads grew to battalion assaults to clear the enemy from the traditional tribal homelands.

But such escalation begat a reciprocal one from the other side; the enemy increased its forces and armaments to preserve its position and continue to assert its power in Laos.

There was one dramatic exception to the rule. Shortly after the first North Vietnamese aircraft was sighted in Laos—an ancient biplane dropping small bombs—an Air America helicopter happened nearby, whereupon the plane turned to attack the helicopter. The latter was unarmed, but it twisted around so that the crewman in the rear could empty a clip of his carbine at his assailant, and shot it down. The North Vietnamese air force did not return, and Air America remained a transport fleet with no combat aircraft or armaments. But nevertheless air support did become a greater element in the Lao war, first by the Royal Lao Air Force and later by the American, and not merely in the Ho Chi Minh Trail area.

A guerrilla force, successful as it may be in making it too costly for a conventional enemy army to control a country, cannot expel that enemy army from its territory. That can be done only by comparable conventional forces. Thus a successful guerrilla force almost inevitably will grow into a conventional army to free the national territory. To help this development in Laos, CIA's Thai friends quietly dispatched "volunteers" to serve in Laos to improve the tribal forces' conventional capabilities against the increased presence of North Vietnamese divisions.

Thus, contradicting the conclusion of Maxwell Taylor after the Bay of Pigs, CIA proved in the Lao war fully capable of the logistics and staff requirements to conduct a major paramilitary operation. But once the scale of the war went beyond the level of clandestine help to tribal patrols behind the North Vietnamese lines, it became virtually impossible to keep the effort secret as Agency doctrine required. Steady and intense combat was taking place in the hills, but it was plain to the casual observer in the lowlands that the Royal Lao Army was not involved in it. The numbers of Air America planes over Laos did not match the smaller number that left Vientiane with loads of rice. The visiting journalist soon realized that the sport-shirted group of tanned Americans at a Vientiane or Bangkok bar quickly fell silent when asked what they did, but their boisterous behavior bore a remarkable resemblance to men on a short leave from dangerous assignments. And it was not hard for an inquiring reporter to develop sources who complained that the Agency's work was not "coordinated" through nor under the control of the massive military staffs covering Southeast Asia.

Thus a problem does arise when the Agency conducts a "large" paramilitary operation, although it is not the one that Taylor had anticipated. The battle was fought without drafting American youth for service in the Lao mountains; the American command structure consisted of the Ambassador and his staff meeting; no large base areas grew to provide the creature comforts required for American troops; orders went through Lao channels rather than American; and CIA officers reluctantly but obediently followed their orders to stay out of combat. But CIA tried to conceal all this from public knowledge and, since it really couldn't, it inspired the growth of myths and legends that bore little resemblance to the facts, and the charge that CIA was conducting a "secret war."

This had some serious effects at home. In accordance with CIA's normal practice, the small group of Congressmen in the committees, who were charged with its supervision, were kept informed of its activities in Laos. As the scale of the operation and the war grew, it required larger budgets, and the committeemen were briefed in detail on this as well. Certain of the members included a visit to Laos on their fact-finding travels and were taken up to the mountain headquarters to see the operation at first hand, and one in particular expressed himself forcefully that this was the way the United States should be operating in Vietnam instead of by the military escalation that was taking place there. But, since the operation was a part of the CIA budget, it had to be kept officially secret and therefore the Agency was denounced by the press and Congress for its "secret war." This led to such results as the Chairman of the Senate Appropriations Committee, Allen J. Ellender, saying on the Senate floor that he did not know whether CIA funds were being used to conduct the war in Laos, a statement that was simply not true; another Senator publicly attacked CIA's "secret war" when he had been fully briefed on it and had actually visited the area; and the Chairman of the Senate Foreign Relations Committee, William Fulbright, asserted that CIA's secret support of the Lao tribal forces was in conflict with our democracy. Taylor's conclusion, then, was valid at least in this regard: that a large-scale paramilitary operation does not fit the secret budget and policy procedures of CIA.

And, in fact, that conclusion was recognized, if somewhat belatedly. The sums required for CIA's paramilitary program in Laos were finally included in the Defense Department's open budget for submission to Congress. There the small total disappeared almost completely from public view among the larger sums that the Pentagon sought for itself. After appropriation, these sums were then transferred to CIA by the Defense Department and, while CIA's internal secrecy still presented some difficulties, the program was no longer a secret to the Congress. In this way the unique CIA combination of intelligence, political and paramilitary expertise could continue to direct the program in Laos under the Ambassador's full control, while the American involvement did not need to be admitted officially, allowing the Soviet Union to ignore it, and at the same time the constitutional authority of the Congress was respected.

CHAPTER SEVEN

Coup and Chaos in Saigon

THE date was May 8, 1963, and the news reports that came in over the ticker at Langley were disturbing and were not made any better by the CIA and embassy cables that fleshed them out. In Hue, the ancient imperial capital in central Vietnam, a demonstration by Buddhists against the Saigon government had flared into a riot, and nine people had been killed by South Vietnamese troops. I was familiar with the Buddhist movement in Vietnam and knew that until then it had never played an important political role, as for example had the Catholic Church and the Hoa Hao and Cao Dai sects in the country's turbulent history. So, as I read the reports I judged that the incident, while certain to fuel the debate then going on in Washington over the Diem regime, would have very little real significance in Vietnam itself. I was totally wrong in my assessment of its effect in Vietnam, for the Buddhists proved able to use the incident as the springboard for a nationwide political campaign. But I was right about its impact in Washington. For the Hue riot led to what I still consider the worst mistake of the Vietnam war: the American-sponsored overthrow of Diem.

In the year since I had left Saigon, the war had continued to grow in intensity, but I still was pretty optimistic about the prospect. What I regarded as the most important aspect of the war, the strategic-hamlet program, had by all accounts taken the initiative from the Communists in the countryside and was going full blast. In fact, if anything, it was going somewhat too energetically, being pushed willy-nilly everywhere rather than following a sensible strategy of gradual expansion of security zones. As a result, hamlets were made "strategic" in areas where they could not be sustained. And too often a single strand of barbed wire around a hamlet was enough for a local official, anxious to please the Palace, to include it in the program's statistics, even when it merely enclosed a passive population that went on attending agit-prop sessions whenever local Communist organizers and guerrillas insisted. But these were problems of implementation that one had to expect in the early phases of such a program, and they could be solved by more rigorous inspection.

To be sure, apart from the strategic-hamlet program, other more substantial problems also existed: the lack of emphasis on the development of a full role for the police in the rural areas, for example, and the continuing tendency of the Vietnamese Army to think in terms of large-scale "operations" against a guerrilla enemy that faded away before it. (One exception to such "fading" had occurred at Ap Bac in the Delta in January, when the Communists took advantage of some confused army units to impose a stunning defeat on the government's forces, leading a peppery American military adviser, Lieutenant Colonel John Paul Vann, to early retirement, after he publicly vented his disgust.) But, while plainly the Communists had not yet begun to lose the war and were still in fact building their forces through local recruitment and infiltration of men and supplies from North Vietnam, they no longer seemed to be winning the race into the vacuum in the countryside. Set against the time frame of several years, which were required in the comparable conflict in Malaya, a start had clearly been made in the right direction in Vietnam, and in my view success seemed possible if the strategy were pursued with forceful leadership, hard work and American support. But all these began to disappear as a result of the May 8 Buddhist riot and deaths.

The various accounts of how the incident occurred and why were impossible to reconcile, and they did not really

matter. Whether it started with an accidentally dropped grenade, a provocation by the Buddhists or Communists, or a
deliberate action by South Vietnamese troops, the demon-
strators were dead and a fatal confrontation between the
Diem government and the Buddhists had begun. And
whether the Buddhists represented most Vietnamese or
stood for only a small portion of the population did not matter either, because the vigor of their political assault on the
Saigon regime electrified America and intensified the debate there over the pros and cons of the Diem government.
Demonstrations throughout South Vietnam followed the riot
in Hue; other political groups opposed to the Diem regime
joined the protests; police squads charged them all with
truncheons and tear gas—and all of it was reported in careful detail by the large American press corps that had gathered in Vietnam to cover the increased American civilian
and military presence.

On June 11, a single event so dramatized the issue that it
made any further thoughtful discussion about it almost impossible. A Buddhist press spokesman alerted American
journalists that "something important" would happen that
morning. And it did. A Buddhist monk, Thich Quang Duc,
lit a match after his fellows had poured gasoline over his
head and body as he sat at an intersection in downtown Saigon, and the horrifying photograph of his immolation
shocked the world. Madame Nhu's callous remark that this
and later self-immolations were nothing more than fanatics
"barbecuing" themselves intensified the revulsion against
the Diem government, which was seen as the root cause of
these terrible religious suicides. As a result, President Kennedy found himself in the impossible situation of supporting
what appeared to be a brutal government. And suddenly the
problem of Vietnam shifted from the countryside, where the
Communists and the South Vietnamese government were
contesting the war, to offices and conference rooms of Washington and Saigon, where the dispute was between South
Vietnamese and Americans, and among Americans, over the
virtues and vices of Diem and his regime.

As a first step toward resolving this dispute, Kennedy announced on June 27 that Henry Cabot Lodge, the Republican vice-presidential candidate in the 1960 election, would become the new American ambassador to Vietnam, replacing Frederick Nolting, the fine foreign-service officer who had become too closely identified with the United States policy of support to Diem. But if Lodge's appointment prevented Vietnam from becoming a partisan issue between Republicans and Democrats, it did nothing to reduce the intensity of the pro-Diem and anti-Diem debate that raged within the American government and increasingly throughout the United States as well.

All during this period I was in daily contact with John Richardson, the CIA chief of station in Saigon, who in his turn was in equally close contact, as was traditional for the Agency's station chief there, with Nhu, as well as with a wide number of political and military leaders and groups in the country. And as a result of our constant interchange of intelligence, I have to say that I didn't then—nor, in fact do I in retrospect now—regard the Buddhist situation itself as quite the serious crisis that it was considered in Washington. Indeed, I agreed with Diem and Nhu that the Buddhists were raising an essentially false issue of religious discrimination, that the Diem regime was not a Catholic government, that the Buddhists were challenging the government's basic authority in a series of escalating demands, and that they had to be met with a firm hand. But most of all, I felt, we must not allow the matter to distract the United States from the main issue in Vietnam: the fight against the Communists in the countryside. And it was apparent that the Buddhist crisis and its repercussions in Washington were doing just that. I did not minimize the turmoil that prevailed, but I remembered that Diem had survived even greater turmoil in 1955, and I believed that he could do so again if the Americans kept a cool head and gave him the support now that they gave him then. And in that context, I believed, we would be able to influence him and work out between us a way to handle the Buddhists' proper concerns and ours, while still pursuing the war against the Communists.

This was the position that I took within CIA with our analysts and estimators and with John McCone, who counted on my personal knowledge of the Vietnamese scene and leadership. And by and large they agreed with me, although they tended to stress the political difficulties more than I did. The military, personified by Defense Secretary Robert McNamara and Maxwell Taylor, now Chairman of the Joint Chiefs of Staff, followed somewhat the same line, at least to the extent that they felt the main problem was winning the war and that we should not be diverted from keeping pressure on it.

But as the Buddhist protests escalated and public opinion against the Diem regime was stirred to a fever pitch of outrage, the State Department's view of the situation came into ascendancy. It was pressed most fervently by Averell Harriman, now Undersecretary; by Roger Hilsman, Assistant Secretary for Far Eastern Affairs; and by Michael Forrestal, son of the former Secretary of Defense and a Presidential Assistant on the National Security Council staff. They fervently believed that the war could not be won unless the Saigon government was reformed to make it more democratic and popular, so as to rally the people to the fight against the Communists. And behind this argument was the persuasive pressure of Kennedy's concern for his political support among the American people, bombarded as they were daily by new shocks in the media about Vietnam. Therefore, the proponents of this view believed that the United States must consider the prospect of dissociating itself from Diem and Nhu, unless their ways could be changed.

While each of the agencies held the official position expressed by the principals as described, none was by any means unanimous within itself on the issues. And this included CIA, where some of the junior officers in Vietnam took an emotionally charged position against Diem, Nhu, and much of their apparatus. In general they were the unilateral officers who were in contact with the opposition and adopted what they thought was the logic of the opposition position. To a degree, the same spirit also spread to some of the officers on the liaison side of the station, who were frustrated with the failure of some of their counterparts to put their best effort into the war programs and who saw Nhu's influence as the source of the difficulty. As the crisis mounted, so did the problem of keeping the channels clear for the reports of these varying views. The raw reports from the unilateral and liaison officers were forwarded uncensored to Washington (and were frequently passed around the Cabinet table as the President searched for understanding) along with Station Chief Richardson's over-all conclusions and judgments. And these very often did not agree with each other—a fact that became known to others in the official community as well as the press.

At CIA headquarters, the same differences existed among the many officers who were by then involved in the Vietnam question. But McCone's careful insistence on hearing out every side before taking a position himself, and his meticulous forwarding of the raw evidence to the other departments and agencies whether or not it supported his conclusions, produced an atmosphere in which the sincerity and integrity of all were respected, and all knew that their case had been made, whether finally accepted or not.

In mid-August, a conference was set up in Honolulu at the CINCPAC (Commander-in-Chief Pacific) headquarters to provide Lodge a final briefing on the over-all Vietnam program before he proceeded to Saigon to replace Nolting, and I was sent along to ensure that he got a full picture of CIA's activities and capabilities. Nolting, who had left Saigon on August 15 after having extracted from Diem an understanding that Diem would call for a reconciliation with the Buddhists, was also at the conference. But barely had the conference got underway when the news tickers reported that South Vietnamese troops had conducted a raid on Xa Loi, the principal Buddhist pagoda in Saigon, and then on others in other cities as well. Despite the various and contradictory stories that shortly circulated about the reasons for the raids, one fact was unmistakably clear. Diem and Nhu had seized the interlude between the departure of one American ambassador and the arrival of the next to try to suppress the Buddhists once and for all by a massive show of force. And in the process they made it virtually impossible for their friends in the American government like myself to do anything but go along with the ideas in Washington to force them to change their methods to ones that did not cause the kind of political repercussion in America that the raid on the pagodas and the burning bonzes did.

Because of the CIA's secrecy and its long-time close relations with Nhu and Diem, the immediate question was raised in many minds whether the Agency might be pursuing its own policy at cross purposes with the official United States position, and even have had something to do with the raids. For, as it developed, the troops who had carried out the raids had been led by the Vietnamese Special Forces, which were supported by CIA, were well known to be independent of the regular South Vietnamese Army general-staff command structure, and reported directly to Diem and Nhu in the Palace. They were particularly feared as a special operational force, shrouded in secrecy for their CIA-assisted clandestine work in North Vietnam and with the CIA-sponsored Citizens' Irregular Defense Groups. In fact, however, they had been assembled for the pagoda raids totally without the CIA's knowledge, and it fell to me to convince Americans and Vietnamese alike that this was so.

But the more immediate problem was with some of the Vietnamese Army leaders. They wanted it clarified that the Army had not conducted the raids, as suggested in the accounts of the Voice of America and the world press, but that the attacks on the Buddhists had been the work of Diem and Nhu's Special Forces exclusively. Moreover, they wanted to know what the American reaction would be if they felt compelled to move against the pair as a result of those attacks.

A hot August Saturday is hardly the day to find all senior policy officials hard at work in their offices in Washington. Yet it was on such a day, August 24, 1963, that one of the most important messages in the Vietnam war was drafted and sent by the United States government. It identified Nhu as the devil behind the pagoda raids and outlined the steps to be taken by the United States embassy in Saigon to make clear that the Special Forces under him and not the South Vietnamese Army had been responsible. Then it went on to state that the United States

> cannot tolerate a situation in which power lies in Nhu's hands. Diem must be given chance to rid himself of Nhu and his coterie and replace them with the best military and political personalities available . . . but if he remains obdurate, then we are prepared to accept the obvious implication that we can no longer support Diem. You may also tell appropriate military commanders we will give them direct support in any interim period of breakdown in central government mechanism . . . Ambassador and country team should urgently examine all possible alternative leadership and make detailed plans as to how we might bring about Diem's replacement if this should become necessary.

That evening, I was alerted that a most important cable had gone to Saigon from the State Department. Knowing of McCone's strong feeling that he be kept intimately advised on all major developments, I went to the CIA Operations Center to read it, and immediately saw its significance. I talked on the telephone with some of the working-level experts on Vietnam in other departments and learned from them that the message had been drafted by Harriman and Hilsman in the State Department, but that it had been "cleared with Hyannis Port," where President Kennedy was spending the weekend. I later heard that Helms, who was the Agency's duty officer that day, had seen the message and cleared it, regarding it as a policy rather than an intelligence matter, in which the Agency thus had no formal role. But when other senior figures learned what the message had said, McGeorge Bundy arranged that I fly on Sunday out to California to brief McCone on it at his home in San Marino, where he was taking a brief vacation.

My concern was well founded. John Richardson reported that Lodge had taken State's message as a direct order to prepare for a coup against Diem and had directed the CIA Saigon station to canvass its contacts and develop a plan for one. And the station did so, following my instructions that it had to take its policy orders from the Ambassador, whether it agreed with them or not. Among the CIA officers involved was my old Jedburgh friend, Lucien Conein, and he and a number of other officers made the rounds of their contacts in the South Vietnamese military. But a policy swing as radical as this one, from American support of Diem to an attempt to overthrow him, required time to translate into an actual conspiracy, especially against a regime accustomed to mistrust the loyalty of its subordinates. We weren't especially successful and were by no means helped when the Voice of America on Monday, mixing up its instructions from State, supplemented its story about the innocence of the Vietnamese Army in the pagoda attacks with the remark that "the U.S. may sharply reduce its aid to Vietnam unless President Diem gets rid of secret-police officials responsible for the attacks."

Vietnamese both in and out of government immediately realized that a threat of this sort could only mean that the Americans were moving to a showdown with Diem and, though the furor this caused subsided somewhat when Voice of America later broadcast that no aid-cut decision had been made, the idea had been planted, and it put Diem on his guard. The station's frantic efforts to make contacts with the Vietnamese military likely to carry out a coup also came to the Palace's attention, while at the same time the Vietnamese military became nervously cautious in dealing with Americans on a subject so fraught with danger to themselves. So by the end of the week, Richardson sent me a cable saying, "This coup is finished," and we braced for the aftermath, which soon came.

Nguyen Khanh, one of the key generals in the plot, suspected that his position had been compromised by the CIA officer who had approached him and said he would speak only through a MACV friend. Nhu began asserting in Vietnamese circles that he was in close touch with CIA and that it had kept him advised of the loyalty of the various generals. And then a few days later Nhu turned full circle and launched a massive newspaper attack against CIA, charging that the Agency was plotting against the regime in collaboration with the Communists. Diem and Nhu had obviously drawn their wagons up against the outside world, especially against the Americans who, they realized, had turned against them.

The tension grew. Lodge attended a Vietnamese ceremony, where he commented that Diem's penchant to dress in the ancient costume of a Vietnamese mandarin showed how far Diem had drifted from reality into some medieval fantasy. Shortly after, Richardson was "reassigned" from Saigon at Lodge's request to demonstrate to the Ngo brothers that they no longer had a sympathetic channel through which to communicate directly with the American government and bypass the United States embassy. And although CIA made its regular September support payment to the Special Forces, the next installment was held up, CIA's flexibility allowing these payments to be turned on and off as a means of exerting further pressure on Diem and Nhu.

And then, in late September, when McNamara led yet another fact-finding mission to Vietnam, on which I accompanied him as the CIA representative, Lodge directed me to have no contact whatsoever with the Palace in order to underscore to Diem and Nhu that their erstwhile special CIA channel to Washington was no longer open to them. As a result, I traveled clear across the Pacific to wind up discussing the situation only with our station officers, as I refused to talk to other Vietnamese if I could not be in touch with my former principal connections. I objected to this situation and appended a footnote to McNamara's recommendation that Lodge be the only contact with the brothers and that he maintain a posture of aloof correctness with them. For I believed that a private CIA channel offered the best way to carry out the President's policy of "pressure and persuasion." And when almost all communication with the Palace stopped, I wrote a memorandum to McCone, suggesting that a "negotiation with Nhu" be undertaken "unofficially" by the CIA to try to convince him that it was essential that he withdraw from the scene (and from Vietnam) in order to permit a resolution of the total impasse the Americans and Diem had reached, offering to undertake such negotiation myself. McCone passed out copies of my memo at a policy meeting in the White House basement, where it was read without a comment. But it was clearly out of tune with the Administration's temper. Pressure not persuasion had become the main theme of Washington's policy.

And the pressure increased. Following up the suspension of CIA support to the Special Forces, a more drastic step was taken and publicized: that of cutting off the monthly AID payments used to finance commercial imports to South Vietnam. Then, President Kennedy stated in a TV interview that he thought the Vietnamese government needed changes in policies and "perhaps" in personnel as well, since it had "gotten out of touch with the people." Ambassador Lodge remained the only person authorized to conduct negotiation on such policy and personnel changes, and he insisted that Diem approach him first.

In the midst of all this, I discovered how CIA and Des FitzGerald, at about the same time, probably got into the revolting (and, I might add, feckless) business of trying to assassinate Fidel Castro. For in a serious discussion with two high-ranking, non-CIA American officials with whom I often discussed CIA activities for policy approval, I was told quite directly, in a tone somewhere between sarcastic and cynical, that if the United States had a really proper intelligence service we would not be going through so much agony trying to decide how to deal with Nhu.

The implication was clear: these officials were suggesting that Nhu should have been disposed of by the CIA long before this. I turned off the conversation without a reply, and took no step to follow up the suggestion. But I can understand how someone else might have taken this as a nonattributable, deliberately ambiguous policy guidance. As I would report in agonizing detail to the Congress years later, some people in CIA took similar expressions of official hostility to a foreign leader as a suggestion, consent or even authority, to mount operations aimed at assassinating Castro. As Henry IV's cry, "Who will rid me of this meddlesome priest?" led to Thomas à Becket's death in Canterbury Cathedral, so the ambiguity with which covert policy vis-à-vis Castro was stated in this period led to vigorous efforts to achieve what the policymakers were *thought* to have meant, however they may have actually phrased their statements. And, of course, in the macho atmosphere of secret operations, a substratum of the violently inclined will always tend to discount normal moral restraints or exceed their original instructions in the heat of action, and any encouragement from above can launch them into horrendous behavior, and once launched, they are difficult to recall or control. In fact the later investigations disclosed that the word *assassination* itself did appear in some official papers of the period, even though John McCone objected to it and apparently was not aware of what was being done with respect to Castro.

My two interlocutors did not follow up their suggestion when I turned them off, and perhaps they were only indulging in some oral bravado. But McCone did react forcefully to a suggestion by General Big Minh around this time that assassination of Diem's brothers, Nhu and Can, might be one way to conduct a coup. At McCone's direction I cabled the Saigon station to abstain from stimulating, approving or supporting any such action or in any way condoning it and thereby engaging our responsibility for it.

To all this "pressure" Diem and Nhu reacted negatively; it succeeded in getting them to dig in their heels only that much more. Madame Nhu came to the United States and appeared on a number of TV talk shows, where she made successively more outrageous remarks and evoked even greater American hostility toward the Diem regime. Meanwhile, rumors of every sort circulated in Saigon, from the allegation that Nhu was in contact with Hanoi, trying to arrange a settlement with the Communists behind the Americans' backs, to the story that the South Vietnamese military had been encouraged sufficiently by the Americans' open hostility toward Diem and were getting ready to try another coup.

On November 1, Admiral Harry Felt visited Saigon and made a ritual call on Diem, with Lodge accompanying him. At the end of the meeting, Diem asked for a private word with Lodge and made what turned out to be a final plea for understanding from the Americans. He conceded that he had perhaps been too inflexible and that he was ready to try to accommodate the Americans by making reforms. But there was one thing he couldn't do: get rid of Nhu. And he asked that Lodge consult with Lansdale and Colby about how much he needed his brother's counsel, as we both knew him. But the cable with this information was sent at routine speed, and by the time it reached Washington, it was too late.

Because as soon as Felt left Saigon, the South Vietnamese generals assembled at their General Staff headquarters, and the coup began. They called in my old friend Lou Conein to sit with them and pass news of the developments step by step to the CIA Saigon station, and from there on to Lodge and Washington. Lou was allowed there, because Lodge had vouched for his *bona fides* directly to one of the generals. The story of the coup is well known and need not be repeated here. It is plain, however, that the American decisions with respect to it were made by the White House, not by the CIA. My instructions to the station were that it work totally under the direction of Lodge, and they were followed to the letter, as both Lodge and the White House later confirmed. Since then it has also become quite clear that the murders of Diem and Nhu were ordered by General Duong Van (Big) Minh, confirming my long-standing doubts about him. And we now know that the equally peremptory execution of Colonel Le Quang Tung, the mild and unlikely chief of the Special Forces, who was totally loyal to Diem, was ordered with the approval of all the generals and can only really be explained by their bureaucratic jealousy of his independence from their command.

The news of the coup arrived in Washington at about 2 A.M., November 1, and the CIA duty officer at Langley phoned me at home to come in and read the traffic. I was not surprised; the pressure had risen so high in the previous weeks that some action was certainly to be expected, and we had received several indications that the generals were moving in this direction. President Kennedy had held a National Security Council meeting on October 29 to review the situation. And the by-then much-hashed-over debate was repeated between the State Department view that the Diem regime had to go because it could not prosecute the war, and the Pentagon's (and McCone's and my) view that Diem was better than anyone on the horizon and that the real American interest was to avoid adversely affecting the war in the countryside by upsetting the political structure in Saigon. The President vacillated in the face of the intensity of argument among his closest advisers, and the only decision reached that day was the usual easy one to seek more information about what was really going on in Vietnam by sending out more cables.

But now the die was cast; a major assault on the regime was underway. Later in the day, the President called an NSC meeting to assess the situation, and McCone had me do a briefing on the geography of Saigon, the disposition of the troops around it, and the indications we had received as to how many were involved in the action. I described these; but, on the basis of my experience with the 1960 coup attempt, I pointed out that the Presidential Guard would be loyal and that the key question was what the reaction of the units outside Saigon would be, and in particular that of an armored unit to the northwest of the city. In Saigon, Diem and Nhu looked at the situation in the same way and spent hours on the telephone trying to rally support from commanders outside the Saigon area. When they realized they could not, they fled the Palace, later surrendered and were murdered by one of Big Minh's aides.

After spending most of that night in the CIA operations center, I went home to pick up a clean shirt before going to McCone's house to brief him. Barbara had already gone to Mass (it was November 2, All Souls' Day), so I dropped by the church and, stepping into the pew with her for a moment, asked her also to pray for the "brothers" in Vietnam, as the news was quite definite that they were dead, although we did not then know how. After briefing McCone, we rode down to the White House in his limousine, and I confessed to him that their deaths had hit me personally; I had known and respected them both, one of very few Americans who did, especially as far as Nhu was concerned. But there was little time for sentiment; I quickly had to go and brief the President and the NSC about how the coup had been carried out and who seemed to be in charge in Saigon.

At the end of the meeting, McCone took me into the Oval Office, where he told the President that he was sending me immediately to Saigon to assess the situation and asked the President's approval (to ensure that Lodge would accept me this time). Kennedy looked drawn, apparently disturbed over Diem's death and anxious to find some way out of the morass that Vietnam now presented. He quickly agreed that I go, at which point I felt I had to interject a word of caution. While I knew all the generals involved in the coup, I also knew that they were well aware of my close relations with Nhu and Diem and they might refuse to see me because of that. Therefore, I said quietly, I wasn't sure how much I could accomplish, but I would certainly do my best. Kennedy understood and wished me well, and I returned home to pack. The first available flight to Saigon wasn't until the next day, so that night Barbara and I had a long-planned dinner with the Noltings and the Richardsons, and there we had perhaps the only Washington wake for the Diem regime and the Ngo brothers.

On the long flight to Saigon the next day, I wondered about the reception I would get from the generals and from Lodge. But both welcomed me. Lodge accepted the President's endorsement of my visit and was fulsome in his praise of the way the CIA station had operated during the coup and had meticulously made clear that it was under his full direction. The generals looked on me as a friend of Vietnam rather than just of the Diem regime and were rapidly convinced by a series of briefings I organized that CIA could help them as much as it had helped Diem and Nhu to meet the challenges both in the war in the countryside and in the chaotic political situation in Saigon. Even Big Minh was friendly on the surface, despite my private qualms that he had neither the force nor the wisdom to lead the country or the other generals. I also probed elsewhere in trying to understand the dimensions of the new problems we now faced. CIA's unilateral officers introduced me to some of their contacts among the opposition politicians who were euphoric about the end of Diem's authoritarian regime but wondered how they could play a role under the generals, who obviously held full power now. And I even had a long and totally confusing discussion with one of the leading Buddhist bonzes, from which I concluded that either I just could not comprehend the philosophical context in which he operated or that he did not have one; there certainly didn't seem to be anything that could be called logic in his views.

But what I was chiefly interested in was the prospect for the struggle in the countryside against the Communists, since the fate of Saigon would be decided there. And it was bad. The strategic-hamlet program had fallen to pieces for a combination of reasons—the Palace's preoccupation since June with the Buddhist crisis and its relations with the Americans; the Communist identification of the program as the main threat to their ambitions and the consequent concentration of their actions against it; Nhu's overly simple advocacy of it everywhere and the bureaucracy's hurried propitiation of him with statistics rather than with actual accomplishments; and now, of course, the impossibility of the new government continuing it, since it was so closely identified with the regime just overthrown. As a result, the Communists had scored substantial gains during the chaotic summer and fall, and now they put in an extra effort to capitalize on the paralysis that followed the coup and death of Diem, which National Liberation Front leader Nguyen Huu Tho termed "gifts from heaven for us." Observing the generals' junta during our briefings, I decided there was little chance that it would stir itself sufficiently to lead a dynamic program in the countryside. And on the American side, with due respect for Lodge's courage and political sensitivities, I realized that each American agency was likely to go on doing its own thing with hardly any over-all control and co-ordination, especially since the new Vietnamese govern-ment had no central policy and Lodge himself showed little liking for the details of administrative management so necessary to control the American bureaucratic maze in Vietnam.

To add to my pessimism, I saw little that CIA could do to help. For November 1 marked not only the date of the coup in Saigon, but the final effective date for the implementation of another crucial event as well: Operation Switchback, the application of Taylor's post-Bay of Pigs recommendations under which CIA's large paramilitary operations were turned over to the Defense Department. I had fully ac-cepted this operation and had worked on the bureaucratic details of transferring our activities to the Pentagon control, offering to send along a number of CIA officers familiar with them so that they could be run in the future without a loss of experience or continuity. Many of our village projects around the country had by this time been incorporated into the strategic-hamlet program. But I thought the American Special Forces teams could still be helpful in training and preparing country communities to undertake their own pro-tection and development, and CIA officers familiar with the politics of the relationships between such villages and local Vietnamese authorities could help the American teams avoid the pitfalls of political problems. But it soon became clear that the military wanted to do its own thing, and nei-ther wanted nor listened to CIA's political ideas of how to fight the war.

As for our operations against the North, I had come to the conclusion that they needed a major overhaul, even before they were slated to be turned over to the military under Switchback. The teams we had infiltrated in North Vietnam, either from the air or from the sea, had been notoriously unsuccessful, having been captured or disappearing from radio contact in a short time after their arrival (except for one or two which quite clearly came under enemy control). And my close friend and deputy, Robert J. Myers, a long-time Far Eastern hand (later to leave CIA and become publisher of *The New Republic*) had vigorously urged me to stop sending them as both unconscionable and ineffective. And he buttressed his argument by pointing out the failure of similar operations in Korea, China and Eastern Europe in earlier years, saying that it was clear from that record and our own, that Communist control of a population was of a different order from the German or Japanese occupations of World War II and thus OSS-type operations successful then were of no use to us now. I agreed with Myers' points and was in the process of developing a new strategy for North Vietnam, primarily propaganda in nature, that would aim at long-term impact of radio broadcasts, leaflet drops and "deception actions" gradually building acceptance among the people and cadres of North Vietnam for the idea that peaceful coexistence, political collaboration, and economic development between North and South was a better policy than the North's armed subversion and violence in the South.

On my way back from Saigon, I stopped off in Honolulu to participate in a conference at the CINCPAC Command Center, where McNamara was holding a review of what should now be done in Vietnam. High on the agenda was Operation Switchback and the Vietnamese operations against the North, transferred from CIA to the military under Switchback. In this conference I told McNamara that putting teams into the North did not and would not work. He listened to me with a cold look and then rejected my advice. The desire to put pressure onto North Vietnam prevailed, and there and then the United States military started the planning and activity that would escalate finally to full-scale air attacks. The CIA's lack of success was dismissed as the result of the small scale of effort that a civilian agency could undertake; by moving to the larger scale possible for the military, McNamara was sure, serious damage to the North's war effort could be wrought. CIA was asked to continue to contribute to this effort in the political and propaganda fields, and several officers were attached to the military program for this purpose.

But on Friday, November 22, all our problems were pushed into the background by a greater tragedy: President Kennedy's assassination in Dallas. As the news came in over the radio in my office in Langley, Myers and I discussed the enormous effect this senseless deed would have on the world he had so inspired with his enthusiasm and charm. I, of course, had no inkling then of the impact it would have on the CIA, forcing it to defend itself against paranoid conspiracy theories that it had a role in the assassination. The intense investigations of later years showed that it had no such role, and I am satisfied from my own knowledge of CIA and its dedicated American officers that no such activity took place or was even possible. And as for the allegation that CIA's actions against Castro stimulated the Cuban dictator to retaliate in this fashion, I have never seen anything but the most far-fetched circumstantial reasoning that could support such a theory.

The fact of the matter is that the CIA could not have had a better friend in a President than John F. Kennedy. He understood the Agency and used it effectively, exploiting its intellectual abilities to help him analyze a complex world and its paramilitary and covert political talents to react to it in a low key. It is, of course, pointless to speculate on what Kennedy might have done in Vietnam had he lived. But I am convinced that he would, at the very least, have recognized the futility of a massive military buildup there as the way to fight a guerrilla war. Despite his vacillation between his conflicting advisers over Diem, I remain satisfied to this day that, given his preference for political action and his appreciation of, and fascination with, counterinsurgency, we would have focused sooner and more effectively on the village-level, people's war had Kennedy been in the Oval Office during those crucial years from 1964 to 1968. Whether we would have won or lost, we would at least not have had a half-million American soldiers involved, nor experienced the casualties they suffered and inflicted by their operations.

Unarguably, Lyndon Johnson inherited a mess in Vietnam, and one not of his making. For he had made clear, albeit from his powerless Vice-Presidential post, whenever he could, that he believed that we would be better off with than without Diem. His judgment proved correct, as Big Minh's junta proved weak, indecisive and incapable of governing, demonstrating the folly of our having concentrated wholly on the weaknesses and evils of the Diem regime to the exclusion of any serious discussion on what would replace it. Johnson also found the situation in Vietnam's countryside a lot worse than had been realized. The six-month political crisis in Saigon had taken its toll, the Communists had exploited it, and Washington awoke to the fact, revealed in reports that CIA had surreptitiously obtained before the coup from Diem's inspectors, that the strategic-hamlet program had ceased working.

McCone came up with the idea of sending out a group of CIA's "old Vietnam hands" to make an independent survey of the situation and examine the reporting system, which had failed to show the weaknesses in the field. They were to spread through the country and contact their old official, personal, and "unilateral" Vietnamese contacts, bypassing the normal reporting mechanisms direct to the facts. They were plucked by me from the faraway stations to which they had been transferred after their Saigon service—Africa, Latin America, Paris—and sent to do the job, much to the discomfort of the military and civilian apparatus then in Vietnam. And, I must confess, I had my own doubts that they could provide anything very useful beyond what the Saigon station was already providing. But McCone's exercise taught me that part of the job of intelligence assessment is getting its results read. And this "special survey" did provide a vehicle to do just that.

Over the ensuing months the Vietnam issues under debate in Washington gradually changed. With Diem gone, all agencies agreed that as much as possible should be done to shore up the series of governments that followed him. And all agreed that the strategic-hamlet concept of building security at the local level should be revived and prosecuted. But a new issue arose to dominate the policy councils—punishing the North severely enough to cause it to draw back from its support of the war in the South. And on this the division among Johnson's advisers broke along different lines from those in Kennedy's day over Diem. In essence, the military argued for bringing the war to the "real enemy" in North Vietnam; the civilians at State, AID and CIA insisted that the major focus should be in the South. Thus began many months of feverish activity in both Washington and Saigon, searching for some stability in government in South Vietnam, trying to mount some consistent strategy and operations in the countryside among all the American and Vietnamese agencies each pursuing its own programs there, and debating seemingly ad infinitum the question of bombing the North.

The ensuing months were a kaleidoscope of meetings in Washington, round trips to Saigon and the inevitable briefings and discussions there, and a cacophony of proposals for ways to strengthen the performance of the Vietnamese government structure, from introducing American advisers as cadre in the Saigon government to warning the Vietnamese against any further coups. One picture remains vividly with me from this period: that of Defense Secretary Robert McNamara in the conference room at MACV in Saigon, on one of his countless trips there, furiously taking notes with his left hand as earnest briefing officers poured forth an endless stream of statistics, statistics through which he sought to assure himself that the massive supply of logistics and forces was having an effect on the course of the war by sheer weight of numbers. There is no need here to try to recapitulate all the steps taken during this period, but some of the major ones did bear on CIA and its role in American foreign policy and programs.

On January 30, 1964, General Nguyen Khanh, whom I had identified as a likely successor to Diem when I left Vietnam in 1962, conducted a bloodless coup to displace Big Minh and his junta, and many Americans heaved a sigh of relief that the lackluster junta was gone. Khanh certainly had weaknesses too, which showed up as the months went by. But perhaps his most difficult problems were to absorb the flood of varying American counsel he received, contend with the Buddhists, who proved almost as difficult to please as under Diem, and furnish Vietnamese counterparts to all the programs initiated by the Americans. It is not surprising that, faced with all this, he proved unable to dominate the situation, and a series of coups and coup attempts followed, until the Vietnamese military formed an Armed Forces Council under Nguyen Van Thieu and Nguyen Cao Ky to try to establish some stability in government in order to carry on the struggle against the Communists.

This political chaos undermined every effort to build strength in the countryside. Such efforts also generally showed inconclusive results, because they were *imposed* from above by the Saigon government rather than *built* from below by local efforts. They were also constantly being disrupted by changes in the Saigon government and, consequently, in local officials. The former CIA program in the highland area among Montagnards suffered special setbacks, first when the American military, deciding it needed an "offensive guerrilla force" to operate along the wild borders of South Vietnam, changed the CIDG program from one of reinforcing settlements to one of manning border redoubts far from any population. Then the American Special Forces' enthusiasm for their highland teams and contempt for the Vietnamese in command of them resulted in an abortive revolt of the Montagnard tribes to secure autonomy from the Vietnamese government, a revolt in which they expected to be supported by the United States.

Partly as a result of the frustration that experiences like these produced in policy circles in Washington, and partly as a result of the dominant role played by the large numbers of American military by now involved in Vietnam, attention turned more and more to the debate over how to bring greater pressure on the North, while the need to build strength in the South received only more and more lip service, but very perfunctory attention to execution in the field. Moreover, the weakness of the Vietnamese government combined with an intense, almost *macho* American determination not to lose the contest with the Communists led Lyndon Johnson to concentrate policy debate and decision-making within American circles to the exclusion of the Vietnamese, with an equivalent tendency to look for solely American means by which the war could be fought.

The high (or low) point of this process came when the Pentagon proposed to send an Army civil-affairs staff to Saigon and, in effect, start down the road to a military-government structure there, under military command, of course. This, fortunately, was vetoed by Taylor, who succeeded Lodge as ambassador in Saigon, but the attitude it reflected was repeated in many other situations and seemed unchangeable. After one of the many meetings I attended at the White House, I stopped McGeorge Bundy outside the Situation Room and told him plaintively that we must get our attention and our programs back to the real contest at the village level, and build up from there instead of endlessly debating where to bomb North Vietnam and what new projects to impose on the overloaded Saigon government. He replied that I might be right in my approach, but that he thought the structure of the American government would never permit it to be applied. And his appreciation of the role of the Pentagon's and the rest of Washington's juggernaut staff machinery was correct at the time.

But the result was the Vietnam war as we now know it. In the autumn of 1964 our intelligence showed the first North Vietnamese troop units (as distinct from cadres and infiltrators) moving south down the Ho Chi Minh Trail. Hanoi had obviously come to the conclusion that the situation in South Vietnam was ripe for a final military *coup de grâce*. But there was another factor in the equation—the Texas tenacity of Lyndon B. Johnson, who refused to accept such an outcome; and in response, an American solution to the crisis was applied: the Rolling Thunder bombing campaign against the North and the dispatch of American combat forces to South Vietnam to provide a shield behind which an effort could still be made to save South Vietnam.

CIA had little say in these events. Through Operation

Switchback its paramilitary work both in North and South Vietnam had been turned over to the military, which permitted only a minor role to be played by the few civilians left with it to assist in the transition. In the intelligence-gathering field, CIA's political contacts and unilateral penetrations did provide some useful insights into the major political developments on the Saigon scene, but as most of these took place in full public view anyway and at such a dizzying pace, they were almost as well reported in the press and by the embassy, leaving the Agency very little to add. And the tension of events was such that the CIA's indirect covert techniques were soon enough supplanted by direct ambassadorial approaches. What's more, the Agency's efforts to work with Vietnamese intelligence services to improve coverage of the Communists in the countryside were almost totally frustrated by the rapid replacement of the leadership of such services with every change in government, and the preoccupation of the new appointees with the much more proximate danger of yet another coup.

Still, the good sense of the CIA officers in Vietnam, their greater familiarity with the country and its people, because of their longer tours of duty there, and their professional tendency to penetrate behind the façades of the situations they faced, all made them valuable contributors in the Country Team discussions, and they provided a useful counterpoint to the optimism of the proponents of panacea programs. And the Agency's analysts in Washington served in a similar way, their estimates on events in Vietnam being by far the most realistic, as shown in the Pentagon Papers, although their conclusions were in great part neither welcomed nor adopted by the policymakers.

During this period I had lots of other things to do as chief of our Far Eastern operations, the largest division in the Deputy Directorate of Plans. The war in Laos was growing in intensity; the pressure was on to develop professional intelligence operations against mainland China; there were spluttering insurgencies in Thailand and the Philippines, where CIA was able to launch some low-key village-level counterinsurgency programs. And Indonesia exploded, with a bid for power by the largest Communist Party in the world outside the curtain, which killed the leadership of the army with Sukarno's tacit approval and then was decimated in reprisal. CIA provided a steady flow of reports on the process in Indonesia, although it did not have any role in the course of events themselves. And all the while I was learning how to handle a second-level management job, directing others to run sensitive operations, rather than running them directly myself, a half world away.

For example, I quickly determined that the number of reports a station submitted to headquarters did not by any means indicate the value of its work. So I cribbed from my grade-school days to set up a grading system for the reports they sent in, from "A" for a valuable one that could have been obtained only by the most professional techniques of espionage, to "F" for one that should not have been sent in (or should have been given to the embassy in the field for its use, since it was only the result of a casual cocktail-party conversation). Then I put out a chart, showing which station produced quality reporting with a small staff and which station produced marginal results with a large staff, and so spurred some intense efforts in the following months in those stations that did not look so good in comparison with their fellows. Moreover, I learned how easy it was to launch new programs when there was truly a need for them, but how hard it was to reduce staffs in areas that, like Taiwan or Korea, had been crucial at one time but were comparatively quiet now and therefore had to yield personnel to higher-priority areas like Vietnam and Laos.

Also, the importance of personal inspection was driven home to me on a trip to Japan, where I saw that an intellectual journal we supported there was crowded out on newsstands by many other comparable publications and thus was useless and even dangerous if it were revealed to be receiving assistance from us. I also was made aware of just how much easier it was to produce excellent inside intelligence on our Asian friends than to produce such intelligence on our enemies. And I once had to insist that our bugging of a friendly political leader's office be turned off as more dangerous than valuable, the danger being its possible exposure by our customers in Washington. And there was the pleasure of helping to develop a new generation of CIA leaders, as when I chose an officer who had served in difficult and dangerous circumstances in the mountains of Laos to be my personal assistant so that he could learn something of the mysterious workings of Washington's policy machinery.

But perhaps the most useful lesson I learned in this, my first real management position, was to accept the varying life styles of my subordinates. A chief of station might live a very flamboyant life style indeed, at least according to my standards, but could use it to maintain warm and close friendships with the leaders of the countries where he was assigned and thus carry out extremely valuable unilateral operations that would otherwise be impossible. One, for example, rigged himself with a microphone and tape recorder to report his conversation with his close drinking buddy, the chief of state, in precise detail. And finally and most of all, I learned to repect and admire the great commitment of the many CIA officers and their wives who served in far-off, uncomfortable and dangerous places not only without complaint but with enthusiasm for the work they did to help their country, and without recognition other than the admiration of their fellow CIA officers.

All was not grim, of course. There were sips of rice wine in tribal-village ceremonies, sophisticated finger-game contests with cultured Chinese officials, late-night discussions of Indonesian revolutionary theory, drinks at the Selangor Club in the Somerset Maugham atmosphere of Kuala Lumpur. My passion for travel was amply indulged with train trips down the Malay Peninsula, across Java and the length of Honshu, showing the officers who worked in the Far East Division, and their local friends, that the chief wanted to see and understand every last place they worked in. I also had a chance to think about the larger questions of intelligence. I arranged the assignment of several Washington-based analysts to stations in the Far East so as to bring their academic assessments of the meaning of the events to the very areas wherein those events were taking place and added their assessments to the spot and raw information being procured by the stations. I became aware, too, of the complex interaction needed among the various agencies involved in technical and electronic intelligence, so that the bits and pieces of data they obtained could be consolidated, their significance could be determined, and the results could then be communicated to the far ends of the earth, where they might be important to an isolated American unit totally unaware of how they were obtained. And once again I suggested to the producers of finished intelligence that they publish their material in a daily-newspaper format for easier absorption by our customers (and was again politely told that it was not such a good idea).

But, of course, Vietnam was the focus of my attention during this period. When I arranged a rotation system for CIA officers there, explaining to John McCone that I wanted to distribute that dangerous and difficult assignment more fairly among the other geographic divisions of the Agency, he looked at me with his steely eyes and said coldly, "Mr. Colby, the President believes that Vietnam is the most important task this nation faces, and wants our very best men assigned there. You will assign the best and most qualified men we have and keep them there, and I do not want to hear any more talk of sharing the duty with less qualified ones." Not long after, the importance and danger of the assignment was driven home when a huge terrorist bomb exploded against the embassy in Saigon and I met the evacuation planes, aboard which were the CIA men and women blinded and cut around the face (and assured them that they would return to meaningful jobs in CIA), and received the parents of twenty-one-year-old secretary Barbara Robbins, who was killed in the blast.

In Vietnam, the station worked hard to improve intelligence on the enemy in the countryside, giving priority to the Viet Cong political apparatus rather than the Communist military units, which the American and Vietnamese army commands concentrated on. We coined the word *infrastructure* to describe the secret Communist political network in South Vietnam and its "political order of battle"—the provincial committees and subcommittees, the organizers and activists and the local guerrilla and terrorist squads who acted as the "enforcers" of the Communist authority in the local communities, executing village chiefs, conscripting young men for training and assignment to main force units, mining roads, and dropping grenades in the morning markets to demonstrate their power and the inability of the government to protect the people. With this phrase to identify its target, the station began to work to get the various American and Vietnamese intelligence agencies, civilian and military, to cooperate and exchange information about this "command and control structure" of the people's war enemy. CIA sponsored and built a national interrogation center in Saigon under the auspices of the Vietnamese Central Intelligence Organization to conduct proper and professional interrogations of Communist captives and defectors, and trained Vietnamese in the right techniques to use in it.

This training certainly did *not* include torture, which is morally impermissible and produces bad intelligence—the subject either confessing what he thinks the torturer wants to hear or deciding to hold more firmly to his information, since he anticipates death in any case, as many French resistance members did under Gestapo torture. There were certainly cases of torture in Vietnam, both by Vietnamese and by Americans, but just as certainly CIA used its influence and its training to stop it. CIA training instead covered the lessons of successful POW interrogation by the military and the similar techniques developed by advanced police and intelligence services. Primarily, these stress the value of cross-checking a prisoner's story with other known facts and gradually convincing him that the interrogator already knows the basic story, and is merely filling in the details. Combining this with the "good guy-bad guy" alternate team challenging and sympathizing with the subject can often lead to the first confidences, which then can be built upon to produce more, and certainly produces more accurate information than torture ever can.*

To carry on the same program in the provinces, where the infrastructure operated, a chain of provincial interrogation centers was set up. The military intelligence agencies, meanwhile, set up a program to translate, analyze and index captured enemy documents in a systematic way. The circulation of the results of these programs gradually built up an awareness of the role of the infrastructure in the war and led to CIA's insistence that any assessment of the "enemy" be expanded from the military units, with which the Pentagon was primarily concerned, to include these important "civilian" components, however amorphous their numerical count and their irregularity might be, compared with the more rigid structures looked for by military order-of-battle specialists.

As the situation in Vietnam deteriorated, the CIA station kept a sharp eye out for activities that might shore up the government's position in the provinces. And it soon gained permission to reenter the paramilitary field. For the demise of strategic hamlets and the metamorphosis of the CIDG to an "offensive guerrilla force," the lack of success in the large-scale "pacification" projects imposed by the Saigon bureaucracy onto regional military and administrative officials, and the steady growth of Communist power made *any* activity that promised to stem the tide welcome to Washington policymakers. What CIA's politically sensitive officers were on the lookout for was a program that had local roots rather than one that had to be imposed by Saigon fiat, a program that could be expanded through CIA's flexible, direct

---

* An interesting indication of CIA's position on this subject can be seen in Philip Agee's book, *Inside the Company: CIA Diary*, where Agee, no friend of CIA today, recounts that he had recommended that a Latin American intelligence official be trained by CIA in Washington so that "the police will be able to recruit agents and pay for information instead of having to resort to torture." (p. 446) The total absence of this subject from the reports of the intensive 1975 Congressional investigations into CIA's past also indicates that CIA was not involved in any such activity, since that certainly would have been brought out if it had.

financial and logistics channels and in a few private chats with senior Vietnamese officials rather than through heavily documented intergovernmental negotiations. And I pressed my fundamental belief in the importance of fighting the war with—and I do mean *with*—the people in the countryside, activating and assisting them to participate in the struggle instead of leaving them to try to avoid harm by yielding to whatever force was closest.

So when Peer De Silva, the station chief I had named to replace John Richardson, returned from a trip up the coast to Binh Dinh province and reported his discovery of an interesting project near Qui Nhon run by the local authorities, I included it in my next visit out to Vietnam. The project was the brainchild of a local Vietnamese officer named Nguyen Be and it consisted of a team of local young men, armed for their self protection, but engaged primarily in mobilizing the village population for self-defense against Communist forces and in a cooperative venture to refrigerate their fish catch so that it could be sent to distant and lucrative markets. The concept, of course, bore a striking resemblance to the "People's Force" project organized by Diem's brother Can in the same central Vietnam area, which CIA supported in 1962 and 1963, but I certainly made no reference to that fact and immediately began to plan how CIA could help Nguyen Be. We talked of the need for a better supply of weapons than Be had managed to scrounge up, of the importance of radios to call for help if the Communists attacked in force, of the ways existing Vietnamese and American programs could be used to back up the effort, and of the need for a training center and wages for the personnel if the project were to grow. De Silva had already sold the idea to the Ambassador, and I had little trouble slipping what seemed only a modest local venture in among the long list of projects and programs that Washington reviewed and approved every day. Since it needed a name to fit the American programing machinery, we called it "People's Action Teams," which I hoped would be more lasting than the 1962 "Citizens' Irregular Defense Groups."

The station arranged for some Vietnamese officials in other provinces to go to Binh Dinh to see Nguyen Be's teams in action and to decide whether that sort of thing could help in their areas. A national training center was set up at the beach resort of Vung Tau, where thousands of recruits, flown there by Air America, were taught that their role was primarily political, that their weapons were only for their own self-defense and that their success would be measured by the reaction of the villagers, not by shooting the enemy. We took a step of symbolic significance when we rejected the idea of a uniform of any sort for the teams. But CIA got into the clothing business anyway by supplying each team member two pair of the traditional Vietnamese black pajamas, to demonstrate that he worked with the villagers, not for the Saigon government. The program was so successful that the Vietnamese government, now headed by Prime Minister Nguyen Cao Ky, adopted "revolutionary development" as its slogan and the name of the teams was changed to "Revolutionary Development Teams," to show that they were carrying out the government's policies. What's more, a Ministry of Revolutionary Development was added to the Vietnamese government to be CIA's counterpart in the management of the program, which grew to number some 40,000 cadre men. When the government suspected the chief of the Vung Tau training center of trying to build a political party with this cadre, he was removed and Nguyen Be was named as his replacement to work under the minister's direct control. CIA's direct financial and logistics support continued, and the ministry tried to bring the other government programs in the countryside into a coordinated effort with the teams.

But, as in the 1962 period, CIA was not wedded to any particular approach; it supported other local projects that sprang from local initiatives. For example, in the Delta, an imaginative provincial chief started a program of sending teams to the area's villages to interview the inhabitants about their grievances and used the information to correct local abuses and failings. Once the villagers were convinced that the process produced results, the teams proceeded to the next stage and asked about local Communist activities and identities to help the province's intelligence service to combat the Viet Cong infrastructure. This program too spread gradually to other areas, thanks to CIA's support. And in some provinces aggressive provincial chiefs supplemented their regular police and territorial forces with special counter-terror units to develop direct sources on the Communist infrastructure and to mount carefully targeted operations based on the intelligence they gathered. Here too CIA provided direct support at the provincial level. But in this case it suffered from the secrecy of its machinery. For an aura of mystery quickly surrounded these units, which operated outside the normal bureaucratic machinery and were subject only to provincial chiefs rather than national control, and outsiders, including the American press, saw in their name, Counter-Terror teams, something sinister and tended to put the stress on the latter word rather than the former.

Even when the name was changed to the more accurate "Provincial Reconnaissance Units," cases of abuses committed by them in the heat of bloody contests in the provinces, when government officers there were fighting for their lives, produced a belief that CIA was cynically fighting atrocities with atrocities. CIA's insistence on discipline and its constant urgings that prisoners be captured whenever possible as valuable sources of information all took place in secret, so little was done to counter this belief. The PRU's ability in providing intelligence and hitting the infrastructure nonetheless evoked enthusiastic support from Vietnamese and American officials close to the battle in the provinces and accustomed to rough behavior on both sides of the struggles there. I regret now not having been more insistent than I was at the time that CIA get these units quickly under better control, but this is a sentiment that I suspect should be shared by the American agencies that supported the Vietnamese military and police as well, and perhaps by the Soviet and Chinese governments on their side too.

CIA was not alone in its enthusiasm for work in the villages. While the effort had taken a back seat during the period of political chaos in Saigon and the initial military commitment of United States forces both in South Vietnam and against the North, the number of advocates of it gradually grew during 1965. The United States Marines soon realized that the danger from Communist guerrillas in the villages around Danang was as great as that from main-force units in the hills, and they developed a program of "combined action platoons," which integrated a few Marines into local Vietnamese territorial-force units to patrol the village areas and fight the Communist guerrilla squads there. The police program of AID, with the support of the remnants of the British Advisory Mission, manfully tried to build a police field force on the Malaysian model, despite the lack of sympathy the idea evoked in military circles, both American and Vietnamese.

When Lodge returned for his second tour as ambassador in August 1965, he became a passionate advocate of pacification—analogizing the CIA-supported Peoples Action Teams to American "precinct workers"—and brought Lansdale along as his pacification adviser with a team of like-minded former CIA officers and others of similar bent and background. And MACV, the military command, joined the chorus with a new staff section called the Revolutionary Development Support Staff to focus on improving the military aspects of the effort in the countryside. But the most important enthusiasm came from the highest level—from President Johnson himself. To balance the huge American military operations underway on the ground and in the air, he demanded results in what he called the "other war," the one to improve the lot of the people of Vietnam.

As can be seen from this listing of activity, most of it frenetic albeit totally dedicated, the opportunities for cross purposes, bureaucratic jealousies, and charges of empire-building were almost infinite. While no-nonsense Maxwell Taylor was ambassador, he kept the agencies under a tight rein. But Lodge's disinclination to become a manager, preferring to be just an observer and policy adviser to the President, allowed almost total confusion to reign, to the extent that the agencies themselves began to call for some coordination of their efforts through some central authority.

In January 1966, a conference of second-level officers of all the agencies involved in the "other war," both from the Saigon mission and in Washington, took place at a CIA facility near Washington to discuss what might be done. The over-all recommendation called for better organization both in Saigon and in Washington, although each agency's specific recommendation carefully preserved its own chain of command over its personnel and operations. But the main point of the meeting was made, and President Johnson in a series of decisions in 1966 progressively forced both the Vietnamese and the Americans to improve their management of the war in the countryside. There was still a tendency to place the stress on statistical and physical measurements rather than on real political accomplishments, but at least there was something other than just the lip service with no follow-up in the field, that had characterized the past two years.

But the major change, in atmosphere, in organization, and in priority came from Robert W. Komer. Quick and intelligent, he had served as a CIA analyst writing national estimates on the Middle East, where he had done so well that he had been hired away to become the Middle East expert on the National Security Council staff in the White House. At one point he had been charged with responsibility for the negotiation that Ambassador Ellsworth Bunker conducted between the Indonesians and the Dutch over West Irian, and I first met him when I briefed him on what the CIA station in Djakarta might contribute in the way of intelligence to help the process along. But he burst onto my life with full force in March 1966, when Johnson assigned him as a special Presidential assistant to energize the "other war" in Vietnam. He demanded to know all about CIA's programs, ideas and possibilities, and he made it clear that he had the President's full authority to do so whether it fitted CIA's professional procedures or not. I soon experienced all the negative adjectives that have been applied to him—brash, abrasive, statistics-crazy and aggressively optimistic—but I also thought he was about the best thing that had happened in the Vietnam war to date. He understood the importance of the war at the village level, he looked at the problem from the level of the White House totally above parochial agency interests and he was fearless and tireless in browbeating the bureaucracy, military and civilian, to do what was needed. And occasionally he frustrated me by contesting CIA's belief that it could win the war alone in its own secret ways, which even I then had to admit was fantasy.

During the next few months Komer lectured and prodded the Vietnam experts in Washington on the need for more precise programs and accomplishments in the field, with measurable goals and standards instead of broad philosophical theories about the nature of the war. How many People's Action Teams would be deployed by the next season, how many teachers would be trained by the Ministry of Education and sent to the provinces, how many tin roofs would be distributed to refugees huddled in slums and camps—the questions came apace, and the answers became commitments to accomplish, or to apportion blame for failure. But more important, he ramrodded the various almost-sovereign independent Washington agencies into accepting an over-all central "pacification" strategy. In particular, Komer identified the fundamental problem—the relationship between the military and civilian components of the war—and produced a solution.

Cutting through the many years of debate—and antagonism—over whether the war was more military or more political in nature, he recognized both the predominance of the American military machine and the fundamental political character of the war. This contradiction he resolved by saying the pacification program should be under over-all American military authority but civilian in direction. In this way, he satisfied the military insistence on unity of command but at the same time reassured the civilians that pacification would not be subordinated to the military focus on searching out and destroying the military enemy, as had happened to the CIDG's and other initiatives. He therefore conceived a complex organizational scheme that recognized the primacy of the new American ambassador to Vietnam, Ellsworth Bunker, honored the principle of unity of command by putting the pacification program under the full authority of the military commander General William C. Westmoreland, but underscored the need for political direction of the war in the villages by inventing the position of Civilian Deputy for Pacification for that commander. Because those involved had come to recognize the importance of this dimension of the war and the need for a central organization to run it, and because of Lyndon Johnson's insistence that they subordinate their agency interests to a broader American responsibility to contribute to it in any way they could, the agencies adjusted to the fact that the new jerry-built machinery would take over the detailed management of the programs they had so jealously guarded until that point. And if Komer found any recalcitrance he quickly overrode it by a threat to bring it to Johnson's attention.

The President rewarded Komer for putting this strategy together in Washington by sending him to Vietnam in May 1967 to make the new structure work there on the ground. And his friends and critics alike watched with fascination when he insisted that his position as Deputy to Westmoreland with ambassadorial rank entitled him to four stars on his limousine as well as a seat at the highest policy councils of the military command and the ambassador's weekly policy sessions. But these externals were only a vehicle for him by which to insist on the essentials of the program to fight the war in the villages. And he accomplished what several years of debate had not done, when he obtained authority over American military support to the Vietnamese territorial forces, had them armed with American M-16 rifles to convince them that they could stand up to the Communist AK-47s after several years of inferiority complex, and he integrated, rather than coordinated, the military and the civilian contribution to the war in the villages. Since everything in Vietnam had to have an acronym he named the new hybrid CORDS, taking its first part from the most recent effort to consolidate the civilian programs in an Office of Civil Operations, and the last from the Revolutionary Development Support Staff, which Westmoreland had set up in the MACV military headquarters.

He made CIA join the team too. Despite the problems this created for the Agency's secret internal procedures, the Revolutionary Development cadre and similar programs were transferred to Komer's direction, with the CIA officers who supported it included. He did, however, recognize CIA's need for secrecy in its unilateral operations and its efforts to build better intelligence on the infrastructure in cooperation with the Vietnamese Special Branch of the police. In the latter field CIA had already been working to improve the collaboration among all the Vietnamese and American intelligence agencies, which was right along the lines Komer was trying to push in other sectors of the battle, so Komer's force was welcome.

By the fall of 1967, then, it looked as though McGeorge Bundy might have been wrong after all, that the structure of the American government *could* be adjusted to meet the need to fight a people's war rather than insisting that war is a matter for soldiers and generals only. And although most of the new activity had so far taken place only in Washington conference rooms and offices, and the work in the field in Vietnam was still largely one of plans and preparations, a sense of momentum grew and replaced the earlier frustrations over the gap between high policy proclamation about the war in the villages and the absence of visible action to carry them out. As the Pentagon Papers concluded its account of the formation of CORDS, "the Mission was better run and better organized than it ever had been before, and this fact may in time lead to a more efficient and successful effort" (Vol. II, p. 622), I was convinced that it would, that finally the United States would be fighting the right war in

Vietnam, at the village level, and that it would be successful if it carried out the long-term strategy that had so long been absent but now finally had begun.

So, when Dick Helms in late 1967 suggested a new job for me, I did not demur. I had been chief of the Far East Division for almost five years and heavily involved in Vietnam for eight, and my ideal time frame for holding the same job had come to an end. While Vietnam had had its disappointments and, in my view, disastrous mistakes, I thought we were at last on the right road thanks in great part to Komer, and that my earlier lonely campaign for attention to the right way to fight the war had now been replaced by a chorus of voices more influential than mine, so I was not that much needed. In the rest of the Far East, I knew we had a first-class group of operations officers, who would carry on the Agency's important work and probably even do better than I at developing the kind of professional intelligence operations against the hard targets that we would need in the years ahead. So I looked forward to new problems and challenges. But I got them, much to my surprise, still in Vietnam.

CHAPTER EIGHT

Fighting the People's War

RICHARD HELMS was now the Director of Central Intelligence. John McCone had remained for a while after Kennedy's assassination, to help provide continuity during that critical period. But, as I had early seen, he and Lyndon Johnson were not really on the same wavelength. McCone one time had pushed me forward at the Cabinet table to show the new President a photograph of a Vietnamese installation. But it was clear that the President did not want to examine it in the way Kennedy would have done, and his only reaction was to caution me sharply to be careful not to spill his coffee onto his lap. McCone resigned in April 1965 and was followed by William F. Raborn, a retired Navy vice-admiral, who had made his reputation organizing and managing the construction of Polaris submarines. He insisted on trying out some new management techniques in CIA, which I for one was impressed by, but he was no intellectual, and his bluff and simple approach evoked first snickers and then rumbles of rebellion from the more sophisticated Agency officers, which spread through the Washington dinner circuit, and he lasted only a little more than a year in the job. Then Johnson named Helms, and he was sworn in at the White House in June 1966, before many of his proud professional colleagues, including me. He was the first insider to get the top Agency post since Dulles.

A year before that, when he had been made Deputy Director under Raborn, Helms had consulted all his senior clandestine operational chiefs on which of them should replace him as Deputy Director for Plans. When I was called into his office he immediately said, "Your time will come later," and so shot down the rumors in the halls that I might be a candidate. I urged that Des FitzGerald be chosen, but I cautioned Helms that he would have to maintain tight control over him to keep him from charging off into some new Bay of Pigs. Helms did choose FitzGerald, who, however, tragically died two years later of a heart attack and was replaced by the other leading candidate at the time, Thomas Karamessines, a careful and meticulous Greek-American professional, who had cut his eye teeth on New York District Attorney Thomas E. Dewey's staff investigating New York corruption.

In late 1967, when Helms had been DCI for over a year, he called me into his office again, this time to suggest that I take over our Soviet and East European Division. I realized that Helms was thinking that my "time" was nearing and so he wanted to give me a chance with this job to show what I could do in the toughest professional intelligence area of all, against the "hard targets" of the closed Communist societies, and to shuck my stereotype as strictly a political and paramilitary operator.

Helms looked on the job as an important one. As a graduate of the FI culture he had been pushing hard for truly professional clandestine intelligence-gathering operations against these "hard targets" ever since he had taken over as DDP. But there was another reason. A few months before, the magazine *Ramparts* had carried its blockbuster exposure of CIA's political and propaganda operations in the international field, with detailed charts of the foundations, dummy sponsors and American organizations through which CIA's help to international fronts like the National Students Association had been funneled. The shock effect of the story, and in particular the impression it gave that CIA was active in the United States, made it clear that CIA's political and propaganda role in the future would have to be much limited. What's more, just about this time, the chairmen of the Congressional oversight committees insisted that the funds for CIA's Vietnam and Laos paramilitary operations be shifted to the Defense budget, so that CIA's activities in the paramilitary field be at least less conspicuous if not in fact sharply reduced. Thus, it was plain that Helms both by preference and as a result of outside pressures like these was putting the Agency's major emphasis on the FI culture and deemphasizing covert-action operations, and nowhere was FI more important than in the Soviet and Eastern European Division. So I accepted Helms's offer gladly, bought a Russian primer and started a series of briefings to learn something of my new job even before dropping out of the Far East at the end of January 1968.

As difficult as were the problems the Division faced in Eastern Europe, I soon discovered that it faced an almost greater problem in Washington. Because there were two schools at work in this field within the Agency, with vigorous differences between them. The division that I was to take over was an adherent of one school, working to develop sources behind the Iron Curtain, interrogate defectors from there, and contend with the bureaucratic problems of running clandestine operations in conjunction with allied intelligence services, especially about Soviet military matters. The other school centered in the Counterintelligence Staff, led by my former Italian-days acquaintance James Angleton. Its charter covered the activities of the Soviet Union's Komitet Gosudarstvennoy Bezopasnosti—the Committee of State Security, or KGB. Angleton and his staff carried on an unrelenting campaign to reveal and to frustrate the KGB's operations against American intelligence, and against America. He concentrated on doing so outside the United States; the task at home, of course, was the job of the Federal Bureau of Investigation, but Angleton worked closely with it in every way the two agencies could help each other.

The problem I saw before me stemmed from the fact that these two schools within CIA were in almost total conflict. The Division produced operations and intelligence, but the

CI staff believed that those operations and intelligence were controlled by the KGB, that the Russians deliberately fed us and manipulated information to mislead the United States in a massive deception program. In Angleton's view, CIA's agents and contacts behind the Iron Curtain were controlled by the KGB, the defectors who escaped were actually dispatched by the KGB with prepared stories, and some of our own officers were suspect of secret KGB links or insufficiently explained associations. I realized the extent of the problem when I learned that Angleton had never accepted the Sino-Soviet split as genuine; he believed it was a careful scenario set up to lead America to relax its vigilance, and he fiercely debated CIA's estimators as to whether it was real or not, well into the 1960s.

I was perfectly aware that the KGB was trying to frustrate CIA's operations, and that we had to count on its being successful to some degree. After all, CIA had seen the forged State Department cables and other documents that the KGB had distributed to African leaders to convince them that the United States was hostile to them. American "truth squads" were sent out to visit those leaders and prove that the documents were forgeries. We had also frequently unmasked false defectors, volunteering to spy for us as double agents, and turned them off. What's more, we knew that the KGB followed American diplomats in Eastern Europe and bugged their bedrooms to discover if they were on intelligence missions. And we were painfully aware that Soviet agents had appeared among our allies in intelligence, from Kim Philby to Otto John.

But even in the limited Division briefings that I received (and I agreed that I should not receive the most sensitive ones until I actually had the job and therefore a "need to know" such information), I sensed a major difficulty. Our concern over possible KGB penetration, it seemed to me, had so preoccupied us that we were devoting most of our time to protecting ourselves from the KGB and not enough to developing the new sources and operations that we needed to learn secret information about the Soviets and

their allies. Indeed, we seemed to be putting more emphasis on the KGB as CIA's adversary than on the Soviet Union
as the United States' adversary. Perhaps the ultimate example of this attitude was our rejection of Russian Colonel
Oleg Penkovskiy's first offer to spy for us late in 1960 in
Moscow, because he was suspected of being a provocateur;
our resistance was overcome only by his persistence in ap-
proaching the British, through whom his immensely valuable material was finally obtained.

Thus, I saw this as my first major challenge in the new
job, even before I could face the difficulties of effective intelligence penetrations in Eastern Europe. A bit along the
lines of my Vietnam experience, I realized that I would
have to try to get attention focused on the main priority
rather than on the subordinate ones. I would have to rally
morale and enthusiasm for the task of collecting intelligence
on what was happening and what would happen behind the
Iron Curtain politically, militarily, scientifically, and techno-
logically. I knew that I would have to pay attention to and
respect good counterintelligence work, and cooperate with
the CI staff responsible for it, but I wanted to consider the
KGB as something to be evaded by CIA, not as the object of
our operations nor as our mesmerizing nemesis. And if that
were to bring me into conflict with Angleton, so be it, but I
hoped I could accomplish what I was after without a direct
confrontation.

But before I got to the most sensitive briefings, or much
beyond the first lessons in my Russian grammar, Vietnam
suddenly intruded into my life again. Helms called me into
his office one afternoon. He had just come from the regular
"Tuesday lunch" of the principal advisers with President
Johnson and was thoroughly disgusted. Bob Komer, he said,
had put a fast one over on him. The President had turned to
Helms at the lunch and out of the blue had said that Komer
wanted that fellow Colby to go out to Vietnam to be his deputy as head of CORDS. And the President's tone had implied that Johnson expected immediate compliance. What
upset Helms was that Komer had not approached him first,

that it threw all his plans for me and for the Soviet operations up in the air, and that L.B.J. had ordered rather than
asked that I be available, and then had immediately gone on
to other subjects. Helms said he was sorry that this had happened, and asked what I thought we ought to do about it.

Stunned, I rapidly checked through the factors that affected the answer. The Soviet Division job was a great challenge, and obviously important to the Agency and to my future, but I had to admit that I had few if any special
qualifications for it. On the other hand, with my long and
intense work on Vietnam, and my repeated advocacy of exactly the kind of thing Komer was trying to accomplish, I
was an obvious choice for that job. I would have to go out to
Saigon alone this time, leaving Barbara and the family at
home, which would put a heavy burden on her. But the
same was true for the wives of the many CIA officers I had
drafted from the other divisions of the Agency to serve in
Vietnam. Moreover, I would have to leave CIA in order to
take the job, to make it clear that it was not just a cover, and
thus step off the regular career path in the Agency, with no
idea what might happen to me thereafter. But none of these
pros and cons produced a simple answer to Helms's question, so I asked for time overnight to discuss it with Barbara,
who after all deserved a full voice in a decision that would
impose a major burden on her. When we talked it out, the
determining factor was my duty to do the best I could for
the country, and that was to use my experience to help Komer's important work in Vietnam. I told Helms the next day
that neither he nor I could go to the President and say I
wouldn't go. So I would. Helms thanked me and told me to
work out the administrative arrangements any way that satisfied me. And he said he would certainly welcome me back
to CIA on my return. He could not have been more consid-
erate.

So I left CIA—really. I took leave without pay, so my
name would remain on the Agency roll, allowing me to
come back some day, and I went through all the procedures
to be hired by the Agency for International Development

and be assigned by it to CORDS in Saigon. This is a point worth underscoring in the light of misunderstandings later that the CORDS pacification program was some kind of cover for CIA. In fact, it was primarily a joint AID-military effort; they furnished most of the funds and people involved, supplemented by a few from the Foreign Service, CIA, and USIA.

As part of my preparation for the new job, I sat in on AID's program reviews when they prepared their new budget for Congress, and I witnessed them wrestle with the differences between the regular AID activities carried out under the direct authority of their office in Saigon and those that had been transferred to CORDS under Komer's authority for which they supplied the funds, matériel and personnel, but not the direction. Similarly, I visited the Pentagon to get to know something of its problems in keeping track of CORDS and its curious mix of civilian and military programs. CORDS itself had little or no funds or people of its own, and was merely the reflection of whatever idea Komer came up with to help win the village war, for which he then demanded that the line agencies supply the wherewithal. My job would be not only to help Komer but also to help the various agencies meet legal and regulatory requirements that applied to their programs worldwide but had few if any provisions for the wartime atmosphere that characterized Vietnam. If we ran into serious trouble in this regard, however, we knew that CORDS would have the full support of President Johnson, Ambassador Bunker and General Westmoreland—enough power to awe even the bureaucracy.

Helms and I arranged that I turn over my responsibilities for the Far East Division at the end of January, spend February briefing and joining AID, and go to Saigon on March 1. We made the schedule, despite the fact that I broke my ankle ice-skating on the C. & O. Canal with the family and shed the cast only the day before I departed. But something more serious occurred before my departure: the Tet offensive in Vietnam, which was to have a crucial impact on the course of the war there.

The 1968 Tet offensive has been studied, analyzed and debated from its very first moments. With some perspective, it can now be seen as an American journalist who was there put it:

> the attack forces—and particularly the indigenous Viet Cong, who did most the fighting and dying—suffered a grievous military setback . . . Because the people of the cities did not rise up against the foreigners and puppets at Tet—indeed they gave little support to the attack forces—the Communist claim to moral and political authority in South Vietnam suffered a serious blow . . . the South Vietnamese government faltered but did not fold, and after the battle became more of a working institution than it ever had been before . . . The irony of the Tet Offensive is that the North Vietnamese and the Viet Cong suffered a battlefield setback in the war zone, but still won the political victory in the United States. [Don Oberdorfer, *Tet*, pp. 329–30]

This "irony" is at the heart of the modern intelligence process. It now is clear that the Tet offensive was not a Communist military success in Vietnam; but it is equally clear that it was indeed a Communist propaganda victory in the United States. The reason this occurred was in part because of the posture of the American government since the earliest days of the military buildup in Vietnam, with its periodic reports of "progress" and its insistence that more and more American military power and machinery would change the direction of the war. It was also, in part, due to the lack of understanding of the Vietnamese by the Americans on short tours there, unfamiliar with the language and applying American psychological standards. And it was a result, too, of the impact of modern journalistic techniques on the American people, who were unable to distinguish whether the events reported were exceptional or representative, and who found it difficult to fit careful assessments of quiet realities into their sensation-filled attention spans. Like the immolations of the Buddhist bonzes, Tet so dominated television screens and the emotions that it equally dominated popular decision-making, and the full reality of what had happened became clear only after the decisions had been taken. Some would argue that the decisions were correct, that the dramatic events merely crystalized what was a long-coming change in the American people's view of the war; and it is, after all, the people's view wherein power rests ultimately in the democratic system of the United States. The problem with this argument is that such a process of decision-making is both delayed and costly. A proper intelligence system should bring the information that would speed up the process, and an American intelligence system should bring it not only in secret to government officials, but also in its essence to the people, who control the ultimate decisions.

Nonetheless, in my view, the decision in fact was correct. For at long last Washington decided that United States military forces were not the answer to the Vietnamese war. And out of this decision came a series of crucial steps: Johnson's withdrawal from the Presidential campaign, the beginning of the withdrawal of American forces in Vietnam, the change of focus from action by Americans to responsibility of South Vietnamese, and—with direct impact on me—the rise to first priority of the Vietnamese pacification program supported by CORDS. Even before I departed for Saigon, on a snowy March 1, I told Barbara and my friends that the first thing I'd do in my new job would be to try to get weapons into the hands of the Vietnamese villagers so they could participate in their own defense. Tet's effect in the United States made this an urgent priority, for it was clear that American assistance to Vietnam was likely to diminish as the antiwar movement, which had been given a large stimulus by Tet, grew. The race now would be between Vietnam's ability to defend itself and the rising American revulsion against the war. If Vietnam could become strong enough to do the fighting itself, American financial and logistics assistance would probably continue; but if the future looked bleak, even that aid would be cut off. With 550,000 well-equipped American fighting men to be taken out of the war, the Vietnamese Army would be hard pressed to provide the military shield against the North Vietnamese forces. And the only possible way it could do it was by being relieved of any responsibility for the countryside of South Vietnam by enlisting and arming the South Vietnamese people in a program to eliminate the guerrilla war there. The sight of a bombing run in progress just off the right wing of the Pan Am plane, which brought me back into Saigon's Tan Son Nhut Airport for my second tour in Vietnam, made dramatically clear just how much work that would involve.

But the first order of business upon my arrival, both for me and CORDS, was dealing with the aftermath of the Tet offensive. The country was in a state of ravaged turmoil and chaos as a result of the attacks. Great portions of the major cities and provincial centers were burned out and in rubble, hundreds of thousands of refugees were homeless, and in many areas transport, markets and other essential services had broken down. Before any of our more sophisticated projects could be contemplated, the awful destruction had to be repaired and the homeless housed and fed—and it was up to CORDS to work with the Vietnamese to do so.

So my first few months were given over to working for Komer on "Operation Recovery"—rebuilding towns, distributing food and materials, repairing bridges, reestablishing electrical systems and restarting all the other elements of people's lives. Tents were shipped in for refugee camps, and the homeless moved into them from where they huddled in temples and public buildings in the major centers. Cement for houses and tin for roofs were distributed for the reconstruction of devastated villages. We worked with the volunteer relief groups, Quakers, Catholics, and the like, to get food to people so that they wouldn't starve. Units of military engineers were seconded to aid in the repair of bombed-out bridges and to sweep roads for mines. Schools were rebuilt, marketplaces reopened, and hospitals and medical-aid centers repaired. And it all had to be done in an atmosphere of concern that the Viet Cong might strike again. So barbed wire was strung around the towns, roadblocks went up at night with defense positions, and food shipments were inspected for smuggled grenades and weapons. Both to see how this program was progressing and as a briefing for my new duties (which included ducking mortar and rocket attacks), I traveled widely throughout the war-torn country, visiting the regional and provincial capitals, renewing some old acquaintances from my previous tour and making new ones and meeting that band of dedicated Americans, some from the military, others from the various civilian agencies, whom Komer had gotten assigned to CORDS. There were some 800 civilians by then, a number that would rise to about 1,200 in the next three years, and about 3,000 military, which would increase to over 6,000 in that same period. About 600 were stationed in Saigon, 150 were assigned to each of the four corps into which the country was divided, about 1,000 to the forty-four provinces, and another 1,500 in the 240-odd districts, working in the villages and hamlets. And among them surely one of the most impressive and dedicated was John Paul Vann.

Vann had originally come to Vietnam in the early 1960s as a military adviser to the South Vietnamese Army. His high personal standards and his assertive personality had made him openly critical of the Diem regime, the Vietnamese Army's performance, and the optimistic statements of his own superiors, and he became one of the key sources for American journalists questioning the effectiveness of United States support of Diem. After his public criticism of the Vietnamese Army's dismal performance at Ap Bac in January 1963, he took early retirement from the U.S. Army. But his commitment to Vietnam and the need to fight the people's war correctly was so great that he had returned in 1964 as a field officer for AID.

We had met once in Washington, when he had criticized the Revolutionary Development Cadre program as much less effective than CIA thought it was. And although I at the time had said I understood his points but nonetheless believed it was a major step in the right direction, he rather feared now that I might have a grudge against him for having dared to challenge CIA. By the time I arrived, he was serving as the CORDS senior official in the Third Corps around the Saigon area. He still hadn't learned to keep his mouth shut; he was terribly sure of himself, always convinced that he had the right answer, and was disliked by those who favored bureaucratic and hierarchical values. But both Komer and I knew he was a man of incredible dedication, bravery and energy, with a detailed understanding of the Vietnamese situation and what needed to be done. He relentlessly roamed the Third Corps area in his helicopter or motorcycle, and stayed in intimate touch with all the levels of the CORDS structure and the Vietnamese officialdom. On one of my first trips with him, we went at night to a village near Bien Hoa to see its efforts to protect itself from the Communists. After we toured its outposts of local young men standing guard, the village chief presented me with a sword. "Do you know what that's made out of?" Vann asked me. I turned the blade over in my hand and shook my head. "It's made out of a Jeep spring," Vann said. "It's the only kind of weapon these people have. That's all they have to fight the Communists with. But they want to fight them nevertheless." The village chief then spoke up and said that their greatest desire was for real weapons—carbines, rifles, anything—so they could protect their village.

Vann's intelligence on me and my interests was perfect, of course; the visit obviously reinforced my conviction that we should arm the people, and it gave me a dramatic argument to use to do so. We agreed that the key to victory in Vietnam was fighting and winning the war on the village level, and that ultimately the most important thing that we could do was to develop an effective program of village self-defense. For the moment we both realized we had to concentrate on cleaning up the havoc wrought by the Tet offensive. But when this effort was well and successfully underway—and all in all nearly a million people were helped temporarily until they could return to their homes or be resettled in new locations—I turned my attention to the matter of self-defense, with Komer's full support.

The idea of arming the population—volunteer or chosen by the village elders to take a turn at night guard duty, but

unpaid, untrained, un-uniformed, and possibly undisci-
plined—sounded like madness to many Vietnamese and
Americans alike. Some believed that the weapons would
simply be passed to or be captured by the Communists, that
the self-defense forces wouldn't fight even if they had them.
Others were fearful that the weapons would be used by political opposition groups against the government, as in the
days of the bandit and armed religious sects; and still others
were sure that a wide and indiscriminate distribution of
weapons would increase the incidence of internecine
crimes. So to each of these objections I had to formulate a
persuasive response. For example, to the fear that the Communists would get hold of the weapons, I replied that the
Communists didn't need our weapons since they had plenty
of better AK-47s of their own. As for the question whether or
not armed villagers would make an effective fighting force
against the Communists, my answer was that wasn't the real
object of the exercise; it was rather to enlist the population
in the war, give them an alternative to conscription into
Communist guerrilla groups, help them defend their home
communities, and provide intelligence and alerts for the territorial forces. On the problem that the weapons would lead
to sect war or crime, I said that a careful and gradual oil-spot
approach would ensure the government's full control; and
by limiting the weaponry to rifles and banning pistols, the
risk that they might be used for burglary or robbery, or political disputes, as in the Philippines, would be lessened. But
my most forceful argument, and the one that Komer used
and President Nguyen Van Thieu accepted, was that the
Vietnamese government had to rely on the active support of
its people if it were to overcome the Communist challenge,
and that putting weapons in their hands was the best way to
dramatize this reliance, for it would let the villager know
that the government trusted him enough to give him the
power to point a gun against *his* enemies, not just the government's.

That I finally did get through with these arguments was
illustrated in an exchange that I had with Tran Van Huong,

then the South Vietnamese Prime Minister and a former teacher in the French school system. When I heard that he was one of the staunchest opponents of the self-defense scheme, I composed a letter to him in somewhat fractured French outlining all my arguments. A few days later I saw him at a ceremony, asked his reaction, and apologized for my French. The French, he said, was "execrable" but he accepted the arguments and supported Thieu's decision to go ahead.

Coincidence helped to launch the program. Komer's program to modernize and re-equip the South Vietnamese Territorial Forces with M-16 rifles was just then in full swing. The Territorial Forces—known on the provincial level as Regional Forces and on the district level as Popular Forces—were a kind of National Guard, or militia, made up of full-time paid soldiers who were assigned to the defense of their home areas. One of Komer's great accomplishments in his first months on the job was to arrange that the American support for these Territorial Forces be transferred from the direct chain-of-command of the military and placed under the management and supervision of CORDS, where they could get better than the secondary attention the regular military had been giving them for years. And now he had also managed to bull through the bureaucracy a program to rearm these forces with M-16 rifles and other more modern weaponry. What this accomplished, besides obviously making the Territorial Forces more potent and effective, was to free their old carbines and rifles for use by villagers.

Perhaps this point needs to be underscored for the sake of avoiding the confusion between Territorial Forces and self-defense forces that often plagued the program. The Territorial Forces were full-time professional soldiers, albeit assigned to the local defense of the provinces, districts and villages, but not to the offensive military sweeps of the regular army. The self-defense forces, however, were the villagers themselves, peasants or shopkeepers who served without pay only on occasion, such as when standing guard duty on the perimeter of their village at night or in the event of a Communist attack. And it was to them that we now had the old weapons of the Territorial Forces distributed, and arranged that they receive rudimentary training from the local Territorial Forces, whom they supported and to whom they looked for help when needed.

Although in the end more than 500,000 such weapons were ultimately distributed, they were not handed out indiscriminately. Rather, the strategy was that of the old oil-spot concept, in which a village or cluster of hamlets was selected as the nucleus of the program and from which it then spread slowly into the surrounding countryside to secure always more and more territory and people—defensive in tactics, offensive in strategy. To get it going, we used the Revolutionary Development Teams that had been organized by the CIA and had since then been integrated into CORDS. These 59-man teams of full-time, paid and well-trained organizers and fighters were sent into the selected villages to help organize the village government and teach the villagers the use of the weapons and the rudiments of self-defense, helping them to build guard posts, stringing barbed wire, demonstrating patrol techniques, and the like. At the same time other members of the team taught new agricultural techniques to improve the rice crops, helped the villagers to rebuild their homes or construct new irrigation ditches, re-established village schools and had teachers sent out from the province center, set up local medical-aid stations, and all the rest that would bring a secure and better way of life to an ever-increasing number of the population. Once the village was self-sustaining, the team would be moved to another village for inclusion in the oil spot and repeat the process.

As Komer and I discussed the CORDS program in the early summer, we agreed that Operation Recovery had done much of its job, even despite a Communist attempt to repeat the Tet assault in May. The South Vietnamese had shown that they could survive a Communist offensive, and the weakness of the May attacks compared with Tet showed that the enemy had obviously been hurt. It was time, then, for the government to take the initiative and counterattack, to press forward on a strategy that would produce permanent results rather than just an interval during which the enemy could prepare another offensive. And that strategy should be pacification—that is, organizing the countryside to participate in a campaign for security and development, so as to take from the enemy any hope for a base in the population from which to fight the government. We also foresaw the possibility of a cease-fire, either from a bid by the enemy or from the pressure of the American public, still shaken by Tet.

We searched around for another name than "pacification," because of its connotation that the population was to be forced into quiescence, when the idea was precisely the opposite, to activate the people in the villages. But we finally gave up; we could find no other simple word and we did not want to come up with a repetition of such artificial phrases as "revolutionary development." ("Rural development" was a possibility, but it sounded more like a program only to improve agricultural production rather than the political and security effort that was really necessary.) In retrospect, I now feel, we should have chosen some single code name and let its meaning grow from the way the program developed in the countryside.

As a step toward promoting our strategy, Komer asked me to prepare a briefing for the September MACV Commanders Conference, with all the leading American military and civilian chiefs in attendance, describing the nature of the war in the countryside and the enemy there. To that audience I set forth something different from the usual rundown of Communist main- and local-force battalions, logistics chains from Hanoi through Laos and Cambodia, and bombing targets in the North. I outlined instead the structure and functions of the Lao Dong Party and its southern section, named the People's Revolutionary Party, the National Liberation Front, the Provisional Government of South Vietnam, the Liberation Committees and National Alliance of Democratic Forces, which had made post-Tet appearances. I pointed out that these had failed to attract much popular support, but they nevertheless were the phantom political skeleton that the Communists would use in any negotiation for a peace treaty or cease-fire.

I then went on to note that this chain of political committees, from local communities up to the national level, constituted the true chain of authority in the enemy organization, the military committees and units merely constituting one of their responsibilities at each echelon. With this understanding of the enemy, it became easy to see that the Saigon government's principal task was to counter every aspect of the Communists' efforts, particularly its political ones, and not concentrate only on trying to crush its main-force military units through "search and destroy" or B-52 bomber strikes.

Thus, I urged the need for us to work with the Vietnamese government to revive village government in the countryside, to demonstrate real hope for a better economic and social life for the people, to show that permanent security for the villager would be possible with his help and with reinforcement from the territorial forces, while the regular army kept the enemy main forces away, and to identify and remove from the population those secret members of the enemy apparatus who threatened reprisal against villagers leaning toward support of the government. Four "campaigns" could carry out this strategy, I suggested: a "spoiling" one in which regular military forces drove enemy main forces away and attacked their bases; a "preemption" campaign to move territorial forces and government presence into areas of enemy threat; a "pacification" campaign to harden important population centers and their lines of communication against enemy intrusion; and a "political" campaign to establish democratic legitimacy through elections from the village level on up and so generate popular support for the struggle against the Communist threat. I ended with an oral flourish, saying that these campaigns should be launched so as to turn the war around by the anniversary of the Tet offensive in February 1969.

One member of the audience listened to me with close

attention and obvious understanding. He tapped his cigar thoughtfully and thanked me for the briefing—and then gave Komer his approval to go ahead and develop the proposal in depth with President Thieu. He was Creighton W. Abrams, who had just succeeded Westmoreland as the commander of America's military forces in Vietnam, and consequently Komer's boss. He was chiefly known as a tough and determined tanker, in World War II with Patton on that dash across France which liberated my *maquis* friends in the Yonne, and since in a series of assignments including the command of the forces sent to help open the University of Alabama to integrated education under Kennedy. He had been given over-all command in the northern Hue area of Vietnam during the weeks of fighting there after the Tet offensive. And he proved to be one of the most sensitive of all Americans in his appreciation of what pacification was all about, and of the importance of the Vietnamese villagers and people in the strategy of the war.

With Abrams' approval, Komer moved. In a furious few weeks of work we sketched out a series of programs that Komer convinced Thieu to adopt as an "Accelerated Pacification Campaign" to seize the initiative of the war in the countryside, and to make pacification the central strategy of the Saigon government. Its key feature was a set of specific, measurable goals, in numbers, to be issued by President Thieu calling for 1,000 hamlets to be brought from a contested to a relatively secure state, 200,000 weapons to be distributed to self-defense groups, 3,000 members of the Viet Cong infrastructure to be put out of action, and the like.

The mention of statistics in connection with Vietnam automatically raises a credibility gap, so a word on this subject is essential. A war is a contest, and traditionally the way to measure whether it is being won or lost is by the location of the forces involved, whether the front lines are closer to the enemy's capital or to the friendly one. Political contests also have indicators by which to ascertain their outcome, through elections in democratic countries or by who is wielding authority in totalitarian ones. But in a political war, where secrecy and subversion are the central facts, these indicators do not work, and the only real measure of who is winning or losing is the attitude of the people rather than the location of troops. For years arguments raged as to how the war was going, and intense efforts were made to determine a way to measure the contest. For a time, McNamara's detailed accountings of American contributions to Vietnam seemed to imply that their volume alone should show the trend of events. But this proved to have the fallacy of not showing the enemy's inputs into the war, which in some cases were the "feeling" that Des FitzGerald had stressed to a doubting McNamara. Then incidental aspects of the war were selected to serve as indicators, from the number of terrorist incidents to the ultimately repulsive "body count." These met competition from more subjective assessments such as John McCone's dispatch of "old Vietnam hands" and the incidents selected by journalists for inclusion in *their* assessments.

In 1966, CIA was asked by McNamara to come up with a technique by which to measure trends in pacification, and it developed the Hamlet Evaluation System to do so. It contained certain "objective" features, such as whether or not a Popular Force platoon was in place, but it also relied heavily on "subjective" assessments, principally to try to measure the quality of life of the hamlet dweller—whether he lived in some tranquillity or was subjected to raids and mortar attacks, whether or not his children attended school, whether he could travel regularly and safely to the nearby market town. Its other major feature was that the measurements were made by the American adviser in the district. Now, obviously, the American was a foreigner, and on a one-year tour at that; obviously he was only a visitor to the hamlet itself; obviously some of the questions were inherently almost impossible to answer with the precision they seemed to call for; and obviously a mathematical compilation of the responses from all the hamlets suggested a false average instead of the wide individual variations that lay beneath it. Thus, for all of these obvious reasons, the HES was roundly criticized as just another attempt to apply American statistical techniques to a primitive society, if not a deliberate attempt to mislead the American public.

But despite that, the HES had some remarkable elements. The fact that an American adviser filled out the questionnaire meant that it was independent of Vietnamese pressure to come up with a favorable report to placate senior Vietnamese officials. The fact that the same questions had to be answered for each hamlet nationwide allowed comparisons between geographic areas on specific subjects, replacing the generalizations that had characterized previous assessments—the broad sweep of the provincial chief's hand accompanied by the comment, "that area is in quite good shape." And the capabilities of the computer allowed the individual answers to be analyzed in an infinite variety of ways, over time, isolating the effects of individual programs.

But perhaps the most impressive effect of the HES was on local officials, from province and district chiefs down to village leaders. They soon became aware that President Thieu was using the system to measure the situation in their areas, and referring to its results on his inspection trips and reviews, so they immediately began to examine how to contend with it. The variety of their alibis soon paid tribute to their imagination, the subtlety of their efforts to influence their American advisers spoke well of their potential as diplomats, but they soon discovered that the easiest and best way to affect the ratings of their hamlets was actually to do some of the things that the system measured—send a platoon to establish a permanent post in the vicinity or train and arm a small self-defense group. And so this measurement system proved to have its main value as a stimulus to action, more effective than orders of the day and exhortations by senior officials.

In the middle of the surge of activity to launch the Accelerated Pacification Campaign on November 1, to give it three full months to show its effect by Tet, Komer received a message from the White House. Lyndon Johnson had by then taken himself out of the Presidential election campaign, and was facing the end of his term in the White House. But one of the things he could still do was to thank the people who had worked long, hard and well for him, and high on the list was Bob Komer. So when the opportunity came to nominate a new ambassador to Turkey, L.B.J. remembered that the Middle East had been Bob's first area of interest, and he named him to the post. On November 6, I bade Komer farewell and thanked him for what he had done for "our" program in Vietnam—in short, making it a reality—and turned away from his plane to make it work. A few days thereafter President Johnson gave me the personal rank of ambassador to ensure that I had the authority to do so. (One of my old CIA associates sent me a message about this high title for a professional intelligence officer, albeit on leave without pay, saying, "Not since Nell Gwynn made it have the rest of us girls been so impressed.")

And make it work we did. President Thieu personally took the lead on the Vietnamese side. He set up a special Central Pacification and Development Council with a staff of its own reporting directly to the Prime Minister and working closely with the CORDS staff in Saigon. He traveled regularly to the provinces and invariably took me along to show that the Americans were as fully committed to the program as he was, and General Abrams forcefully made the same point to the American military command chain. For my part, I decided that I would spend at least two nights a week in the provinces with a local CORDS team to talk out with the American advisers and the Vietnamese provincial officials the problems and the progress the campaign was having. I learned a lot more over a reasonable quantity of alcohol in the evening than I did through briefings and ceremonial visits to carefully prepared hamlets during the day, and I met some devoted younger officers whom I could bring, kicking and screaming, to the Saigon headquarters to expose the staffs there to some field realities—Stephen Young, committed to the revival of the Vietnamese village community; Frank Scotton, fluent in Vietnamese and direct in his identification and complaints about insensitive Americans; and many others. The result on all sides was a feeling that the Vietnamese government had taken the initiative on a new and important campaign, and that it could work, through small and solid steps.

As the three-month campaign gained momentum, we turned some of our attention to the next step: the full-year pacification-and-development program that would follow it. And here I had the chance to try out my idea that political development from the ground up was really the central part of winning a people's war, and not just a supplement to the military and territorial-force activity.

In 1967, as a part of the new constitutional process in Vietnam, elections had been scheduled throughout the country, but the security situation in over half the 2,224 villages had made it impossible to hold them. It seemed to me that this was something on which the government now could put major emphasis, and demonstrate clearly to the rural population how its approach differed from that of the Communists. So, to the other elements of the pacification program I added a series of goals to strengthen local government, including holding elections in all possible villages and hamlets, giving authority to the village council over the local Popular Force unit (instead of having it report to the military district command), and launching a national training program for village and hamlet leaders to be conducted at the CIA-supported training center at Vung Tau, where my old friend Nguyen Be was still director. There the students would be familiarized with their duties, of course. But they would also be assured that, as elected officials, they were the leaders and representatives of their communities, not merely the administrators of central-government programs. And they received more CIA-supplied black pajamas to symbolize their status. President Thieu made a practice of visiting each class to add his assurances to the same effect and, certainly, to capitalize on this unique opportunity to carry his political message to this nationwide collection of influential local leaders.

But the program that perhaps had the greatest impact was

a simple one—giving funds to the elected village leaders to carry out local development programs. During a visit to a rural community up the coast, I had noticed a schoolhouse that had lost its roofing during a typhoon and heard that the local farmers had stripped it and used the remnants on their own property. When I asked them why they hadn't repaired the schoolhouse so their children could go to school, they replied that the school belonged to the government so it was up to the government to repair it. To alter this attitude, which reflected so much of Vietnam's history and culture, I initiated a village development program in which funds were made available directly to village governments (but only after elections were held), to be used as they saw fit for local improvement projects; the program's regulations required public discussion on alternative proposals and strictly forbade district and provincial-level officials from exercising their usual role of approving or disapproving decisions made by village chiefs.

The village officials, who were briefed on this in their training sessions at Vung Tau, were awed at the revolutionary idea that they would actually make decisions about anything as important as money. And I was treated to the spectacle of an impassioned denunciation of the idea in a regional meeting of province chiefs, where one complained that the undependable local chiefs would waste the money on useless projects or siphon it off for their own good—to which the Prime Minister answered in firm and determined tones that the government was committed to a program to build democratic government in the villages, that the province chiefs would be required to support it and that they must learn to recognize the difference between the right of villagers to make mistakes and any cases of outright abuse, which the inspection system could and should catch. Some money was certainly wasted, and some was undoubtedly stolen, but the real purpose of the program—stimulating local leadership and responsibility—was equally certainly achieved. The test of perfection was certainly not met, but the test of the comparative appeal of the South Vietnamese and the Communist approaches was, and that was the object of the operation.

The preparation of an annual pacification plan, for 1969 and each year thereafter, proved to be a vehicle by which the Vietnamese government's entire program was drawn into one national strategy to fight the war and at the same time to develop the country. Since the national plan was supplemented by provincial and even village plans, it became a way for Thieu to stress the programs that he thought important, educate the bureaucracy in how to fit their separate activities together and ensure that all the American agencies worked as a team in support of the effort. The other CORDS projects were easily included: the resettlement or return to their villages of refugees; the gradual expansion of the zone of security of the Territorial Forces; convincing members of the enemy camp that the government's offer of amnesty was both real and safe to accept; assigning the RD Cadre teams more to the political tasks they were originally designed for, rather than having them devote so much of their time to defending themselves and the villages; and moving trained police officers from urban areas into the countryside to serve under village chiefs and to begin the process of normal law enforcement in areas that had not seen it in years.

Similarly, the annual plans provided a way to bring the work of the regular Vietnamese ministries and the American agencies supporting them into the over-all strategy and provided a means of monitoring what they actually accomplished in the countryside while convincing local officials that these activities were what President Thieu wanted, not merely the paper ideas of Saigon bureaucrats. Thus, promotion of AID's new "miracle rice" vastly increasing production after careful briefing in proper fertilizer and irrigation procedures; Thieu's innovative land-reform program to provide title to farmers without payment; agricultural loan banks and cooperatives; training and assignments of teachers; provincial hospitals and local medical services; the dissemination of news through local information cadre; benefits for veterans and their widows and orphans; separate status and development programs for the highland minorities (with highlander and not merely Vietnamese officials); and urban problems—all these were brought into a comprehensive national plan and turned into specific goals at the local level for monitoring and inspection. Each of these had to be negotiated with my AID or USIA colleagues, but the over-all theme remained the one which Clay McManaway, the imaginative AID planning officer for CORDS, and I developed and which President Thieu quickly adopted: Self-Defense, Self-Government, and Self-Development. It was a theme applicable not only to local communities but to all of Vietnam as a nation, and it fitted precisely into the new Nixon Doctrine and its application in Vietnamization.

CHAPTER NINE

Phoenix and "Peace"

O_F all the individual programs that made up CORDS, the one that has received the most attention and publicity is Phoenix, the operation to identify and root out the secret Communist apparatus within South Vietnam, the so-called Viet Cong Infrastructure, or VCI. It is the program that has been most closely identified with me, a fact that I have never chosen to contest, because I have no qualms about accepting responsibility for its activities. But it is also a program that has been equally closely identified with CIA, adding further to the reputation for secret skullduggery under which the Agency labors to this day. On both scores, that is wrong and unfair.

It is true that the Agency did lead the effort to understand the role and combat the activities of the VCI. The Agency's work with the Special Branch of the Vietnamese Police and with the Vietnamese Central Intelligence Organization, for example, involved primarily the collecting of information on, and determining the details of, the VCI's makeup, through penetrations, interrogations, interception of couriers and communications, translation of captured documents, analysis of propaganda writings and broadcasts, and thorough scholarly study and review. Moreover, the Agency also spent much effort trying to organize a series of intelligence centers at which similar work being done by other Vietnamese and American agencies could be exchanged, compared and coordinated, while protecting each Agency's sources from exposure to the others that they did not trust with such sensitive information.

But like the over-all pacification effort itself, the Agency could not do it all, thus the American leadership, and especially Komer, insisted that CIA participate in a larger inter-agency effort rather than quietly work off to the side on its own. So in mid-1967, Komer came up with a joint MACV-CIA program called ICEX (Intelligence Coordination and Exploitation) to work on the VCI, and in December a decree by the Prime Minister enlisted the Vietnamese agencies in the effort. Thus was Phoenix (Phung Hoang in Vietnamese) born. It was set aside during the Tet offensive and then by Operation Recovery, but when Komer and I were able to think about pacification strategy again, we returned to it, and my CIA background (and participation in the debates leading up to the formation of ICEX) enabled me to help turn the Phoenix program into a CORDS operation—with, to be sure, participation by CIA, as well as other intelligence, police and military services, but not as a CIA program. In July 1968, President Thieu issued a decree, which I helped to draft, establishing a series of Phoenix committees at the national, regional, provincial and even district level, to which all the agencies involved had to furnish representation, and which set goals, as part of the Accelerated Pacification Campaign, on how many of the VCI should be captured, induced to rally to the government under the amnesty program, or put out of action by military or police force.

If for no other reason than the turmoil in Vietnam, we knew there was a VCI, but we could not be said to know very much about it. We knew that it was big—the best estimates putting it at well over 70,000—and we knew that it was active, since we saw the assassinations of village chiefs and local officials that it perpetrated, the mines it buried in the roads to blast the busloads of women bringing their produce to early morning markets, the taxes and young men it collected from isolated hamlets, the agit-prop sessions it conducted in remote villages. We also knew that the struggle against it would not be successful if we just blindly struck out into the countryside to ambush anyone slinking along the rice paddies at night in violation of curfew orders or held the kind of mass "screenings" of a community of the type I saw a frustrated American army unit hold in a mood between fury and futility. Since our fundamental strategy in pacification was to enlist the population in the war effort, any case of abuse or mistaken punishment, whether by vicious intent or ignorant error, could only constitute a setback to our program. Action against a guilty member of the VCI might generate regret and sympathy among his family, but it would be understood and accepted as a natural aspect of the war and his role in it. But action against an innocent person would produce hostility and sullen resistance throughout his village, causing a far greater loss to our campaign than any ten proper arrests could compensate for.

Thus, our first step was to make sure that the intelligence we gathered on the VCI was accurate, and for this we set up standards and procedures by which to weed out the false from the correct information. CORDS increased its advisory staff, assigning Phoenix advisers on the national level to help formulate the program's doctrine and procedures and then on down to the district level to help local authorities work up comprehensive card files and dossiers on VCI suspects, separating out the cases with good evidence from those without it. Suspects were assigned to one of three categories: "A" for leaders and formal party members, "B" for holders of other responsible jobs—cadre—and "C" for rank-and-file members and followers. And the decision was taken that those in the "C" category should be ignored, since Phoenix was directed against the VCI command and control structure and not the occasional adherent or supporter. Forms for the dossiers were printed up so that the reliability of the information concerning any individual could be conveniently examined, and the general rule was established that three separate sources must have reported a suspect before he could be put on the rolls. The Phoenix centers at the district level gradually improved their records on the local

VCI and eventually could give briefings of the political order of battle in their areas to match the ones on the military order of battle of the main and local forces and guerrillas. An incidental effect of having CORDS run this program, as well as the other paramilitary operations of the CIA station, was that the station could concentrate on the penetration of the Communist apparatus both unilaterally and with the Special Branch, and I soon saw a real improvement in this regard over what I remembered from my days as Saigon Station Chief and Division Chief. We were getting more—and more accurate—reports from inside VCI provincial committees and regional party headquarters from brave Vietnamese holding high ranks in such groups. They had been first identified by people who knew them, then recruited by our intelligence officers. Some helped because they were disillusioned with their harsh North Vietnamese bosses, others in order to collect cash or favors for themselves and their families, and still others because they saw the war in their areas going against the VC and wanted to be on the winning side at the end.

The object of Phoenix, of course, was not merely to collect an academic treatise on the VCI but to contribute to the fight against it. Here another error is prevalent about Phoenix. Phoenix in fact had no forces of its own, thus it never conducted operations itself against the VCI. The information it assembled and analyzed was turned over to the services that had the forces, authority and responsibility for such operations—the military, the police, the amnesty program, the local administration—and with that information *they* mounted the actions against the suspects identified by Phoenix. The top VCI cadre in a village, for example, might be arrested by the police; a key VCI leader's family might be approached by an amnesty team urging them to convince him to surrender to the government; a provincial VCI committee's guerrilla headquarters might be chosen as the target for encirclement and attack by the province's Regional Force battalion. At the end of each of these operations, the unit conducting it would report its result to the local Phoenix center, the cadre arrested, the amnesties claimed, the prisoners taken, and the identified VCI leaders killed in the attack. The Phoenix committee would then report to Saigon that the arrested, the captives, the amnestied and the killed were no longer on the VCI list of that district—and thus the program was that much closer to reaching its goal of reducing VCI power in that area. Phoenix helped this process, of course, but the supposition that it was an independent force rampaging through the countryside is just wrong.

But didn't Phoenix do something more? Didn't it, in fact, undertake to organize and supervise an assassination campaign in its attempt to destroy the Viet Cong Infrastructure and in the process wind up murdering some 20,000 people, many of them innocents? That is a charge that has been hurled at Phoenix—and at me—repeatedly in recent years. And the short answer to it is: No.

As early as 1969, I issued a directive on the subject of assassination and other equally repugnant activities. I was prompted to do so when I learned that an American CORDS officer, who had been assigned to Phoenix, applied for transfer because he feared that the program was immoral, and my directive is worth quoting in full here, because it bears so directly on the misunderstandings that have plagued Phoenix for so long.

> The Phoenix program is one of advice, support and assistance to the GVN Phung Hoang program, aimed at reducing the influence and effectiveness of the Viet Cong Infrastructure in South Vietnam. The Viet Cong Infrastructure is an inherent part of the war effort being waged against the GVN by the Viet Cong and their North Vietnamese allies. The unlawful status of members of the Viet Cong Infrastructure (as defined in the Green Book and in GVN official decrees) is well established in GVN law and is in full accord with the laws of land warfare followed by the United States Army.
>
> Operations against the Viet Cong Infrastructure include: the collection of intelligence identifying those members, inducing them to abandon their allegiance to the Viet Cong and rally to the government, capturing or arresting them in order to bring them before Province Security Committees for lawful sentenc-

ing, and, as a final resort, the use of military or police force against them if no other way of preventing them from carrying on their unlawful activities is possible. Our training emphasizes the desirability of obtaining these target individuals alive and of using intelligent and lawful methods of interrogation to obtain the truth of what they know about other aspects of the VCI. U.S. personnel are under the same legal and moral constraints with respect to operations of a Phoenix character as they are with respect to regular military operations against enemy units in the field. Thus, they are specifically not authorized to engage in assassinations or other violations of the rules of land warfare, but they are entitled to use such reasonable military force as is necessary to obtain the goals of rallying, capturing or eliminating the VCI in the RVN.

If U.S. personnel come in contact with activities conducted by Vietnamese which do not meet the standards of land warfare, they are certainly not to participate further in the activity. They are also expected to make their objections to this kind of behavior known to the Vietnamese conducting them, and they are expected to report the circumstances to the next higher U.S. authority for decision as to action to be taken with the GVN.

There are individuals who find normal police or even military operations repugnant to them personally, despite the over-all legality and morality of these activities. Arrangements exist whereby individuals having this feeling about military affairs can, according to law, receive specialized assignments or even exemptions from military service. There is no similar legislation with respect to police-type activities of the U.S. military, but if an individual finds the police-type activities of the Phoenix program repugnant to him, on his application, he can be reassigned from the program without prejudice.

The purpose of this directive was to clarify immediately the question of the proper limits of Phoenix activity, and I wanted to do so openly and on the record. For any looseness or ambiguity on this matter was not only unacceptable to me personally but, I knew, could result in the kind of repudiation of our pacification program that had occurred to the French in Algeria, when France's near-victory there was fatally undermined by a French journalist's accusation that torture was an accepted practice in the French Army's prosecution of that antiguerrilla war. Nonetheless many casual readers of the press and of journals of extreme opinion still

believe—and what's more, believe that I have admitted—
that Phoenix was responsible for the assassination of 20,000
Vietnamese, innocent as well as guilty. And this charge is
repeated in some circles whenever my name comes up, bid-
ding fair to become an accepted myth about me. It simply is
not true, as I have testified under oath several times.

To some degree, I am responsible for that 20,000 figure
gaining popular currency. At a 1971 Congressional committee hearing, at which I was asked to testify on Phoenix, I
reported that under the program from 1968 to 1971 some
17,000 had chosen amnesty, some 28,000 had been captured, and some 20,000 had been killed. But the word was
"killed," not "assassinated," and I went on to clarify that the
vast percentage of these—over 85 percent—were killed in
combat actions with Vietnamese and American military and
paramilitary troops and only about 12 percent by police or
other security forces. What's more, most of the latter deaths
occurred in fights when the VCI cadre, whom the police
were trying to round up and capture, resisted arrest, fled, or
otherwise defended themselves. I specifically denied that
Phoenix was a program to assassinate VCI and pointed to
the clear 1969 directive that I had issued on this point.

Nonetheless, the records of the hearings were replete
with horror stories. And, although on examination these incidents turned out to have occurred in 1967, before Phoenix
existed, or to have involved American military units rather
than Phoenix, the word "Phoenix" became a shorthand for
all the negative aspects of the war. And when I was asked
point-blank whether any assassinations or any similar
abuses had ever been perpetrated by Vietnamese (or Americans for that matter) in the Phoenix program, I felt obliged
to say I couldn't be sure, and I conceded that it was possible. This refusal to deny an obvious and honest fact was
then headlined as my admission of an unknown scope of
wrong-doing. Whatever the unfairness of the reporting of my
testimony, I could find no other way to handle the question
than to tell the truth. I was left to wonder how I could put
what I was saying into the context of a war in which we

truly were trying to develop a proper as well as efficient program to counter a deadly enemy, had in fact succeeded to a remarkable degree yet could not testify under oath that we had totally accomplished what we were trying to achieve.

Phoenix did try to eliminate abuses and bring an atmosphere of law and decency to the struggle against the VCI. Beyond the procedures and machinery to improve the accuracy of our intelligence, and thus protect the innocent, Phoenix also developed measures to improve the legal system under which those who were arrested were processed. The first step was to make Phoenix a public program, not a shadowy activity of the intelligence and security services. In fact, it was launched publicly, with the Prime Minister explaining its target as the secret Communist apparatus, its technique of gathering all possible information on the VCI from the public as well as from the government services, and its object of stopping the terrorism that had indiscriminately wounded and killed so many thousands of Vietnamese. Moreover, when local Phoenix units identified VCI suspects, their names and photographs were posted on the walls of the community and an appeal was issued to the villagers to report further data on them. And in an interesting twist of the "Wanted—Dead or Alive" posters of our Wild West, Phoenix put up posters calling on "wanted men" to take advantage of the amnesty program, turn themselves in, and be freed of any punishment for hostile activity. Then too, directives were issued ordering that the elected village chiefs be informed of any operations against the VCI in their areas so that their familiarity with the local community could be used to help or correct these operations.

The next step was to improve the formal legal procedures of the program, with the help of an exceptionally able and determined young lawyer, Gage McAfee, assigned to my staff for the purpose. Phoenix depended essentially on a preventive-detention law similar to those of Northern Ireland, India, Malaysia, and even the United States under a little-noticed provision in our Internal Security Act of 1950.

The Vietnamese law allowed the imprisonment of individuals for a period of up to two years, renewable upon reexamination, on the decision of a Provincial Security Committee. Most captured VCI members were held under this law. Some, however, were referred to the military courts for prosecution for specific crimes. And, in some cases, depending on the circumstances of their capture, VCI would be turned over to the Vietnamese Army as prisoners of war. The effect of the last was to allow the incarceration of VCI for the "duration,"—that is, for an unspecified term; thus, despite the other values of POW status, it actually gave the captured VCI fewer chances of release.

Phoenix's improvements were aimed at the first cases, where VCI were handled by the Provincial Security committees. To begin with, guidelines were set for sentencing according to the status of the VCI: category A were sentenced for two years; category B for one year to two years; and C for a maximum of one year. Extensions of detention after this first sentence were applied to almost all the A's, to only about half the B's, and to only a quarter of the C's.

Another move was the setting-up of time limits for the various steps in the legal procedures—interrogation, investigation of the case, decision on the individual—and so bring to an end the long delays that often resulted in VCI being held in prison indefinitely. A third was to improve the composition of the Provincial Security Committee, which consisted initially only of military, police and administrative officials. In an interview with the Minister of Justice I asked that some of his young "judges" (in the French tradition) be assigned to the provinces to provide legal content to the committee proceedings; the fact that Vietnam had only two hundred lawyers made any hope of ensuring a right of legal counsel for every captured VCI completely impractical. As a result, the composition of the Provincial Security Committee was ultimately changed to include the Province Chief, the "judge" and the elected Chairman of the Provincial Council, with the police and other officials being reduced to the role of advisers, not taking part in making the decisions.

And finally, underlying these changes, was a continual effort to ensure that cases were not lost in a French-style bureaucratic paper maze while the VCI suspects languished in jail.

But was the picture really this rosy? Were all these careful directives followed? Or did not a cynical machinery, despite them, go ahead with its brutal practices? My answer turns on the "art of the possible." I believed that it was important to bring whatever improvements and sense of propriety we could, without either conditioning our help on perfection or washing our hands of what our allies did as of no concern to us. Criticism of and pressure on Phoenix came both from those who questioned how I could support a program that did not meet the standards that I insisted on for Americans under our Bill of Rights (e.g., the right of counsel and open hearing) and from those who bitterly complained that known VCI were slipping through the machinery to resume their terror and killings, because the reforms and improvements, which I was equally insistent about, made it more difficult to take them out of action permanently.

Directives such as mine against assassination were easy to issue and to applaud. But when one of my provincial officers reported that a district chief had shot, out of hand, a woman prisoner and I took the case up with the Prime Minister and had the district chief sacked and punished, the same province officer complained that the district chief was one of the best in the province and should be excused for his action because the woman had been involved in a terrorist attack on one of the chief's own family. When another of my officers proposed that Phoenix's statistics include only VCI actually sentenced rather than merely captured, I agreed, since obviously not every suspect captured would necessarily be proved to be VCI.

But when yet another officer suggested that our figures not include VCI who were killed in battles incidentally and only so identified afterward, and not as a result of careful Phoenix identification and attempts to capture them, I said no, since I believed it would be thoroughly false to pretend that a VCI's elimination didn't matter if he were killed in the course of the very real war going on in the villages and not in a Phoenix-targeted operation. I was not being callous about this. I made my decision on the basis that a fight to the death was underway, that the South Vietnamese government was trying to set and adhere to reasonable standards in the conduct of it with our help and that the alternative before us was defeat by a force that had showed itself many times more cynical and brutal in its approach.

As in the Italian political campaign, I found both Phoenix's ends and our means well within moral limits. We took honest steps to prevent and replace immoral practices, and if our efforts were not totally successful, that did not mean we wouldn't keep trying. And, I frankly admit, all our efforts were not successful. For example, as Pulitzer-Prize-winner Peter Kann graphically described in the *Wall Street Journal*, an alleged VC leader was captured in a raid in a Delta province in 1969 and was summarily executed without anyone applying the careful Phoenix procedures that had been set up for just such cases. But some idea of the success of the program can be gained from the report of another, equally excellent journalist. Robert Kaiser wrote in the *Washington Post* in February 1970 that he had looked in vain for instances of assassinations to report at the time I was testifying on Phoenix before the Senate Foreign Relations Committee. Abuses, unquestionably, did take place but the full truth is that Phoenix went far to eliminate them as an accepted aspect of the war. And another fact about Phoenix is relevant: the testimony of Communist cadre afterward that the worst period for the Communist cause in Vietnam was during the Phoenix campaign.

One of CORDS's activities was the AID Public Safety Program, part of AID's worldwide effort to improve the professionalism of police services in the underdeveloped nations by providing equipment and training in modern (and proper) procedures. This was a major activity in Vietnam, patterned on the successful work the British had done with their colonial police forces in the Malayan and other troubles. A small part of the program involved funds and advice to the Vietnamese civil prison authorities. AID's main concentration prior to Tet 1968 had been on improving the facilities in Vietnam's primitive prisons inherited from the French to meet basic standards and on reforming the paperwork and procedures to give more accurate accounts of who was in the prisons and why. When CORDS took over the program, we stressed the advisory role and the necessity of improving paperwork and procedures. Our public-safety advisers visited the prisons regularly, and so did I during many of my own travels. The American visits showed our concern that proper standards of behavior be followed and gave us a chance to spot and complain about situations that did not meet our standards, such as when I protested finding a twelve-year-old boy in one prison for having thrown a grenade, and a blind man in another.

But one situation we obviously missed; it was the maximum-security section of the prison for incorrigibles and dangerous Viet Cong on Con Son Island. A visiting Congressman, accompanied by a leading American critic of the Saigon government, found the conditions there totally unacceptable. There were shackled prisoners with paralyzed limbs, overcrowded cells, filthy surroundings and whispered pleas for help. The fact that the photos he took of the place implied that the prisoners were held underground when they were not was not the point. In every other respect, the prisoners' treatment could not be justified, even though the prison director had done first-class work in many other aspects of his job. There was no way of minimizing the situation in the light of the other work he had done—nor any point in trying to show the enormity and numbers of difficult jobs that had to be done in a wartime situation.

Such a case of failure or wrong-doing had to be faced in trying to carry out a program of the scope of CORDS, especially in a situation where direct command responsibility was Vietnamese and the American role was one of only moral and political responsibility. Plainly there were other cases of such failures or wrong-doing, and every one was immediately made the subject of worldwide protest, while the enemy's comparable activities were hardly ever noted. We in CORDS tried to prevent such cases from occurring, and although we certainly did not always succeed, I took the position that we had to continue helping the Vietnamese fight the war and at the same time try to raise their standards as far as we could. A refusal to help on moral grounds because of instances of abuse seemed to me as unjustifiable as a callous disregard of standards of propriety and morality; it was essential to push for improvements in behavior while we fought the enemy outside the gate.

But were these goals attainable in a time when the war was so hotly debated? Almost every week I invited one of the resident American newsmen to accompany me on one of my overnight trips in the field. I had only one restriction on what they might write as a result: they had to omit the names of the Vietnamese and CORDS officials who gave us our briefings, ate with us, and discussed how the war and our programs were working. Thus, these newsmen heard of our problems as well as of our successes; they rode up canals that had been under enemy control a few months before; they drove with the morning market traffic over roads no longer blocked by mines. But only a few wrote an account of what our program was doing and the changes it was bringing to the lives of the people in the countryside.

One explained the problem by saying, "There is nothing very dramatic going on to write about." I answered that he might be right as far as a single night's visit was concerned. But surely he must see that the life of the Vietnamese woman in the village we had visited was "dramatically" different from what it had been a year before, when she had huddled in a refugee camp, fearing that mortar attacks would drive her and her family back to her village to provide food, concealment and recruits for the enemy. Now, she had "returned to the village" under the refugee program, was protected by a Territorial Force unit with her son in a self-defense group, had voted for the village council, had participated in a village discussion that had led to the decision to spend its development funds on a bridge across the canal to give her easier access to the local market, and her husband had received title to the land they worked and had made a start in planting the new miracle rice.

Everything was not perfect, of course; she was worried that the Phoenix program might target her other son as VCI. But she had raised that problem with her village councilman and he had told her he had passed it on to a provincial councilman and to the national assemblyman, who would raise it with officials at the province capital and in Saigon if necessary. But these "dramatic" changes apparently could not be appreciated by the American newspaper reader and TV viewer. They were just not "dramatic" enough to compete with the sights and sounds of Vietnam as a military contest. I finished the talk with my newsman friend by saying that in Vietnam he could find anything he looked for; courage and cowardice, dedication and corruption, success and failure— the problem and the challenge were to see them in their true proportion, not to seize individual examples and display them as the whole picture, when they were only a part of it.

The same problem burdened our attempts to explain the pacification program in Congressional hearings. In January 1970, before the Senate Foreign Relations Committee, I arrayed a phalanx of CORDS officers from our Saigon headquarters and on down to the lowest rural level for an entire week of testimony. But most of the interest, and virtually all of the press coverage, focused on Phoenix. In April 1971 I testified before Senator Edward M. Kennedy about the refugee program, which had returned a half million people to their home villages, paid resettlement benefits to a million and a half, and provided short-term assistance to over two millions. Yet the great portion of the questioning was devoted to how little Vietnam had done in the social-welfare field, while a noisy group of antiwar veterans hooted to my rear. And in July 1971, when I testified in detail on Phoenix, my refusal to say under oath that no one had been wrongly killed in Vietnam was headlined as an admission of assassinations. The difficulty was more than the old argument about whether the bottle is half full, or half empty. For too often the most "dramatic" subjects were the ones that got the attention in Washington policy debates as to what should be done in Vietnam and the "undramatic" ones were ignored and had no influence. I never did resolve in my mind how to handle such squeaky-wheel situations. I always refused to overstate what I knew to be the positive aspects of our complex programs, nor would I, in hope of attracting or deflecting "dramatic" attention, deny what I knew to be their negative aspects. My faith that the true balance would show in the end may have been misplaced, but it was all that I had to work with.

But, in the Vietnamese countryside, it was clear that the pacification program was succeeding. Increasingly, I traveled by road or canal, and less by helicopter; often my overnight stays in the field were pleasant evenings in rural communities rather than in tightly buttoned-up defensive outposts. My primary interest still was focused on political growth from the bottom up, and Thieu agreed to my proposal to expand the election process from the village level, which by 1969 and 1970 had included almost every village in the country, up to the provincial level by holding elections for Provincial Councils, an until-then moribund advisory assembly of elderly "notables" in each province. These elections did bring some fresh political blood into prominence, and the council chairmen began to exert some civilian political influence, slightly diluting the power of the pervasive military presence that had so long prevailed. The President and the Prime Minister brought the entire cabinet to the Vung Tau training session to meet these newly elected officials and answer their questions. And their uninhibited nature and their concentration on practical problems of the countryside rather than on fine political theories showed a possible future direction for Vietnamese political life.

I now began to think ahead about solutions not only for the country's rural problems but about those that could move Vietnam toward a permanent political system, which would include the Communists as well as avoid the administratively dominated machinery that characterized the Diem regime. Since this subject was beyond mere "pacification," I felt it essential to be in tune with the embassy, even in the informal think pieces that I concocted. One, for example, reviewed the dangers of setting up a "government party" that the province chiefs would almost surely take over and use as a tool to require membership and control political life in their areas. Instead, I suggested that an American-style party be developed, with "membership" restricted to elected officials or candidates alone, to serve as a vehicle for organizing support during election campaigns from the village up to the national level, but obviously excluding the administrative and military hierarchies. Thieu was interested in the idea, but he was still too dependent on his military structure to abandon or antagonize it, however much his grass-roots strength had grown among local village leaders.

Another of my ideas suggested the possibility of bringing the National Liberation Front into the political process in South Vietnam, but only at the village level and through participation in elections there rather than by negotiation at Paris. The incentive to the local Viet Cong member would be the chance to wield some political power, if only in a minority role, instead of being excluded totally and facing the prospect of being pushed back into the jungle or over the frontier by the pacification program. But this, of course, was a subject then being handled by Henry Kissinger. I did not know whether he ever even heard of my thought, but I could imagine that he might think it quite impossible to convince either Thieu or the North Vietnamese that it would be of any value to either of them. I, of course, thought I would be able to interest Thieu in it, since it was designed to undercut the NLF by going to their grass roots and that was something he would easily appreciate.

To supplement the Hamlet Evaluation System's reports on what was happening in the countryside, I thought it essential to gain an understanding of Vietnamese public opinion as to whether our programs were having the political effects they were designed to have. So we set up a polling mechanism and sent carefully chosen Vietnamese, working for CORDS, throughout the rural areas to discuss with the villagers their opinions on everything from their view of the different military forces in the neighborhood to their "aspirations for the future." The operation could hardly be a secret one. To secure President Thieu's approval, we promised to provide him with a copy of the results but otherwise would not make them public. The results showed that the villagers had a higher-than-expected opinion of the American forces and the Vietnamese Army; a low (and somewhat expected) opinion of the police; a lack of awareness of the Phoenix program, indicating that its public message had not gone over; a growing confidence in and appreciation of the security in the rural communities; and an overwhelming hope for peace. I had arranged that some purely political questions be included in the poll, as a means of at least beginning to measure political attitudes in the country. For example, we asked what kind of individual should be elected president ("A man capable of bringing unity to South Vietnam"), what issue was most important ("National Unity"), and who would be "most likely to run for election to President" (Nguyen Van Thieu swept the field easily over Duong Van "Big" Minh and Nguyen Cao Ky).

USIA ran a separate and smaller poll in the cities, less sharply focused on our pacification program or on Vietnamese political considerations. But together the two polls gave a rough idea of Vietnamese public opinion, which was very useful to the American mission in its planning and appreciation of Vietnamese life. They, and especially CORDS's, were equally useful to President Thieu, of course, helping him to determine his political strategy. This led to criticism of the CORDS poll by American Congressmen, who felt it gave Thieu an unfair advantage over his opponents, although I had directed that the answers, which so directly indicated Thieu's positive position in the countryside, be sharply limited in circulation to avoid their being considered a direct American propaganda effort on his behalf.

To this charge I could only note the inevitable advantage of the incumbent, our need for the incumbent's approval if we were to run the poll, and the fact that the results seemed to show that the incumbent and the pacification program were meeting with the approval of the Vietnamese villagers—a matter of great interest to the United States in its decision-making about Vietnam.

But I soon realized that CORDS was not the proper vehicle for this sort of experiment in political action. It was separate from the embassy, and its close dealings with the Vietnamese administrative machinery inevitably focused its attention on carrying out the programs set by the Saigon government. Moreover, its local representatives had difficulty in detaching themselves from local officialdom to judge the growth of political opinion as an independent phenomenon. The monthly political reports from the provincial advisory teams were thin in content and concentrated on local reactions to CORDS activities and programs, not the identification of new local political talent with a national potential. The great dilemma Thieu faced, how to shift the base of his support from the military to the village and provincial civilian leadership, was nowhere more obvious than in the provinces, where military personnel still wielded the real political power and only the first halting steps had taken place to produce civilians who would eventually replace them. Despite the improvements in the security situation, the conflict was still going on, and Hanoi's determination to resume the war, if it could, lay just behind the scenes of rural peace and development, giving a rationale for not abruptly shifting from the successful civil-military structure that Thieu had developed and so challenging the military's roles and prerogatives. Covert political action was not in the CORDS charter, either in collaboration with Thieu or independent of him. And any such venture would have to fit within an over-all American policy and program, which by now included the Paris negotiation with Hanoi and the NFL and with which I had nothing whatsoever to do.

So, while I dabbled slightly in political action, I put my

real effort into making "community defense and local development" (as we began to call it) work. By the end of 1970, the strategy I had set of concentrating on the Delta, assigning John Paul Vann there and giving it priority on all CORDS work, people, additional Territorial Force units, and hardware, was proving to be successful. On my overnight and weekend visits to the Delta, John arranged that we spend the night farther and farther into areas that had been totally under enemy control as recently as 1969. Once we went up a distant canal to see the successful resettlement of some of the 200,000 Vietnamese refugees who had swarmed over from Cambodia; once we slept in a village that had been an NFL headquarters and still had red-star markers in the cemetery of the NFL men killed in battle. And to celebrate the Tet holiday of 1971, John and I rode two motorcycles alone along the Bassac River across the Delta, seeing nothing more remarkable than "undramatic" rich rice fields, local residents celebrating the holiday by visiting their friends and families and a lone American engineer completing the hard-surfacing of a road that would speed the commercial life of the area in the future. John became so enthusiastic with our progress that he even promised to reduce his criticism to journalists of the American and Vietnamese military, after I had bailed him out of yet another near-firing for insubordination.

In other parts of the country the same changes from three years before were evident. For example, my good friend the provincial chief, who had rebuilt Hue after the 1968 pitched battle there, took the British ambassador and me for an impromptu midnight drive unescorted several kilometers into the countryside, where all we saw were armed parties of nondescriptly dressed local youths—self-defense teams— who waved us on after a cursory inspection of our jeep—the Ambassador and I each later confessed our qualms and our relief at this outcome. An evening tour with the mayor of Saigon of the community centers that CORDS had launched in the city showed them actively engaging the residents in educational courses, sports and social services, in an effort to link even urban populations in community work. Thieu regularly held cabinet meetings on the pacification program and had me attend and sit at the table with his ministers as a full participant. My weakness in the Vietnamese language was compensated for by the presence at my elbow of Jean Sauvageot, an American major who spoke totally colloquial Vietnamese and knew every village chief in Vietnam as a result of his service in the Vung Tau Training Center. The briefings and statistics presented at the meetings were familiar to me, since we in CORDS used very much the same ones, and I was invited—and was expected—to join in the discussions and answer for American shortcomings in the same way as were the Vietnamese ministers. The only trouble I ever had at any of these meetings occurred at the first one I attended. Jean had brought along a pocket tape recorder to help with his translation. I immediately dismantled it ostentatiously, to demonstrate that I was there to participate in the meeting, not bug it. In addition to the cabinet meetings, I accompanied President Thieu on field trips every week or so, sometimes with the diplomatic corps as guests, more often with me as the only foreigner present, but in all cases as a member of Thieu's staff. As the months passed, the subject of these meetings and trips gradually changed emphasis from a review of the security situation and measures to improve the Territorial Forces, to discussions of how to develop new roads and settlements for Vietnamese who never would return to their villages in the demilitarized zone between North and South Vietnam and who needed help in clearing the jungle in new areas entirely. On one of our field trips, we visited one of the highland centers that I had first seen as a part of the same program that Ngo Dinh Diem had sponsored over a decade before.

But the real test of the success of the pacification program came long after I left; in the 1972 and 1975 Communist offensives. In 1972 it proved that we had won the guerrilla war, when the attacks took place only where the Communist regular military forces, with their tanks, artillery and rockets, were active. Elsewhere there was practically no guerrilla activity whatsoever—a sharp contrast to Tet 1968, four years before. This allowed a full army division to be moved out of the Delta to take part in the fighting north of Saigon instead of being held back to protect its bases from local guerrillas. In 1975 the same situation prevailed in the countryside, and the best witness to that is General Van Tien Dung, commander of the victorious North Vietnamese forces, who wrote a long account of his "Great Spring Victory" phrased in almost purely military terms and making only polite mention of the "southern compatriots," the guerrillas, who in fact played little, if any, part in the offensive that toppled South Vietnam. In an ironic asymmetry, the Communists initiated the war against Diem in the late 1950s as a people's war and the Americans and the Vietnamese initially responded to it as a conventional military one; in the end the Thieu government was fighting a successful people's war, but lost to a military assault. The Presidential Palace in Saigon was not entered by a barefoot guerrilla but by a North Vietnamese tank with an enormous cannon.

Robert Kennedy was reported to have once said that there were enough mistakes made in Vietnam for all concerned to have had a share. Certainly the final fall of Saigon cannot be ascribed to any simple or single reason; each of the tragic errors that characterized the long travail there contributed to the final outcome. But the underlying reason, I believe, was the American difficulty in understanding that alien culture, and its insistence that the Vietnam problem could be handled by concepts and solutions that we Americans prescribed. John Vann once graphically complained that Americans did not have ten years' experience in Vietnam—their short tours made them have only one year's experience ten times. Kennedy's vacillation between supporting Diem against the subversion from the North and repudiating Diem's authoritarian Mandarinism; Johnson and McNamara's certainty that Vietnam would respond to the weight of American military pressure; Nixon and Kissinger's formula of a cease-fire and agreement brought about by

American bombs—none of these took into account the determination of the Vietnamese, Southern as well as Northern, to make their own decisions and fight each other to decide what sort of life Vietnam should lead. America's impatience for a clear-cut solution that would meet American standards conflicted with the reality of a civil war longer and more intense than our own, so that even after our own forces were withdrawn, we repudiated the support our erstwhile allies needed to continue the fight. General Dung, again, expressed the epitaph well when he chortled that Thieu was "forced to fight a poor man's war" after having been trained and urged for years to fight in the style and with the profligacy of rich Americans. The Congressional constriction of the military-aid pipeline in the winter of 1974 signaled the Thieu government's inevitable end as plainly as Kennedy's cutoff of the commercial-import program in 1963 signaled Diem's. The tactical errors of the final days, of course, contributed to Saigon's fall, but I believe the root cause to have been the Congressional signal of sharply reduced aid, with its inevitable effect in loss of morale and panic.

It is not particularly profitable, or possible, to isolate individual decisions that might have changed the course of the Vietnamese history. But one can identify several that had large if not totally decisive results, and that can raise warning signals for analogous situations in the future. If intelligence truly constitutes the formulation of knowledge to help decision-making, then some of it can indeed come from seeing the errors of the past. Truman's turn away from Ho Chi Minh's OSS-supported nationalism; Switchback's militarization of CIA's politically oriented paramilitary operations; the American-stimulated overthrow and replacement of Diem's Mandarin government by a series of military juntas; the too-long-delayed process of organizing the American government to support a people's war—whether strategic hamlets or pacification—seeking success, instead, through conventional military and air power; the credibility gap between the American people and their government, which inevitably arose from overly optimistic statistics shaken by dramatic contradictory incidents. All of these are reflections of an intelligence problem: how do you make a faraway and unfamiliar situation understandable and indicate its true proportions despite dramatic and exotic features that seize the popular attention and warp reality out of context? And at the heart of this problem is the fact that the answer must satisfy the American public, not merely the closed circles of government officials, however sincere and committed they may be. After all, the policies of the American government are in the end directed by the will of the people, and any program contrary to that will is sooner or later rejected and repudiated. This was a lesson I learned in Vietnam, and during the intense discussions with my family and friends about it on my visits home every six months.

Jumpmaster (at top) for a training parachute drop in North Carolina, 1943

Identification photos for Jedburgh Team Bruce, 1944

Pointing the trail, Norway, 1945—with Harold Larsen, Herbert Helgesen and Hans Leirmo

Operation Rype—Norway, 1945: Norwegians and Americans together

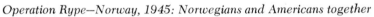

Three volleys and a salute to our crashed comrades—Norway, April 1945

Wild Bill Donovan visits the Norwegian members of Operation Rype—Norway, 1949

September 15, 1945—a happy couple

Another OSS operation, to Ho Chi Minh and Vo Nguyen Giap—Vietnam, 1945

The "diplomat's wife"—and mother—Stockholm, 1953

Ambassador Extraordinary and Envoy Pleni-potentiary Clare Boothe Luce—Rome, 1956

President John F. Kennedy shifts command of CIA from Allen Dulles to John McCone—September 1961 (UPI)

A briefing in the A Shau Valley near the Lao border, Vietnam, 1962—with Generals Nguyen Duc Thang, Nguyen Khanh and Tran Van Don

The Colby family's farewell to President Ngo Dinh Diem—Saigon, 1962

Madame Ngo Dinh Nhu—embattled and outrageous—1963 (UPI)

After a trip to Vietnam, Secretary of Defense Robert McNamara briefs President Lyndon B. Johnson and his senior advisors Averill Harriman, John McCone, Roger Hilsman and McGeorge Bundy visible, with Colby backing up McCone—the Oval Office, December 1963

Home in Washington, 1966

Supplied and supported by CIA, a Lao tribal fighter heads off to the battle, with his rooster—Laos, 1965

Inspecting the Rural Development Cadre team before it takes up the night defense positions—Vietnam, 1968

The Nixons visit the Thieus—Saigon, 1969—wth Assistant Secretary of State and Ambassador Colby at the side

Trying out the new hand plow outside Hue—Vietnam, 1970

Arrival at Chau Doc after a trip across the delta with John Paul Vann—Vietnam, Tet, 1971

Posters around Washington for the newly nominated Director of Central Intelligence—May 1973

President Nixon presides as Judge George Hart administers the oath, with daughter-in-law Susan Colby and husband Jonathan, Joint Chiefs Chairman Admiral Tom Moorer, Henry Kissinger and James Schlesinger watching— September 4, 1973

The National Security Council discusses the Middle East—1974

A friendly visit to Iran, 1974, with American Ambassador Richard Helms

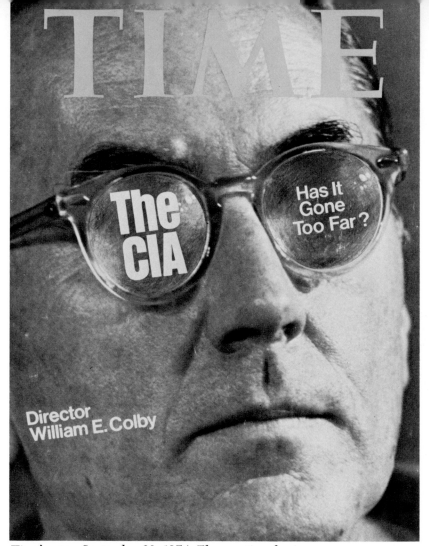

Time's *cover September 30, 1974: The questions begin*

Congress starts to investigate: Senator John L. McClellan calls two CIA Directors to testify—January 15, 1975 (WW)

Daniel Schorr of CBS. His beat: CIA —1975 (UPI)

Congressman Otis Pike, Chairman of the House Intelligence Committee—1975 (UPI)

Senators Frank Church and John G. Tower, Chairman and Vice Chairman of the Senate Intelligence Committee, with the CIA's dart gun—September 23, 1975 (UPI)

A North Vietnamese tank—no barefoot guerrilla—breaks through the Presidential palace gate in Saigon—April 1975

Richard Welch's body returns to the United States from Greece, dawn, December 30, 1975—received by Welch's former wife Patricia and daughter Molly, Colby and Marine Lieutenant Patrick Welch (saluting on right)

At Welch's funeral—January 6, 1976

President Ford pins on the National Security Medal—January 26, 1976
(White House)

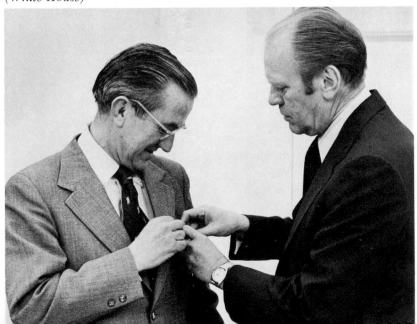

A return visit to the Norwegian mountain where the Rype plane crashed in 1945—July 1977

A new life together—1977

CHAPTER TEN

A Changing Agency— and Watergate

Catherine, our elder daughter, had suffered from epilepsy since early childhood. We had hoped that her condition would improve as she matured and that her seizures would either gradually disappear or be fully controlled by some of the new drugs that were appearing. But this, tragically, was not the case, and the epilepsy, combined with double vision from an early operation to correct the crossed eyes with which she had been born, put her under an enormous strain. Inability to get a driver's license, rejection from an Israeli kibbutz where she had gone to spend a summer, and the social problems that her seizures created for her in high school and college, all produced psychiatric pressures that grew as she reached her twenties.

I feel obliged, for two reasons, to touch on this personally painful subject here. In the first place, it played a part in the chronology of my career at this point. But, far more importantly, I must vehemently refute an ugly and hurtful canard that has floated about in recent years that Catherine's death in 1973 was in some way linked to my service in Vietnam and my role in the Phoenix program. Catherine loved Vietnam, and in fact she once wrote a letter to the *Washington Post* criticizing the shallow way in which one of its writers described the tragedy of compensation payments for children killed there. On my biannual visits home from Saigon, she and I often discussed the war and my work assisting the people of South Vietnam to defend themselves—and she was always supportive. But my absence certainly did not help her, and Barbara faced increasing difficulties as my tour in Vietnam stretched past two and then three years. Barbara's own loyalty kept her from complaining or letting anything interfere with my work. But by the spring of 1971, Catherine's health, both physical and mental, had deteriorated alarmingly, and although Barbara remained resolute in trying to deal with it on her own, our son Paul took it upon himself to force her to make clear to me how serious the situation had become.

I considered the pacification program to be fairly successful by that time. Much of the back country had been freed of guerrillas; roads, markets and schools in many remote hamlets were functioning again; hundreds of thousands of refugees had been resettled; and the ability to travel widely and without armed escorts throughout South Vietnam by then came as a surprise to people who had been there only two years before. Even so, there was clearly still a long way to go before all the political and developmental goals would be achieved. Nevertheless, after a couple of emergency returns across the Pacific because of Catherine that spring, I realized that my first responsibilities at that moment were to my family, and so in June I turned CORDS over to my capable deputy George Jacobson and came home. Catherine went to Johns Hopkins for an extended period, followed by a sequence of alternating hopeful and weakening periods, leading ultimately to her death in April 1973 of a combination of epilepsy and anorexia nervosa.

My unscheduled return to Washington in mid-1971 created something of a conundrum from a career point of view: for the first time, I had moved out of one job without having another one waiting for me to go to. I was then still formally an employee of the State Department (on unpaid leave from the CIA) and one possibility was that I might succeed my old friend Ambassador William Sullivan as the head of

State's Vietnam Task Force. It was not a particularly appealing proposition. Considering that by this time virtually all of the Nixon administration's efforts were directed at phasing the United States out of Vietnam, the job promised to be rather short-lived. And I didn't believe that I could make much of a career at State after that, in view of the dubious reception I could expect the Foreign Service establishment to give an ex-CIA type stepping into a high-ranking assignment at the department. So, not unnaturally, I turned to my first love and old employer, the CIA, to see whether it could come up with something more promising.

Helms welcomed me back with that sense of concern for a veteran member of CIA's clandestine services team that characterized him, and with sincere thanks for the way I had gone off to Vietnam three and a half years before. And as we lunched at his regular table at the Occidental, he said he did indeed have a job for me at the Agency, and one which again suggested that he was thinking in terms of broadening my experience so as to give me a chance to compete for higher responsibilities in the future. But the job he offered was a surprise, one that I thought likely to turn out to be a total dead end in my career.

In my heart, what I had been secretly hoping for was the post of Deputy Director for Plans, to complete my career at the head of CIA's clandestine operations. But, in my head, I was perfectly aware that it was a vain hope for now. My old friend and mentor Des FitzGerald, who had been named DDP after Dick Helms became Deputy Director of CIA, had died in the job, and Tom Karamessines had succeeded him barely four years before. In view of Karamessines' professional ability, his total loyalty to Helms, and the careful way in which he ran clandestine operations, it was obvious that Helms wasn't about to remove him in the near future. So the job Helms offered me was that of the CIA's Executive Director-Comptroller. Now, on paper, this was the third-ranking post in the Agency, below only the DCI and the DDCI, and *above* the DDP. But in reality, I knew well enough, the lines of substantive responsibility went right around it straight from the DCI to the four Deputy Directors in charge of Plans, Analysis, Technology, and Support. I knew that Lyman Kirkpatrick had once tried to make the job into one of a real chief of staff for the Agency, as the regulations described it, but that he had been chewed up in the process and had left the Agency to go off and teach as a result. His successor, the man I would replace upon his long-planned retirement at the end of 1971, was Lawrence K. White, a former Deputy Director for Support, who had sensibly limited his activity to over-all administrative matters and carefully avoided challenging the substantive responsibilities of the Deputy Directors or their direct relations with Helms. So the job looked like one that would give me little possibility to push my own ideas about intelligence and might limit me to little more than ensuring that the grass was properly cut around the Agency's handsome headquarters at Langley.

Thus, I felt myself caught somewhere between the devil and the deep blue sea. On the one hand, there was a futureless job at the State Department; on the other, after a lifetime career as an activist intelligence-operations officer, I could end up in the backwater of CIA administration and management. It was a choice over which I agonized for several days, but after discussing it with Barbara, I finally came down on the side of the Agency, which after all was the place and job that I knew best and where new possibilities might open as people retired in the years ahead. So in September I began my briefings for the post of Executive Director-Comptroller (and looked up the word *comptroller* in the dictionary to find out what it meant).

But no matter how unenthusiastic I originally was about it, it was a job that, in retrospect, I have absolutely no regrets that I took. Because in it I got an unparalleled overview of the profession of intelligence—its problems and accomplishments, its incredible complexities and fantastic potential—of a sort that I could have gotten nowhere else and that was to stand me in good stead in the years to come. Whether Helms was "grooming" me or not—and I think he was—my experience as Executive Director-Comptroller served as a vital transition from the narrow world of clandestine operations to the much wider one of modern intelligence.

I quickly discovered how intelligence—and CIA—had grown from the OSS days of spies and guerrillas to a great enterprise for the collection, analysis and dissemination of knowledge. Although CIA's budget and personnel had not increased much after the original expansion during the Korean and Cold wars, this had been achieved only by shifting many Agency programs and their financing—mainly, as we have seen, in the paramilitary field—to the Defense Department, while the FI and Analysis cultures grew in scope and complexity and its management now used all the techniques of a huge modern corporation, directing the work of thousands of employees spread through the world and handling budgets in the hundreds of millions of dollars. And it also had to work with the "intelligence community," consisting of the intelligence elements of the State, Treasury, Justice, and especially the Defense Department's Army, Navy, Air Force and National Security Agency intelligence services. A young and somewhat brash James R. Schlesinger, as Deputy Director of the Bureau of the Budget, had just finished a study of this intelligence community for President Nixon and had recommended that the CIA director actively assume the role of leader of this community, reviewing the budgets of the various intelligence services and getting them to coordinate their activities with one another.

This idea soon ran aground on the rocks of Washington's bureaucratic realities. Defense Secretary Melvin C. Laird made it clear that he was not about to surrender his control over the various military intelligence services to Helms. And, as Helms recognized that Laird had the political clout to make his position stick, the CIA Director did not force the issue to a confrontation. Nonetheless, although Helms's over-all "leadership" turned out to be a muted one, Schlesinger's recommendation had the effect of opening the programs of the various services to a far wider audience than previously. As the Agency's chief program and financial officer, I was one of that audience, so my new job exposed me not only to every aspect of the CIA's business but also to that of the entire intelligence community and brought me into contact as well with the Office of Management and Budget, the Civil Service Commission, and other top Washington agencies.

I thus had a chance to learn something about the most sophisticated modern management techniques, including "management by objective," "management by exception," and "zero-base budgeting," and how to deal with the problems of program and financial control down through several hierarchical levels to where the real work was done. Elliot Richardson lent me two of his management experts to explain how he had gotten some control of the sprawling Department of Health, Education and Welfare, in hope that some of these techniques could be helpful in the world of intelligence.

But perhaps the most impressive lesson I learned in the new job was that an incredible revolution in the technology of intelligence had occurred during all those years in which I had been running operations in the jungles of Southeast Asia. I had, of course, been aware of the wonder of the U-2 spy plane, if for no other reason than its noisy downing in Russia in 1960 and the vital role it had played in the Cuban missile crisis. But, during my orientation briefings for my new post in the fall of 1971, I went on a tour of the aerospace-technology factories on the West Coast and there had my eyes opened to the veritable science-fiction world of space systems, radar, electronic sensors, infrared photography, and the ubiquitous computer, all able to gather intelligence from high in the sky to deep in the ocean with astounding accuracy and precision. I found that when this information was processed it produced exquisitely detailed reports of secret test centers and experiments deep in Asia; of truck parks and barracks for armored divisions in Eastern Europe, permitting a stunningly accurate reading of foreign military forces. I also learned how electronic machinery could provide detailed information on the existing and experimental potential enemy missiles and aircraft, on the volume and traffic patterns of the communications systems of offensive and defensive forces, and how the massive data banks put together this most secret intelligence with open information to reveal even what was going on politically and socially in the "hard target" areas.

It is impossible to overstate the importance of these astonishing technological advances. They were not just bigger and better toys for spies but the instruments of a profound change in the profession of intelligence, adding immeasurably to the volume of available information from which wise assessments could be made. They did not, I hasten to add, make spies obsolete, as some critics suggest, but they did alter the purpose of spying. Obviously, with technical equipment able to provide, for example, precise information on the quantity and quality of military equipment in the Soviet Union, spies no longer needed to attempt the well-nigh impossible task of infiltrating every Russian military center. They could, instead, concentrate on those jobs that machines cannot handle, such as identifying the political factions and machinations in the closed societies, reporting the new areas into which scientific research there was pressing, learning of the programs being debated but not yet on the drawing boards and revealing the discussions of economic and military strategy going on behind closed doors.

This technology had the additional effect of forcing the over-all intelligence community to work more closely together. Clearly, it would have been grossly wasteful, if not in fact impossible, for each intelligence service to have, for example, its own costly space system. One for any particular job obviously was enough so long as the information it gathered was effectively distributed to all the services. But which service should have it under its control? This question was a subject of constant debate with every new technological advance. And it is very much to Helms's credit that the CIA, by and large, established and maintained leadership in this area. He encouraged that handful of truly brilliant scientists and engineers who worked for the Agency's Directorate of Technology to come up with ever more spectacular innovations in the techniques of intelligence gathering. And when they did, he performed miracles of lobbying in his low-key style to protect them against military competition and even suppression. Perhaps the most spectacular project of all was the most secret: CIA's connections with Howard Hughes's *Glomar Explorer* deep-sea-mining ship, which years later were to be trumpeted in nationwide headlines.

In the clandestine field, because of the shift from Cold War toward détente in international affairs, because of the disrepute into which Covert Action had fallen, and because of Helms's own background, foreign intelligence operations by now had become unarguably the dominant culture over political and paramilitary work. And most significantly, the emphasis of this activity was being placed on the so-called "hard targets." The word had gone out to our officers in stations all around the world that they should focus their efforts on the closed, secret societies of European and Asian Communism rather than on the easier targets of neutral and allied nations, which had taken much of their energies in the past. The results were beginning to be substantial. We were having greater success than ever before in recruiting agents behind the Iron and Bamboo Curtains and obtaining accurate intelligence on Moscow's strategy for a battle with NATO; from China, party members were reporting on the confidential guidance given to the cadres, explaining the factional fights in Peking; in Vietnam we were learning of Communist intentions to mount offensives whenever local forces were briefed on their roles in them; from the Soviet Union, we were acquiring intelligence on secret debates in the senior military circles about future force structures; and in a number of Communist parties in Western Europe and the Third World our friends gave us accounts of leadership discussions on the way to maintain illegal, secret guerrilla networks as well as legal, political fronts in urban centers.

But as I carefully examined these accomplishments, I

found some things that disturbed me. One aspect of the professionalism of this work was strongly stressed: clandestine methodology, which, it seemed to me, often overshadowed the object of the exercise. For example, the collection of what we called "operational intelligence"—the information necessary to identify potential agents, their tastes, their attitudes, and people who had access to them and through whom we could work—often became an end in itself. Enormous effort was placed on learning the makeup and internal details of Communist embassies around the world, recruiting local citizens who had contact with their personnel and selecting agents from among the embassy personnel who were unhappy with Communism, but in minor positions and thus without access to any useful intelligence; those who were in the mainstream of the nation's policy flow were often too high in rank to be likely to work with us. And then, after all this preparatory work, we all too often made "cold approaches" to potential agents only to be rebuffed out of indignation or in fear, and at least once wound up with the uncomfortable result of having some of our officers detained by local police unhappy with our importing the Soviet-American rivalry to their shores. Moreover, beyond all this effort, which aimed only at identifying potential agents, lay yet another expenditure of manpower and resources on what I viewed as preliminary rather than substantive steps toward our proper goals. It was that of Jim Angleton's counterintelligence staff, busily working to ensure that our efforts were not penetrated and misled by a clever KGB.

At this stage, as Executive Director, I had no "need to know" all the complex details of our operations against the hard targets or of the supersecret counterintelligence operations. So I could not form a solid opinion on the merits in the debate whether our operations were totally suspect, as Angleton held, or whether they were being hamstrung by overcautious suspicion. But I did see clearly that a large portion of our effort was wide of the mark that we should have been concentrating on—the recruitment of Communist officials and nationals. It was instead devoted to collecting "operational intelligence" on them or to the very restricted contest between CIA and the KGB, and not to finding out what was happening in policy circles in Moscow. My responsibilities did allow me to know the number of personnel and the resources assigned to accumulating operational and counterintelligence. And while I had no authority to meddle in these matters, I resolved that if I ever did, I would try to shift our major effort to direct contacts between our officers and Communist officials and take the chance of making a few mistakes in return for recruiting a lot more agents than the ultracareful approach allowed.

My new job also gave me my first direct look at the CIA's third key culture—analysis. During my time as head of CIA's Far Eastern operations, I had come into contact with the analysis hierarchy and had learned to respect its ability to put broad masses of detailed information into carefully reasoned assessments. I had not always agreed with them— for example, I thought they had been overly pessimistic about Diem's political difficulties with the Buddhists—but I had approved of the separation of the assessment function from the gung-ho operator types like myself. For they served to warn policymakers that solutions would not be easy and set up a major challenge to the operators to prove the analysts wrong in the final outcome.

While in Vietnam, I had heard of the analysts' courageous and accurate estimates that the war would be more difficult to win than the Pentagon and the White House wished, that the bombing of the North would not cause it to yield and that underlying weaknesses were still present in the South, despite surface appearances of progress. But I had come to wonder whether some of the analysts' opinions had not become too firmly fixed and whether their objectivity had not come to reflect academia's bias that our programs in Vietnam just could not succeed. I had always felt that the analysts had been slow in appreciating the real changes wrought in the countryside by the pacification program, although I blamed some of this on my own reluctance to oversell our progress there. As I looked at a number of their products now, I had a nagging feeling that they were really academic assertions of what their authors believed to be abstract truth rather than contributions to the difficult decision-making process of our national leadership.

One issue especially appeared to me to be an egregious case of analysts insisting on their professional method despite clear indications that their conclusions were wrong—the question of whether the Viet Cong was receiving supplies through Sihanouk's neutral Cambodia. I was in no way involved in the question, but it seemed quite apparent to one who knew something of Southeast Asia that Cambodia was both a natural channel and a porous enough one to permit such a flow whether the Prince agreed or not. But the analysts insisted that there was no "hard evidence" that the flow was taking place, that the supplies could have come down the Ho Chi Minh Trail through Laos and that neither Prince Sihanouk nor the North Vietnamese wanted to compromise his neutrality. After his overthrow, of course, very specific "hard evidence" of such "covert" transshipments came to light, and the case seemed to me an example of overstressing professional techniques in the teeth of good, plain common sense, one of the problems inherent in over-institutionalizing and regulating the process of thought.

I saw something of the same tendency in the enthusiasm of many of the new breed of systems analysts—believing that answers to complex questions could be derived from quantitative processes after an initial assignment of arbitrary values. But I was equally dubious of the opposite attitude, the rejection of all machine analysis in favor of pencil-and-paper wisdom, resting essentially on selected events believed to be representative of more general conclusions. I had no solution to these contradictory impressions about the state of our analytical methodology and expertise. But, just as in the clandestine field, I decided that there was a great deal of work needed to be done here, to probe into new ways of thinking about the world and to open up the somewhat self-satisfied and even sleepy analytical community to changes in its established ways of operating, while at the same time preserving and expanding its exceptional ability to synthesize the kaleidoscopic world around us and to judge the human as well as the technological strengths and weaknesses of foreign cultures.

In my post as Executive Director, I naturally had little or no role in the substantive judgments reached by the analysts. But I found that I could influence their work, if only through such decisions as whether or not to purchase new computer hardware. On one occasion I discovered that a training course in the ways computers could be used in analysis was about to be terminated for lack of students. I protested that this would be nonsense, that we needed to expose all our analysts to these modern techniques, since it was clear that they would be needed even more in the future. So I scrounged up sufficient funds to continue the course for a few more months and arranged to have the course publicized among the younger analysts. And in a short time the course was oversubscribed and became one of the most popular ones offered. On another occasion I suggested that a weekend discussion be organized among all the working-level Agency officers who were concerned with Indonesia. We gathered political, military, economic, biographic and geographic experts and mixed them together with clandestine operators, who had lived and worked in that part of the world, and with technical and scientific personnel. To me, the startling thing was that most had never before met any of the others. But with their new awareness of one another's contributions, they could now maintain direct contact and seek out one another's views instead of making contact only through their bosses.

As for the Covert Action culture, it was rapidly diminishing at this time, almost to the vanishing point. The Agency had cut back on political action and paramilitary operations to the extent that funding for Covert Action had plummeted from more than 50 percent of the over-all CIA budget in the 1950s and 1960s to something well under 5 percent. Through Operation Switchback and then through the mechanism of CORDS, the Agency had turned over virtually all its political-action and paramilitary operations in Vietnam either to CORDS or to Pentagon or to AID financing. A similar transfer was taking place in the CIA's "secret" war in Laos, with the financing for that operation being taken over by the Defense budget (although I helped arrange that CIA personnel continue to play the key role and not be dropped out as they had been in the CIDG program earlier in Vietnam). What's more, since the exposure in the *Ramparts* magazine in 1967 of the CIA's involvement with international front organizations and the National Students Association, the Agency had also been steadily withdrawing from the business of funding international organizations, for example, pulling out of Radio Free Europe, Radio Liberty, and the Asia Foundation, and leaving their financing for the State Department and Congress to work out.

Some smaller-scale vestiges of the Agency's "Mighty Wurlitzer" propaganda capabilities of the 1950s still existed. We still had the capability to pick up and publish in local media in the less-developed world some of the better articles appearing in intellectual organs in Europe and North America; and we were still in contact with a few local reporters and editors of indigenous journals who could assure that a story favorable to the United States would be given space in their publications when it came in over the international wires. But plainly these were hardly major influences on world thinking, and they depended almost completely on material that was prominent and newsworthy in its own right and that opinion molders read anyway; CIA merely provided a nudge to be sure that it did not disappear under a flood of contrary stories or the disdain of those local editors who were likely to discard anything presenting the United States in a favorable light. In addition, a few political contacts existed secretly between CIA officers and local leaders and aspiring candidates around the world. But these were little more than informal friendships, involving almost no substantive assistance. Some long-established support to exile or nationalist groups continued in some regions, but had been reduced in recent years to only token aid to their efforts to express their opposition to the Communist rulers of their homeland.

As for the Agency's larger-scale political and paramilitary programs, most of these were the products of outside pressure, either from a forceful ambassador or a White House directive, and not the brainchildren of CIA officers—the word had gone out in the corridors of Langley and at the stations overseas that the Agency was no longer enthusiastic about pressing for large covert-action operations. And the most elaborate and controversial of these at the time was the one President Nixon himself personally ordered the CIA to undertake in Chile.

In an operation very similar to the one I had directed in Italy in the middle 1950s, the CIA had been clandestinely funneling a wide variety of support to the center democratic parties and political forces in Chile since 1963, in an effort to ward off a Castro-supported Communist takeover of that Latin American country. In Chile's 1964 election campaign, for example, the Agency provided some three million dollars to assist in the election of President Eduardo Frei and his fellow Christian Democrats. In the subsequent years, very much as in Italy a decade before, at least that much money again was spent by the CIA to help keep Frei and other democratic forces in power and block the emergence of the Chilean Left under the leadership of Salvador Allende. Most of these funds were spent on direct propaganda and election activities rather than on the longer-term organizational work and support of social and syndical movements that I had stressed in Rome. But the objectives were the same—to rally support for center democracy.

In 1970, a presidential-election year that marked the end of the Frei administration in Santiago, a rather foolish decision was taken by the Forty Committee of the National Security Council, reflecting the doubts within both the CIA and the State Department about large-scale CIA covert political action and subsidies. Rather than support one of the two non-Communist candidates running to succeed Frei as

President, the National Party's Jorge Alessandri or the Christian Democrat's Radomiro Tomic—and urge the other to withdraw—CIA directed its efforts only into a "spoiling campaign" against the Marxist Allende through propaganda attacks. While this was certainly a cheaper tactic than supporting one of Allende's opponents, at a cost of less than half a million dollars, it also proved to be ineffective. As any of my good New York Democratic friends could have predicted, "You can't beat something with nothing," and the result was a disaster. Allessandri and Tomic split the democratic vote between them, and Allende slipped to victory with a 36 percent plurality.

Nixon was furious. He was convinced that the Allende victory meant a spread of Castro's anti-American revolution to Chile, and from there throughout Latin America. So, after a few days of inconclusive discussion in Washington and Santiago as to what might be done, he called Helms to a meeting in the Oval Office with Henry Kissinger, his National Security Adviser but not yet Secretary of State, and Attorney General John N. Mitchell, and he gave Helms a very clear order to block Allende from assuming office. Called "Track II" to distinguish it from CIA's other actions in Chile, this plan took advantage of the fact that under the Chilean constitution Allende had to be voted into office by the Chilean Congress since he had obtained only a plurality; CIA was to see to it by any means possible that he did not get this vote; and the means specifically included turning to the Chilean military for help. As Helms later said, "If I ever carried a marshal's baton in my knapsack out of the Oval Office, it was that day."

Helms received another order direct from the President: Track II was to be told to no one outside CIA, not to the United States ambassador in Santiago nor to the Secretaries of State or Defense or their Departments, or the Forty Committee. However unusual, this order was fully within the President's authority to order covert action. So CIA went to work to carry it out—sending a special task force of CIA officers to Chile for six weeks of frantic effort, independent of the station, reporting only to Washington headquarters, contacting and assessing political and military leaders to select those who might move against Allende, determining what financial, arms or other aid they might need, and discussing strategies as to how the inauguration could be stopped. Although funds were made available by the Forty Committee to bribe Chilean Congressmen to vote against Allende, they were not spent, because the tactic was clearly unworkable. The only hope seemed to lie with the Army, but any action there depended on removing its commander, General René Schneider, who had made clear his belief that the Army should not act against the Constitutional process. In desperation, an attempt was made to kidnap him, but it was bungled, and he died from wounds he received in resisting it. And the failure of the attempt ended any sentiment in the Army to act. The kidnap attempt was made by a group that CIA had been in contact with but had given up as ineffective. CIA had provided weapons to another group for a similar plan, but it was not involved in the kidnap attempt. In the end, Allende was inaugurated on schedule, and CIA terminated its Track II and its efforts to get the Chilean military to move.

Track II, of course, was well in the past by the time I became Executive Director, and indeed for a considerable time I knew nothing of it, in accordance with the President's directive that it be handled in the utmost secrecy. But I did know that CIA was still active in Chile, since the sums required for its operations there were large enough to affect the Agency's budget considerably. After his assumption of power, Allende carried out a program to squeeze out his opponents, and CIA was trying to sustain them against this pressure in the hope that they would revive and win the next elections in 1976 in a repudiation of Allende's and Castro's hopes. Aid to the center parties, support for free and opposition journals and radios, and assistance to student and syndical groups were all funneled through third-country intermediaries to keep them alive despite the Allende government's moves against their newsprint supplies, their banking facilities, and their activities. Aid in the Chilean Congressional election to anti-Allende candidates in early 1973 helped to bring that body to within two votes of achieving the two-thirds majority that would have permitted Allende's impeachment. And the Chamber of Deputies, the Supreme Court and the Controller General, all issued public attacks on his violations of the Constitution.

Two points need to be made about CIA's assistance during this period after 1970, and both are a contrast to the general impressions abroad about it. The first is that CIA's help was to *center* political groups, and not to right-wing extremists. Of the millions of dollars spent in Chile by CIA the most prominent right-wing group, Patria y Libertad, received some $38,000 during the Track II effort in 1970, about $7,000 more during 1971, and *none thereafter*. The second is that the 1973 coup was carried out by the Chilean military with no participation by CIA—in fact, CIA sent clear instructions to its station in Santiago in May and June 1973 to separate itself from any contact with the Chilean military so that it would not be misunderstood to have been involved in any coup action the military might undertake. The real thrust of CIA's program was to support the center political forces so that they could win the next elections and thus remove Allende through peaceful means.

I am not trying to whitewash CIA's activities in Chile, but only to put in true perspective what the Agency did there. Certainly, in Track II in 1970 it sought a military coup, at the direct order of President Nixon. Certainly, having launched such an attempt, CIA was responsible to some degree for the final outcome, no matter that it tried to "distance" itself and turn away well before 1973. Certainly, its support of the center parties, political groups and media thereafter did produce tension in Chile when Allende tried to suppress them; there would have been no tension if his pressure had not been resisted. And certainly, American policy toward Allende was hostile, including the administration's attempts to rally private capital against Chile, the State Department's efforts to cut off its international credits, and the American military's continued warm contacts with the Chilean military. But to make CIA some sort of scapegoat for all the evils of the present military government in Chile is not only inaccurate and unfair, it is dangerous. For it creates a false image of the United States worldwide and can deprive our nation of an essential tool with which to meet future problems. And an essential step toward the proper use of this tool is to understand what it can do in a careful, long-term operation of supporting local leaders and groups, helping them to accomplish what they do want to accomplish—in short, what it can do when it is *for* some cause and group, rather than being *against* an adversary.

One of the key tasks of Executive Director was that of Comptroller of the funds and programs of the Agency. In any bureaucracy, control of budgets comes close to the heart of the command process, and CIA was no different in this respect. Thus, I knew that any attempt by me to assume control over CIA's funds would be met by stiff resistance from the Deputy Directors. So rather than control, I turned rather to inspection as the means by which to obtain some influence over the budget process, and I learned something about bureaucracy and how to deal with it.

A fundamental difficulty in the budget process was that the offices carrying out operations had to make their requests for funds many months before they would be used, and then defend them not only within the Agency against competing programs but to the Office of Management and Budget and to the Congress. Thus, the offices tried to state their needs in sufficiently general terms, so that they could meet any new situations that might arise in the future, while the reviewing agencies and Congress insisted that each need be set forth specifically so that they could determine its validity. Once, while I was Chief of the Far East Division, I had been indiscreet enough to reply to an examiner's question about an item in a Southeast Asian appropriation that it was (which it was) a "slush fund" to meet future needs; all present were shocked at this blatant truth, and the fund was eliminated from my budget by the examiner. Even after the appropriation was made, however, I found that the problem persisted. Each command level tried to withhold a portion of the approved resources so that it could react to new needs that had not been anticipated when the request for funds was made. But one result of this natural and even essential process was that at the end of the year there was a frantic drive to commit whatever remained of the funds that had been withheld, so that they would not have to be returned to the Treasury. The haste of this process, and the lack of opportunity for careful selection of projects during it, produced contracts and commitments whose value was frequently marginal if not downright dubious.

I thought there must be a better way, and I found it, through the computers and inspection. I discovered that our financial machinery could provide each month a detailed accounting of how much of the funds scheduled to be spent on every activity actually had been disbursed, which activity would need extra help before the year was over, and which ones would not use what they thought they would require. It also provided the information needed to decide which activities should be stopped in favor of others. So I set up a monthly meeting to move the funds accordingly. The Deputy Directors were delighted when I told them that I would no longer withhold a portion of their budgets, that I would be able to find funds they might need for new requirements, and that they would have every opportunity to challenge my proposals to stop some of their activities before Helms. In the first year this procedure caused about twenty million dollars *more* to be available to the Deputy Directors, and it eliminated the last-minute dash to commit withheld funds. And it accomplished this without my having to insert myself into the decision-making process since my role was only one of inspecting what had been done, not of deciding what to do.

Another aspect of the Executive Director's responsibilities was to prepare the Agency's budget presentation to the Office of Management and Budget and to the Congress. And in this process, I learned that normal and strict governmental procedures had replaced the free-wheeling attitudes that had characterized CIA's early years in this regard. A story that my predecessor, "Red" White, liked to tell concerned the original request to the Chairman of the Senate Appropriations Committee for funds for CIA's new headquarters in Langley. Allen Dulles and White gave the Senator a glowing presentation of the need for the building and showed him its plans. "My, that will be a beautiful building," the Senator said; "I suppose it will cost about twenty-five million." "Well, Mr. Chairman, I am afraid it will cost a bit more," Dulles replied; "about fifty million." "My," the Senator said, "that *will* be a beautiful building." And with that the hearing was over and CIA got the money for the building that it had requested.

The story was White's favorite, because it illustrated the dramatic change that had taken place in the way the Agency's budget was dealt with since then. Now we were required to present a detailed breakdown of our funds and personnel, showing the totals of each by organizational component, by activities conducted, and by the targets sought. OMB examiners and Congressional staff experts reviewed all these in detail and came up with sharp questions about, and exceptions to, the Agency's proposals. The Agency naturally put its best foot forward, trying as did all agencies to impress the Congressmen. But it learned that to do this it was required to make full disclosure, to the assigned subcommittees, of the specifics of its activities and give frank answers to the questions the Congressmen might ask. While this was done behind the closed doors of these special subcommittees, which the Congress had established to review the CIA budget, it was plain to anyone who ever participated in these proceedings that our budget received every bit as detailed a review as that given any other department or agency by a Congressional committee.

This new toughness on the part of the Congress vis-à-vis the Agency had increased in direct proportion as the Agency's reputation had declined. That decline, as noted earlier, can be said to have begun in the aftermath of the

Bay of Pigs fiasco. But it had accelerated precipitously during the Vietnam war years. The "credibility gap" that had developed during the Johnson administration and widened under Nixon had made vast segments of the population suspicious of government agencies generally and had spurred the press to a more investigative and hostile approach in their reporting on government activities. The CIA certainly wasn't exempt from either and, indeed, because of the secrecy that surrounded its activities, was a more vulnerable target than most. In a time of growing distrust of government, it found itself regarded as an exemplar of the repugnant clandestine methods and secret manipulations that were seen as characteristic of the Johnson and Nixon administrations. These views were much abetted by the press, of course, which long before had learned the headline value of the initials CIA, but also stirred a deep sense of unease in the Congress.

It is true that, even at this late date, the Congress' role in CIA affairs was very limited. The old command structure of senior Representatives and Senators from the Appropriations and Armed Services Intelligence subcommittees was still the only Congressional oversight with which the CIA had to deal. But, as I quickly saw in my post as Executive Director, dealing with it was now no longer quite the loose and friendly process it once had been. Even the senior Congressional leaders were no longer prepared to automatically approve what the Agency requested. Under pressure from the press, the public, and their more junior colleagues, they felt obliged to assert their oversight function. And in the covert political and paramilitary fields, as we have seen, their influence became increasingly substantial, forcing us to shift the financing of many of our large operations in that area to the open Pentagon budget, so that the remaining ones in our secret budget would be as few as possible. And they sharply questioned us on any and all such programs that did remain in our secret budget, because of their concern that these were the activities, if and when exposed by the increasingly investigative and hostile press, that made the headlines that discredited the Agency and its purely intelligence work, which they believed important in the eyes of the public.

The Agency could not long suffer this growing suspicion and hostility and the concomitant disintegration of its once shining image. The morale of CIA officers was being undermined by it, the recruitment of bright young new officers from university campuses was becoming more difficult, and the Agency's ability to conduct valuable operations was being increasingly circumscribed. The CIA, it seemed obvious to me, was in very real danger of ultimately being crippled as an effective weapon in the defense of the nation's security if not in fact threatened with being destroyed outright—unless something was done to reverse this trend. And that something, in my view, was to lift as much as possible that thick cloak of secrecy that had traditionally veiled the Agency and its operations from the scrutiny—and more important, the understanding—of the public at large.

As we have seen, ever since the CIA's founding—and specifically incorporated in the Congressional act that had founded it—the Agency not only had the special right, but was required, because of the very nature of its work, to operate in the utmost secrecy, with its organization, its functions, the names and numbers of its personnel and its budget known only to the President and his closest advisers. As Dick Helms once phrased it, "The nation must to a degree take it on faith that we too are honorable men devoted to her service." And the nation, in its Congress and press and people, had taken just that on faith for over twenty years.

But the times had changed. In the Vietnam period's atmosphere of rampant cynicism and suspicion about government, secrecy was seen not as a tool necessary for the practice of intelligence, but as a device by which intelligence could hide its bungles and mask its wicked activities. In fact, to a degree, the secrecy itself promoted this view. For those who did not know what the CIA was doing were free, unhindered by the facts, to invent the wildest distortions and fantasies. It seemed manifestly obvious to me that the best and, indeed, the only way to counter the distortions that were ruining the CIA's image was to shuck as much secrecy as possible and let the people, press and Congress know what the Agency was really doing. What was needed, in short, was an educational campaign. In those changing times, when the nation was no longer willing to take it on faith that anyone in government, and especially in CIA, was an honorable man, we were obliged to demonstrate that we were honorable by showing what we were doing. And as Executive Director, I thought I could start the process by making sure that our own CIA employees knew what the facts and the rules were, so they could defend their work in their own minds and to their friends and neighbors. Once this base was laid, we could then consider how to get the message over to the public.

It was, however, not an easy and straightforward task. There were and are, of course, secrets that must be kept in order to carry out effective intelligence work. But there were also some things in CIA's past whose revelation would further undermine the CIA's reputation and add fuel to the anti-CIA fires. For, as I soon discovered, in the secretive, highly compartmentalized world that CIA had been for much of its existence, wherein officers in one section knew little of what was going on in other sections, some very questionable and even improper activities had occurred.

There was one subject on which I was particularly sensitive, and that was assassinations. Some months after my July 1971 testimony to a Congressional committee on the Phoenix program, *Parade* magazine, read in millions of American homes every Sunday, published the statement that the CIA was the "only" agency of the United States government "authorized" to commit assassinations. As I saw it, this was just the kind of canard that was fueling the destruction of the CIA's reputation in the eyes of the Congress and the people. I knew from personal experience that the Agency was not engaged in assassinations in Vietnam; indeed, quite to the contrary, it had been my specific directive as head of CORDS that, for both moral and practical reasons, assassinations were strictly prohibited to Phoenix personnel. And as I was sure that my attitude reflected the thinking throughout the CIA on this matter, I wanted to write to *Parade* and say that not only wasn't the CIA "authorized" to commit assassinations, it was strictly opposed to such activity. But to make the statement broader than my knowledge of the Phoenix program, I decided to do a bit of quiet research around the house. And in the process I learned how hard it would be to clarify such a difficult subject.

I knew the Vietnam side of the question, of course, both with respect to Phoenix and to President Ngo Dinh Diem's death, and I knew that CIA was not involved in assassination in either. But I had heard of a Jack Anderson column of a few years past making some allegations about a plot against Castro. As Castro obviously was still alive, it was clear that CIA could hardly be charged with his assassination, though something may have been tried against him in the early 1960s. When I heard some remarks about possible assassination activity in Africa, I asked a good friend involved in that area of the world and was told that a few steps we may have started at one point there had been stopped and that Patrice Lumumba's death was definitely not a CIA action in any way. I then picked up enough to indicate that there was some further information available in highly restricted circles about Trujillo's death, but that this too was not a CIA action. Nonetheless, it was clear that I was onto a volatile subject, with a number of ambiguities, and I found that no one would discuss it with me in any detail. So I decided that we ought at least put on the record, in the form of a directive from Helms, that CIA would not now or in the future engage in, stimulate or support assassinations in any way. He signed the directive I prepared to that effect as soon as I put it before him. It certainly represented his view. But I had to qualify the letter I wrote to *Parade*. I could not make the flat denial, as I had intended, that any such activity had ever occurred; and as a result, *Parade*'s original sweeping statement was not effectively refuted.

In a not unsimilar fashion I became aware of another

questionable CIA activity. I was, of course, aware that the Agency's legislative charter specifically forbade it from "police, subpoena, law-enforcement powers or internal security functions," and I knew that the doctrine at the working levels of the Agency was to stay away from any operation that snacked even vaguely of such actions. But one day the Agency's Security Director stopped in at my office for a private word. He was obviously unhappy, saying there was something he wanted to make me aware of so that he wouldn't be the only officer with knowledge of what he judged to be an extremely sensitive and explosive operation. He had been instructed to undertake a secret surveillance of a prominent newspaper columnist who had recently published some intelligence material. The CIA surveillance was intended to find out which government officials might have been the source of the leaks.

It was immediately apparent to me, as it was to the Security Director, that a political uproar would embroil the CIA if this operation were ever exposed. But we were both aware that, if questionable, this operation was not patently illegal. There was a gray area in the Agency's charter making the Director responsible for "protecting intelligence sources and methods from unauthorized disclosure," which could be construed to justify it. Even so, I felt constrained to ask a simple question. How many people within the Agency would know about this operation, counting the technicians, secretaries, supervisors and regular field officers who would have to be involved, and I guessed it at about fifty. The Security Director agreed. "Well, let's face it then," I said. "There's not one chance in a million that this is going to stay a secret. Sooner or later, this is going to make the headlines." And, of course, it did. To protect the Security chief's confidence, I decided not to protest the surveillance at the time, but it haunted me as an example of the sort of thing the Agency should not do.

At about this time another CIA operation that was in full swing aroused the concern of many CIA employees—it was later revealed as Operation Chaos—and their constant questions about it soon made it an interdirectorate matter appropriate for me, as the Executive Director, to handle. Young analysts, computer operators and operations officers were all aware that a most secret project was lodged in that most secret of Agency crannies, the Counterintelligence Staff, and that it had a great deal to do with the antiwar movement. And the main concern on the part of these young Agency employees was whether CIA was engaged in an activity that was clearly outside its proper charter—domestic intelligence. They raised the matter first in an advisory group, which management had established to improve communication with the junior personnel, and said they were particularly concerned that CIA not be pushed into some activity that would expose it to outside attack and criticism. So I undertook to look into the operation, and I was to have much to do with it in the future.

Operation Chaos dated back to 1967 and the Johnson Administration. At the time, President Johnson was faced with a rapidly escalating antiwar movement marked by protest demonstrations, bloody riots and a rash of bombings. Feeling himself embattled in the White House, he ordered Helms to discover whether there was any foreign financing or manipulation behind the antiwar movement or behind any of the radical, dissident groups associated with it. Following the President's instructions, Helms launched an operation under the aegis of Angleton's Counterintelligence Staff, so that it could be conducted with maximum compartmentation and secrecy. Moreover, he ordered that it be free of the normal processes of review and approval of its finances, records and methodology. Extensive liaison was established with a similar office set up in the Federal Bureau of Investigation to work on the domestic aspects of the President's directive. Computer files were established, special and private channels of communications to stations abroad were provided, and all were told that the program had top priority. With Johnson's—and later Nixon's—intense interest in unearthing foreign involvement, and displeasure when Helms reported that there wasn't any, the pressure on the operation was enormous, and the cables and computers hummed.

Helms was acutely conscious of the danger of seeming to involve the CIA in a domestic intelligence activity. He knew how easily Operation Chaos could leak to the press, where it surely would be misinterpreted as an Agency effort directed against the antiwar movement itself, rather than its foreign contacts. As a result, his directives were plain: the purpose of the project was to identify *foreign* links to American dissidents, not to spy on the American dissidents themselves, and thus a proper Agency activity well within the CIA's statutory charter. But, as the Rockefeller Commission was later to point out, the momentum of the operation carried it beyond these instructions in some cases. The enthusiasm for having full personal records on individuals readily available, including American citizens who might be contacted by foreign powers, led to the growth of an extensive exchange between the FBI and the CIA, and the buildup of substantial files on Americans. What's more, the need to develop agents who could go abroad with convincing credentials and thus have access to foreign groups who might contact the American antiwar movement resulted in the infiltration of CIA agents into American dissident groups to see what the foreigners might be doing. And there were a few instances—actually only three in number—in which CIA agents, in their enthusiasm, reported on the activities of American dissidents while still in America. This was clearly improper, even though it was only a small part of the overall operation.

By turning Operation Chaos over to the Counterintelligence Staff, which was the most secretive and compartmented element in the CIA, Helms obviously intended not only to prevent the outside world from knowing of it but also to keep it from the rest of the Agency. But by the time I had returned to Langley as Executive Director, the operation had been underway for more than four years and its existence, if not the details of its activities, was generally known. Operations officers abroad who were asked to check the foreign contacts of some American dissident; computer operators conscious of the volume, secrecy and priority of its demands; analysts who were asked to examine foreign intentions and statements about United States dissent; security officers reporting on dissident groups that might be a threat to the Agency—all of them contributed to the gossip about Operation Chaos in the corridors at the Langley headquarters. They also contributed to the rising unease and suspicion about the operation, most especially among younger officers, as to its propriety. It was with this worry that some of them came to me, asking the management of the Agency to make sure that we were not involved in some activity that not only was improper but could destroy the Agency they believed in.

It seemed to me vital that, for the sake of the Agency's morale, a positive response be made by the CIA's top brass to counter the spreading internal suspicion about the operation. So I took it upon myself to have an over-all detailed description drawn up of what Chaos was supposed to be and what it was doing. My hope was that a clear statement of its charter would end the uneasiness over it and that the operation would be accepted as justified. If there were cases wherein the operation had overstepped the CIA charter, it was my hope that the clear description would have the effect of forcing the operation back within its rightful and legal limits—a hope I reinforced by a descriptive memorandum that asked that any deviation from proper activities be called to my attention for correction. Moreover, I believed that this approach would also have the benefit of provoking a reconsideration of the probable value of the whole operation, which by this time seemed less and less significant, since it had become pretty clear that the antiwar movement wasn't connected with any foreign elements—a point Helms had made several times to doubting Presidents.

This tactic worked; Helms in 1972 directed that the elaborate machinery of Operation Chaos be turned away from the antiwar movement to a far more important current threat, that of international terrorism. That target was clearly a legitimate CIA responsibility and a much more pressing one than seeking links between foreign powers and the antiwar movement. It wasn't until more than a year later that I realized that Helms's direction as to the new priority was considered by a few of those devoted to Chaos to be a cover story—a publicly acceptable explanation of their work while they continued to seek counterintelligence targets within American domestic dissent. By the time I learned of this, I was already in the process of dismantling Chaos, so I did not try to ascertain just exactly how this misconstruction of Helms's instructions might have been reflected in actual operations. The experience did demonstrate, however, how the habits and language of clandestinity can intoxicate even its own practitioners and that internal supervision must be crystal-clear and thorough, especially when the secrecy of the operation prohibits external oversight.

But for all my efforts, I found it impossible to do much about righting whatever was wrong with Operation Chaos. Its supersecrecy and extreme compartmentation, and the way its direction depended on Helms's personal attention, kept me very much on its periphery. Whatever assurances I could come up with in response to the questions of the troubled younger officers did little to allay their unhappiness. For the fact of the matter was that the crisis of confidence in government over Vietnam, which was sweeping the nation at large, was beginning to infect the faith of the intelligence community in itself.

Just how serious the infection was soon became clear when a publisher passed along a copy of the outline of a book on CIA being circulated by Victor Marchetti, a former CIA employee, in his search for a publisher. Marchetti, who had started out as an analyst, had been the Executive Assistant to the Deputy Director of Central Intelligence. Sitting astride the paper flow into the DDCI's office, Marchetti had seen some of the most secret aspects of our intelligence operations. His co-author on the book, John Marks, who had served in the State Department Intelligence and Research Bureau, had had almost as much access to sensitive intelligence material there. Both had signed, before they were given access to such material, the same agreement that all intelligence officers sign, to respect the secrecy of the material they become acquainted with in their jobs. But both had apparently decided that they would no longer be bound by that commitment. And the outline of their book indicated that they intended to reveal and criticize a number of CIA's activities, including those that CIA had undertaken with foreigners, with the sincerest understanding that they would be kept secret, since the reputations and even the safety of the foreigners could be jeopardized if they were revealed.

Helms gathered a group of his senior advisers to discuss what we might do about this. We quickly concluded that we would really not be able to prosecute the two former employees if they did publish, since a trial, even if successful, would probably result in the exposure of even more details of the secrets than their book might contain. And it was quite clear that an attempt to enjoin publication on the basis of a threat to national security would be an enormously difficult uphill fight, produce oceans of further publicity, and unite the nation's journalists against us.

But one possibility did exist: an action to compel our former employee to abide by the agreement he made when he joined CIA that he would not publish without first obtaining CIA's agreement that he was not exposing classified information he had acquired during his employment. We knew we would still have a hard fight, but Helms decided we should go ahead, and we all agreed with him, because even if we lost, it would dramatically show how weak our legislation to protect secrets was, and it would give us a basis to ask Congress for something better.

So the Justice Department took the case to court—and won, although only after a long process and appeal. The Circuit Court of Appeals first decided that Marchetti did indeed have to submit his text to us for review. And when he did, by which time I was Director, I told our people to follow the rules meticulously and identify every item that was classified when Marchetti was employed, even though we would not really insist on some of them being deleted in the long run. I also said they were not to object to any of Marchetti's opinions and that we could not object to Marchetti's making a mistake and saying something that was wrong, since by definition something that was not true could not be classified. So our people identified some three-hundred-odd items. Our lawyers made a date to go over them with Marchetti and his lawyers to see whether we could get them to agree to minor changes in the wording of some of the items to make them unclassified, for example, leaving out specific names of people or countries. We also planned to drop our objections to certain of the items in the negotiation, to show our good faith, since some things like Air America had been so broadly exposed that they hardly were secret any more. And we were prepared to accept instances where Marchetti had learned things from sources other than his employment, in which case his agreement with us did not apply. But on some of the items, we knew, we would have to insist that they be dropped. And we hoped Marchetti would agree, as had several other former employees who had written, and written critically, about their CIA experience, but who had been convinced that we were not censoring their opinions and ideas, only protecting the specific and valuable secrets.

But Marchetti said no, not a word could be changed. On about half of the three hundred items, we in CIA dropped our objections, either because we knew they really were no longer secrets or because Marchetti convinced us that he had another source than his employment for the information. But we dug in our heels on the remainder, went to court, testified about their classified nature and, after another appeal taken by the effective Justice Department attorney Irwin Goldbloom, again won. But in a way, so did Marchetti, Marks, and their publisher: they published the book with blank spaces showing the items we had had deleted and with bold type for those items we had initially identified as classified but then had withdrawn our objections. And they made a great publicity campaign out of our "censorship," which certainly added to the book's sale.

As a footnote to this experience, another former employee, Philip Agee, stayed out of the reach of the American court system until he published his story in England, festooned with an alphabetical list of every name of every person he apparently could remember with whom he had been associated during his time in CIA, whether or not that might expose them to danger or damage.

And then in this atmosphere we were hit by Watergate. I first heard of the break-in at the Democratic National Committee headquarters on the radio news that Saturday, June 17, 1972, crowding out the accounts of John Paul Vann's funeral at Arlington the day before, where Komer had led us in tribute to our fighting friend. I must admit that, along with most of the country, I didn't pay the break-in much mind, prepared to believe that it was nothing more than a stupid, third-rate burglary. But by the time of the evening news broadcast that day, when some of the burglars were identified as former CIA agents, and certainly by the following day, Sunday, by which time former CIA officers James McCord and Howard Hunt had been tied to the break-in, I realized that this was trouble for the Agency. Given the intense anti-CIA sentiment of the times, I knew that the Agency was bound to come in for another headline-shrieking pasting. But since the event was as much news to me as to the rest of the country, I felt that it would be soon enough to face the issue at the regular meeting of the CIA's top leadership on Monday morning.

Watergate obviously was topic number one at the meeting, and the first thing Helms did was express his surprise and puzzlement about what was going on. His contacts with the White House were almost exclusively through Kissinger, so he had no real knowledge of the activities of the Haldeman-Ehrlichman circle. He quickly ascertained, by calling on each of his senior subordinates in turn around the table, that everyone was equally surprised, and that thus there was no current CIA involvement with the Watergate figures, despite their earlier employment or other connections with the Agency. The meeting's conclusion—that the CIA had had nothing to do with the break-in—was the absolute, unqualified truth. A number of those around the table did know that Hunt had been hired by the White House for some mysterious and probably improper political machinations, bringing to the task his penchant for unnecessary intrigue. They also knew that McCord was working for the Committee to Re-Elect the President; his background at the Agency had been in security, so his role in this caper was a bit harder to understand. But, although all this offered much material for conjecture, the feeling was that it was beyond CIA's charter to worry about and equally unwise for it to become involved in. Any wrong-doing and the retribution it would bring were for the White House and its employees to handle, not the CIA.

Of course, there was a lively appreciation around the table that morning that because of Hunt, McCord, Martinez, and the others with CIA connections, there was a real danger that the flame of suspicion about the Agency would ignite into blazing headlines, making it seem that Watergate and all that the rubric would come to stand for was at bottom yet another dastardly CIA operation. To prevent that from happening, Helms spelled out a fundamental strategy with which all his associates, myself included, agreed. To protect itself from even the appearance of involvement in Watergate, the Agency was to distance itself from the event to every extent possible. "Stay cool, volunteer nothing, because it will only be used to involve us. Just stay away from the whole damn thing." That was the gist of Helms's advice, and he asked me to coordinate the Agency's efforts in this regard.

My first task was to respond to the requests from the FBI Alexandria office, which had been put in charge of investigating the Watergate break-in, for information on the status and backgrounds of the individuals with CIA connections who had been arrested. The immediate problem was how we could give the FBI facts about the activities of former CIA personnel without revealing the operational jobs they had done in the past and the people with whom they had dealt. We had to be concerned with the protection of legitimate operational secrets and with ensuring that the Agency was not dragged into something it had had nothing to do with while responding to quite appropriate FBI inquiries. It was while I was pondering this problem that Karl Wagner, the executive assistant to Lieutenant General Vernon Walters, the DDCI, drew me aside to say that he had some information that might be relevant. He told me that he recalled that about a year before, Howard Hunt had come to General Robert Cushman, who was then the DDCI, to ask for CIA assistance on a job he was doing for the White House. The assistance, of course, was the famous wig and other material that Hunt obtained. The CIA had provided the assistance, Wagner said, because Hunt's request was backed up by a personal phone call from John Ehrlichman to Cushman. The transaction, Wagner said, was on record, because Cushman had turned on a secret tape recorder, with which the DDCI's office was equipped, during the whole of Hunt's visit. But, Wagner added, the Agency's help to Hunt was cut off a few weeks later, when his requests escalated and Wagner had warned that CIA was becoming involved in some domestic affair of the White House "plumbers" outside its proper jurisdiction.

Wagner's information was obviously disturbing. It showed that a link did exist between CIA and Hunt's activities, and no matter that it had been broken a year before or that it had been forged in the first place by someone as high up in the White House as Ehrlichman, it was exactly the sort of connection that could be trumpeted in the press and by CIA's critics and put CIA smack in the middle of the headlines about whatever stupid enterprise Hunt might have been engaged in in the Watergate building. When I took Wagner to Helms and we all reviewed the details of the contacts, neither Helms nor I saw any need to volunteer this information immediately to the FBI, since it did not have anything to do with the Watergate break-in a year later. Our strategy, Helms stressed, was to respond to legitimate requests by the investigators for information on the individuals involved in Watergate or any other directly related questions. But we had no obligation to rush forward with peripheral information not significant to the investigation at hand and likely to create misunderstandings and public excitement about a possible—and nonexistent—CIA role in the activity under investigation. So I turned my attention to just such a legitimate request.

One of the first reports I provided to the FBI outlined the Agency's association with Eugenio Martinez, stating that he had worked for the CIA during the middle 1960s and that he was still on a $100-a-month Agency "retainer" to report on Cuban exile activities at the time of the Watergate incident. In responding to questions about Hunt and his relations with the Mullen Company, the name of which was found in his notebook, I said that the Mullen Company, a widely known public-relations firm, had allowed the CIA to put two CIA officers on its payroll overseas as cover, and that one of the CIA men was still at his post. Our concern that the CIA would be dragged unfairly into Watergate immediately zoomed. For a few days after I had sent these reports off to the FBI Alexandria office, the information in them was repeated in the press, with the key word "retainer" showing plainly the source, and the Mullen Company characterized as a "CIA front." Clearly there was a leak in the FBI's Alexandria office, and from that point forward I determined that, though we would respond to all legitimate FBI requests, we would do so not to the Alexandria office but only to FBI Washington headquarters, where we could hope that our legitimate secrets would be protected and that the Agency would not be falsely tarred with the Watergate scandal.

But this proved to be no easy job. For, as we now know from the White House tapes, President Nixon, within days of the Watergate break-in, had decided to try to use the CIA to cover up the escalating scandal, which ultimately would force his resignation. On June 23, he agreed to a scheme in which the Agency was to be told to block the FBI's investigation. That day, Ehrlichman and H. R. Haldeman summoned Helms and his new deputy General Walters to the White House. There Ehrlichman expounded on the President's concern that the FBI Watergate investigation—it was now tracking down the money paid to the burglars to where it had been laundered in Mexico—would reveal legitimate CIA operations abroad. Helms replied that he didn't think it would. Nonetheless, Ehrlichman and Haldeman ordered

Walters—not Helms, interestingly enough—to go to Acting FBI Director Patrick Gray and tell him that FBI investigations could endanger CIA operations in Mexico. After the meeting, in the car taking them away from the White House, Helms warned Walters to be sure that, in any conversation with Gray, he merely ask that any connection that the FBI might discover in its Mexican investigations that related to the CIA be brought to the Agency's attention.

Walters, only six weeks in his post, went to Gray and repeated the concern that some revelation of legitimate CIA Mexican operations might occur, and if it did, the Agency should be informed. Immediately after this discussion, Walters returned to Langley and asked me to examine the records to see if any of our Mexican activities might be in jeopardy. I checked with the responsible offices and on June 24 advised Walters that this was extremely unlikely. That was a Saturday and on the following Monday, the twenty-sixth, Walters told John Dean, who was coordinating the Watergate affair in the White House, that there was little possibility of the FBI's running across a CIA operation and causing a problem that the Agency could not handle. With this, Walters felt confident that he had unhooked any possible suspension of FBI investigations that his conversation with Gray might have caused. But on July 5, much to his surprise, Walters received a phone call from Gray in which the FBI chief said that he could no longer hold off the investigation without a written request from the CIA to that effect. The startled Walters replied that no such written or even oral request would be made by the CIA for the very good reason that the CIA, as he had made clear to Dean, didn't feel that there was any basis for it. Apparently Dean had failed to pass Walters' message on to Gray.

With the investigation once more in motion, I received a new request from the FBI for more detailed information about the CIA's relations with Howard Hunt. Conforming to our belief that we had to keep the Agency off center stage in this mess, I drafted a special memorandum that went to Gray personally over Walters' signature (Helms was out of the country). This said that the CIA had provided Hunt with certain technical disguise equipment in 1971 as a result of a request from "a duly authorized extra-agency official." I believed it important that this report be sent to respond to the FBI's question about our contacts with Hunt. But I did not name Ehrlichman as the "duly authorized extra-agency official" for two reasons. The first was to avoid dropping what appeared at the time to be an inflammatory name into a matter that appeared to have no particular relevance to the Watergate affair over a year later. The second was to avoid revealing the existence of the secret taping capability in the DDCI's office, which was the only basis I had for knowing that Ehrlichman was involved (although a separate CIA record was later discovered that confirmed that he was). It was not a wise move.

A few months later, with the Watergate investigations accelerating and broadening to include the over-all activities of the White House "plumbers," Gray turned that memorandum over to the Justice Department and I, along with the CIA's deputy general counsel, John Warner, was called in for a meeting with Assistant Attorney General Harold Petersen and Assistant U.S. Attorney Earl Silbert to discuss the matter. Among the mass of material, they focused on who had backed up Hunt's request for CIA assistance. I first said that the person was from another agency which was authorized to give us direction and then identified the agency as the White House. Finally in response to Silbert's direct question, I named Ehrlichman as the one who had phoned Cushman. I had some hesitation, because the only evidence I had at the time to that effect was the statement of Cushman on the tape, saying, "Yes, he called me."

Ehrlichman heard about this exchange and soon after convoked Helms and me for a session at the White House to go over the matter, with Dean present. Ehrlichman said, and he seemed genuinely perplexed, that he had in fact been away from Washington at the time his phone call to Cushman was supposed to have taken place. I replied that I didn't know any more about it than the one fact of

Cushman's statement on the tape. I then suggested that if it was a question of Ehrlichman's failure to remember the call, he get in touch with Cushman. He asked if I would request Cushman to call him, and I agreed to do so. But to show that I had not thrown Ehrlichman's name out in any sense of hostility, I told him (and later recorded in a memorandum of my conversation with him) that I had "danced around" in order to avoid mentioning his name in the first set of questions put to me by Petersen and Silbert. It was a most unfelicitous choice of phrase and it came back to haunt me during an intense cross-examination by Senator Edward Kennedy in the 1973 confirmation hearings on my nomination to be DCI, where he wanted to know whether I was one of the group that had tried to cover up Watergate and its associated activities.

Another tangential connection between the CIA and Watergate with which I had to deal then involved a group of photographs that were brought to me when I was collecting all the data we had on the Agency's help to Hunt in 1971. He had asked the Agency's technical laboratories to develop a roll of film he had taken with a camera that the Agency provided him when we gave him the wig and other material. The officer who had done the job had made copies of the developed prints before returning the negatives and originals to Hunt. They were very grainy but clear enough for one to make out a series of Xerox shops in the Los Angeles area and an office building and its address, two cars parked out in front, with the names of two doctors on a nameplate on the building and the cars' license-plate numbers identifiable. All of this meant nothing to me, and I thought it adequate simply to mention the existence of the photos in the report I drafted for the FBI on the CIA's relations with Hunt. No FBI follow-up took place.

But after several months, with the Watergate scandal burgeoning into a national trauma, I became uneasy as to what the photographs might signify. I asked our security office to attempt to identify the building, the two doctors whose names appeared on it and the license plates of the cars parked out front. The report came back in December 1972,

saying that the building was indeed in a Los Angeles neighborhood and the names and cars belonged to well-established and qualified psychiatrists, one of whom was Dr.
Lewis J. Fielding. None of this in itself had any significance, and nothing was added to my knowledge; but after a
week or so of rumination, I sent the photographs to the FBI,
along with the information we had gathered on them. They
were, of course, photographs taken by Hunt and Liddy as
part of their plan to burglarize the Fielding offices to obtain
psychiatric material on Daniel Ellsberg. But I didn't discover this until May 1973, when the burglary was revealed
in the Ellsberg trial and resulted in its dismissal.

A footnote to this incident is the fact that John Dean obviously did recognize the photographs and their significance
long before the Ellsberg trial. For early in 1973, somewhat
nervously, he asked that all of CIA's memos (obviously including the photographs) be returned to the CIA from the
FBI, leaving a card in the FBI's file that this had been done.
I recommended that we agree to no such thing since I saw
no legitimate rationale for doing so, although I had no suspicion what might be behind Dean's request at the time. We
reacted the same way as we reacted when Dean approached
Walters shortly after the Watergate arrests with the idea that
the CIA provide bail for the arrested Watergate burglars.
Walters turned that one down flatly, pointing out that this
would be impossible, since the Agency had no funds available for such an activity and if it made some available for
any such action it would have to report the fact to Congressional committees. The strategy was to ensure that CIA
avoid getting involved in Watergate or any other improper
activity, but to do this without taking a hostile position toward the White House, explaining why we could not do
something and not probing into whatever it might be
doing—just staying out.

But this cautious, "distancing" strategy proved to be a
double-edged sword, cutting the Agency in two ways. On
the one hand, the CIA was perceived as withholding evidence as long as it possibly could—then revealing it grudg-
ingly and only what had been specifically asked for and not

a whit more. This clearly generated further distrust and suspicion, and reinforced the hostile questions being asked about the Agency's good faith and its use—or abuse—of its institutionalized secrecy. On the other hand, each disclosure wrung or leaked from the reluctant Agency during this period caused a greater sensation than it would have done if the information had been volunteered. Moreover, each such disclosure fed the belief that more sinister material was still being withheld, and the White House-launched rumors that CIA was the real culprit in the whole affair gained much currency. The over-all result in the long run was to tarnish the CIA's reputation even further.

In the short run, to be sure, Helms's strategy did have the effect of preventing the CIA's tangential connection with the plumbers in 1971 from being blown into sensational proportions by the media before they could be presented in their true context. And more to the point, it also prevented the Agency from becoming involved in the Watergate cover-up, of being used by the Nixon White House to escape punishment for its crimes. Indeed, in this respect it worked so well that the *Washington Post*, surely among the most aggressively investigative of all the media on Watergate, noted in an editorial that the CIA "was the only agency in town that said 'No.' "

Dick Helms paid the price for that "No." In early December 1972, he was invited to Camp David for a meeting with the President. The belief at Langley was that he was being called to discuss the CIA budget, which at the time was under some debate with the Office of Management and Budget. So I arranged a careful briefing on the arguments on our side before he went. But it turned out to be a waste of time. What happened at Camp David had nothing to do with the budget. It had to do with Helms's careful distancing of the Agency from Watergate, his refusal to allow it to be used in the cover-up. And for that Nixon fired him as DCI, sent him packing to Iran as ambassador and named James Schlesinger as the Agency's new chief.

CHAPTER ELEVEN

The Family Jewels

JAMES SCHLESINGER came on strong. Although his was to be the shortest tenure of any DCI in the Agency's history—barely four months—he was to have an exceptionally profound impact on it. He came to the job from the chairmanship of the Atomic Energy Commission. But before that, as noted, while deputy director of the Office of Management and Budget in 1971, on the direct orders of President Nixon, he had conducted a comprehensive review not only of the Agency but of the entire intelligence community. So he was no neophyte when he was sworn in as CIA chief in February 1973. Indeed, quite to the contrary; he knew a great deal about it. More to the point, he had developed some strong ideas about what was *wrong* with it and some positive ideas as to how to go about righting those wrongs. So he arrived at Langley running, his shirt tails flying, determined, with that bulldog, abrasive temperament of his, to implement those ideas and set off a wave of change both in the practice of intelligence generally and in the organization and operation of the CIA specifically. And in my view, he succeeded admirably.

Central to Schlesinger's ideas was his thinking about the DCI's role in the over-all intelligence process. Bluntly put, he believed that he should be unequivocally the head of it, and that "it" included all American intelligence agencies, not just the CIA. One of the key recommendations of the intelligence review he had made while still at the OMB was that the Congress should enact legislation specifically so designating and authorizing the DCI, turning the responsibilities of the day-to-day management of the CIA itself over to the DDCI. Fearful of opening a Pandora's Box—one couldn't be certain what the Congress might do in those days of rising anti-CIA sentiment once it got a chance to start revising the Agency's legislative charter—the Nixon administration turned this recommendation down. But accepting the basic merit of the idea, Nixon issued a Presidential directive (which skirted the need to go to the Congress) to then CIA chief Richard Helms, assigning the DCI formal responsibility for "an enhanced leadership role" over all intelligence activities, including the preparation of a consolidated intelligence-community budget and the coordination of the intelligence activities of the State, Treasury and Defense Departments, the military services and the National Security Agency.

Helms took a game crack at implementing the directive, forming an Intelligence Community Staff within CIA and chairing the United States Intelligence Board on which all the above intelligence services were represented. But there was resistance to his authority, as Defense wasn't about to surrender its control over the Pentagon's intelligence agencies to the CIA's Director. Helms had far too exquisite a sense of political realities to get into a fight he knew he couldn't win, and which could hurt both CIA and himself. And so, with the quiet approval of his key Congressional oversight chairmen, he continued operating the CIA as a separate but equal agency and refrained from trying to assert a dominant position in managing the intelligence community. Thus the Presidential directive rested tranquilly in the records, but had little effect, and some in White House circles considered Helms to have disregarded a Presidential order.

But Schlesinger came with a stronger mandate—Nixon's interest in a better-organized intelligence community—and with a political base to bring it about. He was determined to upgrade the DCI's role and responsibilities, and he vigorously revitalized Nixon's directive to that effect. With Elliot Richardson fairly new as Secretary of Defense—and with nowhere near Laird's political influence—Schlesinger had a much better opportunity to make it work. He shored up the Intelligence Community Staff, appointing generals and other non-CIA personnel to lead it and improve its relations with the other intelligence agencies. He made it clear that he would look at intelligence questions from a position above the entire community, rather than from the point of view of the impact they might have on the interests and independence of CIA.

As for what the CIA itself should be doing under his leadership, Schlesinger believed that the overwhelming emphasis should be placed on the collection and analysis of intelligence—and on using and supporting the ultrasophisticated military technology that so remarkably enhanced the possibilities in this area. Schlesinger thus came down hard on the analytical aspect of the CIA's work as the main element of the modern intelligence process. But when he probed the staffs and offices that produced this work, he found them intensely concerned about the contribution they felt they could make to national policy, so he quickly revised his initial belief that they had grown totally academic and negative, and started listening to these experts, encouraging the young ones to participate, arguing with them as equals and using their ideas to refine his own before making his presentations to National Security Council meetings. He also soon discovered the value of one of Helms's innovations, the post of Special Assistant to the DCI for Vietnamese Affairs, and established a counterpart in a Special Assistant for the Middle East, an expert to keep him up to date on all the aspects of that complicated situation.

But perhaps more important to Schlesinger than even his ideas about the DCI's role in the intelligence community or the importance of analysis and technology to that community was his belief in the need for a major reform in the basic ethic of "intelligence." During his initial briefings, which began directly after he was appointed CIA chief in December 1972 and which consequently often took place (sometimes for six hours at a stretch) in his AEC offices in Germantown, he discussed with me at great length the need to change the concept of a "secret service." He made it clear that he was hypersuspicious of the role and influence of the clandestine operators within the CIA, that he felt the Agency had become complacent and bloated under their domination, that indeed there were far too many of these "old boys" around the place doing little more than looking after each other, playing spy games and reliving the halcyon past of their OSS and early Cold War derring-do days. In his harsh term, Schlesinger regarded them as "dead wood," responsible for maintaining the Agency's severe compartmentalization between its "cultures," which was not only inefficient but resulted in ill-conceived activities and gross mistakes. And it was in his determination to do something about this situation that I became most closely associated with Schlesinger.

Early on I convinced Schlesinger that my post as Executive Director-Comptroller was essentially a meaningless job and ought to be abolished from the table of organization. The ambiguity of my authority made it impossible for me to be a real chief of staff, and I questioned whether one should exist in any case between the DCI and his substantive deputies. What I said to him was this: "Look, where you are going to have your biggest troubles is with the clandestine crowd downstairs. I'm one of them. I grew up with them. I know them. Let me go down there and take care of that for you." By this time, as a totally loyal Helms man, Karamessines had retired from the Agency and so Schlesinger appointed me Deputy Director for Plans, the job I had dreamed of holding when I returned from running the CORDS program in Vietnam, the job I believed would be the highest I'd ever attain in my CIA career. In response to Schlesinger's wish that I help him to some degree with the Agency as a whole as well, I agreed to accept an *ad hoc* arrangement of being secretary of a "management committee" consisting of all the deputies.

The first thing I did on taking over the DDP was to change its name. In the spirit of starting to disperse the atmosphere of intrigue that shrouded the Agency, the meaningless, misleading euphemism "Deputy Director for Plans" became the straightforward, descriptive appellation, Deputy Director of Operations. In the same spirit, Schlesinger erected a green-and-white sign on the parkway leading to the Langley headquarters stating, for all the world to see, that this was the way to the CIA. When the Langley building was first opened back in the Kennedy administration, a CIA sign had been placed on the parkway. But when Robert Kennedy saw it, he thought it ridiculous for a secret intelligence agency to advertise itself, and he ordered the sign removed. So for years one had to know that the sign that read "Bureau of Public Roads" pointed to the CIA turnoff as well as to a tiny highway office. In restoring the CIA sign Schlesinger was symbolically making the point that the day of the clandestine mystique was coming to an end. And for many within the Agency it was a wrenching end.

But a greater impact on the old system came from Schlesinger's determination to carry out a major purge of personnel. About 7 percent of CIA's staff either were fired or were forced to resign or retired. And the largest portion of these, in keeping with Schlesinger's belief that most of the "dead wood" was in the clandestine services, came from my Directorate of Operations (nee Plans). I admit that I agreed with Schlesinger's assessment, especially in light of the minimal level to which covert-action operations had been pared by this time, that the DDO's division had to be reduced substantially in numbers and influence and thoroughly reorganized. It fell to me, as secretary of the management committee, to give the word of departure to a number of senior officers, and it wasn't long before a phone call from me cast a chill on any recipient. The only solace I could take in performing this ugly work was the knowledge that I was able to cushion Schlesinger's abrasive approach somewhat, softening the harsh process for many of my old colleagues by arranging for their early retirement, by transferring them from senior positions to less prominent ones and by otherwise trying to remove them with their dignity still intact rather than in disgrace.

But, to my surprise, there was one senior officer who escaped the purge, and that was Jim Angleton. I make no secret of the fact that I recommended to Schlesinger that Angleton ought to be moved, reiterating my long-held feeling that his supersecretive style of operation had, at least in recent years, become incompatible with the one I believed essential. But Schlesinger wasn't sure. He was clearly fascinated by Angleton's undoubted brilliance and couldn't help wondering if there just might not be something to his complicated theories that deserved further exploration. It may also have been that Angleton's unbending Cold War view toward the Soviets appealed to Schlesinger's own fierce anti-Communism. So he refused to let me move him. But he did agree to allow me to make some major changes in Angleton's operations.

One issue required early resolution. In 1952 CIA had started a program of looking at the mail between the Soviet Union and the United States, and opening selected letters. Over the years this had grown into a major operation that was held in the deepest secrecy by the Office of Security, which did the work, and the Counterintelligence Staff, which received the products and passed them on to the FBI. On various occasions the activity had been discussed with Postmasters General, although memories differ whether these discussions included opening the letters or just inspecting the outside of the envelopes. In early 1973, the project was brought to the DCI's attention for what proved to be the last time. The Chief Postal Inspector, a former CIA officer, who knew the full extent of the activity, was insisting that he would have to stop the activity unless CIA obtained "higher-level approval" for its continuation (as it had done on previous occasions). In my role as secretary of the management committee for Schlesinger, I was charged with preparing the matter for his decision.

Two things bothered me about the project. First was the fact that opening first-class mail was a direct violation of a criminal statute; I looked it up in the law library to make sure. And secondly, I could get nothing beyond vague generalities from the Counterintelligence Staff when I asked what the operation had actually accomplished of any value over the years. So I went to Schlesinger with the recommendation that the project be terminated—and was countered by a strong appeal from Jim Angleton that it be continued, if necessary by getting President Nixon's personal approval. In the session in which the issue was debated, I saw that Schlesinger did not want to override Angleton completely. So we ended with the decision that the project be "suspended." This satisfied me, because in effect that meant it was terminated, since the Postal Inspector cut it off when no higher approval was forthcoming. But it also meant that Angleton's face was saved.

In the same careful way I set about changing the Operations Directorate, trying to avoid directly affronting the people who had built it and who believed passionately in its established patterns. I formed a committee to revise the hoary old split between the FI and CA Staffs, replacing them with a new breakdown into plans, operations and services, and squeezing out those whose contribution I thought minimal. In this process I managed to remove from Angleton's Counterintelligence Staff such functions as CIA's liaison with the FBI, the remnants of Operation Chaos, and its terrorist coverage, and a host of procedural activities, and so reduce his large staff. Moreover, I reformed the enormous paperwork involved in the directorate's system of individual project review and approval, introducing a more general procedure of program direction and inspection of results for each field station, and in the process I learned how hard it is to get any bureaucracy to stop doing something it is used to doing. I set up grading systems for reports throughout the directorate on the model I had developed years before for the Far East Division. And, as a start in breaking down the walls of compartmentation between the Operations Directorate and the Agency's other directorates, I transferred the Technical Services Division, long one of the DDP's most secret elements, providing the microphones to be placed abroad, the psychological advice on how to handle alien agents, and similar applied science and research for clandestine operations, in the past including consideration of the possible uses of drugs either offensively or defensively, to the Directorate of Science and Technology. In return, Schlesinger agreed that the division that overtly collected information within the United States by identifying its officers as CIA and asking citizens to share information with their government, would be turned over to the Operations Directorate, where I thought we could better coordinate this overt collection of intelligence with what we tried to obtain in our clandestine operations abroad.

But, despite these bureaucratic changes, I essentially continued the DDO's activities as they had been run under Helms and Karamessines, giving priority to the "hard targets" of the Communist world, stressing "professional" ways to exert covert influence abroad, building the confidence of ambassadors that CIA was part of their overseas missions rather than a means of conducting independent operations and formulating separate policies, and working secretly with the intelligence officials of friendly countries. I also began, with a great deal of enthusiasm, to get at the job of running CIA's worldwide overseas operations, meeting the Middle East Chiefs of Station at a gathering in Athens, traveling through Vienna and Germany to review our operations in Central Europe (and to feel the impact of the Berlin Wall for the first time) and attending a meeting of my old friends of the Far East Division in Bangkok (after changing its name to the East Asia Division, partly in response to the remark attributed to Imelda Marcos of the Philippines, "Far from where?").

In this process I especially tried to get to know the better younger officers, from among whom I chose replacements for those whom Schlesinger had purged or for those who would be leaving in the near future as the generation that had started CIA in the late 1940s and early 1950s reached retirement age. I lunched every week or two, in a quiet section of Langley's huge cafeteria, with a group of three or four junior- or middle-grade officers, discussing what they were most concerned about and coming as near as practicable to reproducing my overnight provincial visits in Vietnam—but without newsmen, of course.

I also pushed some of my personal hobbies about how our operations should be conducted, from a greater use of technical gadgetry in the collection of "hard" evidence on what our adversaries were planning and debating, to greater attention to the new area of economic intelligence. But I also had to spend a lot of time defending what Schlesinger was doing, trying to fend off the scare rumors that floated out from Langley about massive personnel cuts and the decline of the importance of the old "clandestine service" from its preeminent position. It was clear that the job I had asked for and got was going to be no bed of roses, but I looked forward to it happily anyway, believing that we could settle the turbulence in good time and then could get on to developing the kind of long-term clandestine intelligence service the country would need in the years ahead.

But it was on my trip to Bangkok in early May of 1973 that I read in a newspaper the story that would radically shake up my life, and that of CIA. It was the story that reported that, during Daniel Ellsberg's trial for disclosing the Pentagon Papers, it had been revealed that the office of his psychiatrist, Dr. Lewis J. Fielding, had been broken into by Howard Hunt, using CIA equipment, in search of material that would then be turned over to CIA and from which CIA would prepare a "psychiatric profile" on Ellsberg for the White House. This was a shocker and I couldn't understand how I had never heard of it before, when I was supposed to have been in charge of assembling all the CIA material relevant to Watergate. But more disturbingly, I wondered how the news had hit Schlesinger; for I had assured him that I had told him the full story of CIA's relationship to Watergate on virtually the first day he had arrived at Langley.

I didn't have to wait long after my return home to find Schlesinger's reaction. In a most moving vote of confidence in me, Schlesinger said he assumed that the news was as much of a surprise to me as it was to him. But then he went

on to say that we would tear the place apart and "fire everyone if necessary," but we had to find out whether there
were any other such questionable or illegal activities hidden
in the secret recesses of the clandestine past that we didn't
know about and that might explode at any time under our
feet. To do this, Schlesinger said, he wanted to issue a directive to all CIA past and present employees, ordering them to
come forward with any matter they knew of where the
Agency had engaged in an activity outside its proper
charter. With that directive, which he issued on May 9, the
CIA "family jewels" were born, and led inexorably to a year
of Congressional investigations and a whole new status for
American intelligence.

Schlesinger's memorandum to all CIA employees started
by saying that "recent press reports outline in detail certain
alleged CIA activities with respect to Mr. Howard Hunt and
other parties." Then it went on to state:

> All CIA employees should understand my attitude on this type
> of issue. I shall do everything in my power to confine CIA activ-
> ities to those that fall within a strict interpretation of its legisla-
> tive charter. I take this position because I am determined that
> the law shall be respected and because this is the best way to
> foster the legitimate and necessary contributions we in CIA can
> make to the national security of the United States.

He then ordered

> all the senior operating officials of this Agency to report to me
> immediately on any activities now going on, or that have gone
> on in the past, which might be construed to be outside the legis-
> lative charter of this Agency.

Furthermore, he directed

> every person presently employed by the CIA to report to me on
> any such activities of which he has knowledge. I invite all ex-
> employees to do the same.

And finally

> any CIA employee who believes that he has received instruc-
> tions which in any way appear inconsistent with the CIA legis-

lative charter shall inform the Director of Central Intelligence immediately.

I collaborated with Schlesinger in the preparation and distribution of this memo and, with the Inspector General and his staff put at my disposal, was given the responsibility of seeing that it was implemented.

Partly inspired by this directive, the Security Office informed me of the fact that the Agency had received some letters from James McCord, a loyal CIA alumnus who had been arrested as a Watergate burglar, in which letters he made veiled allegations that an attempt was being made in the White House to pin the blame for Watergate on the Agency. His points had reinforced other indications that stories were being floated that CIA had masterminded the Watergate break-in to strike at Nixon, and that Charles Colson was doing the floating. As in the case of the psychiatric profile, this was the first I had heard of these letters, so I asked that the full story about them be assembled for Schlesinger. But, in the day or so it took to do so, one of Schlesinger's assistants, who had been appointed to help him get on top of the agency that he had come to distrust, heard of the letters and told Schlesinger of them. For the first—and only—time I feared that Schlesinger had become suspicious that I too, as an old Agency hand, was trying to keep secrets from him; I hadn't brought the McCord letters to him quickly enough. The upshot was that we issued yet another order to every employee to report on suspicious matters, and this time made it a specific call for reports on any contact with any of the individuals who had been involved in Watergate.

As for the McCord letters, we learned that the knowledgeable officers had "forgotten" the matter after they had been told by CIA's General Counsel that there was no legal obligation to report them to the Justice Department or FBI. It was the "distancing" strategy that had kept CIA clear of the Watergate mess, but it had also kept the matter from its new Director. His anger over this had to be experienced to be believed, and I experienced it, both barrels. But it reinforced my own concern that the Agency had to find a new way of operating so that the necessary secrecy of our operations abroad did not become a totally unjustifiable clandestinity here at home.

The directives and Schlesinger's forcefulness had their effect. The Inspector General's office compiled a list of "potential flap activities"; it consisted of 693 pages of possible violations of, or at least questionable activities in regard to, the CIA's legislative charter. Presented to the Director so that he would know about them, they were promptly dubbed by a wag the "family jewels"; I referred to them as "our skeletons in the closet." Among them were the Chaos Operation against the antiwar movement, the surveillance and bugging of American journalists in hope of locating the sources of leaks of sensitive materials, and all the connections with the Watergate conspirators and White House "plumbers." (On the last, nothing was added—much to Schlesinger's relief and mine—to what had already been mentioned.) In addition, the list mentioned the mail-intercept program that the Agency's Counterintelligence Staff, under Angleton, had been conducting and some of the bizarre and tragic cases wherein the Agency experimented with mind-control drugs, including the one of a CIA officer who, without his knowledge, was given LSD, which caused a deep depression and eventually his death. (The list in the drug area, however, was far from comprehensive, since the records had apparently been destroyed in 1972.) There were also many instances of the Agency becoming involved in the activities of other government agencies, such as the Bureau of Narcotics and Dangerous Drugs and local police departments. Moreover, the list noted the exchange of information on Americans who were deemed to be threats to the security of the Agency. And, in a separate and even more secret annex, the Inspector General summarized a 1967 survey of CIA's involvement in assassination attempts or plans against Castro, Lumumba and Trujillo.

We could not of course be certain that the 693 pages covered in fact every last one of the skeletons in CIA's closet, since records did not exist in every case or were buried in long-retired files of financial data, arguments over projects, or progress reports on long-forgotten operations. But the list certainly was broad enough in scope and time to suggest that it covered most, and the most serious, of the Agency's questionable activities. And perhaps I revealed my own long career in, and resulting bias in favor of, the clandestine profession, when I concluded that this list of CIA misdeeds over twenty-five years really was not so bad. Certainly there were activities on it that could not be justified under any rule or by any rationalization, were outside CIA's proper charter, and were just plain wrong whether technically forbidden or not. But I was familiar with the procedures of other intelligence and security services in the world; was aware of the kind of encouragement and exhortations CIA received from government leaders and public alike during the Cold War, to be "more effective, more unique and, if necessary, more ruthless than the enemy"; knew the difficulty of enforcing disciplined behavior in an atmosphere of secrecy and intrigue; and knew personally some of CIA's more bizarre characters, such as Bill Harvey, who carried his pistol wherever he went, ex-Marine "Tony" in the high country of Laos so many years, and Peter Lorre–like scientists fertile with ideas as to how drugs might help the "mission."

So, I found that the most remarkable thing about the list was that it was not more serious, that it did not include more widespread dangers to the lives and liberties of our citizens—that, for example, the surveillance of Americans in the United States affected only employees or ex-employees of CIA and five newsmen suspected of receiving its leaked material, that the mail-intercept program involved essentially only the mail to and from the Soviet Union (plus several short-term looks at similar mail with China and Cuba), that domestic wire taps *did* stop in 1965, when the President so directed, and that Nixon had to set up the "plumbers" in the White House, because such activities would not be carried out by CIA.

But my conclusion had one major flaw—the seriousness of the list would not be judged on any absolute scale, but against what the public knew and believed about CIA. A similar list of the failings, and even the positive misdeeds, of the Army, the FBI, or a local police force would be judged against what the public knew and believed about those organizations. And since their functions, successes, and rules of behavior were well known and even well publicized, in heroic war movies and on Sunday-night TV series, their failings and misdeeds—from the Army's My Lai to the FBI's COINTEL—would be seen in the perspective of the whole of these organizations' existence. But the same facts were not known about CIA; the early enthusiasm for its role, as we have seen, had long since been eroded by a series of calamitous exposures, and its fictional image was far worse than the worst of the "jewels." So it had little or no capital of sympathy left to carry it through a public attack. In this situation I thought the best course would be for CIA's leadership to know the past and correct what could not be justified under today's standards, but to let those past misdeeds rest quietly so they could not be used by CIA's many critics to wound it in the present. We should reform the internal traditions and improve the external understanding of CIA by a program of opening up what did not need to remain secret and of educating the public on how modern intelligence had changed.

But just as this process was going on—in fact, just when it was barely started—my career took an astonishing turn. Just as Schlesinger was issuing his May 9 call for the family jewels, I received a phone call from Alexander Haig, who had taken over as White House chief of staff for Nixon after Haldeman had been driven out of the job by the Watergate scandal. "Is your secretary on the line, Bill?" he asked. It was normal procedure around Washington to have one's secretary monitor one's calls, and I said yes. "Could you ask her to drop off, please?" I was somewhat surprised, but Haig and I were friends from my time in Vietnam and I said, "Sure." After she dropped off, Al told me the last thing in the world that I had expected to hear. Richard Kleindienst, because of his involvement in the Watergate mess, had been obliged to resign as Attorney General. Elliot Richardson, then Secretary of Defense, had been nominated to replace him at the Justice Department and Jim Schlesinger was to be nominated to replace him at Defense. "And the President wants you to take over as Director of the CIA, Bill," Haig concluded.

For a few seconds I was at a complete loss for an answer. I had no idea how the President had hit on me. He hardly knew of me. We had met only once, when he had visited Saigon while I was running CORDS, and that was at a formal session with dozens of other people around, so there was no way he could have remembered me from then. The only other remotely personal connection I had with him was the fact that our son Jonathan had been a roommate at Princeton of Edward Cox, who had married Tricia Nixon, and had been at their White House wedding. Surely that couldn't have had anything to do with it. What had, I never really discovered. The best that I ever deduced was that Nixon may well have been aware of my work in Vietnam and that Haig, Schlesinger, and the DDCI Vernon Walters, all of whom were a lot closer to the White House than I had ever been, commented on me favorably and suggested my name for consideration. And undoubtedly Kissinger endorsed it, on the basis of my work in Vietnam and my contacts with him in the middle 1960s, when he was an occasional consultant for the National Security Council on the war, and I had briefed him for CIA. Their suggestions, and the convenience of putting a politically neutral professional into CIA, probably were the determining factors in that period of continued tension over Watergate.

But no matter how my nomination came about, I was both stunned and delighted, and finally managed to blurt out to Haig that I was honored and appreciative and would do the best I could. "That's fine, Bill," Haig replied. "The President would like you to come to the Cabinet meeting on the tenth, where he intends to make the announcement of Schlesinger's and your nominations."

In retrospect, I must admit, there was something rather

disconcertingly casual in the process of elevating me to the top CIA job. At the Cabinet meeting the next morning, after a number of other items of business had been attended to and just before my nomination was announced, I noticed President Nixon lean over to whisper something to Haig and then Haig scribbled a note, which he passed over to me. It asked, "Did you have any connections with Watergate which would raise problems?" I looked across the room at Haig and shook my head no, but it seemed to me a poor way of conducting a security check, and if my answer had been different, poor timing too. A few minutes later, the President announced Schlesinger's and my nominations, and Elliot Richardson turned and congratulated me first.

The casual note about my elevation continued. Mississippi Senator John Stennis, who was Chairman of the Armed Services Committee and thus responsible for my confirmation hearings, had been shot in a holdup and was recuperating in Walter Reed Hospital and, although Stuart Symington was the committee's next senior member, he hadn't been authorized to act on Stennis's behalf in this matter. So it wasn't until July that the hearings were at last convened and the Senate didn't vote to confirm me until August 1. And then, after I had been confirmed, everybody seemed to forget all about the necessity of formally swearing me in as DCI, so that didn't happen until Dick Walters stirred the machinery and I was finally called down to the White House on September 4.

Throughout this four-month period I was in a rather peculiar position. Because my nomination had been announced in early May, all the world knew I was meant to be the next CIA chief. But I wasn't able to accept the responsibility or exercise the authority of the position until I was officially sworn in. In the meantime, I was, if not exactly a man without a job, then one without a title—an absolutely befuddling situation in official Washington, where titles are more important than gold—in effect running the Agency without presuming to do so. For a brief time, while Schlesinger waited for *his* nomination to go through, he and I continued to work together pretty much as before on the Agency's most pressing matters. But he was gone by June, and after he left, Vernon Walters, as DDCI, became acting CIA chief so whatever we did then had to defer to *this* formality. I must say that it could have been an awful mess with anyone but Walters, who handled the odd situation with ease, grace and good humor. We agreed that I could work for him (which I did when I was Executive Director and DDO under him) or he could work for me (which we knew would be the case after I was sworn in) and that we could handle the transition in the spirit of good friendship we had long ago developed.

What was most immediately on my mind after my appointment was announced was still, of course, the family jewels. By May 21 the initial summary of them was available from the Inspector General. Schlesinger and I agreed that I should let our Congressional oversight committee chairmen in both the Senate and the House know that we had assembled them and that we were determined that CIA would remain within its proper limits in the future. In that way we felt that these chairmen could help prevent my confirmation hearings from going off into an anti-CIA extravaganza. Consequently, I visited the courtly Stennis at Walter Reed Hospital, and after a brief oral summary he agreed that I meet with Symington and give him the rundown as well. Similarly, I made an appointment with Edward Hebert, the excellent former Louisiana newsman who had become Chairman of the House Armed Services Committee; he in turn sent me to see Lucien Nedzi, the Michigan liberal Democrat he had selected to chair the Intelligence Subcommittee of Hebert's committee, in order to break out of the tradition of conservative Southern protection of CIA. Three of these men listened to my account of the family jewels without much excitement and accepted my assurances that I would see to it that CIA conducted its activities in full compliance with its charter in the future. There was a general consensus that these matters of the past should be left in the past in order that the Agency could continue to do its positive work in the present and future.

The single exception was Nedzi, who took his new responsibilities as chairman very seriously. He insisted on reading the individual items in the family jewels list in great detail, asked very specific follow-up questions in regard to them and demanded repeated assurances that these kinds of activity would never be carried on in the future. He also asked the toughest question—whether the accounts of these activities could not and should not be publicly released, to serve as a catharsis of the past and a barrier against their repetition in the future. He represented that new and growing approach to Congressional oversight of the CIA that I realized would, in the weeks and months ahead, indeed throughout my term as DCI, be followed by the older, more established chairmen with whom I would have to deal. Under pressure from their Congressional colleagues, the press and the public, they would no longer be willing merely to accept the CIA's accounts of its role and activities but would insist on their Congressional responsibility to supervise the Agency more closely and specifically. More than just resigning myself to this situation, I considered it correct in our Constitutional democracy, but I urged that this new era not be applied to the past. The shock effect of an exposure of the "family jewels," I urged, could, in the climate of 1973, inflict mortal wounds on the CIA and deprive the nation of all the good the Agency could do in the future. And Nedzi, to his great credit (and some later political grief), accepted my arguments, although he made clear that he would hold me strictly to my assurance that a new approach would characterize the future.

But even with the exclusion of the "family jewels" from the agenda, when Symington convened the Senate's Armed Services Committee in July for my confirmation hearings, it was a pretty rough experience. All throughout Washington, mainly on the hoardings around the new subway construction sites, anonymous posters appeared, showing an unflattering photograph of myself superimposed on the Ace of Spades and accusing me of assassinating 20,000 people in Vietnam (a reference to the figure I used in my Congressional testimony as to how many Viet Cong Infrastructure figures were reported "killed" by the Phoenix program). At the same time, my telephone at home—which I insisted remain listed—frequently rang with abusive or obscene callers. Barbara and the children stood up firmly, even to the statement made by one caller to thirteen-year-old Christine that "we'll get your daddy." But I remember feeling, in a curiously mixed-up way, that if our daughter Catherine had to die, I was relieved that it had happened before these attacks began so they could not add to the pressures she suffered. Nevertheless, I forbade the CIA security officers to do anything about the posters, not even to try to determine their authors. Although a few friends tore down some of the posters in anger, I decided the best approach was to ignore them, and I noted that they were never mentioned in the press. I took only one step with regard to the phone calls. It was against one that persisted after most of the others had stopped, the phone ringing at various odd hours but no one speaking when we answered it. I asked the Agency's security officers what someone, anyone, any ordinary citizen could do when plagued by such calls. They replied that the telephone company could trace the calls if it knew the exact hour that they were made. So I noted the times of the calls the next day, reported that to the phone company and soon learned the name under which the calling phone was registered. Again I told the security officers to do nothing; I did not wish to add another CIA surveillance to the jewels. But the next time the phone rang, I picked up the receiver and, as soon as I realized that it was our silent harasser, I said, "Mr. John Doe," using his name. He gasped and hung up, and never called again, probably terrified at what retribution CIA might be about to inflict on him.

Things were hardly less rough in the Senate hearing room itself. The first session was open, with the TV cameras eagerly focused on the picture of America's top spy presenting his credentials to the public. Symington led me sympathetically through a wide range of questions giving me a chance to assert the independence of intelligence assessments from policy control, the fact that CIA is authorized to collect only "foreign" intelligence and that I would quit if required to undertake an activity that was illegal. He pressed me on a few of his hobbies, such as his distaste for military intelligence, the "secret" war in Laos and Kissinger's wide influence. But after I had said that "We are not going to run the kind of intelligence service that other countries run. We are going to run one in the American society and under the American constitutional structure . . ." he said that he was impressed with my answers and looked forward to voting for my confirmation.

A series of witnesses then attacked me for the Phoenix operation and our intelligence coverage in Vietnam. But the main event took place behind closed doors in executive session, where Senator Edward Kennedy spent most of an afternoon dragging me over the coals of Phoenix and CIA's connection with Watergate. The first was simple to deal with—I repeated the testimony I had given on several previous occasions, and welcomed another chance to set the record straight on that much-misunderstood subject. The second was much harder. Kennedy pressed relentlessly on my participation in the "distancing" strategy and my "dancing around" before giving the prosecutors Ehrlichman's name as the one who had asked that CIA help Howard Hunt. But even as I squirmed under the pressure, I admired the constitutional process that so forcefully put even intelligence officials under this sort of tension and made me publicly commit myself to run the Agency in a proper manner; and the final vote of 83–13, I thought, honestly reflected the fact that there were legitimate doubts in the Senate about my appointment. Kennedy was one of those who voted against me. But he replied to a letter I wrote, in which I expressed my hope that he would be proved wrong about me, saying he wished me well and looked forward to my having great success in office.

In the weeks of waiting for the confirmation and thereafter to be sworn in, I decided that it was not enough for me to just hope to run the Agency properly and to collect a file on the wrongs of the past. I had to do something to make very clear what kind of behavior was going to be allowed and what kind was not. Part of the difficulties of the past, I thought, lay in the absence of any clear guidelines as to what was proper and what was improper, allowing various actions to be taken for what once appeared to be good motives or good reasons but which in retrospect turned out to be totally unacceptable.

If the law under which the CIA operated was fuzzy and ambiguous, and it clearly and deliberately had been written that way, at least CIA's internal directives could make clear a set of guidelines for behavior. The directives I had issued in Vietnam against assassination had set the record straight as to my attitude on that subject. Now it was essential to do the same on the subjects that appeared in the jewels collection. So I sat down with the jewels collection and wrote out a series of specific instructions as to how such incidents were to be avoided in the future, then refined the instructions in consultation with my colleagues and future deputy directors, and issued them on August 29. They ranged from stating flatly that "CIA will not engage in assassination nor induce, assist or suggest to others that assassination be employed" to setting the clear limitation on Operation Chaos of "the collection abroad of information on foreign activities related to domestic matters . . . focus(ed) clearly on the foreign organizations and individuals involved and only incidentally on their American contact." They also included a flat bar against opening United States mail and testing drugs on "unwitting" subjects, plus a variety of orders on how CIA should conduct its relations with the other departments and agencies of the government to ensure that it stayed clear of activities outside its proper charter. And with this set of directives signed and issued, I felt that I could take the oath in the Oval Office of the White House on September 4 to "support and defend the Constitution of the United States . . . without any mental reservation or purpose of evasion."

At the ceremony, President Nixon joked a bit by asking that I tell him about foreign developments before he read them in the newspapers, and Schlesinger, Kissinger, and Admiral Tom Moorer, Chairman of the Joint Chiefs of Staff, all wished me and the family well. Now I had an amazing opportunity to put some of the ideas I had accumulated over the years about intelligence into effect.

CHAPTER TWELVE

Director of Central Intelligence

On one of those ideas I had already started. By chance, the membership of the venerable Board of National Estimates, the element of CIA that produced the over-all assessments of world problems for the whole intelligence community, had dropped to only six in June, as a result of retirements among its normal total membership of twelve. Thus, I had the task of replacing them, traditionally from among senior officers of the intelligence community as well as a few representative generals or ambassadors who could bring outside perspective to the Board's deliberations. But I had another idea, based in part on some doubts as to the value of the Board's contributions and in part on my own thoughts as to what intelligence needed and what I would need in the years ahead. I had sensed an ivory-tower mentality in the Board; its composition had tended to shift to a high proportion of senior analysts who had spent most of their careers at Langley and who had developed a "mind-set" about a number of the issues, in opposition to the views of the Pentagon and because of the way Nixon and Kissinger had excluded them from some of the White House's more sensitive international dealings.

They had been right about some of their positions, but they had also been wrong, and I was convinced that change was needed if their inclination toward fixed positions was not to lead to trouble. Moreover, I knew very definitely that I needed help on what I saw as the most important part of the job ahead of me, becoming confident that I, as Director of Central Intelligence, was the best-informed intelligence officer in the government about every one of the major substantive problems that confronted the policy officials I was supposed to assist. In this I was troubled over how badly the machinery was organized to serve me. If I wanted to know what was happening in China, for example, I would have to assemble individual experts in China's politics, its economics, its military, its personalities, as well as the clandestine operators who would tell me things they would tell no one else. Or I could commission a study that would, after weeks of debate, deliver a broad set of generalizations that might be accurate but would be neither timely nor sharp.

Looking at the twelve very senior positions on the Board, six of which were vacant anyway, I hit upon a solution: dissolve the Board and use the twelve positions thus made available to appoint twelve senior assistants to report directly to me on each of the main issues facing me. In short, I would apply to the rest of the world the scheme that Helms had devised for Vietnam and Schlesinger for the Middle East. But this came only after a struggle with the Chairman of the Board, who retired rather than accept the change, saying that he feared that the independence of the national-estimate process would be compromised and would come to reflect strong White House or Kissinger preferences. I responded that these estimates, on their face, were the Director's estimates, so the responsibility for independence was already mine and I intended to meet it. What's more, the United States Intelligence Board already constituted a "wise man" review, so there was no need for an additional one.

Thus, I created the positions of National Intelligence Officers, and I told the eleven men and one woman whom I chose for the jobs that they were to put themselves in my chair as DCI for their subject of specialization. They were to have no more staff than one assistant and a secretary so that they could identify totally with my position and not develop a role of their own. They were chosen from the intelligence community and private life as well as from CIA, and they served as the experts I needed in such subjects as China, Soviet affairs, Europe, Latin America, strategic weaponry, conventional forces, and economics, ranging throughout the intelligence community and out into the academic world to bring to me the best ideas and to press the different disciplines to integrate their efforts. To reply to one charge that has been made about the NIOs, the move was not the result of any direct order or even indirect hint from either President Nixon or Kissinger. I did not consult either on it, considering it a mere matter of internal intelligence housekeeping so that I could produce a better product.

And I am frank to say that I am glad I made the change. I am certain that I could not have done my job without the NIOs, especially when I was later involved so intensely with Congressional investigations. They would call me late in the evening or show up at my desk early in the morning with some development they had plucked out of the reams of material flowing through Langley and say that it presented an unforeseen danger or a novel aspect of a complex problem. Or they would spend the necessary hours assembling the experts from the whole intelligence community to dissect and analyze every detail of some obscure political or weapons change, clarifying the different interpretations of that change by the CIA, the DIA, and the other agencies so that those differences could be put succinctly before the heads of the Intelligence Board, where they could be argued out and dissenting judgments plainly stated before I sent the final estimate on to the National Security Council. They did not work out so well in the management aspects of my responsibilities, but there was no question in my mind that the substantive contribution they made was vital.

For another new venture, I awaited my swearing in. A few days later I told my new subordinates about my suggestion to Allen Dulles twenty years earlier, and my repeated recommendation during the middle 1960s, that CIA's daily intelligence reports be issued in newspaper format to emphasize the more important items and to offer the recipient the choice between a quick headline summary and reading in depth. I told them that the idea had been turned down by Dulles but that I still liked it, and I asked them to take another look. This time, I was amused to note, the reply came back that the new boss's proposal was a pretty good idea and would not be difficult to implement and that they would be glad to do so. I did a customer survey as well, to be told by some that they liked it and by some that they wouldn't; Kissinger said that I should feel free to try anything that I thought would make for a better product, but later declared that he did not like it (although he never suggested that I should stop it for that reason if others favored it, which they did).

So in a few weeks the *National Intelligence Daily* was born, and it became the journal with the smallest circulation (about 60), the largest reporting staff (the whole intelligence community), and the worst advertising in the world (none, since the entire content was highly classified). But it did provide a mechanism for me to ensure that intelligence reports and assessments went to the senior officials and were not screened out by their staffs, that all the key officials were regularly briefed on the major world problems rather than only on the particular ones their own offices might be concerned with and that I myself would build up a backlog of knowledge on the many questions in the world so that I could reply confidently to the most unexpected question during a Congressional hearing. The *Daily* was supplemented by a number of other publications, specialized or omitting highly classified material, but it became the focus of my effort to present our intelligence better and produce it better, since the best intelligence is of little value if it sits on the President's desk instead of getting into his head. On every evening I could, I joined the editorial conference as to what subjects would be carried in the next day's publications, and I used a world map on the wall to jog my mind as to areas and subjects that I thought needed better coverage.

Along the same line, I put a great deal of emphasis into efforts to present our conclusions and assessments in graphic and even pictorial form wherever possible. I launched a number of experiments in seeking numerical terms in which to express the probabilities of the outbreak of war in the Middle East and similar situations and at the same time overcome the danger of giving a false indication of precision. I also managed to end one of the oldest debates in history, the one between the intelligence officer who, after an event occurs, points to the single report that predicted it while the intelligence customer complains that he was not alerted because that report was buried among so many contradictory reports. I told the National Intelligence Officers that we would have a new report form, the "alert memorandum," sent by me to the members of the National Security Council, so that the question of whether or not an "intelligence gap" had occurred could be simply settled by seeing whether or not such a memorandum had been sent, whatever other reporting might have flowed through the community. The box score on these, after a year or so, showed a certain number of "Wolf!" cries. But it also showed many solid warnings, on some of which our customers took the warnings seriously enough to act to ensure that the predicted event did not take place—not a statistically satisfying effect but a credit to the real purpose of intelligence. These kinds of change and experiment reminded me a bit of the pacification program in Vietnam, no one of them very "dramatic," but cumulatively of great importance in adjusting American intelligence to the needs of the future.

But one problem I could not solve—Kissinger's penchant for holding key information so tightly that CIA's analysts continually complained that they could not make proper assessments of foreign problems if they were barred from knowing what was being told to the American government at the top level and what positions the United States was taking in diplomatic negotiations. Kissinger's direct links to the Soviet hierarchy, his negotiations with the North Vietnamese and, of course, his dazzling dances through the Middle East, all were reported in the most secret of channels, with no copies coming to Langley. But while I sympathized with the analysts in their frustration, I saw little hope of any change in the situation. The proliferation of leaks in Washington, from the Pentagon Papers to Kissinger's 1971 "tilt" toward Pakistan against India, had raised the question whether *any* secrets could be kept, and had driven Kissinger into extreme efforts to keep those he thought absolutely necessary for the conducting of coherent negotiations. And I confess that I agreed with his action; after Marchetti and Agee I felt I could no longer say that it was inconceivable that anyone in CIA would be guilty of an information leak, a position we had proudly held in earlier times. Periodically I would raise the subject with Kissinger, who would quickly direct that I be given access to the material on my promise to hold it closely, but in a few weeks the stream would again dry up as some new action started and new ultrasecret indicator was set up for the minimum number of named recipients who had to know of it to execute it, and CIA's analysts were not included. So I finally developed a rationalization for them—that they should produce the best possible assessments based on what they did know; if these agreed with Kissinger's with his added knowledge they would reinforce his belief; if they disagreed, Kissinger would have to decide whether the difference was because of the extra knowledge he had or because he was being deceived. I told the analysts they were making an important contribution by forcing him to answer that question.

Part of the job of presenting intelligence is, of course, getting it to the people who need it. And here again I found a need for change. Lieutenant General Daniel O. Graham, my Deputy for the National Intelligence Community (rather than CIA), stormed into my office one day after a trip to Europe. He told me that he had visited one of our Air Force units and had asked to see the intelligence with which they briefed their pilots. He was shown some pencil sketches of targets that, he was told, had been made from satellite photos but that the pilots were not cleared to see, since they were of too high a classification for personnel exposed to possible capture. Here was dramatically useful intelligence, but we were not getting it to the very people it was most useful to, the pilots who were offering their lives to carry out missions. It was an absurdity as far as the effective accomplishment of the mission was concerned and a blasphemy to the dedication of the pilot. Needless to say, we changed the rules so that most satellite photos became more generally available in official circles. But even I as Director of Central Intelligence was not able to declassify them entirely, largely due to the diplomatic objection that other nations would create great difficulties if they were compelled to admit that many of their tightly protected secrets were in fact not secret at all.

There were other cases in which people who "need to know" a specific intelligence item in order to do their jobs properly did not receive it. "Need to know" has long been a principle for the dissemination of intelligence, but traditionally it has been applied in the sense that those who do *not* "need to know" do *not* receive it. But in the American constitutional system there are many other than senior Executive Branch officials who "need to know" intelligence so they can play a better role in the decision-making process in which they are a necessary element. As a result, some of America's intelligence that never leaves the tightest circles in many countries is revealed not only to the Congress in closed hearings but also to the public in such documents as the yearly posture statements of the Secretary of Defense, the press briefings of the Secretary of State, and even the statements of the President. But these are occasional and are subject to the suspicion that their authors are selectively exposing only those secrets that support their case.

So, in line with my belief in the importance of the constitutional and political role of the Congress in American decision-making, I began a program to supplement the periodic briefings given to the various committees by making daily publications available to them. But it didn't work. Because the material was highly classified, it could be left only with the Committee Staff Chief during the day and had to be

picked up each evening, requiring the Senator or Congressman to visit him to see it. They had only a short time available in the face of their other commitments, and certainly
not enough time to absorb our reports in depth. Some of my
seniors in the Executive Branch were frankly appalled that I
would expose such material to such a place of potential leakage as the Congress, missing the point that the recipients
were restricted to those on the key committees and that the
chairmen had undertaken to be at least as careful with the
information as Executive Branch recipients were. I tried a
variation and developed a special bulletin tailored for the
Congress particularly, shortening the material presented
and concentrating on subjects I knew to be of immediate
interest to Congressmen. But I never really solved the problem of how to move more of the magnificent information and
assessments produced by American intelligence to all of
those who "need to know" so that our final decisions could
be better, although I also never lost my interest in seeking
ways to do it.

Congress has political as well as practical difficulties in
using intelligence information and assessments, difficulties
perhaps best illustrated by my experience with respect to
Diego Garcia. In 1974 the issue arose whether the United
States Navy should substantially improve that island in the
Indian Ocean. The arguments revolved around whether Soviet naval power was growing and whether the United
States needed to have more naval-base facilities to meet it.
Senator Stuart Symington asked me to testify on the subject
before the Armed Services Committee, which would have to
approve any increase in American investments in Diego
Garcia. I summarized, in secret session, the evidence and
history of Soviet naval activities there, presenting secret
photographs and other sensitive information that we had
available. In essence I told the Committee the two key conclusions of a national estimate of the intelligence community: that there had been, over the past several years, a gradual growth in the Soviet naval presence in the Indian
Ocean, that it would continue, and that surges in the Soviet

presence had always followed surges in the American presence. At the end of the hearing Symington said that most of the information I had presented did not seem to be very sensitive and asked me to declassify it for public release. I agreed, removing only the photographs and other such sensitive material, in the belief that here was a chance to make available to America's decision-making process the fruits of our intelligence. And I found myself in the middle of a political crossfire.

Those who urged the improvement of Diego Garcia, including both Schlesinger and the President, stressed the first part of my assessment in their arguments. But those who opposed it, conspicuously including Symington, welcomed the second part as an indication that the improvement would only stimulate more rivalry in the area. Immediately I was asked to "clarify" my assessment to show that I had not "opposed" the improvement. I did this willingly. My clarification consisted of several quotations from my original testimony and reiterated both of its conclusions. But Symington later charged me with having waffled on my earlier remarks under pressure, because I had indeed clarified that I had not opposed the improvement—which was beyond the scope of an intelligence assessment in any event— and I had used an argument that he had intended to use in refuting the improvement proposal. In other words, an intelligence assessment can become the center of a political argument in the Congress between those whose positions have already been stated, instead of helping them to make up their minds. And in such cases it contributes little to the decision-making process and only exposes intelligence to opposition from both sides.

But however much I preferred concentrating on improving the analytical process and its presentation, one major chore demanded a great deal of my attention: producing a better intelligence community. Schlesinger had called for this in his 1971 study and had begun to try to carry it out while he was Director. Now, of course, the job should be easier, because after all the chief saboteur of a strong DCI role in the past had always been the Secretary of Defense, and Jim Schlesinger, the great proponent of the concept, was now Secretary of Defense. And though the temptation might have been great for him, once he took over that department, he couldn't—and to his credit didn't—resist my acting on the very recommendation that he himself had made.

I vigorously used the various organs in which the separate intelligence agencies met—the Intelligence Community Staff, the National Intelligence Officers, and the United States Intelligence Board—as vehicles to open up contacts and discussion among the various components of the community, to stimulate them to work together, to recommend to them what they should be doing, and to review how well they did it. And I quickly learned what every policy-level official who has come to Washington soon learns—that for every hour he spends on dramatic policy-making he must spend at least ten on the business of making the bureaucracy function and moving it in the direction he believes important. Because the appealing concept of "leadership" of the sprawling intelligence community in reality meant many hours of frantic homework, mastering all the finely tuned options as to, for example, which satellite system should be selected and launched five years hence or how the greater funds needed for one system related to the twelve-month delay in coverage of another. It meant discreet pressure on submarine officers, concerned about the safety of their crews and their tactical advantages over their Soviet adversaries, to provide information to CIA analysts seeking to arrive at some over-all assessment of Soviet sea power ten years hence, upon which construction programs could be approved or disapproved. It also meant long hours listening to the arguments why air-attaché aircraft needed to be replaced, why a barracks for an intelligence unit was needed in Korea, and occasionally even why to advance a suggestion that the United States meet its difficulties over foreign bases by once again thinking of using signals-collection ships, despite the tragic experiences of the *Liberty* and the *Pueblo* off Israel and Korea.

And despite strong wording of the 1971 Presidential directive, I learned a few hard truths about the limitations on a Director of Central Intelligence's power—namely, that while he can have a major impact on national intelligence management, the tactical intelligence activities of our armed forces are just too complex, detailed and inherent to the military structure for him really to affect them. The military elements of the 1973 American intelligence community were not hostile to the DCI. But neither were they willing to surrender to him; and I was sure that they would be able to develop under another name, and continue, whatever activity I used my authority to forbid them.

So I turned again to the "art of the possible" in dealing with the intelligence community. As a first step, I outlined what I thought were the important subjects that we should be working on; then I asked all agency heads on the U.S. Intelligence Board to either accept or modify them. My object was to replace an enormous paper exercise called the "requirements" process—which pretended to tell the community precisely what it should be reporting on—with a simple set of general questions about the key problems that we should concentrate on. A wag promptly labeled this the KIQs, or Key Intelligence Questions, which I gladly accepted for its connotation of "kicking" the community along in the right direction. Once each KIQ was formulated, the various agencies discussed what each would do to answer the question. This then was to be followed by a statement of the resources that each agency would apply, so that an initial judgment could be made as to whether too many or too few were involved in the resolution of each KIQ.

This degree of precision about budget allocations was initially met with some reserve, and by the bureaucracy's infinite ability to obfuscate, especially since the fourth step in the exercise was to be an assessment by the National Intelligence Officers of how well each agency had done in answering the KIQs. And this had the hidden danger of serving as the basis for budget cuts for those who had showed marginal results. I recognized the problem, and the negative reaction. But I had been told by business-school experts that every

new management system took three to five years to introduce. So I was content to keep moving in what I thought
was the right over-all direction, hoping to iron the kinks out
along the way. Besides, I wryly commented that by that
time I would probably be gone anyway, and my successor
would try some new system. I did not know how truly I
spoke.

With these new systems, I was content that I now had the
tools to allow me to have some real impact on the community and its direction in the future. One effort to project a
five-year "perspective" on the nation's future intelligence
needs permitted me to call for greater efforts in economics,
point out the need for more research and development in
new techniques of analysis, and insist that the problems of
the less-developed world would require more and more of
our attention. A series of hard-hitting post-mortems of the
Intelligence Community's performance in various crises allowed me to highlight weaknesses and spur steps to overcome them. Moreover, a community annual report to the
President, recommendations to him about the budgets of
each agency, and my acting as spokesman for the entire
community in presenting the over-all appropriation request
to the Congress provided vehicles for pressure on the different agencies to play as members of the community team
rather than as loners.

Meanwhile, there was also the Agency to run. The financial and program-management steps I had started when I
was Executive Director had given it a head start in these
fields, so I saw no need for revolutionary changes there. And
anyway, CIA needed a period of some stability after the
turbulence of the reorganizations carried out under Schlesinger.

But one area still needed attention—personnel management. In this field the separate directorates had been very
much left to themselves because of the quite different types
of people needed for analysis, overseas clandestine operations, administrative support, and science and technology.
But the Agency was politically vulnerable in its poor record

with respect to minorities. While it had some blacks in traditional service positions, their rarity at the professional level was one of the worst in government. And while a substantial number of women were employed at the professional level for editorial and similar work, they reached a ceiling at the middle grades, above which only a token few were ever promoted. So I set up a study group to articulate some new standards and procedures, called upon the senior- and middle-management levels for an extra effort to improve our minority record, changed the rules to encourage the use of part-time women employees by counting them against personnel ceilings only in proportion to the time they worked rather than the same as full-time employees, and instituted an annual planning-and-review mechanism to spotlight the offices that made progress and those that did not.

This effort required the spending of many hours with disgruntled individuals, such as a black woman who had appealed her lack of promotion. The investigator in the case reported that she did not make it competitively, in part because she seemed not to be trying. But in a conversation with her I learned that she had successfully raised three children, put them through high school and into decent jobs without a husband. She certainly had the drive necessary to achieve in that difficult challenge. So I insisted that a program be developed for her training and gave her the challenge of using it to qualify herself competitively for promotion on the next cycle. But I made no promises. Some eight months later I received a happy phone call from her, saying she had just received her promotion. I checked to see that it had truly been awarded competitively and not just to get the Director out of the unit's hair, and I was told that there was no question about her ability or her response. All she had needed was the hope. This one case did not solve the Agency's problem, of course, but it was accompanied by a very substantial number of others, especially by a surge in black professional recruitment.

But there was one area in which I did not move fast enough, to my later regret. I had recommended to Schlesinger that he move Jim Angleton. But by the time the decision was mine to make, I thought the clandestine service had had just about all the personnel turbulence it could take for the moment and that a move against Angleton would be seen as symbolic of lots more to come. Since I had already taken away from him several of his key responsibilities, such as terrorism (ex-Chaos) and the FBI liaison, and had left him with a smaller staff to work on true counterintelligence operations, which was his real forte, I decided not to move him. I spent several long sessions doing my best to follow his tortuous theories about the long arm of a powerful and wily KGB at work, over decades, placing its agents in the heart of allied and neutral nations and sending its false defectors to influence and undermine American policy. I confess that I couldn't absorb it, possibly because I did not have the requisite grasp of this labyrinthine subject, possibly because Angleton's explanations were impossible to follow, or possibly because the evidence just didn't add up to his conclusions. At the same time I looked in vain for some tangible results in the counterintelligence field, and found little or none. I did not suspect Angleton and his staff of engaging in improper activities. I just could not figure out what they were doing at all.

But what really turned me off was the discovery that counterintelligence theories were actually hurting good clandestine operational officers. One had come under suspicion through a gross leap in logic. A defector had remarked that the Soviets were in contact with a CIA officer in a particular city. By a process of elimination, suspicion had settled on this one. But absolutely no other evidence was ever found to support it, even after careful check. Nonetheless, the officer was sent off to a distant and dead-end post for a number of years as a result. On another occasion, the head of a friendly liaison service in a foreign capital drew me aside on a visit to confront me with the fact that our counterintelligence had told him that our chief of station there was a Soviet agent. After I recovered from the shock and looked into the case, I discovered that similarly vague coincidences had once been used to bring him under suspicion. But the matter had been

exhaustively investigated several years before, and the officer, a brilliant and effective one at that, was given a totally
clean bill of health. But our counterintelligence had never
accepted the conclusion. I read every document in his file
and conducted my own inquiries to be sure, following
which I wrote a memorandum that I, as Director, had done
so and had total confidence in him and wanted no trace of
the earlier suspicions to remain with him. And I told my
foreign colleague that I had done so—and resolved that I
just had to get a better handle on our counterintelligence.

Angleton had one major responsibility other than counterintelligence—Israel—which he had traditionally handled in
the same totally compartmented fashion as counterintelligence. He had been one of CIA's earliest contacts with
Israeli Intelligence and had played a valuable role in the
exchange of intelligence between Israel and the United
States during the years of his highly personal and special
relationship with them. But however appropriate that may
have been in past quieter years, the artificial segregation of
CIA's contacts with Israel, which inevitably accompanied
Angleton's secretive management style, from its officers
working in the Middle East as a whole, and to a considerable extent the analysts, was impossible at a time when the
Middle East had become one of the crucial foreign-policy
problems of the United States. So I resolved to move the
Israeli "account" from the Counterintelligence Staff. In the
process I hoped Angleton might take the hint and retire in
time to secure certain retirement benefits which closed in
June 1974.

But he dug in his heels, and marshaled every argument he
could think of to urge that such an important contact could
not be handled in the normal bureaucratic machinery. I
yielded, in truth because I feared that Angleton's professional integrity and personal intensity might have led him to
take dire measures if I forced the issue of either his Israeli
relationship or his continued employment. But I knew that I
would have to face up to the necessity of moving him out,
sooner or later.

The outside world also pressed in and took much of my

time from whatever I might have wanted to do within the intelligence community and CIA. On September 11, 1973, just six days after I was sworn in, the Chilean military rose against Salvador Allende, bringing a great chorus of world-wide accusations that CIA had engineered the coup, a charge that I would have to answer in detail later. But even more important, on October 6, a month later, Egypt and Syria launched a coordinated attack against Israel, and the cry of "intelligence failure" went up, with some basis. Some months previously a State Department intelligence memorandum had concluded that, if there was no substantial political and diplomatic progress toward a Middle East peace by the fall, the chances for an outbreak of war would increase substantially. Separate estimates reckoned that the Israeli would win such a conflict in a short time. By early October, a flow of contradictory evidence flooded the analysts. The Egyptians had moved to the Suez Canal, but they had done so in previous maneuvers. Some clandestine reports suggested that an Egyptian and Syrian mobilization was in process, since operations and signal intercepts indicated a high state of alert and preparedness. But soothing words came from diplomatic circles. Then, when the attacks actually began, the intelligence community's "watch committee" focused on what the Arabs, in their opinion, *should* do rather than what they were doing and came to the conclusion that "there was no hard evidence of a major, coordinated Egyptian–Syrian offensive," which the post-mortem I arranged for later called "quite simply, obviously and starkly—wrong." It was obvious that the intelligence process had failed notably in this performance.

Several weeks later, on October 24, my silent pocket buzzer wriggled while I was at dinner with friends in Virginia. I phoned the CIA Operations Center and was told that Kissinger wanted to see me right away at his State Department office (he had just added the Secretary of State title to that of Assistant to the President for National Security Affairs). I left Barbara with a promise that someone would drive her home and went off to the State Department. There

Admiral Tom Moorer and I were told that the meeting had been transferred to the White House basement "situation room," so we drove over together in my beat-up Skylark. There we learned that Brezhnev had just sent a tough message to President Nixon proposing that both Soviet and American forces be dispatched to the Middle East to prevent the Israelis from crushing the Egyptian Third Army, but that if the Americans would not, the Soviets would go alone.

Long into the morning hours Kissinger, Schlesinger, and the rest of us discussed how to handle the danger that Soviet troops might enter the Middle East. The intelligence job was to say whether they could (yes), would (possibly, but not really likely except in purely token quantity—which, however, would be enough to raise the specter of Israelis fighting Soviets), or were in the process of doing so (airborne forces were alerted and prepared to move and the Soviet airlift planes had gone to USSR bases, where they could quickly pick up the troops, but none seemed yet to be on the way). Aside from what I knew when I walked into the meeting, of course, I spent considerable time during the evening on the secure telephone with the CIA Operations Center and our Middle East and Soviet experts who had been assembled, and they in turn were in contact with the other elements of the community, in DIA and especially NSA with its worldwide electronic nets.

Kissinger later asked me whether I thought we had overreacted with the worldwide alert of our forces, Defense Condition 3, the lowest level of real alert. I replied that I basically thought not, especially as SAC and a good portion of the Pacific Command were already at that level, although the public-relations impact may have been greater than the act itself. But I came away with the conclusion that the collection machinery of the intelligence community, when focused as it was in this case on a known problem area, can be superb. The real challenge I saw was to make the analytical process function with the same degree of excellence, both with respect to identifying dangers lurking behind contradictory evidence and with respect to winnowing the valuable items from the masses of information available from the collection machinery.

In addition to crises like these—and there were others, from coups in Cyprus and Portugal to a nuclear explosion in India and a left-wing and possibly antagonistic government in Australia—the regular business of intelligence had to go on as well. Each new item of intelligence on Soviet strategic weapons had to be examined with meticulous care, to determine whether it was compatible with or a violation of the 1972 SALT agreements. Hours were required for preparation and participation in discussions in the White House as to possible new subjects of agreement as these negotiations continued. Intelligence targets had to be changed. For example, Portugal had been such a quiet backwater that in 1973 I suggested closing our station there, but by 1975 it had become the center of a struggle for power by a hard-line Communist Party in the heart of NATO. Africa in the 1973 edition of the Key Intelligence Questions hardly rated a mention in comparison with the priorities of Indochina, but by 1975 it had risen to a principal area of attention. (Even if some of these look like mistakes in hindsight, I thought that preferable to listing everything as a top priority item just so we could never be wrong on paper—we had to try to be both selective *and* right.) Entirely new subjects rose in importance, from the economics of the oil trade to detailed geographic and economic briefing papers for Law of the Sea negotiations to the dangers ahead in overpopulated, underdeveloped and bitter ministates in the Caribbean.

Just as I had believed in traveling in Vietnam, as Director, I believed it essential to visit the world. I made quick day or weekend trips to neighboring areas to meet the foreign officials with whom CIA dealt and to assure them that we valued the cooperation and knowledge they provided us. I made a longer trip through Europe to reinforce our NATO relationships. And I made a particularly fascinating tour of the Middle East to look at the 1973 Suez battlefield from both sides and appreciate the dominating geography of the

Golan Heights to Israel (and to suggest the possibility of electronic listening posts on both sides so as to ensure early warning of real troop concentrations and dispel suspicion and misunderstanding from false alarms—which I was later told was incorporated in the negotiation process and finally accepted on the Sinai line between Israel and Egypt).

CIA's ceremonial work had to be done, too, meeting and greeting visiting foreign intelligence chiefs whose services gave us valuable intelligence or access to geography that enabled our technical machinery to cover vital targets; and giving medals to officers who had distinguished themselves throughout the world in current operations, and to Jack Downey, who was finally released from more than twenty years in a Chinese prison and aroused the admiration of us all at the calm and cool way in which he picked up the threads of his life in a totally changed America.

On a typical day in 1974, the alarm rang at six-thirty, and I crawled out of bed and went down to get the *Washington Post* at the front door. I went through it carefully to see what foreign stories were top news, what issues were hot in Congress that I might be asked about, what the editorials and columnists were saying about the political scene in Washington and whether Jack Anderson had some juicy story about CIA. Calisthenics, shower and English muffin, and it was eight o'clock and Mr. Galloway, the driver, and one of the security officers were outside in the blue Chevrolet with its unobtrusive armor plate. They had *The New York Times* and the *National Intelligence Daily* and I went through the latter first to pick up the wide range of information that wasn't in the public domain and check how the summary of a particularly difficult National Intelligence Estimate had been presented, with the dissenting position of one of the agencies. *The New York Times* I went through fairly rapidly, not rereading the news that had been in the *Post* but picking up its additional coverage and its editorial pages and noting how it was presenting some of the politically charged items. We pulled up to the front of the Agency about eight twenty-five and I walked rapidly through the marble entrance hall and up to the private elevator. Into the office, where Barbara Pindar had pulled the classified material out of my safe and tried to arrange it on my desk in some sort of order, separating the studies I had squirreled away to get at some day when I had time from the papers I had to move right away. Jenonne Walker, my executive assistant, came in to tell me of the cable traffic she had screened and to show me one or two I had to read, and quickly summarized one when I grimaced at its length.

At nine precisely I went in to the conference room, where the dozen senior officers of the Agency (plus General Danny Graham for the Community) were assembled for our daily morning meeting. Dick Lehman led off with a summary of the main news, plus what had arrived after the *Daily* had been printed at 6 A.M., and we chatted about one or two of the major developments in the Middle East or Southeast Asia. Then Bill Nelson alerted us about a problem in his Operations Directorate; it concerned the exposure of the bright exploit of one of our officers in Thailand who sent to the Prime Minister a letter purportedly from a Communist leader in hiding, the object being to stir up dissension among the Party's chiefs. The Thai youth whom the officer sent to post the letter unfortunately had an excess of conscientiousness and registered the letter with his own return address. The exposure of the ploy was turning into a *cause célèbre* among the Bangkok students denouncing CIA "interference" in Thailand, with our ambassador no less irate. Ed Proctor for the Intelligence Directorate then told us of a National Security Council study that needed contributions from our economic, political and military experts on Latin America, and he predicted some sharp differences between CIA and DIA on parts of it. Carl Duckett for Science and Technology said that tomorrow's meeting of the Executive Committee of the National Reconnaissance Office (which I would chair) would see a big fight over whether to delay an electronic sensor system in order to find the funds to keep one of our photo systems functioning at peak schedule with the increased costs that inflation had brought. Jack Blake for the Administrative Directorate said that the load on the Agency's computers was still increasing and that it seemed inevitable that more would be needed.

The General Counsel and the Inspector General passed, but the Legislative Counsel said that a subcommittee of the Senate Foreign Relations Committee wanted a briefing on Southeast Asia next week; so I asked Proctor to start drafting it. Danny Graham spoke for the Community to say that his staff had gotten the comments of all the agencies on the new ideas for an intelligence center in the Pentagon for crisis periods. Angus Thuermer dropped the request of a hard-driving newsman for a backgrounder on South Asia, and Ed Proctor said that one of his better analysts could handle it— who could not expose our operations there because the Operations Directorate had never told him of them. Dick Walters then ended by reporting that an old friend of his had been appointed chief of a friendly intelligence service, so he would invite him for a visit to make sure that our station chief got off to a good start with him. I said that we should "no comment" the Thai-letter story when it hit the press, in order not to make it any more of an issue in Thailand than it already was, and just take our lumps on it as necessary, but to try to satisfy our unhappy ambassador.

Then at ten o'clock the U.S. Intelligence Board, the heads of each of the agencies of the intelligence community, met to review and argue out a few differences over the pending national estimate on Chinese advanced weapons for the next ten years and to discuss the post-mortem the community staff had produced of intelligence performance during the Yom Kippur War. At noon, I presided over a ceremony to award a medal to a clandestine-operations officer for his courageous activities in the mountains of Laos, although the citation was written in generalities to keep the details secret. Then down to the cafeteria to lunch with four young economic analysts and share their excitement as they saw interest in their product growing in Washington and their problems move to the top of the list for policy discussions.

Back to the office and a final review with the authors of

the briefing I would be reading to the three o'clock meeting of the National Security Council committee wrestling with what to do about Southeast Asia and then the drive down to the basement entrance to the White House to sit and wait for Kissinger. Finally he arrived and I opened with my briefing—the North Vietnamese continuing to build their logistics structure to support their forces still in South Vietnam. The discussion ranged around the table as to what could be done about it, without conclusion, and Kissinger directed State to develop some options for what we might do by the next meeting. Back to the Agency, this time in rush-hour traffic, but I had some extra paperwork along so I read it in the car.

Now a series of short meetings on particular issues for each directorate, reviewing the chief-of-station nominees for the changes due in the coming summer, approving the appointment of a committee to look over the personnel-records system and improve it, talking with the National Intelligence Officer for China about some new trends there, walking down to the *Daily* office to review the stories planned for tomorrow, and receiving a new American ambassador on his way to his post—telling him that CIA gets along very well indeed with strong ambassadors and badly with weak ones, and hoping that he will take the hint and be strong. Finally, the flow stops about seven o'clock, and I go down the elevator the last time for home, but with a thick book of homework for after-dinner reading (and locking in the safe for the night) on the options to be talked about for the decision tomorrow on the photo versus electronic system, but preferring that kind of quiet evening to accepting invitations to the diplomatic world's busy round of parties and small talk.

If all this makes it appear that the Director is a juggler of many different things at one time, it is a true picture of his activities. But my main point is that his responsibility for substantive intelligence is the most important thing he is charged with. And that requires that he be helped by having as many as possible of his remaining jobs done by deputies and other subordinates. For to the extent this can be done, he is freed to devote his time and energy to understanding the world and the trends and developments there that affect the people of the United States for good or for bad. He can, as I think he should, and as I tried to, do the necessary homework and discuss the basis for their assessments with the analysts and experts, and so be able to speak with conviction and precision not only when he presents the opening intelligence assessment at National Security Council meetings across the table from the President, but when he has to defend it against a Kissinger or a Schlesinger challenge during the course of the ensuing policy discussions.

This kind of expertise can make the Director more effective if the President seeks his personal counsel. Kennedy certainly did from McCone, who pushed his way into the President's office, and Johnson obtained it at his regular "Tuesday lunch" (which sometimes took place on Friday), at which Helms was a regular participant. Nixon, however, preferred detailed papers and made his decisions from them, and neither Helms nor Schlesinger nor I really saw him outside formal or ceremonial meetings. I remember only one private conversation with him; it occurred when he phoned to ask what was happening in China and I provided a quick summary off the top of my head. And by 1974, with the Watergate hearings and disclosures coming to a crescendo, he became increasingly withdrawn and inaccessible. I recall one National Security Council meeting, when I was giving a briefing on some aspect of Soviet missilery, the blank look in his eyes convinced me that he was not listening to a word I said. When Gerald Ford took over, he was accustomed to the daily briefing and publications that I had arranged for him to receive as Vice-President, and he continued these for a time. But my own reluctance to push into the Oval Office unless I was invited or had something that I thought demanded my personal presence, combined with a lively awareness of the probable reaction if I had tried to elbow past Henry Kissinger, kept me from pressing for personal access to either Nixon or Ford.

In retrospect, I consider this one of the errors I made as Director, although I am not sure how I could have done any differently. I know that our intelligence material did reach the President in the form in which it was sent. (Ford rather liked the *Daily*.) But some material can best be advanced only personally and informally in the give and take of conversation. What's more, the Director is much better able to direct the intelligence community if he has heard the President's concerns personally and shares some of his closely held communications. It might even have relieved the frustrations of my uninformed analysts. So I am pleased to see that President Carter has a weekly intelligence session with Stansfield Turner.

Such direct meetings also could keep a director confident that he is in tune with the President's sensitivities as he decides on intelligence initiatives from day to day and that he can seek policy guidance on the inherent risks they raise. With Nixon and Ford the Presidents during my tenure, I had to handle these with Kissinger in informal moments before and after meetings of the many NSC committees we attended, checking, for example, whether a CIA approach to a foreigner to become our agent would constitute a diplomatic catastrophe if exposed. To his credit, Kissinger was invariably supportive, wishing us good luck and asking only some months later how it had worked out and if he could see some of the resulting reports, and expressing his admiration when they turned out to give an inside look at a difficult target. I grew to enjoy my private and committee sessions with him, listening to him berate the State Department— and even Intelligence on occasion—while sometimes forcefully warning him that the odds were against an outcome he hoped for.

Kissinger was obviously brilliant, vain to such a degree that even he himself joked about it, canny in his husbanding and selective exposure of secrets and stern in his insistence on the prerogatives of a great power. He tried to relate all his actions to an over-all strategy. For a period, I must confess, I was awed by his command of, for example, the more esoteric aspects of the SALT negotiations and the confusing array of weapons, options and trade-offs that he juggled brilliantly at National Security Council meetings. As I became more confident on the topic myself I found myself increasingly supporting Kissinger's efforts to keep the *process* of *détente* moving ahead with the comparatively cooperative Russian leadership then in power, and increasingly impatient with the Pentagon's insistence that all concessions be made by the Soviets. Thus, I used intelligence to try to expand the subject under debate from narrow weapons counts to the politics of over-all Soviet policy. And I successfully resisted the attempt to use intelligence to block negotiation on such matters as the cruise missile. I asserted that our intelligence was comprehensive enough to assure that we would catch the Soviets at any attempt to cheat on any agreement before their actions could give them a strategic advantage over us. With Washington's tendency to focus on and debate minutiae, I believed it proper for intelligence to try to raise the level of the discussion to the strategic relationships facing us over time and space. Kissinger understood this and perhaps best expressed the contribution intelligence can make to policy when he returned a particularly secret report we had compiled for him with a rare compliment on its quality and the request to "Keep giving me things that make me think."

Obviously too close and personal a contact with the President and his White House staff has its dangers. The Director is likely to be sucked into the President's orbit and feel obliged to look not only for how intelligence can help a President to choose policies but how it can justify his choices. In my case, I was never close enough to either Nixon or Ford for this to happen. And Kissinger, while meticulous in telling me what topics he wanted assessed or what would be on the National Security Council agenda, never—and I repeat never—suggested what positions I should take or even asked what I would be saying before the meeting itself. Even if his approach had been different, however, the geographical separation of Langley from the

White House and my close relations with the indepen-dence-proud analysts at CIA would have exerted an influ-ence on me. And it is for this reason that in all the discus-sions about how the intelligence community should be organized I took the position that the Director should retain direct control and responsibility for CIA so that he can de-pend on it for his support and positions on substantive ques-tions, whatever other arrangements he might make with re-spect to the management of the community as a whole.

One job certainly cannot be passed off to anyone else— the DCI's job of speaking for intelligence to the American public. In line with the conclusions I had drawn about the public's lack of understanding of modern intelligence and about the need for a change in the old traditions of total secrecy, I started a process of bringing intelligence out of the shadows and explaining what it really was all about. I began in the conventional way with a few quiet background discussions with knowledgeable newsmen and columnists, who actually needed no education but were interested in knowing something about who I was and what my approach to my new responsibilities would be. To these I added the equally conventional lunches with the editorial boards of some of the leading newspapers and weekly magazines, again for general background discussion, which I hoped would help them to put CIA stories in some proper context and to play down the sensational approach to intelligence. These went reasonably well, and I began to think of ways in which CIA could make more of its information and assess-ments about the world available to the public through the press, and build some better comprehension of what the real focus of intelligence work was. So I signed up for a few speaking engagements at which I hoped to reiterate some of the points I had made during my confirmation hearings. None of these was novel, of course, as Dulles, McCone and Helms had done the same thing, but I saw the need to speak more often directly to the public than their occasional for-ays, since the new political atmosphere, to my mind, de-manded full attribution and public accountability to get our message to the American people.

I knew that my credibility was at stake in the process, and that any long-term success in my venture into public relations depended on maintaining it. At one of the editorial board lunches, I was asked whether CIA used American newsmen in its work abroad. I knew we had done so in the past, but I also knew that the employment of those whom I had handled had been terminated, and I thought this meant that the practice had ended. So I answered, "No." But when on my return to Langley I checked to be sure that my answer was correct, I learned that while most had indeed been phased out, there were about five staff members of general-circulation media and about twenty-five in the stringer or free-lance category still working. To protect my credibility, I felt it essential to return to that editorial board and correct my answer, pointing out that we had always avoided influencing what these newsmen wrote. I also said that I was arranging to end the arrangements with the five who remained, since they perhaps cast some question on the integrity of the American press, although I said I would continue to use the free-lance journalists since the purchasers of their copy were under no illusions that they worked only for them. I learned a lesson about dealing with the press the hard way on that occasion. The numbers I had given to demonstrate how minimal the relationship between CIA and newsmen was at present provided the journal with a banner headline, and it resulted in a storm of breast-beating about the purity of the press that is still going on today and bids fair to spread to a claim that CIA should not only not have any contact with the American press but with any journalist at all, including presumably a TASS correspondent overseas. This despite the fact that almost every other country's intelligence service, including several impeccably democratic ones, uses the overseas representatives of its press services with the enthusiastic support of all concerned. But, despite these problems, I thought the period long past when I could follow Allen Dulles' example when he faced the same question, puffed his pipe a moment, and answered flatly, "No"—and was never the object of an investigative reporter's campaign to prove him false.

On another occasion, I invited a group of journalists to Langley for what I thought might be the first of monthly backgrounders on the situation around the world. It proved to be the last one. The assembled journalists asked hardly a question about the world situation but breathlessly bore in for a headline about CIA's operations. As I fielded these with increasing dismay, one asked whether CIA used businessmen in its work abroad, or as a cover. Naïvely believing that this long-established and well-documented practice of all intelligence services, real as well as fictional, was hardly a secret, I replied, "Of course." The newsman kept pressing: "How many? Thousands?" "Oh, no. Nothing like that." "Less than a hundred?" And in some exasperation, I finally blew it by saying, "Around two hundred"; and that was the single story to come out of the session. It not only taught me *never* to use a number when talking to a newsman, but ended my experiment in regular CIA press conferences. I continued, and even expanded, the practice of informal and off-the-record discussions between our analysts and knowledgeable newsmen, but dropped any attempt to institutionalize the process.

I did, however, keep up pressure to get our story out to the American people. To the annual "family day," which brought employee families to see where Daddy or Mommy worked and reduce CIA's air of mystery among its own personnel, we added "alumni day" to bring retirees up to date on the Agency and to arm them with the answers they needed to defend the institution to which they had given their loyalty. One of the programs that bring top high-school seniors from every state for a briefing visit to the national capital suggested that a stop at CIA be included, and every Tuesday evening in the spring hundreds of young Americans now arrived for a question-and-answer session in the Langley auditorium. A number of colleges and universities also arranged to visit and discuss the intelligence profession, from Princeton's Whig and Cliosophic Society to Malcolm X College. I also brought tears to the eyes of a Yalie employee when I arranged to have a copy of the statue of

Nathan Hale, expressing his only regret that he had but one life to give for his country as America's first spy, placed in front of CIA headquarters to show that intelligence is as old as the Republic it serves. I accepted, and encouraged a number of our other officers to accept, speaking engagements around the country to explain intelligence and answer questions about it.

But this gradual strategy, I must admit, could not keep up with the rising criticism of the CIA, spurred by Watergate and then sharply exacerbated by Allende's overthrow and death in Chile. A determined effort was launched to link the Agency publicly with what had happened there. One Congressional investigation had been started as an extension of Senator Frank Church's study of the activity of multinational corporations, and particularly covered the links that had existed between I.T.T.'s people in Chile and the embassy and CIA station in Santiago. In the spring of 1973, Schlesinger had handled this probe, and under his direction we had reported to CIA's oversight committees on the relations between the Agency and I.T.T. with particular reference to the 1970 Chilean election campaign. But we did not go into its Track II aspects. The subject had also come up in Helms's confirmation hearings as Ambassador to Iran, and the press had kept the subject simmering throughout this period, then brought it to a crescendo when Allende was actually overthrown on September 11, 1973.

The principal protagonist on the subject was Congressman Michael Harrington, of Massachusetts. He pressed the subcommittee on Inter-American Affairs of the House Foreign Affairs Committee to hold a hearing on Chile on October 11, and I was called to appear before it. I made clear that I could testify only in executive session if I were expected to discuss any substantive intelligence on what had happened in Chile and that I would not testify at all on CIA's operations there, in deference to the long-standing arrangement with the Congress that CIA's operations would only be discussed with the oversight committees the Congress itself had established. The hearing amounted to little more than a fencing match between Harrington and myself; I limited myself to statements of what had occurred in Chile, while he pressed for information about what CIA had done, and I refused to answer. Frustrated by this, Harrington put pressure on the oversight committee, Nedzi's intelligence subcommittee of the Armed Services Committee, to hold a full hearing on what CIA had done in Chile. Nedzi, of course, knew at least in outline CIA's Chilean activities and wasn't particularly eager to comply, but finally under Harrington's pressure he did call the Intelligence Subcommittee into secret session in April 1974 (without Harrington) and asked me to testify.

Now I was in something of a dilemma. I had no problem testifying and answering questions on all of the CIA's covert political-action operations up to Allende's election and since his installation in office—our so-called Track I activities. But there was Track II, the operation we undertook on the direct personal orders of President Nixon during the six weeks between the time Allende won his plurality in the 1970 presidential elections and the time he was formally voted into and installed in office by the Chilean Congress. Although it lasted only six weeks and was cut off after Allende was inaugurated, in Track II we had indeed looked for a coup. But President Nixon had ordered Helms and the Agency to keep that activity in the strictest confidence, reporting it to absolutely no one.

After I had completed my testimony on Track I and answered all the Congressmen's questions on it in full detail, however, I felt I could not in good conscience leave it at that. Before and after my confirmation hearing, I had undertaken in all sincerity to give assurances to the Congressional chairmen, Nedzi included, that I considered it my responsibility to keep them informed even about CIA matters that they would have no way of even suspecting, and therefore would be unable to question me on. And now here was just such a case—and a personal test for my conscience of that assurance. So, once the business on Track I had been concluded to everyone's satisfaction and the session was adjourned (and the transcript closed), I approached Nedzi, who had only the committee counsel still with him, and in a quiet voice told him there was one other thing I had to tell him. I said there was an aspect of our effort in Chile which President Nixon had ordered and which he had also ordered be revealed to no one including the ambassador and the secretaries and departments of State and Defense. And then I gave him a summary of Track II in a very few words. He listened, asked how this related to the Track I story I had testified on and then sternly demanded my assurance that Track II had been cut off in 1970 and that I had been accurate in my testimony that CIA had not been associated with the military coup in 1973. I gave these assurances, and we let the matter drop. On my way home, I felt good about my conscience and my loyalty to the Constitutional role of Congress, but I recognized a dilemma in that I had violated a direct and, when he gave it, legal order of my boss, the President. I added this problem to the contradictions I was somehow going to have to resolve between the American Constitution and the traditions of intelligence.

But this was not the end. Harrington kept the pressure on, now turning to a rule of the House that said that any member is entitled to review the transcript of any committee of the House; and he wanted to review the transcript of my testimony on CIA's Chilean operations. A few weeks later Nedzi phoned me to say that he and Hebert had decided they had no choice but to accede to Harrington's request. But they planned to get and were prepared to enforce his commitment to respect the secrecy of the testimony. I replied that the decision obviously had to be theirs and that I had no basis on which I could effectively object to it. Harrington signed that he would "agree to honor" the committee rules that the information he received remain secret, and he read the transcript. At that point I thought the matter had ended and went on about my many other chores. I had that summer, even somewhat defiantly, accepted an invitation to appear before a thoroughly hostile "conference" on CIA and covert action in mid-September; there I thought I could at least give CIA's side in reply to the allegations and exaggerations that were running through opposition circles.

I got more than I bargained for. For a few days before the conference, in plenty of time for maximum press attention, a letter Harrington wrote summarizing my secret testimony "leaked" to *The New York Times* and raised a storm about CIA and Chile. But I went through with the appearance and got a chance to deny to Harrington's face his claim that I used the word *destabilization* in my testimony, as a description of our program in Chile. Nonetheless the word has circled the world as a dramatic catchword for CIA activities, just as I knew it would, as soon as I saw it in Harrington's letter. As an illustration of CIA's problem with such imagery, my denial at the "conference," my letter in *The New York Times* making the same point and a public statement by Nedzi's committee that the word was not used by me, all were totally unable to reduce the political impact of this single word.

One result of the Chile storm came in the Senate. A bill that came to the floor would have forbidden CIA any function beyond pure intelligence—that is, no political or paramilitary action whatsoever. The Senate voted it down by a decisive vote of 68 to 17, but it passed an amendment to the Foreign Assistance Act that said that any CIA activity other than intelligence gathering could be undertaken only if the President "finds it important to the national security . . . and reports, in a timely fashion . . . to the appropriate committees of the Congress." In this way, CIA's covert-action function received its first legislative recognition, and my dilemma after telling Nedzi about Tract II had been solved. I mentioned to my friends in the White House that this law meant that CIA never again could undertake a Track II without telling the "appropriate committees of the Congress." But it was not until the following year that I would learn that this law in effect had virtually eliminated the "covert" part of CIA's covert action that year.

Harrington's letter, and the ensuing uproar about CIA and Chile, had another effect, and one more personal and painful for me. Because that uproar produced an undercurrent of charges that my predecessor, former boss and sponsor in my preparation to become DCI, Dick Helms, might have broken the law. At the time of the Senate confirmation hearings on his appointment as ambassador to Iran, Helms had been asked some specific questions about the CIA's activities in Chile. In light of what had now been revealed, the question had arisen whether his answers were accurate. Within CIA a middle-grade officer who was aware of Track II, responding to the Schlesinger-Colby directives that all "questionable" matters be reported, submitted a memorandum saying that an investigation was needed to determine whether Helms had committed perjury. It was about as welcome on my desk as a cobra, and as hard to handle.

Here I was in the middle of another conflict between the past and the future. Helms as a totally loyal servant of his President and his intelligence profession had manfully tried to keep the secret he had been directed to keep. But that middle-grade CIA officer had equally properly reacted to my very specific instructions that he should present to me anything about whose propriety he had the slightest doubt. If I accepted the one, I repudiated the past; if I accepted the other, I compromised the future. In my own mind I was, and remain, fully convinced that Helms did nothing for which he could or should be condemned. At the same time, I realized that if I took upon myself the decision that the matter should be dropped without further inquiry, I would be saying that Schlesinger's and my directives and all my brave words about a new era of American intelligence contained the reservation that they would not apply if I thought they should not. To avoid granting myself the sole power to make a decision and to indicate that I took such reports seriously, I asked the Inspector General to assign three officers to examine the record of Helms's testimony in detail and to submit to me their findings, so that it would be clear and on paper how the matter was treated and that it was not pushed aside.

After several weeks the three officers submitted to me a

report that made my life no easier, because it did not come to any definite conclusion. The trio reviewed the testimony and the evidence that lay behind it and recommended that, as they could not say whether or not the facts were really in conflict with the testimony, I was legally obliged to consult with the Attorney General to make the final determination.

I have to say I didn't like that recommendation one bit and looked around to see whether I really had to comply with it. I turned first to the Agency's General Counsel and asked him to review the affair and give me his advice, also in writing. In due time he agreed with my view that Helms most certainly had not committed perjury. Then he went on to call my attention to an agreement that had been struck between the CIA and the Justice Department in 1954, that the Agency, because of the necessary secrecy of its operations, could decide alone and on its own whether CIA would report possible criminal charges to the Justice Department, since a trial might risk the exposure of intelligence sources and methods. On the basis of this advice, I drafted a memo stating that in my mind no perjury had been committed and that unquestionably intelligence sources and methods (including Track II and its contacts) would be revealed in any court action. The draft concluded that the matter should be dropped.

But I had to do one more thing—submit the draft memo to the three officers who had made the review, so that they would know that their work had not just disappeared somewhere in my office. But they, courageously and unanimously, retorted when they read my memo that it would not stand up. They stated flatly that the 1954 agreement between the CIA and the Justice Department could no longer govern, if it ever had any validity. And I could see as I talked the matter out with them that if I insisted on my "solution" I could expect the matter to leak eventually to the press (not necessarily by any one of them, but certainly nevertheless), with the implication that CIA in general and I in particular were "covering up." So I took a deep breath and made an appointment to see Acting Attorney General Laurence Silberman.

It was late December, just the week before Christmas, when I went over to have that chat with Silberman. I had not yet made up my mind whether to turn the Helms material over to him. What I really hoped to do was get a reading from him about the validity of that 1954 agreement between the CIA and the Justice Department, whether it still had any legal standing. But no sooner had I described it than he cut me off. "Come on, Bill," he said. "You're a lawyer. You know better than that. I don't care what the past arrangements might have been. In this day and age, there's no way in the world the CIA is going to be given the extralegal privilege of deciding unilaterally which of its employees should be prosecuted and who shouldn't. That's just plain nonsense. Sure, I understand the danger that your legitimate secrets could come out in a trial, and that there are instances where a trial would have to be avoided in order to protect them. But that isn't something the Agency has the power to decide on its own. It's something the Agency can come to the Justice Department and argue about, but it's something for us to take into consideration and decide, not you. So, come on now, let's get down to cases. Who or what are you talking about?"

I didn't argue with him; in fact, I really agreed with him. It was indeed impossible, if one believed in the Constitution, for a government official like myself to be given the power to determine unilaterally and secretly whether or not a criminal charge should be prosecuted. So, with some prompting, I described to Silberman the questions that had been raised about Helms's testimony and my theory that it was not perjury. He listened, but ended up by insisting that the files on the matter be made available to the Department of Justice. Since this meant, among other things, turning over the secrets of Track II operations, I insisted that he guarantee that the material be handled within the Department in a highly classified and compartmented manner. He agreed, and the next day I made the necessary arrangements to have the files forwarded to Silberman.

In the months and years ahead I would be condemned for this action. A number of colleagues and senior officers in the

Agency would say that I had turned against my friend, bene-
factor and predecessor. But I am satisfied that I did what I
had to do. Times had truly changed since 1954. The arrangement then between the CIA and the Justice Department,
struck in good faith in that time's atmosphere where the traditional role of intelligence allowed it to operate in almost
total secrecy, had to collapse in the new times where no
one, not even the President, was allowed to put himself
above the law. In what was by then the post-Watergate climate—Nixon, of course, had been forced to resign a few
months before, in August—subordinate CIA officers, in this
case the three young officers who had made the review,
were no longer content simply to accept what their seniors
might decide, and it was their respectful but insistent pressure that, I realize, obliged me to act as I did. I was persuaded that I had no right to make a decision on this matter
alone or to preempt a ruling by the proper authorities,
whether the dangers to intelligence security would prevent
prosecution or investigation in the case. And I am glad they
did, requiring me to uphold my oath to the Constitution and
really demonstrate that a new and American intelligence
had been born, not just talked about.

Besides, I was convinced that no fair jury in the land
would conclude that Helms had committed perjury, and that
therefore he would not be indicted for it. And the subsequent long silence from the Justice Department, despite occasional press rumblings, seemed to confirm my original assessment. Indeed, the final outcome, with Helms avoiding a
show trial by not contesting a lesser misdemeanor that he
had not "fully, completely and accurately" testified to Congress, specifically eliminated the perjury charge. One can
only wonder how often that "fully, completely and accurately" standard is breached in Washington, and consequently whether the Justice Department's using it against
Helms reflected more of a political than a legal attack on his
directorship of CIA. But some would say, therefore, that I
should never have presented the matter to Silberman, since
that started the process, and I accept the blame for that as

the cost of my belief that intelligence must operate according to new rules.

I had another chore to accomplish in that week before Christmas, equally unpleasant and Scrooge-like. Because another retirement deadline had been set by the Civil Service Commission for the end of December, I was determined to face up to my responsibility to remove Jim Angleton before it, so he would not miss out on its benefits.

During my trip to the Middle East I had learned to my shock that the CIA stations in Israel and the neighboring Arab countries were not allowed to communicate with each other because the Israel relationship went only to the counterintelligence staff. Therefore they could not compare notes and impressions and help each other to come to better assessments as to what was happening in that delicate area. I knew that Angleton had been most upset when I acceded to Kissinger's request that I not visit East Jerusalem under Israeli auspices in order not to give any unconscious political signal to the Arabs. But I found the Israeli officials I met either not greatly disturbed by it or too polite to criticize it. Out of that trip and from a lot of other impressions I had come to the conclusion that I was not doing my job as Director unless I insisted that I, rather than Angleton, make the decisions about Israeli relations and counterintelligence. And I was reinforced in my belief that a change in management and the manager of both was essential.

So, I called Angleton to my office to talk the matter out with him, saying that I had come to the conclusion that a change was necessary in both jobs, the Israeli liaison and counterintelligence, but that I wanted to retain his talents for the Agency, and especially his experience. I offered him the prospect of separate status, where he could summarize for us the many ideas he had and conclusions he had reached about counterintelligence, and where he would be consulted on, but no longer be in charge of, our Israeli liaison. Not unexpectedly he resisted both ideas with the strongest arguments he could offer. And thinking that a day or so of reflection might make it easier for him to accept the inevitable—and in my mind this time it was inevitable—I asked him to think over the matter for a couple of days to decide whether he would like to stay on in the way I described or whether he would choose to retire completely before the deadline for the benefits.

But on the next day—it was December 18, 1974—I received a telephone call that knocked all my plans into a cocked hat, ruining not only the Christmas season for me but nearly all of the next year as well.

CHAPTER THIRTEEN

Investigating the CIA

THE telephone call was from Seymour Hersh, the Pulitzer-Prize–winning investigative reporter for *The New York Times*. He rang me up to say excitedly that he had "a story bigger than My-Lai" (which, of course, was the story for which he had won his Pulitzer), concerning illegal CIA domestic activities. Now, although Hersh and I could usually be found on the opposite sides of any issue involving the CIA, I had every reason to respect his journalistic integrity. Earlier that year, in February, I had learned that he was inquiring about a rumored deep-ocean CIA operation (later to be revealed as the *Glomar Explorer* project). I had gone to him then and had requested that he not only not write whatever he knew but that he not even speak of it to anyone, and he obviously honored my request. So now I felt that I owed him the interview he requested and could trust his responsibility both as an American and as a hard-driving newsman. I invited him to come to my office at Langley to discuss the matter. I also warned Brent Scowcroft at the White House and Congressman Nedzi that something was up.

Our meeting took place on Friday morning, December 20. From what Hersh told me—that he had learned from several sources that the CIA had been engaged in a "massive" operation against the antiwar movement involving wiretaps, break-ins, mail intercepts, and surveillances of American citizens—I realized immediately that he had come upon some disjointed and distorted accounts of several items on our highly secret "family jewels" list. I did not ask him how he had come by the information, or from whom. For one thing, I was perfectly aware that a journalist of Hersh's standing would protect his sources as fiercely as would we in intelligence. But more to the point, I didn't have any trouble imagining just who or what they might be. After all, there were enough former CIA officers around, especially among the thousands fired or retired during the Schlesinger purge of the Agency, who had been privy to one or another of the "family jewels." With the unease prevalent in the Agency about Operation Chaos, a journalist of Hersh's skill would not have found it difficult to get a lead on CIA's activities concerning the antiwar movement and quickly build from there admissions about individual wiretaps and other domestic surveillances used by the Agency. Anyway, my major concern at that moment was not to try to identify the leakers but to deal in some sane and rational way with the exaggerated way Hersh had put together the information leaked.

"Look, Sy," I began, "what you're onto here are two very separate and distinct matters that you've gotten mixed up and distorted." I then went on to try to explain—and put in proper perspective—the two matters that his sources had confused and exaggerated for him. First, I said, there was an operation that the Agency had conducted to discover whether the American antiwar movement was being supported or manipulated by foreign powers, and that such matters were properly within the CIA's charter. Moreover, I stressed, after having concluded that no foreign power was involved with the antiwar movement, the operation had been terminated. As for the talk of mail intercepts, wiretaps, and surveillance of American citizens, that was something entirely different and in no way connected with the antiwar movement. What he had come upon here, I explained, were some cases in which CIA had acted under its responsibility to protect intelligence sources and techniques against leaks, and on some few occasions in its twenty-eight-year history it had used such surveillance techniques in the United States and in so doing had overstepped the boundaries of its charter. But the important point, I emphasized, was that the Agency had conducted its own review of such activities in 1973 and had issued a series of clear directives making plain that the Agency henceforth must and would stay within the law. "So, you see, Sy, you would be wrong if you went ahead with your story in the way you've laid it out. What you have are a few incidents of the Agency straying from the straight and narrow. There certainly was never anything like a 'massive illegal domestic intelligence operation.' What few mistakes we made in the past have long before this been corrected. And there is certainly nothing like that going on now."

But, as subsequent events amply demonstrated, Hersh didn't see it my way at all. Indeed, the main thing he took away from our meeting that Friday was the sense that I had confirmed the reports he had heard. And so there it was on Sunday, December 22, 1974, splashed across three columns of the *New York Times*'s front page: "Huge C.I.A. Operation Reported in U.S. Against Anti-War Forces, Other Dissidents in Nixon Years." And that was followed by the shocking lead paragraph: "The Central Intelligence Agency, directly violating its charter, conducted a massive illegal domestic intelligence operation during the Nixon Administration against the antiwar movement and other dissident groups in the United States, according to well-placed Government sources."

A press and political firestorm immediately erupted. The charge that the Agency had engaged in domestic spying, the inference that it had become a Gestapo, proved the fatal spark. All the tensions and suspicions and hostilities that had been building about the CIA since the Bay of Pigs and had risen to a combustible level during the Vietnam and Watergate years, now exploded. What was to be called the Year of Intelligence in Washington began, a year in which the CIA came under the closest and harshest public scrutiny that any such service has ever experienced not only in this country but anywhere in the world.

I have to admit that I didn't immediately foresee these traumatic consequences. After all, the CIA had been emblazoned unfavorably in newspaper headlines countless times in the preceding years, most recently in regard to its Chile operations, and had weathered those storms. And it seemed to me that we could do so again—if we handled the present crisis in a calm and sensible way. In my view, the calm and sensible way in this case was to counter the distortions and exaggerations of Hersh's article by publicly telling the true story of Operation Chaos and the rest, conceding the Agency's few misdeeds in the past, explaining how they had come about, emphasizing that they were few and far between and relatively small and, above all, stressing that they had been terminated by the Agency itself and reported to Congress in 1973 and that nothing of the sort was going on now, nor would anything like them take place in the future. More than anything else, it was the CIA's experience in Watergate that led me to this strategy. It seemed to me that our ultracautious "distancing" attitude during that crisis, our reluctance to reveal anything more than we were specifically asked, had caused us to withhold information in hope of keeping the Agency clear of the scandal, and had created the very climate of suspicion and implied culpability that we had been, justifiably, trying to avoid. Thus I felt that this time we must take exactly the opposite tack, coming clean straightaway on those few activities in the Agency's past that admittedly were questionable, in the hope that they then would be disposed of quickly and not become the subject of a long series of titillating, reluctantly revealed individual exposures, each making a new sensational headline.

But when I contacted the White House that Sunday, I found that there was a great deal of concern over there on how to respond to the *Times* article which had come out much more seriously than I had expected it would when I first discussed Hersh's call and Friday interview with Scowcroft. One of the President's aides suggested that I phone the President to give him a basis for some comment on the story. He was at the moment en route to Vail, Colorado, for his Christmas vacation, so the White House operator put me on an open circuit to Air Force One, readable by any listening foreign intelligence-intercept operators and so hardly conducive to detailed discussion of intelligence affairs.

"Mr. President," I said, "on the story in the *Times* this morning, I want to assure you that nothing comparable to the article's allegations is going on in the Agency at this time." I then went on to tell him that Hersh had mixed a few disconnected aspects of CIA's past but that any such actions had been fully terminated. I concluded by offering to prepare a memorandum, detailing in writing what I had sketched out for him orally and documenting the truth of my assurance that all misdeeds of the past had been corrected in 1973.

Ford thanked me for the call and asked for the report as soon as possible. And then, on arriving in Vail, besieged by the press corps clamoring for a reaction to the Hersh article, Ford issued a statement which, in effect, repeated the assurances I had given him over the phone—that is, that the CIA was not engaged in domestic spying or any other illegal activity at the present time, and saying that he was asking Kissinger as his National Security Assistant to obtain a report from me on the subject.

Meanwhile, back at Langley, I set about drawing up my report to the President "in response to your request for my comments on the *New York Times* article of December 22, alleging CIA involvement in a 'massive' domestic intelligence effort." It took only two days to prepare, summarizing the relevant items on the 1973 jewels list, and I appended a hefty appendix of the Agency directives that ordered a halt to such actions. When it was done, I topped it off with a covering note that pointed out that I had prepared the report in unclassified form (omitting any reference to individuals or intelligence sources and methods) and was thus suitable for the President to release forthwith to the press, to counter the grossly exaggerated impression of the matter given in Hersh's article. But I did not make an issue of the possible release, as I did not believe in "crowding" a Presidential boss.

In the middle of preparing this summary, I received a call

from Jim Schlesinger, and I went over to the Defense Department to show him how I was going about handling the crisis. Schlesinger, of course, was aware of what was going on better than most. He knew all about Operation Chaos and the Agency's other questionable domestic activities on the "family jewels" list, since he himself had ordered it compiled in the first place. Therefore he had immediately recognized how and where Hersh had gotten his story and what a distorted concoction of partial truths it was. Thus, too, he understood what I was trying to do and fully backed me in the strategy I had adopted for handling the crisis that the story promised to stir up. But what he also realized—and I had totally overlooked—was the fact that neither President Nixon, nor Ford, nor Kissinger had ever been apprised of the family jewels list.

Now it is important to recall here that the "family jewels" consisted of nearly 700 individual items of which the domestic activities covered in the New York Times story represented only a part, although the major part. The list, for example, also included the CIA's assassination attempts against Castro, which had not leaked to Hersh. To be sure, at the time the list was originally drawn up—after my appointment as DCI but before my confirmation hearings—Schlesinger and I had agreed that I take it around to the Congressional committee chairmen and fully brief them on it, assassinations and all. But we had not done the same for Nixon or Kissinger, which I cannot explain to this day other than by saying it fell between Schlesinger's directorate and mine, during our transition, and that it was deep in the past by the time Ford became President. Schlesinger remembered this and told Kissinger that he had to know the full story about CIA's questionable activities before he decided how to handle the Hersh article. I couldn't have agreed with him more. That Tuesday evening when I went over to Kissinger's office at the State Department to give him my memo to take to the President in Vail, I also brought with me the complete "family jewels" list.

Kissinger went through it hurriedly. But when he came to the part about the assassinations he slowed down. "Well,

Bill," he said, looking up, "when Hersh's story first came out I thought you should have flatly denied it as totally wrong, but now I see why you couldn't." He then took my report to Vail, where Ford and his staff discussed the next step and Kissinger filled him in orally on the rest of the jewels. I hoped Kissinger's greater knowledge would now change his criticism of my strategy, which had been sufficiently strident in Washington circles to cause an old friend to warn me that Kissinger was no friend of mine, that he had been making caustic comments about me in the past two days.

Barbara and the children had left for some Christmas skiing in Pennsylvania, and the plan had been for me to join them as soon as possible. But the way things stood, I felt that there was no way I could leave Washington. Obviously, Ford and Kissinger would spend the next day or so discussing my memo and the "family jewels," and I thought it likely that I would be asked to join them in Vail. But even if I weren't, I figured that I had best be at my CIA post during this period, because I hoped the President would release my memo to him, clarifying and countering the distortions and exaggerations in Hersh's article, and I wanted to be on the scene to handle the deluge of press inquiries that that would surely cause. So I settled down to a bachelor's Christmas week in Washington, waiting to hear from Vail. I waited in vain.

Not that I didn't have plenty to keep me occupied. For example, during the Christmas season I found myself once again engaged in a disconcerting legal conversation with Larry Silberman, the Acting Attorney General. As noted earlier, I had turned over to him some material on CIA's Chile operations relating to Helms's testimony at his Senate confirmation hearings. When Hersh's story broke in *The New York Times*, Silberman called me and said it looked like we had some further business to discuss. "What else have you boys got tucked away up your sleeves?" he said by way of greeting, waving Hersh's article at me as I walked through his door. "What's this one all about, Bill?"

I told him, much as I had told the President, and in the

course of my explanation I revealed the existence of the family jewels list. "That's very interesting," Silberman said after a moment. "Tell me, did you turn that list over to the Justice Department?" "No," I replied, nonplused. "You know what that amounts to," Silberman said. "You're a lawyer, Bill. You have had in your possession evidence of illegal actions. As a public servant, you're obliged to turn such evidence over to the proper authorities, in this case the Department of Justice. In withholding that evidence for a year and a half, Bill, you may have committed a crime yourself." I was shocked at the suggestion. After a moment, when I had recovered a bit, I said, "The thought that the jewels should have been reported to Justice never crossed my mind. I reported the list to the chairmen of our appropriate Congressional committees and issued the directives that corrected the situation. I thought that was sufficient." "Well, maybe," Silberman said. "But in any case you better let me have that list and I'll see what we should do about it." And in the period since that very bad moment, my belief has been vindicated that no fair jury would convict CIA officers for these long-past activities, which had been undertaken in totally different circumstances and atmospheres than today's, and the Justice Department has decided on its own not to prosecute them.

It was also during this period that Angleton's retirement broke on the AP wire. On Friday, December 20, after hearing Hersh's story from him and trying to show him its true proportion, I had called Angleton back and had told him that I must make clear that my decision to remove him was firm, whatever the Hersh article might say. I told him that no one in the world would believe his leaving his job was not the result of the article. But both Jim and I would know it was not, which was the important part to me. The news of his retirement added to the furious press storm that raged throughout that Christmas week. *The New York Times* followed up Hersh's original piece with a story nearly every day, playing the issue so hard as a major exposure of massive wrong-doing that many felt the newspaper was trying to use it to make up for having been consistently scooped by the rival *Washington Post* on the Watergate scandal. The rest of the media, equally anxious not to be caught napping on a major news break, rushed out with their own versions of Hersh's reporting. Television programs were staged, editorials written, everyone and anyone who might have had the remotest connection or opinion was interviewed. Under the steady drumbeat, the Congress was roused to a high state of indignation, and a demand for a wide-ranging investigation of the CIA swept Washington.

Inside the intelligence community tensions grew. One retired professional asked me sharply whether I was going to try to save the Agency. "Yes," I replied, "but I won't lie and I won't do anything illegal." "Does that mean I would?" he hotly challenged. "No, I don't mean that, but I want my limits to be clear," I said, trying to mollify him. A week after Hersh's story appeared I gathered the leadership of the Agency in the auditorium at Langley to try to reassure them and, chiefly, keep them working on their real jobs. I briefed them on the jewels and the way they had been exaggerated and distorted by Hersh's piece, on the fact that the directives of 1973 were clear and that I believed that they were being followed today and that the Agency would survive if it could just get its story across. And I urged them to let me worry about dealing with the Congress and the press and to make their contribution to the Agency's future by continuing to produce the best intelligence in the world. In the weeks ahead I would have to repeat the exercise many times, answering some officers who asked in fury how a nation that had assigned them difficult and dangerous work in the past could be discussing prosecuting them for doing it today, and others who wanted me to square the ugly revelations of CIA past behavior with their plea, "What am I going to tell my children?"

Yet, during all this uproar I hardly heard a word from Vail. Nor was my memo to the President released, as I had suggested. The silence from there was deafening. Ford, Kissinger, and a number of top White House aides had gathered in the Colorado ski resort, and the press reported daily their discussions of the burgeoning CIA crisis and their strategy on how to handle it. But I was not included. As the week wore on, I felt myself increasingly out in left field while the infield was making decisions well out of my hearing. I concluded that the White House planned to "distance" itself from the CIA and its troubles (as the CIA had distanced itself from the White House during Watergate), that it was going to draw the wagons around—and leave me isolated and exposed on the outside. I felt very lonely, but I saw a certain logic in the Ford administration's determination not to take on almost thirty years of CIA's sins. I decided that if I would have to fight the problem out alone, I at least would be free to use my strategy to save intelligence and not have to defer to every tactical move concocted in the White House.

On January 3, 1975, a day before my fifty-fifth birthday, Ford returned from Vail, and that evening he summoned me to a meeting at the Oval Office. Kissinger, Don Rumsfeld, Phil Buchen, and one or two others of the President's closest advisers were there. We quickly went over my "Vail Report." I had brought a summary of the family jewels and we went through them, including the assassination plots, in some detail. The fact that these activities had been terminated before Ford took office gave little solace in view of the political difficulties they would nonetheless surely raise for him.

I was then told that Ford was considering appointing a "blue ribbon" commission to conduct an investigation of CIA's domestic activities to answer *The New York Times* charges, and hopefully to still the outcry and thus prevent a full investigation of intelligence from getting started. No one mentioned the possible release of my Vail report, and I decided that the President had turned my idea down. So I accepted the idea of the commission as another way to clear the record, being certain that it could only conclude, as I had, that although some things had been done wrong in the past they were few and far between and had been corrected in 1973. I insisted that I not know the names of the individuals selected to serve on it until they were announced publicly, so that I could not be accused of influencing the choice of the investigators. But I was also convinced that the blue-ribbon commission would not be the end of the matter, and that the President's carefully circumscribed investigation of CIA's domestic affairs would not stop Congress from conducting its own probe. It was clear that our failure to respond to the *Times*'s charges after two full weeks had only added to the rising clamor. The atmosphere in the nation had far too radically changed—in the aftermath of Vietnam and Watergate—for the Executive Branch to get away, as it always had in the past, with keeping the cloak-and-dagger world of intelligence strictly its own prerogative and affair. Intelligence was entering a new era, and the country was in the process of redefining its correct position under the Constitution. The Congress would have to be answered, I believed; the Congress, having found and demonstrated its power in the Watergate affair to the amazing extent of having forced the President to resign, would demand to be answered. And I was right.

The formation of the Rockefeller Commission was announced on January 6, and January 13 was the date set for its first hearing, with me, my predecessor Jim Schlesinger and his predecessor Dick Helms as the first witnesses. But virtually at the same time, the intelligence subcommittees of the Senate's Armed Services and Appropriations Committees announced that they too would hold investigations into Hersh's allegations against the CIA, and *their* first joint hearing was set for January 15, with the same trio of present and former DCIs called upon to testify. Not to be outdone, the House of Representatives let it be known that it also wasn't about to be put off by the Rockefeller Commission and intended to look into the matter for itself as well. And so began a year in which I found myself called to testify before one committee or another two or three or sometimes even five times a week.

The Rockefeller Commission stayed in existence until

May, its original three-month mandate extended by two months once its investigations were underway. Its charter had been carefully drawn to authorize it to look into only the CIA's alleged improprieties in the domestic field—Operation Chaos, the mail-intercept program, and so on—and to stay away from the other "family jewels." Thus, although I was called back several times in the ensuing few months, in fact, my testimony came down to little more than reiterating and reviewing (and sometimes updating with later-revealed details) the memorandum I had prepared for the President when he was in Vail. Only Erwin Griswold, the former Solicitor General, of all the members of the Commission, was anything that could be called aggressive in his questioning of me. I had the sense that he felt that I was tending to minimize the gravity of some of the Agency's improprieties and from time to time he would climb on me fairly hard. But even in his case I had no trouble in giving him the full answers he sought. Indeed, if anything, as it turned out, I discovered that I was being somewhat too open and candid for some people's tastes. After my second or third appearance, the Commission's Chairman, Vice-President Rockefeller, drew me aside into his office at the Executive Office Building and said in his most charming manner, "Bill, do you really have to present all this material to us? We realize that there are secrets that you fellows need to keep and so nobody here is going to take it amiss if you feel that there are some questions you can't answer quite as fully as you seem to feel you have to." I got the message quite unmistakably, and I didn't like it. The Vice-President of the United States was letting me know that he didn't approve of my approach to the CIA's troubles, that he would much prefer me to take the traditional stance of fending off investigators by drawing the cloak of secrecy around the Agency in the name of national security. So I mumbled something appropriate and went on to give the Commission what it needed to get a fair picture of CIA's history, and I was pleased when its final report essentially reiterated my Vail report conclusions, that:

A detailed analysis of the facts has convinced the Commission that the great majority of the CIA's domestic activities comply with its statutory authority.

Nevertheless, over the 28 years of its history, the CIA has engaged in some activities that should be criticized and not permitted to happen again. . . .

Some of the activities were initiated or ordered by Presidents, either directly or indirectly.

Some of them fall within the doubtful area between responsibilities delegated to the CIA . . . and activities specifically prohibited to the Agency.

Some of them were plainly unlawful . . .

The Agency's own recent actions, undertaken for the most part in 1973 and 1974, have gone far to terminate the activities. . . .

If this had been the end of the investigations, I would have thought it a fair epitaph on the past and a fair outline of the approach that should be taken in the future. But it was not to be the final word in any sense; the constitutional separation of powers had taken control of the subject of intelligence, and the Rockefeller Commission hearing proved only the opening scene.

The first move by Congress occurred on January 15, two days after my first appearance before the Rockefeller Commission, when the intelligence subcommittees of the Senate's Armed Services and Appropriations Committees called me to testify at a joint session under the cochairmanship of Senators Stennis and McClelland. Now here, I must say, I was facing a reasonably friendly panel. These Senators, after all, had been performing the oversight function for years; they were that senior command structure that had been faithfully and patriotically protecting the CIA from public prying during all that time. They perceived of their duty now as what it had always been: to hear me out on the facts concerning the CIA's improprieties in the domestic field and then to stand up for the Agency, warning of the dangers to national security if the intelligence service was too much tampered with. So here again my testimony essentially amounted to repeating my Vail report. But there was one crucial difference. These fine Senators perceived the intensity of the public clamor and the strong views of their fellow Senators, and they knew that a public answer was needed. So they requested that my testimony be released and since I had testified in terms that in my mind were not classified, I consented. I was, of course, privately delighted. Ever since I had prepared the Vail report I had been hoping to get it out—believing it the most effective way to counter the misconceptions fostered by Hersh's article. But on my way down from the Hill that afternoon, I realized that I had not told the White House what was coming in the press next day, so I stopped there to give Brent Scowcroft a copy of the statement the Committee had released; the substance was well known to them, but the fact of its public release was a new bombshell.

My testimony was reported in the media the following day, January 16, and the effect was enormous. *The New York Times* devoted two full pages to the text of my statement. And I have to admit that it did not, as I had hoped, begin to quiet the storm whirling around the Agency. The years of total secrecy had made the CIA extremely vulnerable to suspicion and sensation. Public ignorance of modern intelligence, the false popular picture of it gleaned from spy novels, and the twisted romanticism of people like Howard Hunt and Gordon Liddy provided a poor framework in which to understand my disclosures. Journalists tended to believe that what I had revealed about the CIA's past misdeeds was just the tip of the iceberg, that a great deal more of comparable activity must still remain concealed. So, the improprieties I had conceded dominated the media, overriding my assertions that they were few and far between, and the storm continued unabated.

But surely the most important factor in all the furor was the radically altered nature of the Congress. There had been a time when the joint hearing held by the Senate's intelligence subcommittees would have been deemed sufficient and would have signaled an end to the matter. Senators with the seniority and clout of McClellan and Stennis then could easily have squelched any demands for further action on the part of their junior colleagues. But this was no longer the case. This was the post-Watergate Congress, with new and even some old members exultant in the muscle that they had used to bring a President down, willing and able to challenge the Executive as well as its own Congressional hierarchy, intense over morality in government, extremely sensitive to press and public pressures. This Congress was not going to be satisfied with the single hearing held by Stennis and McClellan. And on January 21, less than a week after the joint session of McClellan's and Stennis's committees, the Senate voted to create a Select Committee to Study Governmental Operations with respect to Intelligence Activities. It took as its precedent the Senate Select Committee that had investigated the Watergate scandal and set as its task an inquiry into all CIA activities—not just the matters raised in Hersh's article—past, present, and future. Its chairman was Frank Church of Idaho.

The lesson was clear. The old power structure of the Congress could no longer control their junior colleagues and hold off their curiosity about the secret world of intelligence. In this new era, CIA was going to have to fend for itself without that long-time special Congressional protection. Indeed, as it became ever more obvious that the nation's attention and the media's limelight were now to be focused mercilessly on the Agency, a number of other Congressional committees discovered that they too had some jurisdiction in the intelligence area and moved quickly to get their share of the headlines. CIA's former Congressional protectors helplessly asked me to go ahead and testify before those committees and not claim any exclusive responsibility to the old watchdogs. In this fashion I ended up adding such audiences as the House Post Office Committee to the groups I had to tell about CIA's past activities and the fact that they would not be repeated. And I had to go before the redoubtable Bella Abzug to explain CIA's need for protection of its sources in legislation she was pressing to open government files, taking in the process a day-long tongue-lashing over why CIA had included her name among our reports from Paris about visitors to the Vietnamese Communist Delegation headquarters there, and telling her we would do it again if she visited an office abroad of an organization CIA was covering and which our troops were fighting.

I cannot pretend that I was happy with this exposure. I was perfectly aware of the troubles it would cause, the delicate matters that were likely to be unearthed and revealed and the sensations created by everybody and his brother engaging in cheap TV theatrics at the expense of the CIA's secrets. But I must say that, unlike many in the White House and, for that matter, within the intelligence community, I believed that the Congress was within its constitutional rights to undertake a long-overdue and thoroughgoing review of the Agency and the intelligence community. I did not share the view that intelligence was solely a function of the Executive Branch and must be protected from Congressional prying. Quite to the contrary, I felt that as the Constitution grants the powers of legislation and appropriation to the Congress, the Congress was entitled to conduct an investigation of the intelligence structure. And one of my friends who knew me well correctly stated another of my considerations. He said to a newsman that I had analyzed the Washington scene in exactly the way I would have approached a problem of understanding and influencing another nation's capital and had realized that in 1975 the center of political power had moved to Congress and saw that CIA's survival depended on working out satisfactory rather than hostile relations there. It was out of this belief that, as soon as I learned of the formation of the Senate Select Committee on Intelligence, I phoned Senator Frank Church and offered him and his staff my full cooperation, saying that I was fully available for discussions on how we could go about assisting in the comprehensive investigation he had in mind while at the same time protecting the necessary secrets of intelligence work.

The Church committee's approach was to set its staff to

collecting data and documents and generally laying the groundwork for the investigations and only then to call witnesses to testify before its membership. Since this would take several months, the first hearings of the committee—and my first appearance before it—didn't occur until May. But that didn't mean I wasn't heavily involved with the committee well before then. From the onset, I had to spend a great deal of time negotiating the ground rules by which the Agency was prepared to turn over material to the investigators. As I pointed out to Church and his committee cochairman, John Tower of Texas, there were essentially three categories of material that they would want: unclassified, which of course they could have freely; classified, which they needed, but which they had to protect from leaking; and finally, certain material that should not be subjected to any risk of exposure, mainly involving the names of sources and the details of technology that could allow the Soviets and other targets immediately to frustrate critical and costly intelligence-collection systems.

I explained the rationale for each category and requested that the committee assume for itself the same security discipline that we in the intelligence profession accept as a matter of course. I asked, for example, that in the exchange of information and documents, the names of agents and staff officers be excluded routinely; that we establish at the outset the rule that our contacts with foreign intelligence services not be brought into the investigation, and that their material and even their cooperation with the CIA not be exposed; that special arrangements be made so that particularly sensitive activities would be handled by the committee according to special compartmented systems—that is, so that every staff member would not have access to every bit of information passed to the committee; and that on certain highly sensitive activities we be allowed to brief only the chairman and ranking minority cochairman. I made a particular point of requesting that the committee's staff (although not its elected members) be required to sign secrecy agreements and that some arrangement be worked out for the final disposition of the committee's records to protect those records in the future as well as during the life of the committee. I also asked that procedures be set up to protect Agency employees, including taking testimony from them without recording their identities on public documents, to prevent the exposure that would end their ability to serve in clandestine work abroad in the future.

Now, these obviously were delicate negotiations, since they could easily be construed by the committee as an attempt by me to seal off information to which it should have access. But I stressed that I was not taking a hard line on these matters. I said I believed I could justify every case in which I desired to withhold specific information, to the committee's satisfaction without revealing the information or raising a point of principle as to the committee's right of access. I pointed out that the separation of powers under our Constitution is, in many respects, ambiguous, and any attempt to get a clear ruling in principle on whether Congress has the right to Executive Branch secrets usually founders on the strong views of each branch of government. So I suggested that we apply the English case-law system, resolving individual disputes on the merits of each separate situation.

As had been my experience with the Rockefeller Commission, I reached a fairly good, although not complete, understanding on these matters with Church and Tower, and thus I felt comfortable in instructing my subordinates to cooperate with the committee's investigators. I must say, though, as in the White House, many long-time professionals in the Agency were anything but happy with my approach. Raised in the old tradition, some argued that intelligence was inherently a Presidential function and that the Congress should be kept out of it. Others warned that the Congress could not be trusted with intelligence secrets, that release to it was the equivalent of release to the world at large. And still others, while eschewing such extreme stances, asserted that each item that the investigators requested should be fought over tenaciously and turned over only when there was no alternative.

I could not and would not agree. Drawing on my legal experience at Donovan and Leisure many years before, I explained to my CIA associates that the investigation we now faced was like a major antitrust action. In those cases, an enormous number of documents are demanded by the prosecution, meticulously examined and then three or four specific papers are extracted to prove the case. The only real defense in such actions, I pointed out, was not to fight over the investigators' right to obtain the documents, as the courts would almost invariably rule against you, but to come forward with documents and information so as to place in proper context the documents selected by the investigators and to explain that they had another significance than guilt. Since this strategy often required the revelation of even more material than the investigators sought, it was greeted with very little enthusiasm within both the administration and the intelligence community. But I remain satisfied that it was the correct approach, pragmatically and constitutionally, and eventually resulted in the Church Committee coming to fair conclusions about American intelligence, reflecting proper differences and not merely the hysteria that I had feared might take over.

I cannot say the same for the House's equivalent Select Committee on Intelligence. Compared with the Senate, the House was a far more raucous and unruly body with many new members voted into office in 1974 at the height of the nation's anger over the Watergate scandal and hypersuspicious of CIA's secrecy. It had a devilish time getting its act together. Its first move was made by George Mahon of Texas, the respected chairman of the Appropriations Committee and a long-time friend and protector of the CIA. Having just survived the freshman revolt that led to the fall of Edward Hebert from the Armed Services chairmanship, he phoned to tell me that he would have to end the long practice of reviewing CIA budget requests only in a small informal group of senior committee members, and would have to ask me instead to report to the newly established Defense Subcommittee, which would mean an initial over-all briefing on the intelligence community and budget for its new members. But the subcommittee, as it turned out, wanted to start with an account of the Agency's domestic activities that were so much in the news—and do it in open session on February 20. Far from objecting, I welcomed the opportunity to put CIA's case before the TV cameras, in the hope that this would settle the issue in the House and that the representative group of members in the new subcommittee would prove to be the kind to whom CIA could report its secrets in the future and thereby generate the kind of Congressional support it would need. So we had the public session in which I essentially repeated the Vail report and then a closed session in which I obviously startled some of the new and suspicious members with a frank and full description of the community budget and intelligence activities, secrets and all. My only real problem was staying out of the cross fire when some of the new members took verbal potshots at the established leadership of the committee and the House as a whole.

But, as had been the case in the Senate, the House wasn't about to be satisfied with the single hearing of Mahon's subcommittee. It too wanted to set up a Select Committee with a mandate to conduct a total, no-holds-barred review of the CIA and the intelligence community. But the problem for that large and wildly heterogeneous body was agreeing on who should head it. The natural choice would have been Lou Nedzi, the chairman of the intelligence subcommittee of the Armed Services Committee. But some of the maverick, nonestablishment Representatives were opposed to him, regarding him, like Mahon, too much of a friend and protector of the CIA to have the stomach for doing the kind of hatchet job on the Agency that they were spoiling for. Since they were numerous enough (though clearly not in the majority), they were able to provoke several months of ferocious infighting in the House over the chairmanship, which ended in a 290–44-vote vindication of Nedzi by the full House but an arrangement by which he would step aside from the investigation. Thus it wasn't until July that the House Select Committee on Intelligence was formed, and Otis Pike of New York was finally selected as its chairman, with members spanning the political spectrum from staunchly conservative Robert McClory of Illinois to California's flamboyant Ronald Dellums.

But well before this happened and my troubles with the Pike Committee began, the CIA crisis suddenly exploded far beyond Hersh's charges. Ironically, the White House, which had been the most concerned that this should not happen and had invented the Rockefeller Commission to prevent it from happening, was responsible for the devastating turn of events. In late January, not long after the formation of the Rockefeller Commission, President Ford hosted a luncheon at the White House for the publisher and top editors of *The New York Times*. It was strictly off-the-record, and during its course, according to a later report, one of the *Times* editors criticized the composition of the Rockefeller Commission, saying it didn't seem to be the sort of group that would do the hard-nosed investigation that the public expected. Ford is reported to have replied that he had chosen the membership with extreme care because he had learned from me (obviously referring to my briefing of him on the "family jewels") that there were CIA activities that the members might come across in their investigation that were a lot more sensitive than those Hersh had reported on and that, in the nation's best interest, he felt had to remain secret. "Like what?" hard-driving managing editor Abe Rosenthal is said to have asked. "Like assassination," the President is said to have responded, "off the record."

This juicy tidbit of information, in the atmosphere of those times when virtually all the media's efforts were concentrated on ferreting out any CIA activity, was almost impossible to keep from leaking. And finally, leak it did, to Daniel Schorr of CBS, who in the middle of a background interview with me on February 27, said that the President had told *The New York Times* that he was concerned about CIA assassinations and then asked me whether CIA had ever killed anybody in this country. I was so stunned at the President's

opening up this topic that I retreated to the long-time practice of answering only the specific question asked. "Not in
this country," I replied to Schorr. To his follow-up questions
I limited my remarks to simply pointing out that assassinations had been formally barred in the "jewels" exercise in
1973, partly because I didn't know how far the President
had gone and partly because I had long decided that denying that CIA had ever assassinated anyone (which is true)
immediately evoked the question whether it had tried
(which of course it had, against Castro). But in my unease I
compounded the President's mistake in this instance. My
first answer left open the implication that CIA assassinations
had actually taken place abroad. On the following evening,
February 28, Schorr broadcast on CBS that "President Ford
has reportedly warned associates that if current investigations go too far they could uncover several assassinations of
foreign officials involving the CIA."

There was no stopping the press or Congress now. My
hope that a gradual and comprehensive description of modern intelligence would come out of the investigations, that
in fact the investigations could serve the useful purpose of
educating the American public to the value of intelligence
and thus help it enter a new era under the Constitution, collapsed on the subject of assassination. A hysteria seized
Washington; sensation came to rule the day.

From the moment of Schorr's broadcast, I flung myself
into a struggle to prevent an investigation into the subject of
assassinations. I belatedly pointed out that in fact the CIA
had never assassinated anyone; that clear prohibitions
against assassination now or ever in the future had been issued in 1972 and 1973; that the record on this matter was
exceedingly imperfect and could not in particular clarify the
degree of encouragement and pressure from the White
House to conduct such operations under earlier Presidents;
and that the only thing an investigation into the matter
could accomplish was to do serious harm to the good name
of the United States, nothing else. But my arguments were
in vain. The Rockefeller Commission decided that it was

duty-bound to look into the matter and immediately demanded full access to all of the CIA's documents on the subject—and it wanted them unsanitized. I tried to make a last-ditch stand on this score. Recognizing the awful problems that could be caused by the release of such documents—cables with names of Americans and foreigners involved in the operation, memoranda of Washington conferences in double-talk and euphemisms, and similar confusing and dangerous material—I protested that some reasonable degree of precaution should be taken, at the very least by the sanitizing of names to protect the identities of the individual agents involved. But the reply I received to this was that since the Rockefeller Commission investigation was being conducted under the authority of the Executive Branch I need not concern myself about the security of the materials in question, that they would be treated as the Agency itself would have them treated and returned. And so I was obliged to order turned over whatever unsanitized documents the Commission demanded, hoping that would be as far as they would go. But, as was probably predictable, that wasn't to be the case.

The Rockefeller Commission's mandate, even with the two-month extension, ran out before it had completed its investigations into the assassination attempts. And, much to my dismay and over my vigorous protests, the White House passed over to the Church Committee all the unsanitized documents we had turned over to the Rockefeller Commission, and it set off on an investigation into assassinations of its own. This lasted some six months and generated endless sensational headlines; and in the end it came to the conclusion I had predicted: It convinced the world that the United States and CIA had used this tactic widely, that Presidents may have been involved, while obscuring the fact that no assassination had taken place and that the practice was now clearly proscribed.

The launching of the various investigations had a devastating impact on the normal work of the CIA—and on my regular duties as DCI. Apart from the fact that I and any number of my senior associates were constantly being called away from Langley to testify before one committee or another, the Agency over-all was diverted from its proper responsibilities by the deluge of demands from the hordes of investigators, with literally hundreds of CIA officers reassigned from normal intelligence operations to handle the mechanical and clerical chores of locating requested documents, sanitizing them to remove names of agents and particularly sensitive operational material, and then negotiating whether or not the information could be publicly released.

But unquestionably the greatest impact was on the morale of the Agency. With every new sensational headline, with every new damaging revelation, nerves frayed, emotions erupted. Officers were incensed that charges of CIA misdeeds, which they had constantly and loyally denied over the years, were now being conceded to be true. They accused the Agency's top command, myself included, of misleading and even lying to them. Others were furious that attacks were now being made on officers who years before had loyally followed their superiors' directives in the belief that what they were doing was proper for an intelligence service. They remonstrated bitterly that to be pilloried now and even subjected to possible criminal prosecution was hardly what they had expected from a grateful nation for their dedicated and sometimes dangerous service. One of our best operations officers, David Phillips, who had run an exceptionally successful series of political operations in Latin America, decided what CIA really needed now was an outside voice of support, similar to the support the FBI had received over many years from its society of former agents. So he retired, and went out with my hope that he could succeed, but our joint understanding that he could have no special help from or relationship with CIA or we would be pilloried for attempting to run a covert operation on the American public.

Nevertheless, despite all the disruption, the CIA people as a whole followed my urgings that they put their main effort on their intelligence duties. Indeed, paradoxically perhaps, this was one of the most operationally active periods in the Agency's history and one of the most demanding on me in this regard in my tenure as DCI. For this was the period when the *Glomar* project blew sky high, South Vietnam fell to the Communists, the *Mayaguez* crisis erupted, support for the Kurdish rebels reached its height, the Angola operation was launched, and intense debates raged within the administration over what to do about SALT, the Turkish suspension of our intelligence-base operations and the Panama negotiations, just to mention a few of the more noteworthy things that preoccupied me while I was dealing with the relentless investigations into the Agency's past.

Glomar happened first, just a couple of weeks after Schorr had broken the assassination story, and I must say it pulled me away from the latter problem in a hurry.

The *Glomar Explorer,* built under the cover of Howard Hughes's Summa Corporation, and operated as a member of the well-established Glomar Marine Corporation's fleet, had been completed and taken on sea trials in the spring of 1974. Deemed fit, and represented to the world as a far-out experiment by the secretive Howard Hughes in the possibility of mining manganese nodules from the depths of the vast Pacific, it had sailed that summer on what was accepted by all observers as a purely commercial enterprise. The security on the project at that point was perfect, so much so that while it was busily at work at a key stage, a number of foreign ships came near, including one particularly curious one, observed its activities closely, and then sailed away apparently without suspecting it of being anything more than it professed to be.

But, for reasons I cannot describe in detail, it was essential that the *Glomar*'s activity be extended to another summer's fair weather in the surging ocean. Exasperating as this was, the Agency did not lose hope in the *Glomar*. The cover *had* worked, and the incredible technology had proved that it was possible to work 16,000 feet deep on the floor of the ocean. Problems that had caused difficulties could easily be remedied, and the lessons of the first year's experience made it certain that the *Glomar* would complete its tasks at a marginal increase in cost over the original effort. So, after a full and detailed review, the go-ahead was given. But a mysterious incident intervened.

In June 1974, just about the time the *Glomar Explorer* was on its initial shakedown voyage into the Pacific, the Los Angeles headquarters of Hughes's Summa Corporation was broken into and burglarized. No one to this day can say for sure who the burglars were or what they were really after. But what they got was $70,000 in cash, some artifacts, and four footlockers full of documents, files, and sundry papers. Among the latter reportedly was a single-page memo, from a senior Summa official to Hughes, sketching out the CIA-Summa project. When we in the Agency heard of this supposed memo, we immediately got in touch with the FBI, briefed a few key officers on what was involved, and asked that the agents and the Los Angeles Police Department investigating the burglary be especially on the lookout for this sensitive document and ensure that it would not be exposed if found.

For a time it seemed that our luck was holding out and no harm had been done. But the burglars were not apprehended and the document was not found; and—what was worse—the importance of that paper, and the fact that we were looking for it, leaked, probably from the Los Angeles police, to two investigative reporters in the Los Angeles area. A few months after the break-in, someone saying he was associated with the burglars put out a feeler to see if the government was interested in buying back the memo—for a healthy sum. The FBI arranged a meeting with an intermediary, but at the last moment the latter apparently got cold feet and pulled out of the deal. But the two Los Angeles newsmen were relentlessly probing for more data, and on February 7, 1975, they were ready to go into print with what they had found. The *Los Angeles Times* splashed on a page-one headline: "US Reported After Russian Submarine/Sunken Ship Deal by CIA, Hughes Told." Before the newspaper hit the streets, however, we heard that it was on the way and I arranged for a CIA officer to get in touch with the paper's editor, to see if he could get it killed. We were too late for the first edition, but the editor, as soon as we had explained the importance of keeping the project secret, managed to drop the story back to page eighteen in subsequent editions and then ordered the reporters off doing any follow-up pieces. A *New York Times* story was also datelined February 7, but would not actually appear until the following day so I had the chance to get to the *Times* in time to get it to bury the story on page thirty in the first edition and kill it outright subsequently.

Now we faced the problem of whether the *Glomar* had really been exposed. The two pieces, I felt, hadn't necessarily done it, as foreign governments hadn't necessarily accepted them. This wasn't just wishful thinking on my part. I remembered that, during World War II, the *Chicago Tribune* had run a front-page story revealing that the United States had broken the Japanese top-secret naval code, to which President Roosevelt had reacted in great fury. Nonetheless, the Japanese continued using that code—and the Americans kept intercepting and deciphering it; apparently the Japanese High Command had not gotten word of or hadn't believed the *Chicago Tribune* story. But even if the two *Glomar* stories had been noted, there was a fair chance, I felt, that not much significance would be attached to them, because both were garbled and error-ridden enough to throw anyone off the scent. For example, the *Los Angeles Times* story talked of the North Atlantic rather than the Pacific, where the *Glomar* had worked. The *New York Times* story concentrated almost entirely on the robbery of the Summa Corporation's headquarters and only got around to mentioning the CIA connection in the thirteenth paragraph and then only passingly. So there was a real chance that the stories would be dismissed as just another of the hysterical tales about the CIA then crowding the press, and if *Glomar* was careful to follow the manganese-nodule-collection scenario it could even escape another close inspection next summer.

So, for the moment at least, my concern was really with the American press. Although I could reasonably hope that foreigners had missed the story I realized there was no chance at all that any number of hard-nosed investigative reporters would overlook the tantalizing references to the CIA in the *Los Angeles Times* and *New York Times* articles and that they wouldn't start digging and ultimately unearth the whole truth. Moreover, they would surely be led by Seymour Hersh, who could claim that the story had now broken, so that his year-old agreement with me to stay away from the subject was no longer in effect. But it was clear that it did not matter how many Americans learned of the project as long as we could keep it from foreigners. So, in the next few weeks I found myself racing around from newsrooms to editorial offices to television stations, trying desperately to plug any leaks on the story and feeling as if I were rapidly running out of fingers and toes with which to do the job. Every time I got a tip that a newspaperman or television correspondent was asking questions about the project I would hare off to see him or his superiors and personally request that they withhold the story. I realized well enough that journalists, justifiably, were mighty skeptical of government since Watergate and, these days, of the CIA especially, and I didn't think legal action against the press would do any good at all. So, in order to convince them of the legitimacy of what I was asking in this case, I took the gamble of responding to their questions to the minimum degree necessary to show my good faith, and only then, when I was sure they comprehended the seriousness of it, did I request that they hold back stories on the *Glomar*. In practically every instance, my urgings paid off and the press held back. But finally, on March 18, despite my last-minute telephoned entreaties five minutes before air time, Jack Anderson blew the *Glomar* on national TV.

Now, I don't say that Anderson was any less responsible or patriotic than the other journalists. On one occasion in the past, in fact, he had responded to just the sort of request I made of him on the *Glomar* project, and I wrote to him, thanking him for that. But this time he said that the *Glomar* was far too widely known throughout the press corps for it not to blow sooner rather than later, and by someone else rather than him. And I have to admit that it was becoming the subject of chatter around the Press Club bar. Once I knew for sure that he was going to air it, I called all the other journalists who had agreed to hold back on their stories at my request. I had made a commitment to them that if I discovered that I could not persuade any one newsman to withhold the story I would let them all know that they were free to go with their stories so that none of them would be scooped. So, on March 19, newspapers and television programs bannered these stories from coast to coast. There was not a chance that we could send the *Glomar* out again on an intelligence project without risking the lives of our crew and inciting a major international incident.

But one further step needed to be taken, deciding what the government would say about the story now that it was out. To decide this, a White House meeting was called on the morning of March 19, and I attended carrying a copy of Khrushchev's *Memoirs.* I pointed out that, in describing in detail his side of the 1960 U-2 incident, Khrushchev said that he had known of the U-2 flights for some time and that he was preparing to blast our "weather plane off course" cover story. But what had really upset him and had led to his cancellation of the Paris Summit meeting was President Eisenhower's admission that he had indeed approved the mission. So I argued that the government's reaction to the exposure of *Glomar* should be a strict "No Comment," and this was the decision. Thus, my previous willingness to brief newsmen and their publishers was replaced by a refusal to say a word about the subject, a matter of considerable puzzlement to a number of them. But it worked, and our public silence was matched by a similar silence internationally, so that the *Glomar* never became the subject of international acrimony.

There have been a number of published post-mortems on the *Glomar,* and the more prevalent of these were a measure of the disrepute to which the CIA had sunk at the time. For they tended to impute a deviously manipulative motive to my handling of the events. For example, there were those who were convinced that the *Glomar* project was completely successful and that then, in order to keep this a secret, I deliberately went around to all those newsmen to plant on them a false story that it wasn't, fully aware that if I told enough people the story was bound to leak eventually. And there are others who are sure that I put the story out solely for public-relations reasons. According to this view, I reckoned that it would do the Agency's image a world of good at a time when the headlines were scourging it for assassination attempts and illegal domestic activities to get the press to report on a project of such daring and brilliance as the *Glomar* certainly was. I must say that this is all nonsense. The *Glomar* project stopped because it was exposed. A real significance of the affair, however, is its indication that most American publishers will cooperate in maintaining a national secret if they understand it really to be one, provided that it does not spread so far as to be uncontrollable.

But no sooner had the flap over the *Glomar* subsided than I was caught up in another world-shaking and heart-rending event: the fall of South Vietnam. With Congress' refusal to supply the military aid needed by the South Vietnamese Army to carry on its forward defense, the situation grew increasingly more ominous there during March and April, and the meetings of the National Security Council's Washington Special Action Group—WSAG—under Kissinger for crisis handling proliferated. My own initial hopes that the Thieu government could meet the challenge soon declined in the face of the evidence of the increase in North Vietnamese divisions and the loss of morale in the Southern army. So I had to take the unhappy position that further North Vietnamese success and even the fall of South Vietnam was the most probable outcome. This followed an earlier estimate we had made that the North Vietnamese would make a probe in 1975 but would save their main effort until 1976 unless a target of opportunity opened; and it quite obviously had. The WSAG meetings became increasingly sharp, with me allied, a novelty, with Philip Habib, the brilliant and knowledgeable Assistant Secretary for East Asia, whom I had admired and disputed with for years over how to deal with Asian military leaders. But, as I pointed out the threatening developments and urged that we remove from Saigon as many Americans and their Vietnamese co-workers as possible, I fully understood the fears of Ambassador Graham Martin that a mass evacuation could trigger a panic and anarchy, which would make it impossible for any to escape. In this kind of situation, Kissinger's argument that only the man on the spot can deal with all the unreported subtleties of a situation was exactly right. And his tactic of pressing Martin but supporting his decisions, in my mind, allowed at least some 130,000 to escape instead of the smaller number that would have survived earlier collapse.

I could take only one consolation out of the disaster. One of the analysts, with whom I had many times argued that South Vietnam had more hope in the long run than he conceded, told me that his colleagues and he had been fearful that my own long and close relationship with Vietnam would affect my presentation of their gloomy conclusions in those days of crisis, and they were pleasantly surprised at the tough stand I had taken with Kissinger. I gave the analyst credit for his assessments and said I appreciated his thought that I had become an analytical, as well as an operational, professional. At the same time I made clear to our operational machinery that they were to help CIA's Vietnamese colleagues and co-workers as much as they could, in their resettlement abroad and in the arrangements we made to end our contact with a valuable secret source within the Viet Cong, assuring him that we would absolutely guarantee that his help to us over the years would never be revealed.

A few days later, I was awakened in the early morning of May 12 by the CIA Operations Center with a report that an American ship called the *Mayaguez* had been captured by the Cambodian Communists, also newly victorious. I absorbed the sketchy details, was assured that our collection machinery was alert for any further news and that the responsible National Intelligence Officer had been advised, so he could begin to organize the intelligence picture. I asked whether the same report had been passed to the White House, State and Defense. It had, so I thought that all the necessary alerts would be handled by the operations centers and situation rooms there. I was wrong.

President Ford heard of it first in his normal morning intelligence briefing at seven-forty, and Kissinger not until his regular session sometime after eight. Apparently their operations-center people had thought there was little that Ford and Kissinger could do on the basis of the sketchy information available and decided to let them alone until the regular briefings. Needless to say, I changed the procedure so that the CIA Operations Center would advise me not only that such messages went to the White House, State and Defense, but also whether or not the centers there planned to alert their principals, so I could decide whether the Director of Central Intelligence should call them himself.

Once they *were* alerted, Ford and Kissinger wanted fast action; and I saw again one of the problems of our intelligence machinery. When a problem becomes tactical, the vital detailed information to make judgments about it flows first through operational command channels, and the elaborate intelligence analytical structure is pretty much cut out of the main action, only able to follow it at second hand. The same thing had occurred in the Cyprus crisis the year before, when Kissinger's phone conversations with foreign ministers and premiers went faster than the analysts could follow. So, in the *Mayaguez* situation, I found myself being briefed on new developments along with the President in the Cabinet Room by Acting Joint Chiefs of Staff Chairman, Air Force General David Jones, and making assessments of probable Cambodian Communist reactions on the basis of the opinions and judgments I had formed by reading the *National Intelligence Daily* over the previous weeks and by studying Cambodian character and Communism over the years. After the affair was over, I called for a post-mortem on the intelligence contribution and resolved that, if I could get time away from the Congressional investigations, I really would like to figure out how better to organize ourselves for crisis management, so that we could keep up with the need for fast action but at the same time benefit fully from the depth of knowledge and understanding of our analysts.

In addition to these intelligence activities, the Agency during this period was also conducting a number (albeit a much reduced number since the 1950s and 1960s) of covert-action operations. Perhaps the most significant of these were the ones in support of the Kurdish rebels in Iraq and of the non-Communist black nationalists in Angola.

The Kurds are a primitive mountain people in the area where Iran, Iraq and Turkey meet, with the largest group in Iraq. They have struggled for autonomy for centuries, asking and receiving assistance from wherever they could find it. The assistance generally reflected the interests of the country giving it. For example, the Soviets helped the Kurds when the USSR saw them as a useful force against Iran. But in 1972, the problem was Iraq, while Iran and the United States were concerned about Communist influence there. So the Shah of Iran asked President Nixon to share in his program to help the Kurd autonomy struggle against Iraq, as a way of demonstrating that the United States was truly allied with Iran against the danger of expanding Communist influence in the area. With the best clandestine techniques, CIA provided that share—and it was only a minor share—of the aid requested by the Kurds to carry on a defensive struggle against Iraqi suppression. But in March 1975, the struggle was going badly, and the Iraqi were clearly winning despite the outside help to the Iranians. So the Shah changed course and arranged a settlement of his border disputes with Iraq and cut off Iranian (and American) aid to the Kurds. CIA's cable traffic suddenly was jammed with requests to help the refugee and exiled Kurds instead of shipping arms and military supplies to them clandestinely.

In Angola, late in 1974—before Angola's independence, but after Portugal had announced that it would be granted—

our intelligence revealed that Soviet arms were moving to the Popular Movement for the Liberation of Angola (MPLA), not to strengthen the group in its liberation efforts (since that was no longer an issue) but to bolster it against its rival liberation movements, the National Front for the Liberation of Angola (NFLA) and the National Union for the Independence of Angola (UNITA). In light of the Soviet Union's growing position in Somalia, the Indian Ocean and Guinea, and against the backdrop of its aborted attempt in the middle 1960s to establish a position in the Belgian Congo (now Zaire), this intelligence looked ominous. So, early in 1975, the National Security Council's Forty Committee authorized a secret program of political, nonmilitary assistance to the NFLA, to be handled by the CIA and funneled in from neighboring Zaire, which was equally concerned over the danger of a Communist Angola. But this, as quickly became apparent, proved quite insufficient. Russian support to the MPLA was building that group up so rapidly that it was clear that, unless something more were done, the Marxist-oriented MPLA would gain full control after independence and put Angola under Communist domination.

Thus in June the Forty Committee approved increased CIA backing, including military hardware, not only to the NFLA but to UNITA as well. And CIA responded quickly, moving arms to the two groups, helping with their training outside Angola (as no CIA officers were permitted to engage in combat or train there) with such effectiveness that the tide was completely reversed, and it was the MPLA that became embattled in the capital city of Luanda (thanks in part also to support to UNITA from South Africa, which CIA stayed well away from, knowing that this would discredit UNITA among other black African nations). In their desperation, the MPLA called for open help from their Soviet and Cuban allies, who responded with a massive airlift of tanks, artillery and rockets and the dispatch of some 12,000 to 15,000 Cuban military personnel to join directly in the battle. The tide was again reversed, but the battle was not over. CIA had run out of funds to supply the additional equipment and forces the NFLA and UNITA needed to meet this new situation. So, I requested an addition to our appropriation. And in the course of this, the operation exploded into the public print—a few months after the fall of Vietnam and in the middle of the Congressional investigations and hearings on CIA—and was sensationalized to suggest that a new terrible Vietnam-like American involvement, not mere assistance to black nationalists who wanted to fight for their own version of liberation, was being cooked up in far-off Africa. The Congress turned down our requests for more aid, and in a short time the MPLA's victory over its opponents was plain.

Now, on both these operations—as indeed on all of the CIA's covert-action operations—I was obliged to keep the Congress well briefed and regularly informed. For as noted, in October 1974, after the Chilean uproar, a law had been passed requiring the DCI to report on all CIA covert-action operations to the "appropriate" Congressional committees. And there were, by this time, *eight:* the Appropriations, Armed Services, Foreign Affairs, and Select Intelligence Committees of both Houses. Thus, by mid-1975, appearances on the Hill had become a pervasive aspect of my job as DCI, and I was going up there to report on every new step taken in the Angola, Kurdish, and other covert operations currently underway as well as testifying on practically everything the CIA had ever done during the last three decades to the Select Committees investigating intelligence. Sadly, the experience demonstrated that secrets, if they are to remain secret, cannot be given to more than a few Congressmen—*every* new project subjected to this procedure during 1975 leaked, and the "covert" part of CIA's covert action seemed almost gone.

But I was determined that the real work of the Agency would go on. I arbitrated a debate between CIA's Latin America analysts and Dick Walters, who had known for decades the leaders they were assessing. I asked that our economic reports carry unemployment indices as well as monetary ones, because of their political significance. I pointed out to our weapons experts that the Soviet Backfire Bomber *could* be used against the United States even if it could not make a round trip from the Soviet Union since, as General George Brown had pointed out, our B-52's planned only for a one-way mission. And I approved the use of a microphone "bug" as part of our intelligence coverage of an independence movement in Micronesia. The last would be criticized later by the Senate Intelligence Committee, probably correctly, but I did it in part to show our people that the Agency would not pull in its horns and only undertake safe and easy operations just because it was under pressure. If the impression arises that I was jumping from frying pans to fires during this period, it is correct. But I was exhilarated doing it.

CHAPTER FOURTEEN

Survival

B Y May, the Rockefeller Commission's extended mandate
expired and it went out of business. It had, of course, failed
to preempt Congressional investigations of intelligence,
which I never believed it could, but it did produce a sober
and useful summary of CIA's domestic activities as a backdrop to its conclusions set forth above. It confirmed the position that I had taken in the Vail report and ever since, that
the CIA's misdeeds domestically were truly few and far between—certainly not the "massive illegal domestic-intelli-
gence operation" that Hersh had reported—and that they
had been corrected in 1973. Its report gained currency, and
so much of the sting was taken out of Hersh's December
story that the Pulitzer Prize Committee was said to have
passed him over, judging him to have overblown his reporting.

But on one point the Rockefeller Commission's report
did add—unintentionally—to the sensationalism swirling
around the CIA. That was on the matter of the death of
Frank Olsen. Indeed, even the CIA professionals, myself included, were shocked and shamed to learn of the true circumstances around this CIA officer's suicide, as revealed in
the report, following his being administered LSD without
his knowledge in 1953 in a joint CIA-Army test program. I
had been aware that a death had occurred in this program.
The program itself, which was designed to determine the

effects and possible uses of LSD by hostile intelligence or political forces, was listed among the "family jewels" as one of the CIA's past questionable activities. But the Agency's records indicated that steps had been taken in 1953 to ensure that Olsen's suicide was treated as a line-of-duty death and that appropriate arrangements were made to take care of his family.

Thus, it came as a shock when the Olsen family, identifying the incident from the published Rockefeller Commission report, stated that this was the first they had heard of the circumstances and specifics of Olsen's death. The official reaction was immediate. President Ford extended his and the nation's regret and instructed that recompense be made. I made a particular point of contacting the family and extending the CIA's very sincere apologies for the tragedy and did everything I could to push through the appropriate and acceptable recompense. But one of the most difficult assignments I have ever had was to meet with his wife and his now-grown children to discuss how to give them the CIA records and thus open up and overcome a twenty-year secret that had had such an impact on their lives.

Virtually at the time that the Rockefeller Commission was winding up its business, the Senate Select Committee on Intelligence, under Frank Church, was at last ready to begin calling witnesses to testify before its membership. Since its formation in January, the Church committee had been engaged in collecting and collating data and documents and generally laying the groundwork for its investigations. I had worked with Church and his cochairman, Senator John Tower, during the preceding months to develop the ground rules for the investigation, and I was anxious that they get off on the right foot. After a number of tries, I ultimately got all the committee members and their senior staff out to Langley for an extensive introductory briefing, giving an overview of the intelligence community, the types of its operations, the budgets of its programs, and its procedures for approval and review. I concluded by saying that I believed that it was in the CIA's best interest that the committee obtain a full and clear understanding of the world and methods of intelligence, since in this way we could debate, on the basis of knowledge, the scope of their investigation and could avoid going off on tangents with respect to one or another individual activity.

The second thing I did was retain the services of Mitchell Rogovin as the Agency's counsel for the investigations. The CIA's own General Counsel, John Warner, had recommended this move to me, having clearly foreseen the enormous demand for legal advice and representation that the investigations would place on his office. It was, perhaps, the smartest move in the entire exercise. Rogovin was a highly independent, exceptionally brilliant, Washington-wise attorney with a background ranging from representing Common Cause to work in the Internal Revenue Service. Within a matter of days after his appointment, he had won the respect and admiration of all the contending forces in Congress, the administration and the intelligence community, and in the ensuing months he did a great deal to smooth the process of getting the more extreme members of each of these groups to accept the fact that others also had legitimate concerns and rights, and to work out compromises to avoid confrontations. On many occasions he and I would sit patiently through tough-talking denunciations of Congress by the members of the interagency coordinating group in the basement of the White House, then drive back to Langley agreeing, with resigned smiles, just to take the heat from the Congress for a few days for being dilatory until the White House realized that the material in question really had to be delivered to the Congressmen.

On May 21, I made my first appearance before the Church committee. Anxious to establish an aura of responsibility and seriousness, Church ordered the session closed to the press and public. The topic under discussion was assassinations and I had come prepared to testify on the matter as compiled in the "family jewels." But barely had I been sworn in than it looked as though all our preliminary talk about sweet reason was going right out the window. The committee's counsel, Frederick A. O. Schwarz, set out to "clarify" just what the committee wanted to know, and he proceeded to read off a series of all-encompassing definitions, which included everything from any direct participation by the Agency in a plot to most of CIA's paramilitary operations. It became clear that what Schwarz really was up to was to lay a basis for a great foray into Phoenix again; the "definitions" read like a criminal indictment; all that was missing, it seemed, were the handcuffs on my wrists. I confess I was angered, but I did my best to maintain my cool and told Schwarz that I would be delighted to testify about Phoenix, as I had done three times before, but that I thought it would be more useful for me to outline the CIA's relationship to the cases included in the "jewels" and the others about which we had been asked, such as Ngo Dinh Diem in Vietnam. My anger must have been more transparent than I thought, because I heard afterward that Schwarz's opening remarks were generally considered a disaster, threatening to launch the committee into a confrontation with me instead of starting the serious review of the past that the Congressmen wanted. And I heard no more of Phoenix during the hearings.

The Church committee stayed with assassinations throughout the summer, calling me and others to testify several times and then, in the fall, brought out an interim report on the subject. Despite its strong rhetoric, it really vindicated the position I had taken at the outset. For example, its second "finding" was that "No foreign leaders were killed as a result of assassination plots initiated by officials of the United States" (Castro is still alive and CIA's few steps in regard to Lumumba had nothing to do with his death), although Americans were privy to or encouraged coups that resulted in deaths (Trujillo, Diem, Schneider) and certainly tried against Castro. In two cases, that of Rafael Trujillo in the Dominican Republic and René Schneider in Chile, the report confirmed that the CIA had provided weapons to the groups that assassinated these men but concluded that those weapons were not in fact used in the killing. And the report noted Helms's directive of 1972 and mine of 1973, against any CIA involvement in assassinations.

Furthermore, the Church committee report acknowledged that the record was exceedingly unclear as to the level in the White House at which authority, consent or knowledge of the CIA's actual assassination plotting existed. Something of a bias crept into the report on this score, with the case strengthened against the Eisenhower and Nixon administrations and somewhat softened with respect to the Kennedy administration. Nevertheless, I found the report's account of the CIA's activities themselves reasonably fair and straightforward, and I certainly agreed with its basic position that the United States should *not* be involved in assassinations, with the single exception of an active war situation, where, I said, I would happily have helped to carry the bomb into Hitler's bunker in 1944. If our young men and an enemy's young men are killing and being killed, the older leaders can hardly be immune, and the committee accepted this point as well.

For all of this, though, I was not happy with the report. In the first place, as a matter of principle, I thought it wrong and unwise to issue such a report, since it would tarnish the good name of the United States at home and abroad and provide the basis for an extended anti-American campaign by our adversaries. I was specifically unhappy about the inclusion of individuals' names, and protested that those identified might be subject to retribution or at the very least held up to public opprobrium for things they had done years ago under the direction of their superiors. We struggled intensely over this issue, even including my going before Judge Gerhard Gesell in District Court to testify to my belief that the inclusion of one officer's name could subject him to possible violence, and in the end the Committee relented with respect to some twenty of the thirty-odd names they had originally included. And I must accept that the committee's position was not unreasonable with respect to the remainder, since they were either very senior CIA officials who must bear some public accountability for their actions, or in the one category that I was most uncomfortable defending—members of the Mafia. Because during the efforts against Castro some CIA officers had the godawful idea that the Mafia still had contacts in Cuba and would be happy to try to get him out of the way; a collaboration had been set up to do the job. It failed, in part because it was ineptly planned, but in part also because Mafia greed is not the stuff of which self-sacrificing revolutionists are made. It brought the predictable, but not predicted, complications in its train: requests to call off prosecution of Mafia hoods because the CIA operational background might be revealed. I made the appropriate arguments against including these names in the Committee's reports to demonstrate that the CIA will always protect its sources, but my heart was hardly in it, and I really didn't protest much when the committee included them. An amusing sidelight to this incident was the committee's own effort to protect the identity of "a close friend of President Kennedy" who was also a "close friend" of the Mafia figures involved—Judith Campbell Exner.

From assassination the Church committee moved on to Chile, and on this topic too it issued a separate staff report. And, to my way of thinking, although the rhetoric was stronger to the contrary, here also the facts essentially vindicated the CIA. Not surprisingly, it skipped quickly over the years of assistance to the center democratic forces and put its main emphasis on the Track II operation and the military coup that overthrew and killed Allende. The report gave a fair and accurate account of the Agency's Track II six-week effort, personally ordered by President Nixon and kept secret from even the State and Defense departments, to prevent Allende's inauguration as president after his victory at the polls, which, among other things, resulted in an aborted kidnap effort in which General René Schneider was killed. But then, as I had maintained all along, the Senate report stated that the CIA had turned to a program of supporting center democratic groups against Allende and, in its careful and somewhat grudging language, "found no evidence that the United States was directly involved" in the 1973 coup.

While the Senate committee was pressing ahead in this essentially orderly and responsible fashion, the House was still trying to get itself organized, so that it could get into the act. It wasn't until the beginning of June that it managed to form a Select Committee on Intelligence equivalent to the Church committee. On June 12 I was summoned to testify, with a quite obviously hostile panel waiting to pounce on me, including such figures as Michael Harrington, Ronald Dellums, and the new chairman, James V. Stanton. It promised to be a donnybrook, with me at the bottom of the pile. But the House was still embroiled in its own struggles, and in the end I left without saying a word, because the minority Republican Representatives decided to boycott the hearing at the last moment, making it impossible to hold under the House rules. It was well into July by the time a compromise was struck at last and Otis Pike, a fellow graduate of Princeton and of Columbia Law School, was put in charge.

As I had done with Church, I immediately got in touch with Pike after his appointment, offered my full cooperation, and suggested that we get together to work out the procedures by which his committee's needs could be met without endangering the Agency's legitimate secrets. But perhaps because of all the tugging and pulling that had preceded his appointment, and his determination not to be accused of being a CIA patsy, Pike looked on his role as that of my adversary in the investigation process. Thus, he at first flatly refused to apply to the House committee or its staff the practices that had been accepted by the Rockefeller Commission and the Church committee. For example, he vigorously complained that the compartmentation system that I urged was just a device by which to withhold information. Moreover, he refused to accept any classification system for the committee's documents, no matter how sensitive the material might be, nor would he require his staff to sign secrecy agreements binding them to protect the sensitive material they would learn. But ultimately and most seriously, he accepted without change the ragtag, immature, and publicity-seeking committee staff that had been gathered for the investigation, a bunch of children who were out to seize the most sensational high ground they could and could not be interested in a serious review of what intelligence is really all about. Only after the most intricate negotiations were we able finally to work out some sort of arrangement to allow the investigation to proceed, and then at the cost of my sacrificing some of our normal security procedures.

A herald of our troubles with the House committee occurred even before it managed to get itself organized enough to hold its first hearings. As part of the preparatory process for its investigations, the committee staff was shown a copy of the "family jewels." One of the items included was the fact that over the years the CIA had detailed officers to various government agencies, including the White House, on a rotation basis to serve as liaison officers and to improve the CIA's knowledge of those agencies since it often had to work with them on intelligence matters. The head of each of those agencies was perfectly aware of the CIA officer's presence and assignment. Nevertheless, in 1973 when I reviewed this practice along with the other items on the "family jewels" list, I concluded that a few specific situations were questionable since they could be construed as involving the Agency in domestic activity. One of my 1973 directives on this subject stated that the CIA "will not develop operations to penetrate another government agency, even with the approval of its leadership."

When the House committee got hold of the "family jewels" list, all the other, more juicy items—Operation Chaos, assassinations, the mail-intercept program and the like— were already by then widely known and as such no longer material for sensational headlines. But one of the committee staff members seized on this item and breathlessly circulated it to the members, who in turn hastened to pass to the press, the utterly distorted and false charge that the CIA had "infiltrated" the White House. And this stirred a retired U.S. Air Force colonel, Fletcher Prouty, who had served for a time as liaison officer between the Air Force and the CIA, to allege—and allege it to Daniel Schorr on nationwide television—that Alexander Butterfield had been his CIA "contact" in the White House. I immediately replied that the tale was "outrageous nonsense" and Butterfield categorically denied it. But Butterfield, of course, was the man who had revealed the existence of the Nixon tapes, which had brought President Nixon down, and so a nationwide uproar was created, doubtless satisfying egos of the House committee staffers even though, once the facts were out and Prouty was discredited, it lasted for only three days.

One good thing that the Pike committee did was to decide *not* to get into the subject of assassinations, leaving that to the Church committee. It chose instead—and I credit Pike himself with the good sense in making the choice—to focus on three simple questions about intelligence: How much does it cost? How good is it? And what are the risks involved? In theory, these seemed to me to be right on the button as worthwhile and sensible, and I was confident that intelligence would come out with a good grade, albeit not a perfect one, and that the result would contribute to the educational process I had long thought needed, with the main intelligence mission in the forefront and the sensational derring-do tales in their real perspective. But in fact the adversary atmosphere and the committee staff (and a few of the members) turned the exercise into a pretty awful mess.

Rather than attempt to recount all the myriad controversies with the Pike committee over the next six months, one issue can serve as representative of what I mean by a pretty awful mess. This particular one pertained to the committee's stated goal of determining how good was the CIA's intelligence, and its staff thought it had struck on a gold mine when it found the Agency's own post-mortems on various incidents, those we had drawn up ourselves to evaluate the errors we had made. The fact that these covered only our faults and not our successes did not concern the staff, since they knew that only the former made good headlines.

One of the most dramatic and hard-hitting of these post-mortems was on the CIA's intelligence assessment, made for the Watch Committee on October 6, 1973, that there would

not be a major war between the Arabs and the Israelis. As
we have seen, the post-mortem called it "simply, obviously,
and starkly—wrong." And my staff had made a careful study
to determine the reasons for the mistake, so we would not
repeat it. The House committee obtained this post-mortem
and, after using it as part of their evaluation of the CIA's
intelligence performance, requested that it be declassified
for public release. I agreed that its conclusions could be,
since they did not reveal the sources of our assessments, although some of the material quoted in the post-mortem
might.

But the conclusions were not enough; the committee
wanted to spice up their public release by quotes of the
original material. So a committee meeting was called on
September 11 to vote on the public release of the material in
question, with Mitchell Rogovin attending for me. The Congressmen, abetted by their staff, argued that I had made the
deletions less to protect intelligence sources than to save
ourselves from public embarrassment. As the session became more acrimonious, Rogovin telephoned me several
times and, as I was determined to be as forthcoming as possible, I agreed on point after point to allow our deletions to
be restored, rationalizing in some instances that while they
did reveal that signals intelligence had been the source of
information, they at least didn't fix the specific signals inter-
cepted. On others, however, I felt obliged to dig in my
heels, stressing that they revealed that we knew the item at
the time it was reported and thus revealed just what we
could read of the traffic involved, which the countries in
question even now could use as a basis for reviewing their
security procedures and improving them, to our disadvan-
tage. For hour after hour, it went back and forth in this manner, the committee agreeing on some deletions and I agreeing on some restorations, until we came to a sticking point
on four words.

The four words were "and greater communications security," referring to our coverage of an increase in the security
procedures applied to Egyptian signals communications.
The committee didn't believe that these four words re-

vealed anything more than our over-all signals-intelligence
capability. But after Rogovin read the words to me over the
phone, I thought that they might refer to changes that had
occurred in Egyptian signals procedures, and I believed that
this could assist a careful communications-security officer to
identify possible weaknesses or strengths in his procedures
by reviewing each step he had taken at the time. Thus, without the opportunity to check the actual basis of the four
words to determine whether they hurt our collection capabilities or not, I made a decision that the four words must be
deleted. Since that day I made a full review of my decision
and have been reinforced in the position I took. The problem was best illustrated in an exchange that took place between a journalist and myself during a press conference I
held the afternoon of the controversy. He said that the average person could not see anything particularly significant in
the four words. I replied that it was not merely the average
person who studied such matters, but trained communications-security officers who could deduce lessons from four
such words to improve their security and consequently deprive us of information.

But the committee voted to release the four words nevertheless. Obviously we had reached a critical moment in the
investigations. For the committee to flatly ignore my protest
and release what I regarded as legitimate secrets placed all
our classified material and sensitive information at hazard.
As soon as he learned of this, President Ford directed that
no additional classified material be turned over to the Pike
committee until some satisfactory arrangement could be
worked out for the protection of our material. And since I
was aware that the situation could be presented in the most
negative way in the media, I called a press conference in
the CIA auditorium in Langley to explain the basis for the
President's action. I avoided taking any ultimate position
as to whose authority—the Congress' or the Executive
Branch's—was dominant in the issue, merely saying that I
thought the constitutional process would, in good time,
work out a solution to the impasse.

Several days elapsed while the House committee drafted

a citation declaring me in contempt of Congress for refusing to turn over further documents, and I bemusedly wondered if this would be the way my name would go down in history. My sense of isolation, of being out on a limb all on my own, was rapidly growing by this time. I did not believe that, in the long term, the Executive could hold to a position that blocked a Congressional committee from pursuing an investigation of intelligence. But nothing seemed to be happening in the White House or its interagency coordinating group to resolve the paralysis in which we had landed. So for the first time I felt that I had an issue I had to take up directly with the President, and phoned for an appointment, which he quickly granted, and Rogovin asked Philip Buchen, the President's legal counselor, to join us. I counted on the President's long experience in Congress to make him realize that some solution had to be achieved to remove the impasse. I stressed that no solution would come out of negotiations between the CIA and the Pike committee, that as this was a battle between the Executive and the Congress, the White House and the Congressional leadership had to get involved. "We've got to do something. We simply cannot be in the position of blocking the investigation," I said. "Please, Mr. President, could you make contact with the Congressional leadership and put someone in the White House in charge of this thing?" The next day Ford appointed Jack Marsh, a Counselor to the President and an experienced former Congressman, to manage the Executive Branch's approach to the investigations of the intelligence community by both Church and Pike committees, rather than have the contest debated among the various people involved.

There were still some pretty sharp differences of opinion as to the degree to which requests by the Congressional committees should be met. Kissinger, Schlesinger and Scowcroft, for example, were hard-liners, repeatedly arguing for a tough attitude and questioning anything more forthcoming. Buchen, because of his legal background, and Marsh, because of his Congressional experience, realized that stonewalling would never work and argued for some measure of cooperation with the Congress. Among them, I was certainly among the "doves," holding that the committees should be given the material they requested with the exception of those that revealed the identities of our officers and agents, our relations with foreign intelligence services and particularly sensitive technological data about our systems. And I argued again and again that it was in our interest to respond to the investigation in a responsible manner and endeavor to develop an understanding of intelligence, rather than an adversary relationship, on the part of the committees. It was when I had finished making this argument one time that Kissinger made his crack about my going to "confession" when I went up to the Hill to testify. And once when we decided on a particularly tough position to put to one of the committees, Schlesinger said that I should not be the one to go up to the Hill to express it "since you don't really believe in it, Bill." And I had to admit he was right.

But my initiative with the President at least resolved the impasse with the Pike committee. On September 26 the President gathered House Speaker Carl Albert, Minority Leader John Rhodes, Pike and his committee's ranking minority member Robert McClory, Kissinger, Rumsfeld, Buchen, Marsh and me in the Oval Office. After we discussed the issue involved without conclusion—whether the Congress had the right to release something that the Executive Branch had declared a secret—Pike indicated that he was prepared to accept an arrangement by which the flow of classified material would be resumed subject to an understanding that the material would not be declassified by the committee without an opportunity for the CIA to object. If agreement could not be reached, Pike agreed, the President would personally review the material, and his decision on whether the material could be declassified and released would be controlling, although the committee would retain its right to proceed to a judicial review and resolution of the dispute in the courts. Pike stressed that he was speaking for himself and not the entire committee, but the meeting disbanded with the understanding that this solution would be adopted if the committee went along with it.

It was on this basis that I resumed the flow of classified material to the committee. I forwarded it "on loan with the understanding that there will be no public disclosure ... without a reasonable opportunity for us to consult with respect to it. In the event of disagreement the matter will be referred to the President. If the President certifies in writing that the disclosure of the material would be detrimental to the security of the United States, the matter will not be disclosed by the committee, except that the committee would reserve its right to submit the matter to judicial determination." The committee never formally voted to accept these conditions, but essentially they unblocked the impasse we had reached, until the final round of battle over the House committee's release of its final report.

I had urged all along that the CIA be given a chance to look at the final report before it was publicly released so that we could catch any serious security exposures that might occur in it. As a result, we were provided with an early draft for this purpose and did indeed find in it material that we strongly felt should not be made public. The three most serious had to do with Agency covert operations in Iraq, Angola and Italy, in all three of which the committee's release could present major difficulties to friends of the United States who had counted on our continuing secrecy. As a separate matter, when I saw the draft report, I was incensed at the totally false impression it gave of the effectiveness of our intelligence by cutting and pasting our own post-mortems to focus on whatever failures or mistakes we had identified and analyzed. It was, in my view, an utterly unbalanced and contentious piece of work, presenting an extremely unfair picture of the Agency and the intelligence community.

With respect to the materials that I felt should not be released for security reasons, I insisted that Pike adhere to the procedure he had agreed to, in which the President would be the final arbiter of what could or could not be made public. And President Ford had made it quite clear that he felt that disclosure of these materials would be detrimental to the United States. But Pike refused to abide by the agreement, contending rather lamely that it had applied only to the basic documents acquired from the CIA and not to the committee's own final report, as though the latter could disclose something he had agreed the former should not.

Now, just at this time, the report itself was leaking profusely and in fascinating detail to the press. There was some suggestion that it was the CIA that was in fact the source, leaking the material in order to discredit the committee and undermine the report because of its almost totally negative view of the Agency. This was arrant nonsense, and one of the leaks proved that conclusively. It had to do with the fact that Senator Henry Jackson had been consulted in 1973 by the Agency on how best to handle a particular problem the Agency had with the Congress, when he had quite properly advised us on whom to approach in the matter. This piece of information appeared as a footnote in a version of the Pike committee draft report that the CIA had *not* received; the draft that we did get didn't contain it. So there could be little doubt that the leak came from the committee itself or, more likely, from members of its rather irresponsible staff. But as the leaks continued flowing, first the House at large became increasingly uneasy and embarrassed, and then the committee itself split on whether or in what form the report should be released. Pike was determined to go ahead, arguing that "To say that this committee of Congress can't write a report and file a report without clearing it with the Executive Branch is preposterous." But his cochairman, McClory, felt that "It would be a violation of our agreement with the White House and with the intelligence agencies if we were to use materials that were submitted to us under an agreement of confidentiality." Some effort was then made to negotiate changes in the report to make its release more acceptable, but before these were concluded the House of Representatives voted by a 246 to 124 majority to shelve the work entirely. The key issue for the House was its obligation to abide by an arrangement one of its committee chairmen, Pike, had made with the President, and the effect a refusal might have on future relations with the Ford or any administration.

Although, after I had left office, Dan Schorr arranged for the report's publication in the *Village Voice,* the fact of the matter is, at least in my view, that the entire Pike committee work wound up being a thoroughgoing waste of time and money, when it might have served the useful purpose of educating the public to the true nature of the intelligence community and its value, despite its admitted failures, to the nation's security. Ironically, one of the best post-mortem critiques of the Pike committee performance was made by Pike himself, in a newspaper interview published on February 10, 1976, when he said "he should have had tighter control of the staff" and that "most of the staff members had been aware of all the committee investigations and that he should have compartmentalized investigations and thereby limited the number of persons with sensitive information about any given inquiry."

All the wrangling and the sensational leaks from the Pike committee provided it, not surprisingly, with the lion's share of the headlines vis-à-vis the more orderly, responsible Church committee. Equally unsurprisingly, the members of the latter committee got a bit envious. So, in September, after some four months of serious closed sessions, the Church committee threw open its hearings to a suitably spectacular, headline-grabbing subject. And I, unwittingly, handed the committee a corker on a silver platter.

As part of my continuing determination that any illegal or questionable activity of the Agency, past or present, be exposed and halted—in short, that the "family jewels" list be completely comprehensive and up-to-date even after its initial compilation in 1973—I had issued a standing order that all CIA officers be on a constant lookout for any such activities and report them to me. Thus, in the spring of 1975 Carl Duckett, the Deputy Director for Science and Technology, informed me that he had discovered several bottles of lethal substances—eleven grams of shellfish toxin and eight milligrams of cobra venom—along with some associated equipment with which they could be administered including a dart gun and other devices, which had been squirreled away in a little-used vaulted storeroom in his directorate. Now, the possession of these materials was unquestionably improper. In 1970, fulfilling a treaty commitment, President Nixon had ordered that all such materials be destroyed, except for research quantities, which the amounts Duckett had come up with clearly exceeded, as they were capable of killing thousands of people. Duckett had learned of the existence of the poisons from an officer in his Office of Technical Services and, after a bit of investigation, had discovered what had happened. At the time of the Presidential order, the Office of Technical Services was still a part of the Directorate of Operations and a middle-grade officer there had decided, in an excess of zeal, that the potential value of the toxins was too great to allow them to be destroyed and so he stored them—safely, thank heaven. Sometime thereafter, the officer retired. His successor assumed that the storage had been approved by his superiors until one of the repeated calls to report any questionable activity led him to make sure—and Duckett and I became aware that we had something we should not have. As soon as we had the facts clearly in hand we reported them to the White House and, with its approval, to the appropriate Congressional investigating committees.

With this splendid example of the effectiveness of its "investigation" and with its competitive instincts fully aroused, the Church committee decided to hold its first *open* hearing. So, on September 16, I found myself with some wonderment describing the story about the poisons and dart gun before the TV cameras. I tried to explain that the failure to destroy the poisons as ordered had been more a bureaucratic oversight by a middle-level officer than a sinister CIA plot; that the toxins and the dart gun (which my hastily prepared statement called a tongue-twisting "Nondiscernible Microbioinoculator") had never been used; and that, in any case, it was the CIA itself that had brought the matter to the committee's attention, which surely indicated the innocence of our error and the degree to which we too wished to put an end to such questionable activities.

But none of what I said mattered very much. With the lights glaring and the cameras turning, and with every Senator eager to play with the dart gun and get his picture taken holding it, the over-all impact was of the wildest hugger-mugger of the cloak-and-dagger world. The only consolation I had—and this I credit to Mitch Rogovin's careful foresight—was that I, as the Director of CIA, wasn't photographed holding the weapon, because he grabbed it and passed it to the Senators instead of letting a staff member plop it on the table in front of me. An idea of the total confusion that the session produced can be acquired from the "subway story." In the CIA files, a description appeared of an experiment *conducted by the Army* years before, using inert material to determine the vulnerability of the New York subway system to hostile bacteriological attack, and one of the Senators asked me a question about it. The result was a series of stories in New York papers giving the impression that CIA was somehow romping wildly through the subways spreading poison.

In fairness, however, I have to add that this ghastly day was an exception to the otherwise generally responsible and serious approach taken by the Church committee and characterizing its final report (not issued until well into the spring of 1976). For despite some sanctimonious hyperbole about the failure of CIA to reflect the highest standards of American life, the final report in general was a comprehensive and serious review of the history and present status of American intelligence, with its faults shown as an aspect of the nation's historical experience in the Cold War rather than as the sins of intelligence alone, and a substantial degree of its attention was directed to the need to improve our analytical capabilities. I certainly did not, nor do I now, agree with every one of its conclusions and recommendations. But I certainly welcomed its repudiation of the image of CIA as a "rogue elephant" by the statement that "The

CIA, in broad terms, is not 'out of control' "; the finding that American intelligence agencies "have made important contributions to the nation's security, and generally have performed their missions with dedication and distinction" and that "the individual men and women serving America in difficult and dangerous intelligence assignments deserve the respect and gratitude of the nation"; the conclusion that "the Congress has failed to provide the necessary statutory guidelines" and finally, the view that "the United States should maintain the capability to react through covert action when no other means will suffice to meet extraordinary circumstances involving grave threats to U.S. national security" instead of totally banning such activity. The committee made the expected criticisms of the "jewels," of the traditional intelligence culture, and the need for tighter controls. But when I compare the final report with my initial fears of what it would do, expressed in my remarks to my CIA colleagues that the question was a simple one of "survival," and heightened when my old Jedburgh colleague, Tom Braden, wrote in his newspaper column that CIA was a "monster . . . shut it down," I confess a sigh of relief at the outcome. Most important, this committee's basically responsible approach has been followed by a permanent Senate Select Committee on Intelligence, which has demonstrated that effective Congressional supervision can be accomplished while the essential secrets are kept.

Nonetheless, to a large degree, the circus that the Church committee and the media made out of the poisons and dart gun was the last straw for the White House. From the outset I had been, of course, aware that many in the administration did not approve of my cooperative approach to the investigations, and I had felt myself increasingly isolated from the White House "team" as the year progressed. I had been blamed for not categorically denying Hersh's story at the very beginning; I had been criticized for turning material on Helms over to the Department of Justice; I had been chided for being too forthcoming to the Rockefeller Commission; I had been scolded for not stonewalling at every Congressional hearing. But the impact of the toxin spectacular, and especially the fact that I had delivered the dart gun when Congress demanded it, blew the roof off.

From that day forward, gossip and rumor spread like wildfire throughout Washington that my days were numbered. Newspaper columnists reported that the incident had triggered the White House into a vigorous search for a new CIA chief. At every public appearance I made, reporters clustered around me to ask whether I expected to be fired. Again and again I found myself repeating a carefully rehearsed statement, that the Director of Central Intelligence served at the pleasure of the President and that whenever he no longer pleased the President he would, of course, cease serving. Although, as I must admit, I steadfastly tried to deny the truth of it to myself, I knew that my days were numbered, and I began to talk of the possibility of a new face at the head of CIA when the investigations were over, so it could resume looking forward instead of backward.

But I could not and would not change my basic approach. I believed in the Constitution; I believed in the Congress' constitutional right to investigate the intelligence community; and I believed that, as head of that community, I was required by the Constitution to cooperate with the Congress. I also believed that any other approach just wouldn't work. So, I pressed on with my strategy, responding to Congress' legitimate demands while at the same time I tried to get it to protect intelligence's legitimate secrets. And so the struggle went on.

The staffs of the committees seemed inexhaustible in their ability to write requests for "all documents" dealing with broad categories of subjects. The intelligence professionals reacted with alarm and indignation at such fishing expeditions. Negotiations would then try to boil the requests down to some reasonable degree. The material would be gradually collected and carefully examined with a view to sanitizing it. The delays involved would arouse suspicions and frustrations on the part of committee staff members that nothing was forthcoming. Then the sanitized material would be passed on to the committees. And sooner or later, chances were better than even, a spectacular headline or TV program would explode.

The spectacular TV program on November 1, a Saturday, was Daniel Schorr's CBS evening news description of the CIA's Kurdish operation, making the point that it was arranged between President Nixon and the Shah of Iran and had been abruptly suspended, leaving the Kurds to their fate at the hands of their Iraqi enemies. The operation had been described to the Pike committee only a few days before, so there was very little doubt in any one's mind where the press had got hold of it, and Pike himself was shaken and disturbed by the leak. I spent that morning in the White House with Marsh and others concerned with the investigations, discussing whether we could get the Church committee not to publish its report on assassinations, as well as wringing our hands over the way the House committee was leaking. After the session adjourned, I went out to National Airport to catch a plane for Jacksonville, Florida, where I was scheduled to meet with Egyptian President Anwar Sadat to discuss intelligence matters in the Middle East. The meeting, as I noted earlier, never took place, because Barbara Walters had completely captured the Egyptian President's attention. When I returned to Washington that night, I was greeted by a message from Marsh asking me to be in the Oval Office at eight the following, Sunday, morning. It was there and then that the President asked for my resignation as DCI.

After Barbara and I had alerted our family so they wouldn't be shocked at the news, we went over to visit the Schlesingers that Sunday evening, to hold a bit of a joint wake, since the news was now out that Jim too had been fired as Secretary of Defense. He was surprised, and a bit pleased, that I had also turned down the consolation-prize job that Ford had offered; he smiled at me and said, "It looks like Dick Helms outlasted both of us." Later I turned my thoughts to the future and decided that I would write this book to try to present a real picture of American intelli-

gence to contest the sensational and hostile image that dominated the media, and then I would return to the law and
resume the profession I had interrupted more than a quarter
of a century before. And I decided the time to start moving
ought to be right away; in my view, as soon as the word was
out that the President had fired me—and it was out in blazing headlines that Monday morning—and thus by definition
no longer was "reposing special trust and confidence" in
me, as my commission read, my authority as DCI was
ended. So I cleaned out my office and planned to depart
Tuesday.

But then Dick Walters, the DDCI, intervened. He had
made the obvious observation that Ford and everyone else
around him had overlooked. And that was that at the very
height of the investigations the CIA was about to be without
a chief. To be sure, George Bush had been named by Ford
as my successor, but he was in Peking at the moment and it
would take him a month or more to disengage from his duties there (which included accompanying Ford on his early
December visit to China), process through the Senate confirmation hearings and be sworn in as DCI. In the meantime
the hearings were still going on; in fact, I was scheduled to
testify before one committee or another right on through until the New Year. It was an impossible situation, and Walters
realized this and told me he was going down to the White
House to say so. I certainly didn't ask him to do so, but I did
say that I had no problem with staying, but on the necessary
condition that President Ford make it clear that I could
speak with authority in the interim period. Walters translated this into a statement that the only way I could be convinced to stay would be for the President to ask me personally.

On Wednesday, then, November 5, Ford called me again
to the Oval Office. Since I knew exactly what the meeting
was for, I took the initiative and said, "Mr. President, I don't
want to make this in any way difficult. I am fully prepared to
stay on until George Bush can get here, but the DCI serves
at the pleasure of the President. In order to be effective he

must have the President's full authority to act. If I have that from you, that's all I need." "Certainly, Bill," Ford responded with some relief. "You have my full authority, of course. Do you want me to put that into writing?" I replied that it wasn't necessary, that I was satisfied to have his word on it. Nevertheless, he released a statement to the press saying that he had asked me to remain as DCI until George Bush returned from Peking and could take over the assignment, and that during my "lame duck" term I would have full authority in the job. And that was how I conducted myself—as if I would be there forever.

Bush got back to Washington in mid-December but wasn't sworn into office until January 30, 1976, and those final three months of my career in the CIA were among my busiest. For example, it was during this period that many of the most serious battles with the Congressional investigations came to a head, especially over the release of the Church committee's assassination report and over the Pike committee's final report. And it was also during this period that a comprehensive new charter was finally developed for the intelligence community—Executive Order 11905.

Shortly after I became DCI I had determined that one of the problems that had caused the "jewels" as well as the difficulties in managing the community was that there was no clear charter for the community and its agencies, or rules by which they should act. There were the fuzzy and ambiguous words of the National Security Act of 1949, a series of secret and top secret National Security Council directives, which were a hodgepodge of bureaucratic language, the internal regulations of each of the agencies, and a large number of memoranda agreements and guidances such as the President's 1971 letter to Helms about taking the leadership of the Intelligence Community. Out of all these, one was supposed to be able to derive some idea of the rules of the game, but in fact most intelligence officers like myself operated on the basis of a feel for what their job was and on how individual problems should be resolved in the bureaucratic machinery.

So I decided that there was real need to produce an "omnibus" National Security Council intelligence directive, so that we could review the charters, relationships, and rules of behavior of the community and its agencies, and ensure that they were realistic and proper in today's world. The task proved to be interminable, in no way speeded by the fear of many agencies that it might result in some diminution of their power or functions. I finally overcame some of this by promising Schlesinger, who was as suspicious of my motives as the rest, that the directive would merely try to codify the existing situation and make no changes whatsoever during this phase of the action. But I ran into more fear when I incautiously revealed that I thought that, once the secret codification had been made, it should be screened and an unclassified version developed for public release as part of the process of educating and reassuring the public as to what intelligence was all about.

Thus, the intelligence bureaucracy ground along slowly with successive drafts and studies, with minute differences argued over until Michael Raoul Duval, assistant to Jack Marsh and the President, picked up the subject, making the sensible argument that the President should assert his authority over intelligence by straightening out its charters and rules rather than let the Congressional committees take all the initiatives after the investigations. Thus, during my lame-duck period I found myself not only handling the day-to-day problems of CIA and the community but also participating in meetings and discussions on how intelligence should be organized and run in the future, ending in a long Saturday-afternoon National Security Council session with President Ford on January 10, at which all the options were reviewed and discussed in depth and the decisions taken that resulted in the Executive Order issued on February 18. Before the session Marsh told me to be free to take full part despite my peculiar lame-duck status. I did, and I was glad that the main lines of the final order very much followed a number of the points I argued for. In effect, the order constituted that "omnibus" intelligence directive I had started working toward so many months before.

But the most satisfying development during this final phase in my career came with the growing recognition that my approach to the turbulent Year of Intelligence had been the correct one—that it was, in fact, working. In the beginning, clearly, it had seemed that my policy of candor was only worsening the crisis and further endangering the intelligence community's future, as every admission I made of past misdeeds was irresponsibly leaked by the Congress, ruthlessly exploited by the press and emblazoned in sensational and misleading headlines. But as the year ended, a very real calming note began entering the national debate over intelligence, to a certain extent helped by my being fired. The Congress and the media, by and large, gradually became convinced that I and my colleagues were genuinely endeavoring to be responsive to the constitutional process, that we wanted truly to be as forthcoming as practically possible, that we had made and were willing to continue to make the reforms that the changing nature of the times demanded. To be sure, the press remained excited by any reference to the CIA—as it does, indeed, to this very day—but the more serious journalists and the more serious journals eventually learned to distinguish between the sensational and the real, the legitimate secrets and the boondoggles. And the Congress learned to appreciate that, whereas it had the right under the Constitution to have access to information classified as secret by the Executive Branch, it had the corresponding responsibility to exercise self-restraint with those secrets in the legitimate interests of the nation's security.

To a very large degree, the steadily changing attitudes of the media and the Congress were the result of steadily growing pressure from the public at large. The extensive testimony of my colleagues and myself to the Congressional committees, the frequent press conferences and backgrounders that I held and the speeches I continued to give throughout the country played a part in this. But fundamentally the pressure reflected the good sense of the American people who understood the nation's need for intelligence and grew increasingly uneasy that those services were in danger of being destroyed. A growing volume of mail arrived at the CIA's headquarters from worried Americans expressing concern whether the Congress and the press were going too far in their revelations and assaults on the intelligence community. Gradually the true dimensions of what the CIA had done wrong—some, but not much—began to emerge through all the clamor, and gradually an increased sophistication developed as to what intelligence was all about. By the latter days of 1975, the pendulum had begun to swing back, and perhaps the ultimate encomium that I received came when Henry Kissinger, sometimes my severest critic, took me aside after a meeting in the Oval Office and said, "Bill, I feel required to say this to you. For the longest time I believed that what you were doing was wrong, that what you should have done was to cry havoc over the investigations in the name of national security. But I have come around to believe that your strategy was really correct."

But a single and terribly tragic event did more than anything else to cap the American public's desire to see the pendulum swing back and an end brought to the hysteria over the CIA. And that was the brutal murder, by three unknown terrorists, of Richard Welch, CIA chief of station in Athens, on December 23, 1975. The shock effect was enormous. Suddenly the nation was reminded that intelligence is a serious and dangerous business and that its officers are exposed to real risks. There followed a series of charges and countercharges about who was responsible, and I am afraid I lost my temper when a scruffy group of anti-CIA activists attempted to absolve themselves for having published the identities of a number of CIA officers, including Welch, by saying that the CIA was responsible for his death by sending him to Greece "to spy and perhaps even to intervene in the affairs of the Greek government." I blasted back that the group, "without even an expression of human sympathy, has issued a statement which can only be called a shocking attempt to use the death of a dedicated American as fuel for its irresponsible and paranoiac attack on other Americans serving their country here and abroad." In fact, whatever the individual actions of that group or the weaknesses in CIA's cover arrangements, it was clear that the main cause of his death was the sensational and hysterical way the CIA investigations had been handled and trumpeted around the world, and the American public began to demand that it stop.

Welch's body was flown home on December 30, and I went out to Andrews Air Force Base in the cold dawn to meet it and do the best honors a civilian service could provide, lining up at the tail of the plane with Phil Buchen from the White House, Assistant Secretary of State Arthur Hartman, and Welch's former wife and his three children. President Ford had directed that Welch be accorded the full honors of an American killed in battle and himself attended the military funeral held in the chapel next to Arlington National Cemetery, where he was buried. The dignified posture of his family, especially his oldest son, Patrick, a newly commissioned Marine lieutenant, powerfully portrayed to the TV-viewing public the kind of people who serve the nation in its intelligence service.

As the Senate went through its confirmation procedures for George Bush during January, my work didn't die down at all. National Security Council meetings on SALT, the Middle East, and the Executive Order on intelligence came apace. Congressional hearings continued and I tried to wrap up a number of unfinished items in the normal business of the Agency and the Community so they would not land immediately on Bush's desk. I did have the chance to introduce him to the senior officers of the Intelligence Community and begin his briefings to the limited extent appropriate before the Senate acted (so as not to presume upon its prerogatives). A series of journalists came around for interviews to sum up the experience, and I was able to use the authority I still had to award a Distinguished Intelligence Medal to James Schlesinger for what he had done for the Community, and to Carl Duckett for what he had done for intelligence technology. And on January 27, President Ford brought my family to the Oval Office to award me the National Security Medal and add my name to a very distinguished list including Bill Donovan, Allen Dulles and John McCone. But even then I wasn't finished, as I hurried from the Oval Office to a press conference I had called at CIA to blast the Pike committee's leaked report both for its content as "totally biased and a disservice to our nation, giving a thoroughly wrong impression of American intelligence" and for the irresponsible manner of its dissemination.

The next day, January 28, the Senate voted to confirm Bush, and my authority ended. I arranged to cancel my clearances to see classified information, packed up the mementos on my desk and left the office. Barbara and I came back the next two days for a reception and handshakes from hundreds of our friends and colleagues, and a dinner with a series of jokes and farewell presents from the senior officers. And, finally, on Friday, January 30, I received President Ford and Bush in the CIA auditorium for Bush's swearing in, opening it by saying only, "Mr. President, and Mr. Bush, I have the great honor to present to you an organization of dedicated professionals. Despite the turmoil and tumult of the past year, they continue to produce the best intelligence in the world," and was met by a storm of applause from my old associates, which embarrassed me despite its sincerity and warmth. After the speeches, I followed Dick Walters' final bit of good advice and slipped away and drove home alone in Barbara's somewhat dusty Skylark, trying to put my thoughts in order about where American intelligence—and Colby—had come from and where they both should be going in the future.

Constitutional Intelligence for America

As I drove along the George Washington Parkway toward home and a new life, I decided that I was not bitter about being fired. I understood and accepted President Ford's need to assure the American public that he had taken charge of CIA after the year of investigation, and to do so by putting one of his own "team" in as its new chief. I thought CIA was lucky in the choice he had made, George Bush, and felt that the President had certainly extended himself to be nice to me after making that choice. I had to confess, though, that I was sorry to go, since I was going to miss the fantastic coverage of world affairs in the *National Intelligence Daily*. I also believed there was still a lot I could have done to bring CIA and the whole of the Intelligence Community up to its real potential—in particular, in making improvements in the intellectual and analytical procedures, which I had barely had a chance to touch but which fascinated me in what might be tried, thanks to the contributions that modern technology could make to our thinking processes. But I was satisfied, if even a little stubbornly so, that I had done well in working out a wholly new relationship between American intelligence and the Congress, one which in my mind finally resolved the previously unacknowledged contradiction between the old tradition of intelligence and the Constitution, even though it did reduce the President's power and would make the lives of my CIA colleagues more difficult in requiring them to obtain Congressional approval as well as acquiescence for their operations in the future.

Nonetheless, I realized, the most important part of the job was still ahead: the need to build *public* understanding and support for modern intelligence, which the investigations had not helped and may even have hurt. I did not see that I could have done very much differently, except in some details such as how I handled the dart-gun incident before the Church committee or by removing Angleton before he became an apparent scapegoat. But I saw that American intelligence still had to get rid of its James Bond—or Maxwell Smart—image, and that America's debates about intelligence still had to fix on improving its quality rather than excitedly dwelling on its past sensational adventures and misadventures. I wondered what I might still contribute in that process, and I realized that now, as a private citizen, I could say and write what I thought about these issues.

American intelligence had come a long way since my World War II OSS days in France and Norway. Its scholarship, its technology, and its new generation of professionally trained and experienced operations officers produce fantastic information and assessments of our world. And these enable our leaders to make foreign policy and defense decisions on the basis of knowledge rather than in the haze of ignorance and suspicion in which they operated in so many situations in the past. America's scientific and technological genius applied to intelligence, the integrity of its academic discipline, which has become the intellectual heart of the process, and the courage and resourcefulness of the officers who trained and built an operational service during my lifetime to match and better older foreign organizations—all were a credit to the nation they served with such dedication and skill. I had been lucky to be a part of their efforts, and I was especially honored to have been named to lead them. I certainly had a life of challenge among them, in the physical, the intellectual, and the political senses, and I can look back happily to the decision that Barbara and I made those many years ago when we accepted Gerry Miller's invitation to join CIA and went off to Scandinavia.

But I realize that my view of American intelligence and of its leading element, the CIA, is much different from that of the ordinary citizen, and even from that of the well-informed minority. Their harsh opinion, in part, is of course the result of those questionable activities that have come to light and have cast a shadow of meanness, cynicism and amorality over the intelligence profession. Drug experiments on unsuspecting Americans, prying into the lives and mail of American citizens, concern only about "flap potential" instead of legality and discussing with Mafia hoods how poison could be administered to Fidel Castro—none of this could be condoned with the argument that the use of abhorrent means is justified by the end of protecting the nation. The nation has a far better image of itself, strong enough to reject such behavior and survive without it. Equally unsavory recent revelations about the FBI, tarnishing the reputation of that once universally admired institution, have had the effect of rubbing off on CIA and compounding the image problem. While we in intelligence knew such activity to be exceptional and were often as much surprised by it as was the public, we have to admit that this activity was both bad and a natural outgrowth of the clandestine ethos, which held that if an activity could remain secret it could be justified by its role in the Cold War contest. Even my own action of issuing directives against such behavior was done without disclosing the history that had led to the directives; in effect, I was trying to "distance" CIA from its own past, but thereby only added to the impression of the institution protecting itself through secrecy.

But the public's image of intelligence was formed and exaggerated by more than CIA's own missteps and misdeeds. Intelligence's tradition of total secrecy had served to conceal its virtues as well as, or better than, its vices, a fact no longer compensated for by President Kennedy's sympathetic remark that "Your triumphs are unheralded, your failures trumpeted." And two events overturned America's tolerance and even encouragement of intelligence's secrecy: Vietnam and Watergate. Public confidence in government generally was shaken, producing among some a total turn-off and among most an end to the patriotic acceptance and support for what the leadership and the experts asserted they did in the public interest. A new revisionist history arose to question the premises and the wisdom of policies and activities that had once had the fullest public support, from the Cold War to America's economic and commercial role in the less-developed world. The revisionism had its impact on intelligence, in greater questioning from the Congress and opinion leaders of the projects and procedures of intelligence, and in a sustained public appetite to see the initials CIA in the headlines.

To meet this new challenge, and indeed to enable American intelligence to survive in this new world, only a bare start on a new approach has been made. My own 1973 directives prescribed that certain obvious abuses no longer be permitted. President Ford issued, in 1976, Executive Order 11905, which for the first time publicly described our intelligence community and the restrictions on it. Together these solved part of the problem of the past, when intelligence practitioners had no clear-cut guide as to what was permissible and what was beyond the nation's conscience, so their judgment in some cases plainly was warped by rationalizations in support of what seemed to be a contribution to the security of the nation or the greater efficiency of the intelligence machinery. But these small steps toward a set of rules for intelligence have to be filled out in the way that the American people traditionally express their consensus on how their affairs are to be conducted: through an Act of Congress defining the roles and rules for American intelligence.

Such an act need not go into the precise details required for internal CIA directives. But it should state the broad principles and prohibitions under which American intelligence must operate. The division between CIA's *foreign* intelligence mission and the FBI's internal-security activities; the use of NSA's and other agencies' capabilities for electronic surveillance and message intercept against *foreign* nations and *their agents* and not against Americans (unless authorized by judicial warrant); clear prohibitions against involvement with assassination, torture, or weapons barred in treaties to which the United States is signatory; and the obvious but previously muted truth that American intelligence is bound by American law—all this should be plainly stated, and then would be reinforced with the other laws going beyond Executive Branch directives, that such activities would bring legal penalties to those undertaking them. In the course of the hearings and debates leading up to such an Act of Congress, a number of other principles could be debated and the line carefully could be drawn between what is too great a limit on future flexibility and what is too little reflective of American ideals. One example, for instance, for such debate is whether no covert political action should be undertaken "to subvert democratic governments" (as the Church committee concluded, producing an almost impossible definitional task to determine whether a regime like North Vietnam's "Democratic Republic of Vietnam," or CIA's aid to Socialists in Western Europe in the 1950s, would have been included) or whether a simpler—and lesser—restriction such as a bar against assistance to "military" attempts against "civilian" governments would be a better over-all restriction on future United States options (barring a repetition of the Diem coup, Track II in Chile, and the 1958 Indonesian operation—but not CIA's help to the restoration of the Shah of Iran, to Christian Democrats in Latin America, or to Magsaysay in the Philippines).

Many intelligence activities are better criticized on the basis of specific circumstances than on broad principles, however, and statutory bars are not the way to deal with them. Procedures rather than prescriptions can separate activities that might be required and fully justified in the nation's interest in some cases, from those that should be rejected in the specific circumstances of the moment. The

Executive Branch has long had means to permit intelligence decisions to be reviewed by senior officials, for example, the National Security Council committees established by every President since Eisenhower, the Office of Management and Budget review of requests for appropriations, and the outside panel of wise citizens on the President's Foreign Intelligence Advisory Board. But the weakness of Executive Branch procedures was shown in Chile's Track II, when the President, under whose authority these review bodies were established, directed that they be bypassed.

Congress, which for years had exercised its review functions in only the most perfunctory manner, roused itself in 1974 to insist that any activities of CIA abroad, other than intelligence gathering, be reported to the "appropriate committees" of the Congress as a first step toward assuming its full constitutional role of reviewing and approving or disapproving the actions of the Executive. The 1975 year of investigation was a convulsive attempt, after the fact, to perform this function for the twenty-five years during which it had been neglected. But its outcome, nonetheless, was to establish a proper procedure in the Senate (and finally in 1977 in the House) by which continuing review could be accomplished by special committees that could know the secrets but be small enough to keep them from exposure. In 1776 the Committee on Secret Correspondence stated that "fatal experience has shown, that there are too many members of Congress to keep a secret," and today's 535 are no less leakage prone than the 50-odd then. So, Congressional review today must be accomplished by a small, representative body of the Congress and not by exposure of the secrets to all. These committees, with the clear responsibility for reviewing intelligence activities, can replace previous Congressional "oversight" (in both senses of the word) with the kind of Congressional consultation and responsibility in American decisions about intelligence operations called for by the Constitution, bringing perhaps a new meaning to the initials CIA—Constitutional Intelligence for America.

Behind the two elected authorities over intelligence, the

Executive Branch and Congress, stands the ultimate source of its power, the people. And any improved structure for American intelligence must recognize that the American people are no longer content to provide blind support for the secret work of intelligence, whatever may have been the traditions of the past. It is, therefore, equally essential that the relationship of the people to our intelligence apparatus be redefined and made appropriate to modern America; the American people must not be expected to continue to follow an intelligence tradition built for other times, realms and establishments.

Part of this will be accomplished by the legislative process of adopting a new and clear statute for American intelligence, since the debates about its provisions will allow the public to influence the concepts and limits to be set for American intelligence. Just as clear legislation will give direction to the practitioners of intelligence, so it will also give information to the public as to the tasks assigned in its name and the limits of behavior it has authorized. Thus, statutory text can replace adventure fiction as a guide to behavior and supervision, and provide reassurance of propriety. Part of the process will also come as a result of serious Congressional supervision, with its inevitable public comments about intelligence, both its successes and its failures, placing in discussion matters that in the past would never have been revealed.

But the major part must come from a new responsibility of intelligence—educating the public in its ways and values and educating it in world affairs through its products. Intelligence must accept the end of its special status in the American government, and take on the task of informing the public of its nature and its activities as any other department or agency. The public can no longer be expected to follow Helms's 1971 admonition that it "must take it on faith that we too are honorable men devoted to the nation's service." Even though the men and women of CIA had been honorable to themselves and in their service to their nation (with the very few exceptions that occur in any collection of fallible human beings), Americans have long looked to a government of laws and not merely of men, and CIA must fit within this if it is to continue. Thus, the public must be informed of what intelligence is doing in its name and how this contributes to the general welfare of the nation. This can be accomplished, in part, by the kind of public-information program usual in other departments and agencies, brochures, lecture engagements and tours of Langley, raising the volume and priority of activities of this sort already underway.

But by far the most effective manner of accomplishing the task of public education is by letting the public benefit directly from the products of intelligence, its information and assessments, and thus building an appreciation for their excellence and their importance to decisions about American policy. Simple as this concept is, and even given the fact that most of the important conclusions and assessments of intelligence today do reach the citizenry through official releases or unofficial leaks, it evokes fears of wholesale exposure of intelligence and its total destruction as a result. But a perusal of *The New York Times* on one side and *Aviation Week* on the other soon reveals the American assessment of the strength, today and projected into the future, of Soviet missiles, submarines and armored divisions in Eastern Europe, our understanding of the factions that will contend for power after Brezhnev, our estimates of the policies that Arab oil producers will follow, and of the conflicts of tribal factions in the African continent against its colonial frontiers.

Thus the material is made public already. But its source in the intelligence community is obscured from the people who use it. This proves that intelligence substance can be disseminated to the public while its sources are kept secret. The similarity to journalism is striking. Deep Throat's identity remains a secret, but the nation has benefited from his information. Journalism has long since seen its function as bringing information to the public, and protecting its sources as a means to that end. Intelligence now faces the challenge of recognizing that in America its true function is the same. It must view the protection of sources as a means to that same end instead of almost an end in itself, which so long characterized its ancient traditions of secrecy.

It is not enough, however, only to make the practice of intelligence proper, important as that may be. Intelligence must also be improved to meet the very real challenges of the world ahead. It must be comprehensive and reliable enough to provide a positive verification that arms-control agreements we may reach with adversaries are complied with, or early warning when they are not. It must eliminate the wastage of exaggerating possible danger, resulting in needless expenditures on defense, just as much as it must avoid complacency and so encourage an adversary to think he can take advantage of us. It must expand its concepts of what constitutes the national interest of the American people from purely military security to their economic well-being, and what constitutes a threat from those posed by nation states to those presented by anarchic terrorists and multinational cartels, from those arising from political decision-making to those growing out of sociological and cultural forces.

The easiest field in which to see both the need and the likelihood of improvements in intelligence is in the technological. Even a straight-line projection of the changes that have occurred in this field since the U-2 grew into the space system, sonar grew into the *Glomar* and radar grew into the incredibly sensitive sensors of today, produces awe about what kind of technology is ahead. Since it is clear that technological improvement is accelerating, not merely growing, the changes are apt to be even greater than we can now project, and as startling and dramatic to the new generation of intelligence officers and customers as the advent of space technology was to the first. A few "science fiction" thoughts that are well within the possibility of development can illustrate this: constant visual surveillance of all areas of the globe despite weather, darkness, or camouflage; instant translation of electrical messages and oral transmissions anywhere in the world; electronic sensors searching out and identifying dangerous concentrations of metals, chemicals and organic substances. Some equally spectacular innovations will be available to allow our clandestine intelligence operations to penetrate attempts by hostile groups or nations to keep secrets that could threaten us. Miniature machinery to carry away photographs or recordings of secret discussions and documents threatening our safety and welfare; proved psychological techniques permitting a high degree of accurate assessment and prediction of the likely actions of foreign leaders and political movements; instant machine analysis of the background of a potential source and comparison of his information and alleged access with previously collected material to provide confirmation or raise doubts as to his *bona fides*—these and many comparable improvements in our clandestine operations abroad will plainly be available. The increasing integration and eventual "marriage" of the technological and the clandestine cultures into a single intelligence approach will produce many more.

Some of these technological improvements might, of course, be blocked by a fear that they might be used to take us to George Orwell's totalitarian world of 1984. But the clear guidelines and constant supervision of a constitutional approach to American intelligence can prevent this, and ensure that our use of such capabilities will be as much within the standards of our society as our restricted and legally controlled use of weapons and military facilities.

But it is in the analytical area of intelligence that I see the greatest potential for improvement, and the greatest need. And it was in this area that I was disappointed that I had so little time and opportunity to press for change. We have barely begun to bring the "two cultures" of science and the arts into real alliance, despite my few gestures in this direction, encouraging the use of computers, experimenting in techniques to bring greater precision and utility to estimates by refining their presentation into specific probabilities rather than subjective verbal statements, and funding research and development projects to try out wholly new approaches to analysis. But continued pressure in this direction, in the academic and commercial world as well as in government, will and must improve our techniques of analysis for the positive benefits they can bring to our understanding of the world around us and allow us to keep up with the information explosion, which can bury us otherwise.

For example, our disciplines and techniques of just plain thinking and communicating obviously need improvement. Individual facts and events must be placed in their true position and proportion vis-à-vis the whole of a situation, both *horizontally* within all the relevant factors in other disciplines and situations and *vertically* in time between the past and the future. A myopic focus on the wrongs and weaknesses of Ngo Dinh Diem, not seeing them in the context of South Vietnam's contest with North Vietnam and of the change he was leading from a French colonial society to a modern nation, led to President Kennedy's approval of his overthrow and the disaster of America's direct military involvement in Vietnam. A similar myopic distaste for Nguyen Van Thieu's unwillingness to turn from his army political base led to Congress' refusal to send the South Vietnamese the aid they needed to continue to fight the far more totalitarian North. And a myopic fascination with the old intrigue-filled traditions of intelligence and its essentially few missteps and misdeeds over a quarter of a century almost led to the destruction of what is clearly the best intelligence service in the world. Similar myopia threatens in the future, for example, the selective application of human-rights criticism to America's client states like South Korea without viewing the alternative of Kim Il Sung's draconian rule in the North, or an anachronistic focus on our military security while the real dangers to the future grow in the sociological frustrations of the Third World's massive populations and underdeveloped economies. It is one of the challenges to "intelligence," both in the human and in the institutional sense, to find new ways of thinking to avoid such problems.

Part of this process of improvement involves experiments in new techniques of analysis, imposing more rigorous discipline to ensure consideration and evaluation of all the "horizontal" and "vertical" factors. For this, simple procedures, checklists, review techniques, and the aid of machine systems can obviously be helpful. These could include the "red" and "blue" teams in war games applied in political and economic as well as military situations. Subordinate National Intelligence Officers should be appointed to cover smaller and smaller geographic units such as individual African nations and the constituent republics of the Soviet Union, thus providing the basis for a moot Central Committee meeting reflecting the separate local interests of the component units. Outside panels should be increased to bring in critics and consultants from academia and the private world to contest the intelligence bureaucracy's comfortable conclusions and force it to look for the unexpected and the improbable. Intense research and development in these fields might come up with important new concepts and avoid immature enthusiasms for apparent panaceas that might produce more harm than good. In the process, our intellectual and philosophic "culture" can lose its ingrained distaste for, and even fear of, technology by appreciating its help to precision, discipline and reduced drudgery. At the same time we can hope that the scientific and technical "culture" can accept the finite quality of machinery and find fulfillment in providing new platforms from which the human mind can climb to new heights.

As these two "cultures" merge, so must the others that characterized the initial years of American intelligence. Far from separating the analyst and the technician from the rough clandestine officer, all three must become aware that they are fellow members of the same profession, working together to learn and to understand all they can of the complex world around us. The analyst must value the informal "feel" of the operations officer, who is immersed in a fast-moving and subtle situation, not merely his formal report. The operations officer must sense the larger frame into which the analyst fits his observations. The technician must be close to both to provide the tools they need and will use and to supplement their work or overcome their handicaps with technological breakthroughs. And all three must reach out openly and frankly to the other professions working toward the same goal of knowledge, whether the other services be in government or the private world of academia, journalism, or commerce. The more the information of all of these can be shared and debated, the better it will be screened and refined for the public good, for which all are working.

Yet another part of the process of improving intelligence involves changes in its presentation and in its service to all the participants in the American decision-making process. American intelligence must serve the Constitution as well as abide by it. By circulating its improved information and its assessments it can lead the government and the people to a broader appreciation of the problems facing our nation in the world of the future; it must expose the fullness of intelligence analysis rather than have single features of situations selected and exaggerated to support or conflict with competing policy choices. We must develop a new and positive meaning to the old intelligence doctrine of the "need to know"—that those who *do* need to know to make wise American decisions must receive the information and assessments of intelligence.

This is perhaps one of the most difficult tasks ahead for intelligence. It must develop the distinctions between protecting the secrecy of its sources and techniques and making available the substance of its information and its conclusions. It must face public criticism and political challenge of its assessments. It must maintain the independence and objectivity of its judgments apart from the policies and programs they may support or question. Internationally, we must insist that an intelligence judgment is a step toward policy, not a reflection of it. In a political debate where knowledge can be power, intelligence judgments must be supplied impartially to all factions, to help the best solution to emerge, rather than the favored one. Photographs must be declassified, backgrounders attributed, publications edited to protect the sources but allow the substance of the reports and assessments to circulate to Congress and the public. The estimates will then be debated and the sage unanimity of the cloistered world of intelligence will be challenged by those close to the struggle and fearful of irrational and foolhardy, but real, surprises. Out of the process will come a better understanding of the role and value of modern intelligence, as well as better intelligence itself.

Out of this better understanding must come a better appreciation that the real secrets of American intelligence need protection, and better protection than they have today. George Washington once wrote that upon "secrecy, success depends in most enterprises" of intelligence. While his statement reflects the old tradition of total secrecy about intelligence, it also shows that secrets about intelligence are fully compatible with American tradition. We respect and protect many secrets because certain American institutions cannot operate without them: the ballot box, confidences between attorneys and clients, advance crop statistics that might upset the free market. Under present law, however, intelligence secrets are essentially protected only against the foreign spy, not against the current CIA employee who quietly leaks an item to a friendly newsman because he differs with some policy, or the former employee whose memoirs suddenly appear on the newsstands with the names of his former agents and friends. As we saw, the protection the Agency got in the Marchetti case depended on the chance that we learned of his intention before he and Marks published, and thus we were able to enforce his contract not to do so without the Agency's clearance. And one ex-employee and his publisher escaped the procedure by keeping their publication a deep secret until the release of thousands of copies.

But again the Constitution must be the guide. A criminal sanction could indeed be established punishing an intelligence employee who violates his undertaking to protect the secrets he must learn as a part of his intelligence duties. But in my view the sanction should apply only to him and not to the newsman or publisher or some other person to whom he tells the information. To obviate a fear expressed by Daniel Schorr that the newsman could be subpoenaed to identify his source, a provision could be added that no third party repeating the information in the exercise of his First Amendment rights could be enmeshed in the case. And since I am well aware that the charge can be made that such a statute could be used to chill the "whistle-blower" against abuse or wrong-doing, I believe that the government, before it could prosecute, should have to satisfy an independent judge that the secret revealed truly did expose a legitimate intelligence source or technique. With these two provisions, both the rights of the employees and the interests of the American public in preventing any intelligence cover-up can be protected, while at the same time the sources and techniques essential for obtaining the information necessary to defend them in the world of the future can also be protected. And if they were passed by Congress, I now believe that CIA should have no right of prior review or restraint of such a publication, and should depend solely on the deterrent effect of these carefully circumscribed criminal sanctions.

With this better understanding of the reality of modern intelligence through this greater disclosure of its functioning, limits and products, a new division can be established between the aspects of intelligence that should be known and discussed in the American political arena and those whose secrecy must be respected and protected. Necessary cover for clandestine-operations officers will again have public acceptance and cooperation and not be the basis of a game of hide-and-seek. And I believe that the public will continue to accept and even expect covert political and paramilitary action in those situations requiring some American response more effective than a diplomatic protest and less violent than sending the Marines. With the dangers foreseeable in the world ahead from delirious terrorist groups, megalomaniac local despots and frustrated demagogues, all with access to modern weaponry and even possibly to advanced methods of destruction, some quiet assistance from America to more responsible elements in their countries may enable them to secure and retain power, solving without danger or damage what otherwise might grow to major and violent confrontations. These techniques should be used only rarely, when no other, less risky means exist, and it should be clear that our effort should be one of support *for* elements offering the prospect of responsible and friendly policies for both the United States and the area concerned, and not merely *against* some individual or group viewed as promoting policies uncomfortable for our selfish interests. If the operations meet these standards, the Executive Branch and Congressional committees required to be informed of them will accept their propriety and respect the need for their secrecy. If a proposal is so dubious that this cannot be counted on, the operation will not be launched. In some situations other experiments may be needed to devise *ad hoc* overt or nonofficial corporate machinery to meet large-scale challenges in novel and informal but not necessarily secret fashions, similar to CORDS and to the quasi-independent public board to which Radio Free Europe was transferred after its CIA sponsorship was exposed. Through such structures, CIA's expertise and even personnel could contribute openly, but CIA itself would not be assigned missions inappropriate to its secret procedures and machinery.

One subject that will continue to be discussed and debated about intelligence is its organization, especially whether the Director should be named an intelligence czar above the entire community with full authority over it or merely be the first among equals of the heads of the various intelligence agencies of the different departments. This is the sort of issue that can fascinate the Washington bureaucracy and power brokers for decades. But I confess I consider it a very subordinate question to the major ones I have outlined on how to keep our intelligence proper and how to make it better. The elements of the argument are obvious: the desirability of a single focus of responsibility for the wide world of intelligence; the efficiency of a single authority over the overlapping interests and needs of the different departments and services for intelligence; the danger that a czar would slip into the orbit of the White House and tend to support its policies instead of pressing for independent assessments; the separate needs of the different departments for special types of intelligence support and their ability to invent other names and continue them if barred from "intelligence"; and so forth *ad infinitum* (and perhaps *ad nauseam*).

Since this debate can—and will—go on forever, I propose to stay out of it and assert my belief that American intelligence can work, however it is likely to be arranged on the organizational wiring diagrams, because its professional development since World War II has produced such a cadre of experienced and expert practitioners and body of doctrine that the Community will drive toward excellence and service beyond narrow bureaucratic interests. If the Director fulfills his substantive responsibilities to know and improve our intelligence information and assessments so he can provide them to the President, the National Security Council, the Congress and the people of the United States, he will be in the best possible position to task the members of the Community with real requirements that they will recognize as important, whatever their hierarchical relationship to him. He will also be best able to measure the value of their contribution and thus the ideal size of their budgets and to advise the President and Congress. He will be so challenged and occupied that he will have to depend heavily on deputies and subordinates to handle whatever managerial tasks he may be assigned, and he will soon discover that organizational questions lose any appeal that they might have had initially.

The future of intelligence has a further dimension. On June 22, 1973, I was invited to the White House to attend the signing of the United States–USSR Agreement on the Prevention of Nuclear War and go through the receiving line thereafter. When President Nixon introduced me to General Secretary Brezhnev as Mr. Colby of the CIA, Brezhnev drew back in mock alarm and teased, "Is this a dangerous man?" President Nixon assured him that I was not and that I fully agreed with the Treaty they had just signed. I decided to make my first, and still only, venture in summit diplomacy. "Mr. General Secretary," I said, "the more we know about each other the safer we all will be." I wish I could say he agreed with me, but he listened to the translation and turned without a reply to the next person President Nixon presented to him.

But the point is valid. Ignorance, suspicion and misunderstanding have been the sources of too many wars, either because they generated hostility and hatred or a false belief that the other side could be easily defeated. And of course, surprise after complacency has cost millions of lives that might not have been sacrificed if warnings had generated preparations to deter or repulse an attack, from the Japanese's on Pearl Harbor to Hitler's on Russia.

Recent years have brought a major change in the role of intelligence in this regard, from the old effort for strategic or tactical advantages to a new contribution to reassurance and understanding. The most dramatic example occurred in the SALT negotiations between the United States and the USSR. Agreement on limiting nuclear arms had been sought by the United States for decades. In 1946 the Baruch Plan proposed passing America's monopoly of nuclear weapons to the United Nations, but the effort failed because no satisfactory assurances could be developed that other nations would abandon the field if the United States did. In the 1950s Eisenhower sought mutual restraints and offered a program of "Open Skies" to monitor them, with unarmed photoreconnaissance aircraft from the United States and the USSR flying over each other's territory, but the Soviets rejected the idea. In the 1960s Kennedy and Johnson tried to arrange the exchange of inspection teams free to investigate the territory of both sides, but this too was turned down. But by 1972, overhead photography had been sufficiently developed on both sides so that each could rely on its own "national technical means of verification" of the limits agreed. And SALT I was signed.

One of the aspects of that agreement shows what intelligence can offer a future world. Both the USSR and the

United States were considering the next strategic step of deploying nationwide antiballistic-missile systems to destroy incoming hostile missiles. But agreement was reached that neither would do so, leaving both sides vulnerable to retaliation and thus deterring a first use. Aside from the stability this brought to the strategic balance between the two nations, and the incremental value of this individual step in the arms-control process between them, the cancellation of the program saved the United States from expenditures estimated at between fifty and one hundred billion dollars in the next several years.

In many other situations around the world this sort of accurate and dependable intelligence is already helping to avoid the frictions and disputes that have so many times in history led to violence and agony for so much of the world's population. From the Sinai Desert, as we have seen, to the DMZ in Korea, to our certainty that there are no offensive missiles in Cuba, assurance and confidence from knowledge have replaced fear and suspicion of the unknown, even with respect to areas closed to outside visitors and operating in the closed and secretive ways of a police or totalitarian state. The contribution is not only in the field of military security, since careful scholarship and collection of intelligence gives early alerts of economic, resource, political and terrorist trends that permit advance preparation to minimize the impact or negotiate away a confrontation. International statesmen are gradually becoming accustomed to conducting their negotiation on the basis of common understandings of the facts and factors involved rather than believing they can profit from private and secret knowledge withheld from the other side (although Soviet military officers still try to persuade their American counterparts to keep from civilian negotiators on both sides "secret" military information about Soviet weapons systems, and still insist on using the American names for the Soviet weapons being negotiated over, since the Soviet weapons are too "secret" to discuss with Soviet civilians, despite the fact that they are known in detail to American intelligence).

This, then, is the future dimension of intelligence. It must become an international resource to help humanity identify and resolve its problems through negotiation and cooperation rather than continue to suffer or fight over them. To the extent that American intelligence provides its products to help the American people make better decisions, it will lead this process, and its material also will become available for others in the world to use. But I believe we will see, and should welcome, an institutionalizing of this process on the international level, so that information and assessments about world problems can be made conveniently available to all, applying to intelligence as a whole the techniques and experience of such specialized world information centers as the United Nations Food and Agriculture Organization, the International Labor Organization, and the host of semiofficial and private centers and services that are contributing to this same process in their particular fields. This does not mean that intelligence should in any way be consolidated into one gigantic intelligence center, which would collapse of its own weight, but rather that the concept of the intelligence "community" of separate agencies in the United States gradually be expanded to the world level, recognizing specialization where it is appropriate, exchanging different appreciations to seek better comprehensive judgments, and ensuring that each item appears in its appropriate horizontal and vertical proportion in final over-all assessments.

As the nations move into this new era of international dissemination of information, they will come to appreciate the benefits of the greater knowledge they will gain. They will also be dissuaded from attempting to conceal information for strategic advantage, realizing the futility of any such attempt in the face of America's intelligence machinery. And then the words from *John* (8:32), which Allen Dulles prized so highly and placed in CIA's entrance hall, will truly characterize the role of American intelligence: "And ye shall know the truth, and the truth shall make you free"—free of war, misery, and ignorance.

ACKNOWLEDGMENTS

A book must have structure and content. Initially this one had its present content, and the structure of a treatise. But my wise friend and fine lecture agent, Harry Walker, sent me to Morton L. Janklow to be introduced to the world of publishing. Effective literary agent, but imaginative counselor as well, he arranged a meeting with Richard Snyder and Michael Korda to convince me that someone as clear and cogent as Peter Forbath could help me shake off the habits of twenty-five years of impersonal bureaucratic prose and write an account of my adventures in intelligence instead of a series of academic essays. So to all of them with great appreciation, but especially to Peter, who produced the structure in which my story could be told, I confess my debt if this book is an effective expression of what I have experienced and believe. They are all true professionals in communication, as I hope I have been in intelligence, and both intelligence and I have much to learn from their profession, and I certainly have done so. And another true professional in both intelligence and communication, Helen Kleyla, made a major contribution with her rapid and precise production of perfect texts from scratchy drafts.

But the book depends on other contributions to its—and my—story. To my parents, who taught me duty; to my wife, Barbara, who gave me love; to my children, who showed me loyalty—only I know how the life recounted here reflects their contribution rather than anything I could have accomplished alone, and how much I have depended upon their unstinting support during dark days as well as bright. So the words may be about me, but any merit in the story is theirs.

One acknowledgment is negative. Many years ago I agreed that the CIA should review any material I might wish to publish to ensure that I not reveal any classified information without proper authorization. Of all who signed such an agreement to keep the secrets I was about to learn, I believe that I must abide by this twenty-five-year-old commitment, so I submitted this manuscript to the Agency. I do not agree with all the excisions the Agency required, but I have conformed to them because I thought them reasonable even if mistaken. I believe them well within the proper limits of concern for the legitimate secrecy of our intelligence sources and for the avoidance of diplomatic conflict over intelligence operations. The final judgment over such reasonable differences should be the Agency's, not each former employee's—whether he was Director or intelligence officer in rank. Thus this acknowledgment states that the CIA has reviewed this manuscript to determine that it does not improperly reveal classified information. However, the CIA expresses no position of approval or disapproval with respect to the ideas and opinions the manuscript contains; these are mine alone, perhaps formed during my intelligence career but articulated only after separating from it.

And a final acknowledgment: to the honorable "company" of men and women of American intelligence, whose courage, devotion and brilliance have produced the best intelligence in the world, and to their younger successors, who willingly and cheerfully embrace a future of American intelligence under law and who ask only that their contribution to a safer and better world—and America—be better understood by their fellow Americans. I hope that this book may help them all to receive the respect and appreciation their service truly deserves.

Index